Liberalizing Contracts

In *Liberalizing Contracts* Anat Rosenberg examines nineteenth-century liberal thought in England, as developed through, and as it developed, the concept of contract, understood as the formal legal category of binding agreement, and the relations and human practices at which it gestured, most basically that of promise, most broadly the capitalist market order. She does so by placing canonical realist novels in conversation with legal-historical knowledge about Victorian contracts. Rosenberg argues that current understandings of the liberal effort in contracts need reconstructing from both ends of Henry Maine's famed aphorism, which described a historical progress "from status to contract." On the side of contract, historical accounts of its liberal content have been oscillating between atomism and social-collective approaches, missing out on forms of relationality in Victorian liberal conceptualizations of contracts which the book establishes in their complexity, richness, and wavering appeal. On the side of status, the expectation of a move "from status" has led to a split along the liberal/radical fault line among those assessing liberalism's historical commitment to promote mobility and equality. The split misses out on the possibility that liberalism functioned as a historical reinterpretation of statuses – particularly gender and class – rather than either an effort of their elimination or preservation. As Rosenberg shows, that reinterpretation effectively secured, yet also altered, gender and class hierarchies, there is no teleology to such an account.

Dr. Anat Rosenberg is an Assistant Professor (Lecturer) at the Radzyner Law School, The Interdisciplinary Center (IDC) Herzliya, Israel. She had been a visiting research fellow at Columbia Law School, and is currently a visiting scholar at the Faculty of History at Cambridge University, and a visiting fellow at the Institute of Advanced Legal Studies, the University of London. Her research brings together law, literature, sociology and cultural studies, to study the history of late modern capitalism.

Discourses of Law

Series editors: Peter Goodrich, Michel Rosenfeld and Arthur Jacobson
Benjamin N. Cardozo School of Law

This successful and exciting series seeks to publish the most innovative scholarship at the intersection of law, philosophy and social theory. The books published in the series are distinctive by virtue of exploring the boundaries of legal thought. The work that this series seeks to promote is marked most strongly by the drive to open up new perspectives on the relation between law and other disciplines. The series has also been unique in its commitment to international and comparative perspectives upon an increasingly global legal order. Of particular interest in a contemporary context, the series has concentrated upon the introduction and translation of continental traditions of theory and law.

The original impetus for the series came from the paradoxical merger and confrontation of East and West. Globalization and the internationalization of the rule of law has had many dramatic and often unforeseen and ironic consequences. An understanding of differing legal cultures, particularly different patterns of legal thought, can contribute, often strongly and starkly, to an appreciation if not always a resolution of international legal disputes. The rule of law is tied to social and philosophical underpinnings that the series has sought to excoriate and illuminate.

A full list of titles in this series is available at:
www.routledge.com/law/series/SE1036

Masculinity and the Trials of Modern Fiction
Marco Wan

A Mosaic of Indigenous Legal Thought
C.F. Black

The publisher gratefully acknowledges the support of the Jacob Burns Institute for Advanced Legal Studies of the Benjamin N. Cardozo School of Law to the series *Discourses of Law*.

Liberalizing Contracts

Nineteenth Century Promises Through Literature, Law and History

Anat Rosenberg

Routledge
Taylor & Francis Group
LONDON AND NEW YORK

First published 2018 by Routledge

2 Park Square, Milton Park, Abingdon, Oxfordshire OX14 4RN
52 Vanderbilt Avenue, New York, NY 10017

Routledge is an imprint of the Taylor & Francis Group, an informa business

First issued in paperback 2018

British Library Cataloguing-in-Publication Data
A catalogue record for this book is available from the British Library

Library of Congress Cataloging-in-Publication Data
A catalog record for this book has been requested

ISBN: 978-1-138-92370-6 (hbk)
ISBN: 978-0-367-15083-9 (pbk)

Typeset in Baskerville by
by FiSH Books Ltd, Enfield

To my parents.

Contents

Acknowledgements

Acknowledgements tend to begin with talk about accumulated debts. In a book on contract there is a strange irony in using the language of debt, yet this study's findings actually sooth the irony, for they tell a story about relationships, with their hopes and suffocations. The debts I want to acknowledge have been all hope to me (as Victorians' debts were not to them), but have often suffocated others who have been generous enough to be involved in this book. I hope they will sense their share in it, and forget all suffocation.

This book began in my PhD. Like a child it is now both strange to its early stages and constituted by them. The intellectual friendship and keen interest I enjoyed then and since have been a *sin qua non* for whatever it is now.

From early on I enjoyed the mentorship of three wonderful intellectuals and friends. The remarkable Roy Kreitner has been there from the beginning. A reader both demanding and generous, ever able to move between minute detail and overarching vision even when I was not, and never tired of intellectual exchange, my work would not have taken the routes it has without his wisdom, and would have been all the worse for it. Ayelet Ben-Yishai has been indispensable to this study from the day I met her. A brilliant Victorianist and skillful reader, she has offered insight and perspective which have inspired me these past years and challenged me to make this study the best I can. Uriel Procaccia early on initiated me into the cultural study of law. I owe that early choice to him, and he saw me through with unflinching support.

My colleague and friend Galia Schneebaum has attended this study from its early iterations when we were both just finding our ways through academia. She has thought and astutely commented on different parts more times than I can remember, always improving my work. My many conversations about this study with Galia, and with Eliav Lieblich, Moran Ofir, and Adam Shinar at IDC have become part of this book. They have all been both willing listeners and voices of reason. Other colleagues and friends at IDC have enriched my work. I am particularly grateful to Lior Barshack, Amnon Lehavi and Yoram Shachar, who have generously commented on various parts and often shared in my dilemmas. I am also grateful to Avinoam Cohen, Hanoch Dagan, Amos Israel, Assaf Likhovski, Menachem Mautner, Christopher Tomlins, Avishalom Westreich, and Steven Wilf for offering their advice and intellectual acumen at various stages. The two readers of my PhD, Nan Goodman and Bernadette Meyler, had early on shared knowledge and advice which informed and encouraged my work on this book.

I have presented parts of this study in many forums, and have benefited from them all. I am particularly grateful to my thoughtful commentators at IDC's Law & Humanities workshop of 2015-16, Alex Feldman and Noam Yuran, who have contributed to the final result, and to the participants in that discussion.

Special thanks go to the library staff at IDC for their excellent professional support, especially to Yael Nesher who has made everything needed available with speed and willingness. I am also thankful to Tal Shulzinger for her committed assistance as I was preparing the manuscript.

My nearest family, my parents and parents in law, my brother and sister, and brothers and sisters in law, and my partner Ariel, have made me realize this pregnant little fact (to borrow from the immortal George Eliot): there are people who believe in whatever I do; who know – or think they know – that if I write a book it will be worth reading. I could hardly ask for more, yet they have also offered their time, patience, and emotional backing. My children, Nitzan, Nitai and Eylon, have had the different contribution of often pulling me away from work – and as often surprising me by taking care not to do so even as they deserved my attention, inadvertently preserving a much needed sense of proportion. My larger family and my friends have kept me on track with their ardent interest and care.

Ariel's share in this study is greater than I can acknowledge. A reader, critic and fountain of original thought, this book would not have been written without his loving patience, his commitment in things large and small, and his unwavering insistence that I follow my intellectual convictions and worry not about disciplinary and theoretical straightjackets. I hope to have met the challenge.

I dedicate the study with love to my parents, Zvia and Ami.

Anat Rosenberg
June 2017

* * *

An early version of Chapter 1 appeared in *McGill Law Journal*, of Chapter 5 in *the Cardozo Journal of Law and Gender*, and of Chapter 6 in *Nineteenth Century Literature*. I thank the editors for their permission to use the materials.

Introduction

From Status-to-Contract.[1] You will have heard Henry Maine's aphorism to the point of apathy, but if pressed you likely have something to say about its historical meaning, and the discussion will soon heat up. You might argue that status-to-contract captures dramatic shifts in the basis of the social structure, political power, and cultural discourse in the Victorian era. You might think that it accounts for increasing social mobility and dynamic options that emerged in political, economic and intimate life as persons became less constrained by ascribed social roles and structures of hierarchy. Or you might think that status-to-contract was a genuine but in the final analysis failed effort in these directions. Or perhaps you tend to see status-to-contract as an ideological feat serviceable in keeping masses of people immobile under capitalism while appeasing them with individualistic fantasies. Most likely you hold a complex version of social struggle and compromise, and of ideological complexity. Since Maine's incredibly popular anthropological foray, his generalization assumed a life of its own in popular and academic debates about liberal modernity. Conversations invoking it contain assumptions about "contract," "status," and the commitments that "status-to-contract" implied, which inform historical understandings of Victorian liberalism.

This book is a study of Victorian liberalism in contracts. It examines liberal thought as developed through, and as it developed, the concept of contract understood as the formal legal category of binding agreement, and the relations and human practices at which it gestured, most basically that of promise, most broadly the capitalist market order. It treats status-to-contract very seriously, yet intervenes in some accepted assumptions about its elements. Victorian liberalism was a serious effort to imagine existence beyond status, that is, beyond much that had made it meaningful for centuries; such a world, as Raymond Williams put it, "had no new forms, no

1 "[W]e may say that the movement of the progressive societies has hitherto been a movement from Status to Contract." Henry Sumner Maine, *Ancient Law: Its Connection with the Early History of Society and Its Relation to Modern Ideas* (New York: Henry Holt, 1906), 165.

significant moments, until these were made and given by direct human actions."[2] Status-to-contract is a historical construct without which the content of various elements of liberalism in contracts cannot be understood. Yet current understandings of the liberal effort in contracts need reconstructing from both ends of the formula. On the side of contract, historical accounts of its liberal content have been oscillating between atomism and social-collective approaches, missing out on forms of relationality in Victorian liberal conceptualizations of contracts which this study seeks to establish in their complexity, richness, and wavering appeal. On the side of status, the expectation of a move "from status" has led to a split along the liberal/radical fault line among those assessing liberalism's historical commitment to promote equality. The split misses out on the possibility that liberalism functioned as a historical reinterpretation of statuses, rather than either an effort of their elimination or preservation. That reinterpretation effectively secured, yet also altered, status hierarchies. There is no teleology to such an account.

To examine liberalism in contracts beyond prevalent debates, this study places canonical realist novels in conversation with legal-historical knowledge about Victorian contracts.

Novels and Liberalism

As I introduce the logic and arguments of the chapters that follow, my methodological assumptions and terminological challenges will become clearer. Two clarifications, however, I want to offer upfront so as not to obscure the introductory discussion. One is the study's methodological focus on novels. The cultural significance of realist fiction is too well established in scholarship on Victorian liberalism to require justification. I do, however, want to emphasize elements of particular relevance for the book.

Accounting for the place of fiction in modernity, and as a specifically modern idea, a dominant line of theorists, among them Lennard J. Davis, Robert Newsom and Catherine Gallagher, explains literary realism as an assertion of truth of a particular order: that of the probable or credible. Realist novels established a cultural standing and claimed to be realistic by describing factual events that did not happen – an openly admitted element of fictionality, but could have – hence different from mere deception.[3] This order of truth claimed insight into the historical conditions of

2 Raymond Williams, *The English Novel from Dickens to Lawrence* (London: Hogarth Press, 1984), Introduction.

3 Lennard J. Davis. *Factual Fictions: The Origins of the English Novel* (New York: Columbia University Press, 1983); Robert Newsom, *A Likely Story: Probability and Play in Fiction* (New Brunswick, NJ: Rutgers University Press, 1988); Catherine Gallagher, "The Rise of Fictionality" in Franco Moretti, ed., *The Novel, Volume 1: History, Geography, and Culture* (Princeton, NJ: Princeton University Press, 2006): 336–63. On the communal extension

social existence, examined in concretized form. The novel's focus on the ordinary, the average and breaches of the average, its interest in both social expansiveness and depth psychology, its obsession with the tension between uniqueness and representation, the conventional forms underlying realist effects which came to be at once admitted, even centralized – as the history of aesthetics reveals, and yet overlooked, all were tied up with a focus on the immanent conditions of self in society. Representing that which could have happened constituted, by claiming to represent, historical subject positions, motivations and responses, patterns of relations, and social structures. In all of this, promissory relations became both formal and thematic infrastructure. As a genre, realist novels were a cultural site which recognized the centrality of promises for the liberal outlook and worked out the implications with painstaking attention. As I elaborate in Chapter 4, this is no surprise. Theories of literary realism often recognize its formal dependence on relationships, and promises were only the most formalized cases.[4] Promises, in other words, lay at the core of the artistic modeling and interrogation of the Victorian capitalist order that realist novels were.

Sophisticated historical work examines liberalism in contract law in terms that resonate with these insights about literary realism. Contract law is understood as a substantiation of a capitalist social order premised on claims to already find that order: to develop doctrine and rules, to judge practice, and to institute legal relations, by claiming to observe the already-existing choices of individual agents within relationships and social structures fitting a liberal vision of the world. And of course promises were at the heart of this project, a point I will revisit below as I clarify the contract/promise relationality.

Both contract law and novels are appropriately viewed as sites that attempted to provide cultural scripts for the reading – and living – of contractual relations in a capitalist world. Such efforts are habitually understood in legal theory in terms of normativity, yet as work in the inter-discipline of *Law and Literature* often demonstrates, normativity is generated ideationally no less than materially. Law has not been the sole

of this theory see Ayelet Ben-Yishai, *Common Precedents: The Presentness of the Past in Victorian Law and Fiction* (New York: Oxford University Press, 2013).

4 One theory that Chapter 4 does not examine is the so-called author-reader contract. At stake is a relationship between author and reader which some theorists have suggested is the very center of realism. See Brook Thomas, *American Literary Realism and the Failed Promise of Contract* (Berkeley, CA: University of California Press, 1997). I do not examine discursive uses of the author–reader contractual metaphor in Victorian culture at large and therefore cannot dispute its significance, then again, theoretically I do not want to accept or assume a-priori a particular meaning of contract or promise that would inform my treatment of the author-reader relationship, for that meaning is my basic question. As my discussion in Chapter 3 implies, if one is inclined to use contractual language for the author-reader relationship, relational liberalism might be fruitful.

or even the most important mode of norm-making in capitalism. Visions of human experience are produced in various sites of culture, of which the novel was in Victorian times of the most central.[5] The novel's centrality does not in itself tell us anything a priori about its position vis-à-vis law. I will later have more to say about the implications of this study for accounts of law and literature. But it does imply historical relevance. As Bradin Cormack suggests, "legal analysis becomes critical by reopening the exclusionary discourse of law onto a more complex scene than that remembered as the image the law produces through and as its own historiography."[6]

Yet novels have remained oddly marginalized in contracts histories. In examining the question of liberalism in contracts, research drawing on literary sources (among others) which *has* formed conversations with Victorian contracts histories, unusual as it is, has been important for my work. It includes Margot Finn's work on credit relations, Irene Tucker's work on the problem of historicity in contractual liberal subjectivity, and work on the promise of marriage, for instance by Ginger S. Frost, Saskia Lettmaier, and Randall Craig. I draw on their and others' work in the following chapters, as well as on the broader field of Victorian liberalism, where cultural and literary histories habitually examine themes relevant to the history of contracts without directly addressing contracts histories. My analysis is narrower than much of this work in that its primary sources are novels, and broader in terms of its investigation of promissory types and conceptual concerns in contracts. The methodology is geared to reopen existing understandings and loci of debate in contracts histories.

In the chapters that follow I examine seven novels by different authors, published across the high Victorian era. The methodology is by no means exhaustive; I do not claim a comprehensive historical account. Rather, I have focused on a number of rich cultural expressions of liberal concerns with contracts across an era of rapid change and intense debates about the capitalist order. I do suggest, however, that the common streaks emerging across artistic diversity reveal something beyond isolated individual cases.

In Part I, I point to the liberal problematization of status-sociality in contracts, and to a dominant style of relational liberalism which emerged as an alternative to status, on the basis of six novels. The novels are viewed, as Claudia Klaver puts it in another context, as themselves historical

5 See for instance Sara Murphy, "The Law, the Norm and the Novel," in *Studies in Law, Politics and Society: Special Issue – Law and Literature Reconsidered*, ed. Austin Sarat (London: Emerald, 2008): 53–78.

6 Bradin Cormack, *A Power to Do Justice: Jurisdiction, English Literature, and the Rise of Common Law, 1509–1625* (Chicago, IL: University of Chicago Press, 2007), 28.

7 Claudia C. Klaver, *A/Moral Economics: Classical Political Economy and Cultural Authority in Nineteenth-Century England* (Columbus, OH: Ohio State University Press, 2003), xix.

events.[7] That these novels are canonical, at least arguably so, is important. The canon has become contested not only due to controversies about borders emerging from divergent theories of realism, but also because canonization is troubling as a process of hegemony-consolidation. Yet that is the minimal generalization I do seek. Precisely the historical force attributed to the canon by its critics explains why reading it is justified in dialogue with legal history interested in hegemonic norm-making.

In Part II I work under the assumption that, as John Kucich puts it, "[w]ithout a sense of the interplay between individual creation and general cultural structures, we belie the complex ways in which experience is actually shaped for the sake of polemical convenience."[8] I read individual texts alongside broader historical developments in law that legal histories have recovered, so as to get a glimpse at, indeed, general cultural structures, as I explain further in a moment.

I have consciously avoided a delimitation of novels to those especially concerned with legal institutions, or whose authors had profound legal knowledge. I concur with Brook Thomas who, in a study of contract and realism in America, observes that "[w]hat fascinated ordinary people … was not the legal doctrine … but the idea of contract as a mode of social organization …"[9] The interest of this study is liberal thought as implicated with contract as a social relation and organizing principle of order. Legal mechanics of enforcement do at some points become important, but are not at the center of the analysis.

A second clarification concerns my use of "liberalism," a concept almost hopelessly morphing into the theory of everything, the Humanities' closest response to the ambitions of Physics. If, as Lionel Trilling argued, liberalism is "a large tendency rather than a concise body of doctrine,"[10] at once historically concrete and wonderfully encompassing, then some specification is in order not by way of conclusive definitions, but rather as a matter of analytic choices and emphases.[11]

In invoking "liberalism" I do not gesture at a specific political philosophy nor institutional politics of the Victorian Liberal party. Instead I gesture at an accumulation of ideas that manifest in dominant sites of Victorian social thought like law and novels which, through their generic structures, put abstract ideals under pressures of ongoing concretization. As a minimum,

8 John Kucich, *Repression in Victorian Fiction: Charlotte Bronte, George Eliot, and Charles Dickens* (Berkeley, CA: University of California Press, 1987), 33.

9 Brook Thomas, *American Literary Realism*, 1.

10 Lionel Trilling, *Liberal Imagination: Essays on Literature and Society* (New York: Viking Press, 1950), xi.

11 As Goodlad has recently urged, Lauren M.E. Goodlad, "Liberalism and Literature" in *The Oxford Handbook of Victorian Literary Culture*, ed. Juliet John (Oxford: Oxford University Press, 2016), 103–23.

these ideas revealed an interest in conceiving a social order no longer predominated by statuses, and in giving shape to processes of individualization involving some measure of discomfort with ascriptive accounts of human existence based on social place and role. This is close to what David Wayne Thomas describes as liberalism's assumption that individuals act within "a sociality to which they adhere through their own volition." However, as he also notes, in this phrasing there is already an overdose of atomism that I will want to complicate, hence my emphasis on the alternative of status-sociality against which liberal thought defined itself.[12] Within this status-problematizing project, I am interested specifically in the relation of individualization to Victorian concerns with the capitalist market order and its accommodation.

Novels, like contract law, have been repeatedly associated with Victorian capitalism. W.J. Harvey once argued that "[o]ne of the few Marxist generalizations about literature to hold up reasonably well when put to the test of detailed historical examination is the thesis that the development of the novel is intimately connected with the growth of the bourgeoisie in a modern capitalist system. From this social process derive the assumptions and value we may conveniently if crudely lump together as liberalism."[13] There are endless echoes to this view in literary histories, similar ones about law in the histories of contracts – many of which are discussed in the chapters that follow, and increasingly in the past two decades, challenges and complications too. The liberalism I explore often complicated the ideological commitments and worldviews classically associated with the Victorian bourgeoisie, be they idealized domesticity and sphere separations, the meaningfulness of the private, the security of psychological interiority, the authority of classical political economy (in its popular versions at least) or else. Yet the positions which concern this study were not about external critique. By engaging questions about capitalist ethics like work or thrift, capitalist articles of faith like the market's promise of prosperity or the relation of economic to cultural capital, processes of identity formation under Victorian capitalism, or indeed material life in an industrializing and financializing economy, the texts I examine were at once interrogating and spinning the conditions of possibility of their emergent capitalist world.

In all of this, contracts and promises were central elements of thought and expression.

12 David Wayne Thomas, *Cultivating Victorians: Liberal Culture and the Aesthetic* (Philadelphia, PA: University of Pennsylvania Press, 2004), 14.

13 W.J. Harvey, *Character and the Novel* (London: Chatto &Windus, 1965), 24.

Victorian Liberalism and Contracts in History

The Victorian era is commonly described as "The Age of Contract." This was the era in which the law of contract assumed its modern shape and became the conceptual center of private law. It was also the era in which liberalism came to hinge on contract as the basis of the economy, or more broadly relations in civil society, as opposed to contract's much more salient role in earlier modernity in terms of political obligation and obedience to sovereign power, in the philosophy of the social contract.

I begin by examining what we know about liberalism in contracts from the most dominant strands of existing contracts histories. Chapter 1 reviews legal histories in the inclusionary sense of scholarship on Victorian contract law and contractual relations broadly understood, drawing on diverse historical schools – doctrinal, internalist, liberal, feminist, critical and cultural. I critically read between the lines of controversies for the implicit narratives that histories of contracts have generated from the late Victorian era to the twenty-first century. My interest in Chapter 1 is to clarify how histories provide an account of the concept of contract in Victorian liberal thought in terms of atomistic individualism, often despite an overtly critical perspective. In this account, promise represents a socially-disembedded expression of an individual will; the social structure is described in terms of separate spheres, with the market as a distinct domain driven by economic motive; and the promising person in the market – or the contracting person – is a rational agent. Contract's "social" rivals – status included, have been collectivized and relegated to the role of external challenges, their operations for the most part unacknowledged in terms of the Victorian *liberal* conceptualization of contract itself, and certainly not in individualized terms, even as social alternatives sometimes aligned with the welfarist goals of political liberalism of late nineteenth century. A relational liberal vision of contract is almost completely absent from the dominant strands of contracts histories (with possible exceptions I note).

The following chapters, divided to two parts, begin a revision of our historical knowledge about Victorian liberalism in contracts.

From Status: Relational Liberalism in Contracts

Part I, *From Status*, argues for the historical significance of relational sociality as a liberal construct informing visions of contracts. By "relational sociality" I refer to a primary and fundamental explanatory and normative role for interpersonal and discrete relationships, with those individualized elements in them exceeding statuses emphasized. Relational liberalism in contracts challenged status-sociality, was indeed attractive *as* an alternative to status, but was also a challenge to atomism. The implications of relational liberalism therefore require a dual emphasis: When read against the pressures of status ascriptions, the individualizing tendencies of relational liberalism should be acknowledged, yet its social tendencies should be kept in view when read against the histories of atomistic individualism.

To clarify the conceptual place of relational liberalism I open Part I with a discussion, rooted in the work of Mark Granovetter, of the analytic significance of making distinctions between forms of social embeddedness, particularly between status- and relational embeddedness, that theorists and historians of relationality tend to collapse together. Although, for reasons I explain, "embeddedness" is often a misleading term for my purposes, Granovetter's distinctions are essential to the argument. I isolate relationality in order to explain its historical appeal for the liberally-oriented. Yet, for the same reason I do not propose to disperse it completely to its multiple individualized contexts, as some theories of relationality invite us to do: the liberal turn lay in the abstract idea of existence constituted by individualized relationships, frequently captured by the Victorian image of the web.

The chapters of Part I include readings in novels which engaged with promises intensively. My analyses straddle a wide array of promissory contexts, for instance, those of commerce, employment, land, and familial intimacy. In examining a multiplicity of promissory types I acknowledge and test the liberal aspiration of the Victorian era, described in contracts histories, to create a general category of contract based on a generalized idea of promise. Historians have repeatedly observed an imperialistic tendency in classical legal thought, first to recast a multiplicity of relations in promissory terms, and then to apply to them all a single set of ideas. Readings across various promises allow me to examine the scope described in contracts histories, and touch central concerns of Victorian culture invoked by contract. As the following account should clarify, my analytical position does not deny differences of promissory context, parties, or subject matter, nor does it overlook the insights of scholarship focused on particular promissory types. Indeed it draws on them. Across the diverse range of concerns and by virtue of its broadness, certain persistent understandings of capitalist existence can be observed in their full historical significance. The pervasiveness of these understandings, and their implications for liberalism in contracts beyond context-specific differences, would be difficult to appreciate in a study limited to a particular promissory type. Relationality, rather than either status or atomism, emerges as indeed a wide-ranging, context-crossing liberal effort.

Chapter 2 tackles the question of the economic domain's construction as a separate sphere, the basic concern of contracts histories, speaking to liberal contracts' relation to Victorian capitalism. I examine the question in William Thackeray's *Vanity Fair* (1847), and Anthony Trollope's *The Way We Live Now* (1875). My reading alternates between the two novels while I focus on a central axis in both: credit-based efforts to gain social capital by two parallel protagonists, Becky Sharp and Augustus Melmotte. Thackeray and Trollope both pointed with displeasure to contracts' entanglement in status relations, particularly gender, class and nationality. Gender and class are familiar in historical contracts scholarship as Chapter 1 clarifies, yet contract's role as an exclusionary nationalist construct has gone almost unheeded despite the extensive literature on liberalism's nationalist or at least Eurocentric entailments.

The credit contract's entanglement in statuses led both Thackeray and Trollope to differentiate it from money, a process I read with current theoretical debates about money. Credit, both novels suggested, preserves a social memory contradicting the obliteration of history that the rule of money encouraged. The credit contract, often taken as the paradigm instrument of the Victorian market economy, was paradoxically construed by novelists as a cultural obstacle to a rational market.

Thackeray and Trollope understood at least some of contract's status entanglements as a problem. The critical impulse drove them to seek alternatives, but here differences are more telling than commonalities. The ideology of a rational economy premised on epistemological certainties was finally articulated in *The Way We Live Now* as a never-materialized alternative; Trollope was unable to see how contract could be a tool to such a market even as he coveted it. *Vanity Fair* preferred a moral vision of the social whole inflected by relational intersubjective intimacy, again one which remained unrealized in the narrative. Thackeray and Trollope represented, I suggest, two polar conceptual alternatives for the social order, located at the two ends of high Victorianism: the social order as metaphoric family, and the social order as separate spheres. The next chapters argue that the solution of novelists to pressures to imagine a contractual society often lay somewhere between these two unrealized alternatives. Relationality became a favored focus of promissory representations in the effort to shake statuses off. It was removed from a sentimental morality of *Vanity Fair*, but was also far from the vision of demarcated spheres that *The Way We Live Now* aspired.

Chapter 3 engages with the question of abstraction, a recurrent theme in contracts histories. The liberal atomism that histories describe transpired in various abstract iterations of individual agency, supporting a view of a rational market economy. Reading two mid-century novels, Elizabeth Gaskell's *Ruth* (1853) and Charles Dickens' *Bleak House* (1853), I argue that both exhibited a dramatic recoil from abstraction. In *Ruth* abstraction was treated literally, as a possible state of existence considered dangerous. In *Bleak House* abstraction was a moral choice rather than a factual condition, emerging in an (im)moral economy. Gaskell's and Dickens' positions complicate the argument that liberalism was prone to abstraction in consequence of social realities that had themselves become abstract under capitalism.[14] The experience of social life as abstract was then as now a matter of mediation. As Amanda Anderson's work on modern practices of detachment, discussed in the chapter, shows, abstraction was never an easy project. The alternative to abstraction, Chapter 3 argues, was a relational liberalism.

In *Ruth* we see a heroine (Ruth) falling from virtue in consequence of two continuous processes: a detachment of economic from relational concerns – a staging of a disembedded economy, cast as a generalization of the principle of prostitution – sex coupled with money, without love; and a consequent detachment from social meanings – a radical staging of Ruth as an abstract individual. These processes and their relational reversal, when Ruth is socialized by relationships, and learns to resist money without love, were dramatized through her evolving promissory agency. The novel's relational solution, however, was ultimately unstable, because Gaskell inflected her art with a competing transcendent morality. Gaskell's difficulty with liberal solutions assumed other forms with other novelists, but all of them betrayed how unsure a project liberalism was.

Bleak House's critique of abstraction was far reaching. My reading focuses on the web of credit in the novel, which was informed by Dickens' obsession with relational interdependencies – *Bleak House's* famed "connexions." The moral imperative to always connect, never abstract, that Dickens posited in the narration of credit relations, I argue, made the web of credit disappear as a system: it was dispersed among the multiple relationalities of which it was made. It is therefore a small surprise that the credit web has not been a significant focus of readings of *Bleak House* concerned with its critique of systems and its political economy. *Bleak House's* narration of credit stood in direct opposition to the state order represented in the court and the police. The novel's liberal turn, I argue, depended on that implicit opposition between state and market, from which the credit web, for all its rapaciousness, emerged as a more attractive mode of social organization.

Representations of a relational economy, as both Gaskell and Dickens developed, thus should not be read as resistances to the capitalist order. They cannot be read into a history of the Polanyian "double movement" in which relationality was a defensive embedding response to an emergent market system. Instead, they were a form of implementation of a market economy. We should be able to see two implications: Novelists' emphases on the relational constitution of the economy serve as correctives to assumptions in contacts histories about the hegemony of atomism. At the same time, precisely the nonabstract mode of novelistic liberalism made the capitalist order alluring in its potential responsiveness, its complex creation of opportunities to exercise whatever agency could be got.

14 Recently made by Andrew Sartori, *Liberalism in Empire: An Alternative History* (Berkeley, CA: University of California Press, 2014).

Chapter 4 engages another theme of contracts histories: the liberal association of contract with freedom, supposedly the heart of contract's appeal as a principle of social order. With George Eliot's *Middlemarch* (1871) and Thomas Hardy's *The Mayor of Casterbridge* (1886) we see a move from the mid-century project of impressing on readers the importance of relationality for individual agency and for the morality of choice, toward explorations of the constraining implications of living in a web of relationships. The consciousness of constraints highlighted relationality as the basis of the liberal contractual order, yet reversed associations of contract with freedom.

In *Middlemarch* I read the parallel stories of three protagonists, Lydgate, Dorothea, and Fred, where the fictionalization of promises – most significantly the men's contractual debts and Dorothea's deathbed never-made-promise to her husband – is pivotal to the unfolding of plots dealing with relational interdependence, with all the suffocation involved. Eliot, I argue, gave artistic expression to the concerns of liberal philosophy with voluntary submission as an everyday necessity. Her tool for negotiating promissory suffocation was the practice of economy. While Dickens and Gaskell made room for the capitalist market through relational socialization, Eliot incorporated popular political-economic advice about economic prudence into the terms of meaningful existence in the web of constraints. Yet the advice finally falters and reveals Eliot's hesitation. Her ultimate achievement was in forming a non-naïve liberal consciousness: Eliot's liberalism offered a sense of hope that one could embrace without thereby being the fool who does not realize how limited it is, a position that resonates with us still.

Hardy, writing at the outskirts of high Victorianism and the margins of realism, was far more pessimistic. *The Mayor of Casterbridge* examined contractual constraint through the problem of masculinity in contracts. Reading Hardy's protagonist, Henchard, with histories of Victorian masculinity, I observe how an atomistic approach to contracts is associated with a particular vision of conventional masculinity, and represented as ruinous in a capitalistic world of tamed passions, where relational awareness is key to prosperity. I begin with the novel's brutal opening scene of wife sale, which foretells Henchard's downfall both causally and symbolically. The downfall plot is then narrated through junctions of promissory overload, in which the character of Farfrae appears as a foil for the novel's protagonist without the rigid masculine debasement. Viewing conventional masculinity as a victimizing imperative in modern capitalism, Hardy's art compensates for a blindspot in contracts histories, which have read the gender of contract from the perspective of women's exclusions, and have too often left the positive content of contract – its inclusions, to nongendered readings. Hardy highlighted the inescapable relationality of the capitalist order, but viewed it with suspicion.

Part I reassesses the history of liberalism in contracts, but is also in implicit dialogues with theoretical concerns in *Law and Literature*, and in contract theory, on which I would like to briefly comment.

Law, Literature and Relational Liberalism in Contracts

It is not my intention to frame literature as a corrective to law. I am not methodologically positioned to deny that the insights of relational liberalism I highlight in literature were marginalized in law, as existing histories imply, because this study does not compare novels with primary legal sources. However, I am inclined to speculate in another direction.

To contend that law developed a distinct liberalism is possible. Indeed, there are good reasons to think that generic differences between law and literature, particularly differentiated author functions, bolstered atomism in law.[15] However, to imply that a dominant liberal view of contracts, which permeated a hegemonic cultural site like literary realism, was almost missing from law, is unconvincing even if one accepts the significance of genre differentiations, and more generally concedes a level of autonomy to law. The body of research on Victorian law and fiction has already dispelled any claims to unbridgeable distinctions between them on the level of ideology. A better hypothesis for the too-stark absence of relational liberalism from Victorian contracts histories, is that the narrative structures which have typified debates among contracts historians (explored in Chapter 1), have diverted attention from relationality as a distinct mode of liberalism. This has been the case even as the findings of some work in the field, particularly feminist history, already point to the presence of relational liberalism. At least in some areas of law prone to liberal idealizations, at least some of the time, relational liberalism must have inflected contracts.

Part I's contribution cannot be framed as a literary corrective to law even if we were to assume that atomism dominated law to the exclusion of other liberal visions, at least not in the romantic sense that the role of the literary sometimes assumes in *Law and Literature* scholarship. For instance, in a recent book Alison LaCrois and Martha Nussbaum associate novels with movements of social recognition which challenged the legal neglect of weakened social groups, and so argue that "[o]verwhelmingly, the eyes of the law were opened by novels."[16] My analysis of relational liberalism in contracts can hardly fall into this framing. At the very least, if law was committed to atomism while novels embraced relationality, at stake were two ideological attempts to construe the capitalist order. My readings are

15 Anat Rosenberg, "The History of Genres: Reaching for Reality in Law and Literature," *Law & Social Inquiry* 39, no. 4 (2014): 1057–79.

16 Introduction to Martha C. Nussbaum and Alison L. LaCroix eds., *Subversion and Sympathy: Gender, Law, and the British Novel* (New York: Oxford University Press, 2013), 4.

interested as much in the manner of making capitalist structures attractive through the relational mode of thought, as they are in pointing to the blindspots of atomism. From this perspective, my claims offer correctives not to law but to views of literature as a subversive counter to law, in which law alone assumes the role of the suspected hegemony.

At the same time, Part I also diverges from another ideal position in *Law and Literature* scholarship, in which law and literature are described as ideologically convergent, mutually supportive hegemonic discourses. Hegemonic though they were, and entangled with the capitalist order, they were not speaking to a single and shared idea of liberalism. For generic reasons as well as due to liberalism's messy history as such, we should acknowledge internal complexity which does not easily align with a single delineation of liberal ideology. Complexities in liberalism have been increasingly elaborated in the cultural histories on which I draw in the following chapters.

Relational Contract Theory and Relational Liberalism in Contract

Contracts scholars are familiar with relational contract theory which originated with the American theorist Ian Macneil in the 1960s. Macneil framed his theory as an express alternative to the Victorian classical school which placed at the center of contracts the imaginary of the discrete transaction, rather than ongoing relations. Readers might fairly wonder if I am reading the theory back into history. I am not resistant to such a project in principle, and Macneil himself argued that his concept of contract was "the oldest of contracts."[17] Moreover, one is never free from presentist concerns, and certainly without relational contract theory, and also, more broadly, present-day relational liberal philosophy, my language and imaginative frameworks in Part I would have been different. However, too quick a collapse of relational contract theory with this study's claims is probably unwarranted. The book is not structured by the analytic categories of relational contract theory but is rather a study of cultural meanings. More fundamentally, on the more abstract level of liberalism in contracts, Macneil's work in the twentieth century appeared to miss the novelistic point before it began. Everything associated with promises in novels, Macneil attributed to "non-promissory" elements. His exposé in *The New Social Contract* began by arguing that "promises are inescapably but fragments of any contractual relation."[18] Yet a great part of relational liberalism in novels addressed promises.

17 Ian R. Macneil, *The New Social Contract: An Inquiry into Modern Contractual Relations* (New Haven, CT: Yale University Press, 1980), xii.

18 Macneil, *The New Social Contract*, 8. He expressed the same distinction much later, see Ian R. Macneil, "Relational Contract Theory: Challenges and Queries," *Northwestern University Law Review* 94 (2000): 877–908.

My readings of fictionalized promises purposely do not distinguish unenforceable from enforceable ones (i.e. contracts), and locate relational concerns in contracts already at the level of promise. To reexamine Victorian liberalism in contracts one would have to start with promises, for on many accounts, including Macneil's, they were the conceptual heart of the atomistic project. To clarify this point, consider briefly the place of promise between the history and theory of contracts.

Legal scholars generally agree that a contract is an enforceable promise (or set of promises), or, to relax the formulation – that contract involves a promise. The actual act or relation of promising, in other words, is a necessary element of contract. As Chapter 1 explains, historically it was classical legal thought, with its celebration of the individual will, that centralized contract around promise, itself understood as self-imposed obligation. Around the same time, Nietzsche articulated the radical implications of this assumption in forging a historically novel consciousness: "To breed an animal with the prerogative to promise – is that not precisely the paradoxical task which nature has set herself with regard to humankind?" Promise, he said, is "the *will's memory*"; the prerogative to promise underlay Nietzche's account of the historical emergence of the "*sovereign* individual," whose mastery-in-responsibility was an internalization of social straitjackets which he then wore with pride.[19] Nietzsche had in mind earlier contractual discourses, but in 1887 he was cognizant of the power of promise to breathe life into the idea of the individual will. His radical reminder of the social process behind the celebration of the will recalls the not-too-distant history in which the English were rigorously debating the meaning of promise. As Victoria Kahn's history of early modern contractual discourse reveals, in the seventeenth century, when the language of contract became prominent in political theory, the English were acutely aware of the poetic power involved in the feat of the promising individual, and of the instability of such contingent emergence of obligation, rather than already convinced by liberal notions of autonomy and liberty, the stabilizing power of self-interest, or the presence of instrumental rationality. Promise and contract had not yet been liberalized.[20] By the Victorian era, the role of promise in contract as it is described by contracts histories, appears to have relied on a forgone conclusion that left an earlier richness and elasticity of concepts behind.

19 Friedrich Nietzsche, *On the Genealogy of Morality*, trans. Carol Diethe, ed. Keith Ansell-Pearson (Cambridge: Cambridge University Press, 2006), 35–6 (emphases in the original).

20 Victoria Kahn, *Wayward Contracts: The Crisis of Political Obligation in England, 1640–1674* (Princeton, NJ: Princeton University Press, 2004). On Kahn's account contract in fact first transformed promise, essentially secularized and conventionalized it. Ibid., Chapter 4.

Within contract scholarship, the implications of the process of "promisizing" contract are easiest to grasp not through Victorian histories alone but through some of the theoretical debates that followed them in the twentieth and twenty-first centuries. If promise is a human relationship integral to contract, which is little contested, theories that challenge the atomism of the classical legacy, like Macneil's, and that seek to instate communal and relational aspects in contract law, suggest that there are, or should be, other components or meanings to contract which exceed promise – exceed individual will; these theories therefore deny that promise is, or should be, the source of contract's binding nature. Put differently, in theoretical debates over contract, promise often functions as a byword for the atomism associated by historians with classical legal thought. Implicitly accepting the historical association of promise with the individual will, such theoretical positions displace the basic question of promise history and philosophy about the meaning of promise, which was never entirely put to rest,[21] onto contract; the question becomes: is contract exhausted by acts of individual will?[22] The debate begins, however, with the historical process which made promise central for contract while implicitly assuming that it was a self-imposed obligation. This is a point Macneil did not challenge, but is central for this study's analysis of Victorian liberal conceptualizations of contract.

Given the legal identification of the meaning of Victorian contract in promise (read: self-imposed obligation) which emerges from contracts histories, conceptualizations of promise are a necessary part of the analysis. Dealing only with enforceable promises in novels (a doubtful effort in itself), would overlook the locus of conceptualization. A Gordian knot between contract and promise was indeed pervasive, but not on the atomistic terms familiar from contracts histories.

21 I will not engage the extensive debates about promise in moral philosophy for my interest is in the particular way promise has been crystalized in thought on Victorian contracts. Suffice to mention the way that Arendt, who was indebted to Nietzsche in attributing to promises a central place in *The Human Condition*, also departed from him in keeping upfront the relational dependence of the promising person, whose own identity continually depended on recognition by others: "Without being bound to the fulfilment of promises, we would never be able to keep our identities; we would be condemned to wander helplessly and without direction in the darkness of each man's lonely heart, caught in its contradictions and equivocalities – a darkness which only the light shed over the public realm through the presence of others, who confirm the identity between the one who promises and the one who fulfils, can dispel." Hannah Arendt, *The Human Condition* (Chicago, IL: The University of Chicago Press, 1958), 237.

22 Jody Kraus, following up on the ongoing debate sparked anew in recent years, calls for an assessment of the basis of promise itself before moving on to its relation to contract. Kraus's account, however, relies on a deontic moral theory to ground the familiar assumption that a theory of promise is necessarily a "theory of *self-imposed* moral responsibility," under which obligations are created by virtue of the individual will. Jody Kraus, "The Correspondence of Contract and Promise," *Columbia Law Review* 109, no. 7 (2009): 1603–49.

Beyond these points of difference from relational contract theory, it is worth observing that in seeking to show what contract meant "beyond promise" Macneil pulled together various forms of sociality, as other theorists of relationality often do, among them status and interpersonal relationships. For purposes of the historical argument of Part I, I re-differentiate these forms, as Victorians did.

With Status: Liberal Complexity Reassessed

Problematizing status, as explorations of relational liberalism did in novels, hardly meant statuses' elimination. Thinkers today still face the problem of reconciling hard-wired group identities which had never disappeared and have in fact regained some of their charm – partly because they appear inescapable, partly on substantive grounds – with liberal ideals of universality, mobility, equality or autonomy.[23] In Part II I put aside the tensions between relational and atomistic liberalism in contracts, in order to examine the terms of coexistence of liberal ideals – contract among them – and status hierarchies. These hierarchies posed challenges for liberalism of any hue, as they still do. The difficulty that interests me in Part II in fact exceeds the problem of statuses, and touches the question of complexity as such, that is, the existence of apparently contradictory yet intertwined conceptual commitments in liberalism.

Victorianist scholarship has increasingly moved away from binary oppositions toward complexity across the full scale of questions that the concept of contract brings to the fore. Philosophies of individualism have been subjected to the scrutiny of diverse strands (as have varieties of capitalism in global perspective); political economy as well as its external critiques have been broken down to internal divides across time, among writers, among influences religious and secular; gender ideology is no longer seen as merely oppressive for women, but complex, with varieties and uncertainties which imply opportunities for women as well as obstacles for men. The same goes for particular systems that dominated the Victorian social order, like marriage and credit. The widening engagements with complexity have been implicated with a theoretical move beyond suspicious hermeneutics. These developments provide rich grounds for Part II, which seeks theoretical terms for historical complexity in Chapter 5, and examines their aesthetic enactment in Chapter 6.

Part II relies on two liminal sites: the promise of marriage, and Emily Brontë's *Wuthering Heights* (1847). I therefore open it with a brief discussion of liminality in cultural analysis.

23 Benhabib for instance seeks to situate "reason and the moral self ... in contexts of gender and community." Seyla Benhabib, *Situating the Self: Gender, Community and Postmodernism in Contemporary Ethics* (Cambridge: Polity Press, 1992), 7.

Chapter 5 examines the coexistence of liberal ideals and statuses in the promise of marriage. Unlike previous chapters, my discussion turns not only on contract as a liberal ideal but also on romantic love, a liberal ideal central no less than contract in this context. To discuss the role of love I return to *Bleak House* and *Middlemarch*, where the love matches of female protagonists – Esther and Dorothea – are central to the plot, as are problems of class and gender from which love is inextricable. In discussing contract, however, I turn back to law, and explore findings of historians concerning broad legal processes, like developments in the doctrine and litigation practice of the promise of marriage. With both love and contract, literature and law, I examine the continuing power of gender and class hierarchies.

Debates among historians who address hierarchic power and inequality have oscillated between liberal and radical interpretations. At one pole the persistence of class and gender is treated as a matter of slow and difficult progress, at the other as the very essence of liberalism. Chapter 5 seeks a new interpretation, relying on the move between close readings and analyses of broad processes to observe shared structural responses.

The central possibility explored in Chapter 5 is that the coexistence of liberal ideals and statuses was a conceptually-patterned one. I examine two patterns: containment and withdrawal. Containment refers to efforts to rationalize and assimilate considerations of status within the conceptual frameworks of contract and love. In consequence, those considerations were reduced in magnitude, their effects and relevance redirected. By contrast, under withdrawal, the application of the liberal framework (contract, love) was bordered rather than expanded, leaving areas beyond it to forces of status, but the delimitation was construed as inconsequential because liberal ideals retained relevance in areas treated as the core of social relations; cultural energies were accordingly rechanneled. Both containment and withdrawal repositioned statuses vis-à-vis liberal ideals, at once preserving hierarchic powers and undermining their ability to serve as explanations and goals of social relations. These two effects allow us to view Victorian liberalism as, ultimately, a new interpretation of statuses. Containment and withdrawal functioned like cultural codes – historically contingent, unplanned, not coherently serviceable to any interest, power or normative aspiration, yet sticky through their embeddedness in culture. With these patterns there was no single trajectory to be expected, as present-day debates about identity politics, discussed at the close of the chapter, clarify.

Chapter 6 argues that in *Wuthering Heights* (1847), Brontë offered an early and sophisticated argument about the pattern of containment as a dominant liberal mode for handling internal tensions. *Wuthering Heights* hinged on promissory junctions, crucial among them Heathcliff's arrival as a broken promise. The novel's representations of promises clarified the implications of containment as a patterned manner of handling, and maintaining, conceptual tensions in liberalism. At stake in *Wuthering Heights* was not only the problem of status hierarchies, but a messier set of ideas often considered problematic for liberal idealizations, among them irrationality, untamed passion, and the supernatural. My motivation in observing these tensions is not just to extend the argument about containment, but also, and more importantly, to point to an aesthetic enactment of the anguish that liberal structures of complexity were to evoke for the decades that followed. That anguish was registered in *Wuthering Heights*' troubled reception.

At the close of Chapter 6 I discuss some of the theoretical implications of ideological dysfunction, to which the patterns discussed in Part II speak. The implicit assumption of the functionality of ideology has dominated debates about the status-to-contract formulation. It should be abandoned if we are to take the formulation seriously as an effort to instate a new social order, yet acknowledge that statuses were never left behind.

The components and framework of status-to-contract were historically dramatic, yet on terms that have remained too often unacknowledged, and otherwise only partially and inconsistently conceptualized in contracts histories of the Victorian era. The following chapters endeavor to both demonstrate and conceptualize correctives.

Chapter 1

Contract's Liberalism in Contracts Histories

If you were inclined to search for ghosts in Victorianist scholarship, the atomistic individualism of Victorian contract law would be a promising start: a historical construct holding present understandings of Victorian contract in its grip despite continuing critique and reevaluation. This book, too, is a reevaluation, yet in opening with this chapter I risk resurrecting the ghost. I acknowledge the risk, but ask you to bear with me. The aim is not merely an account of the most dominant scholarship within Victorian contracts history – hence the risk, but one which explains why the ghost has been so persistent by analyzing the narrative structures typifying scholarly dialogues. I bring together accounts of contract law written from the nineteenth century to our own time, and critically read between the lines of their controversies to examine an overwhelming consensus among historians about a single meaning of liberal contract in the nineteenth century. The possibility that there was more than one liberal, individualist version of contract going around has been closed off in consequence, as has reevaluation of the integral role of statuses in liberalism; these are unintended consequences of intellectual investments channeled through particular foci of debate. They are unwarranted within the broader field of Victorian historiography which has been examining complexities in liberalism in political philosophy, economic theory, institutional politics, and Victorian culture at large.

In reading across varied histories I apply to a field of history Hayden White's suggestion that historical work is "a verbal structure in the form of a narrative prose discourse that purports to be a model, or icon, of past structures and processes in the interest of *explaining what they were by representing them.*"[1] While White's analysis of literary form and style cannot be easily transferred from individual works to the field they form together, I proceed by examining how a discursive field attains important effects in terms of historical comprehension narratively, drawing on White's sensitivity to the

1 Hayden V. White, *Metahistory: The Historical Imagination in Nineteenth-Century Europe* (Baltimore, MD: Johns Hopkins University Press, 1975), 2.

narrativity of historical work together with familiar aspects of discourse analysis. My interest is a narrative *effect* that emerges from the accumulation of conversations in contracts histories.

The discussion breaks down the narratives of contracts histories and isolates at the outset a conceptual structure of atomistic individualism in contract which might appear, when viewed by itself, reductive. The analytic benefit by the end of the analysis hopefully justifies the choice and remedies any a priori concern that I am doing injustice to existing scholarship. For readers still skeptical, there is a weaker way to read my analysis that will still be enough for this book: You might read not a consensus around a specific version of liberalism in contracts, but rather an absence: A relational liberal version of contract is almost completely missing from contracts histories of the Victorian era. So is an account of liberalism as a reinterpretation of statuses. "Social" elements in Victorian contracts have been both collectivized and relegated to externalist positions understood as working outside contract or otherwise devastating it. I make a case for the stronger claim of implicit consensus around atomistic individualism, yet I am also at peace with the weaker reading: search for contract as a reinterpretation of statuses, or search for the relational if you can.

Metanarratives

Contracts histories have long conversed with two metanarratives of the nineteenth century. One is the liberation of the individual from the ascriptions of status. In this story, contract rose to prominence in the Victorian era as a conceptual alternative to status. Less celebratory versions do not view the development as progress, or view the displacement of status as only partially or tenuously achieved, but otherwise agree on the conceptual conflict at hand: status versus contract.

A second metanarrative is the rise of the welfare state, or the move from individualism to collectivism. In this story, contract, as the preferred mode for determining social relations, rose with individualism and sank with collectivism. Here, too, there are alternative versions. One version doubts whether any effective socialization was achieved through these changes, at least from the narrow perspective of contract. Another version questions the linearity of change (first individualism, then collectivism) and suggests a messier story. But the conceptual opposition – individualism versus collectivism – in which contract is associated with the former, remains intact.

2 E.g., Roscoe Pound, "The End of Law as Developed in Juristic Thought (Part 2)," *Harvard Law Review* 30 (1917): 219–21; Robert W. Gordon, "*Britton v. Turner*: A Signpost on the Crooked Road to 'Freedom' in the Employment Contract," in *Contract Stories: An In-Depth Look at The Leading Contract Cases*, ed. Douglas G. Baird (New York: Foundation, 2007), Chapter 7 (a critical account of the status-contract-status narrative).

Combined, the move of the nineteenth century is sometimes described as *status-contract-status*.[2] As Carole Pateman observes, such claims gloss over two meanings of status: status as ascription, a preassigned social position based on ascribed characteristics; and status as reference to state, as opposed to individually-determined content of relations.[3] The common grounds which prompt these claims is the abstract point that communally-based definitions of social relations are superseded by individually defined ones, and then revert back again. Whether the story is one of progress and decline, vice versa, or just an amalgam of normative visions competing for dominance, the conceptual picture emerging from histories is of status and collectivism as the two historical Others of the Victorian view of contract, each entrenched in a commanding narrative of the century.

The "contract" of this narrative bears a specific and too familiar idealist meaning, that of the classical legacy: an act of an autonomous individual will in the market. The meaning of contract makes up part of a broad consensus among historians about Victorian contracts. To bring the consensus into full view I break the story down to three narrative strands that inform historical contracts scholarship.

The first and most familiar strand of the story concerns the meaning of contract. It involves three idealist pillars: promise as a socially-disembedded expression of an individual will; the social structure as one made up of separate spheres, with the market as a distinct sphere driven by economic motives; and the promising person in the market – or the contracting person – as an autonomous and rational agent. This is the atomistic version of liberalism associated with the classical legacy. The next two strands of the story speak to the stability and hegemony of that version.

The second narrative strand concerns contract's conceptual Others, status and collectivism, which histories concede were the predominant alternatives to atomistic individualism. Histories show, however, that status and collectivism functioned in the nineteenth century as external critiques – as alternatives *to*, not *of*, contract; these critiques eroded contract in practice without substituting *its meaning*, and so left contract's conceptual link with atomistic individualism intact.

The third narrative strand turns to the relationship between contract's atomism and the wider cultural scene. Histories suggest that the atomistic individualism grounded in contracts enjoyed a wide cultural resonance: it was part of its era. I review discussions of the cultural terrain in the third part of this chapter, after having reviewed legal developments, purposely reversing the standard analysis in which "context" comes first, in an effort to flesh out the nontrivial connection made by historians between the atomism of classical contract law and broader cultural mores.

3 Carol Pateman, *The Sexual Contract* (Stanford, CA: Stanford University Press 1988), 10 and Chapter 6.

Each strand of the story – individualism; the Others: status and collectivism; and the broader culture – is all too familiar, yet their cumulative effect in grounding a shared consciousness concerning contract's historical meaning, one excluding the possibility of alternative liberal meanings of contract in Victorian times, and assuming a dramatic conflict (or otherwise hidden cooperation) with status, has not been adequately grasped. The historical debate which has grounded the shared consciousness is heated on virtually all other questions: the explanation for contract law's individualist bias; how old this individualism is – here positions range along a timeline of some six hundred years; and, closely related, what were the minimal features which made any particular constellation of contract rules, doctrines, or theoretical rationalizations distinctly individualistic. It is possibly the breadth of these debates that renders the picture of classical contract law so obvious and its individualism so dominant. Just below the heat of debates, the story of a single liberal meaning of contract serves as common ground. A hotly contested field has managed to produce an uncontested historical consciousness, entrenching a questionable artifact at the heart of modern capitalism's history.

Narrative Strand I: Contract's Meaning, Or Classical Contract Law's Atomistic Individualism[4]

Undisputed Point # 1: Contract law in the nineteenth century embodied an elaborate version of individualism.

The following discussion covers histories that have dealt with various aspects of Victorian contracts, like case law, contracts theory, legal thought or consciousness, and legal practice. I refer interchangeably to "law," "legal discourse," or "legal thought" although, as I will note, theory and academically-minded explications of doctrine were, as one might expect, far more coherent than practice, judicial application or practically-oriented

4 I focus on the law in England. However, these origins have been crucial for American contract law as well and are examined by its historians.

The term "classical" is prone to different uses. For example, Atiyah focuses on a theory he interchangeably calls "will theory" and "classical theory," which emerged by 1830. P.S. Atiyah, *The Rise and Fall of Freedom of Contract* (Oxford: Clarendon, 1979). Kennedy and Kreitner refer to "classical theory" as a way to distinguish it from pre-classical thought, and argue that it rose in the last three or four decades of the century. Duncan Kennedy, *The Rise and Fall of Classical Legal Thought* (Washington, DC: Beard, 2006); Roy Kreitner, *Calculating Promises: The Emergence of Modern American Contract Doctrine* (Stanford, CA: Stanford University Press, 2007). The difference depends on the extent to which the expulsion of relations from contract, rather than just increasing focus on the will, is perceived as crucial. Given my interest in the final result, on which these and other historians generally agree, I treat the move from the will theory to the classical formulation as a process of intensification, and use the terms interchangeably.

explications of doctrine. I will address important implications of these divergences within law in discussing status and collectivist influences on contracts.

I start by clarifying the meaning of "individualism" in historical accounts of contracts, which is in fact atomistic individualism, and then review and refocus histories to elaborate on its content. While the consensus traced in the next two parts of this chapter may be less obvious to readers, the story of this part, that of classical contract, has been told many times over; I therefore recount only core elements while focusing on the underlying human picture: the promising individual in the market.

Individualism in Contracts Histories

When historians discuss the individualism of classical contract thought of the nineteenth century, they analyze different things. Some writers discuss basic ideals underlying individualism, such as contract's commitment to negative liberty (Steven Lukes' "autonomy"[5]); others refer to specific doctrines of individualism, like economic individualism; still others refer to patterns of human behavior and consciousness, like the calculating promisor.[6] The point of convergence and underlying concern in the varied uses of "individualism," is an ideational construct: a picture of the social order at the center of which lies a sphere of "free" competitive economic activity conducted by autonomous individuals who are rational maximizers of economic interest. This notion is surrounded by corresponding conceptions about the role of politics (not necessarily laissez-faire, but tending to view government economic activity as "interventionist," and channeling it to encourage individual competition and self-reliance) and the judiciary (viewed as a protector of rights, the goal being to ensure mutual respect of rights among individuals and, thus, adequate spaces for self-realization). The diverse accounts of classical contract law all suggest, from different angles, that contract law assumed and reinforced this specific liberal worldview.

The following account explains the salient features making up the tie. As I weave different histories into a single account I adopt the emphases of specific historians on specific points which might not be conceded by others. In dealing with historical details this is unavoidable, yet should not obscure the main argument: the end result, namely, the picture of contract, enjoys a wide consensus even if not every detail of how and when law got there does.

5 Steven Lukes, *Individualism* (Oxford: Blackwell, 1973), Chapters 7–11.

6 For an account set in terms of the ethics of human interaction and patterns of behaviour, see Duncan Kennedy, "Form and Substance in Private Law Adjudication," *Harvard Law Review* 89 (1976): 1717–18, 1738.

Individualistic Bias in Contracts

General: The Classical Model of Contract

"As every contract derives its effect from the intention of the parties, that intention, as expressed, or inferred, must be the ground and principle of every decision respecting its operation and extent, and the grand object of consideration in every question with regard to its construction."[7] Such was Pothier's classical formulation of the will theory of contract, the basis of the English formulation of the theory.[8] As classical contract doctrine gave meaning to this formulation, a specific picture of the contractual relation emerged: The relation represented a meeting point between two individuals with separate interests. Each of them was a person assumed able, for all relevant purposes, to choose for herself, and who rationally chose that which could best serve her own economic interest.[9] The meeting point was achieved through the exercise of each person's will, expressed in a promise. That exercise, or the moment of formation, was the core of the analysis which proceeded by assuming its exclusive meaningfulness. Importantly, the discourse of rights and duties, seeking to describe what one party need or need not do for the other, and is or is not entitled from the other, relied on a distinction and even opposition between the parties before, at, and after formation, focusing attention on each in isolation rather than on the fact of their relation. The same discourse relied on the isolation of both parties from a broader social environment. Their contract belonged to a separate economic sphere ideally composed of such persons and the relationships they in fact choose, and of nothing else. This picture, finally, was of general applicability, ideally representing any and every contract.

Promise had an important conceptual place within this vision of contract: Promise is the basic human relation underlying contract, a notion which became almost incontestable in the Victorian era.[10] Classical treatises

7 M. Pothier, *A Treatise on the Law of Obligations, or Contracts*, trans. William David Evans, 3rd ed. (Philadelphia, PA: Robert H. Small, 1853), vol. 2, Chapter 5 in A.W.B. Simpson, "Innovation in Nineteenth Century Contract Law," in *Legal Theory and Legal History: Essays on the Common Law* (London: Hambledon Press, 1987), 190.

8 See Simpson, "Innovation," 247–78; Atiyah, *Rise and Fall*, 399–400; D.J. Ibbetson, *A Historical Introduction to the Law of Obligations* (Oxford: Oxford University Press, 1999), 222; Warren Swain, *The Law of Contract 1670–1870* (Cambridge: Cambridge University Press, 2015), 182.

9 The female pronoun might seem awkward given grave limitations on women's contractual capacities in the nineteenth century and the masculine imaginary of contract law, but women were never absent. Since gender cannot be avoided in language, I prefer this default.

10 See Kreitner, *Calculating Promises*, Chapter 1, for a discussion of the nineteenth-century centralization of promise as the heart of contract. Atiyah, *Rise and Fall*, 146, describes the nineteenth-century understanding of the entire field of contractual relations around promises; until the nineteenth century, argues Atiyah, a promise was neither a necessary

on contract reveal the centrality of promise to contract thinking. Take, for example, Pollock's leading treatise: "[T]he expression of intention … includes the particular kind of expression which is called a promise. We have as the proper groundwork of contract a promise determined by the acceptance of a proposal."[11] Or take Anson: "We are always in the habit of considering that an essential feature of a contract is a *promise* … A promise which a man is legally bound to perform creates an obligation …"[12] The crucial point is that the centrality of promise was based on understanding it (often with little engagement in the philosophy of promise) as a self-imposed obligation.[13] This understanding informed classical contract thought, and was reinforced through the centralization of the will in contract law doctrines. (From this perspective, observe, insistence on reciprocity or "agreement," which some historians emphasize, was not in fact inconsistent with the centrality of promise. The basis of legal contractual liability could exceed the reasons for seeing a promise as in itself morally obligatory, but the understanding of promise as issuing in the individual will was important nonetheless[14]).

Conceptual Tendencies in Classical Contract Law: Centralizing the Individual Will

A number of points are widely viewed as central to contract law's individualism. Most generally, the will theory brought about a tendency to attribute all the consequences of a contract to the will of those who made it. Thus, for instance, restrictions of capacity existed because some persons lacked free will; duress was the overbearing of the will, undue influence its subversion; mistake meant that the wills of the parties had miscarried; the measure of damages was defined by the will of the parties with respect to

nor a sufficient condition for the existence of a legal duty. A less dramatic formulation might suggest that the process by which promise became the focal point of contract had reached its zenith in the nineteenth century. See e.g. Allan E. Farnsworth, "The Past of Promise: An Historical Introduction to Contract," *Columbia Law Review* 69, no.4 (1969): 576–607; see also Brook Thomas, *American Literary Realism and the Failed Promise of Contract* (Berkeley, CA: University of California Press, 1997), 33–4. Thomas argues that the link between promise and contract emerged in the second half of the eighteenth century.

11 Frederick Pollock, *Principles of Contract at Law and in Equity* (London: Stevens and Sons, 1876), 5.

12 William Reynell Anson, *Principles of the English Law of Contract* (Oxford: Clarendon Press, 1879), 4.

13 As I noted in the Introduction, precisely this understanding made the promise-contract relation a contested theoretical issue for twentieth-century critics.

14 This point goes to explain Swain's finding that English law insisted on agreement (meeting of wills) but that at the same time promise became theoretically central. Warren Swain, "Contract as Promise: The Role of Promising in the Law of Contract. An Historical Account," *Edinburgh Law Review* 17, no. 1 (2013): 1–21.

the extent of liability; and so forth.[15] The locus of each party's liability was the promise, that is, the act of will involved in contract formation, whatever else happened before or after it was made; and it was to be equally protected in all cases through the expectation measure.

Contract law thus became abstract. Its doctrines seemed "to describe phenomena in a manner one step removed from concrete particulars of the persons and subject matters appearing in the cases."[16] Abstraction is often contrasted with an older view of contract as a status relationship which treated different types of contracts (landlord and tenant, master and servant, principal and agent, and so forth) on different terms. At the core of the opposition between status and contract in classical thought was a contrast between the mandatory terms of the status relation, prescribed by law or custom according to the parties' social roles, and the freely chosen content of the contractual relation. Contract became an abstraction specifying the general conditions under which individually-willed content would be enforceable.[17]

Closely related was a tendency to reify contract, that is, treat it as a thing intentionally made by the parties.[18] The nineteenth century gave rise to the rules of offer and acceptance, determining how a contract was made. Once reified, contract, and more specifically the moment of formation through the exchange of promises, could be an independent source of rights and duties, a definitive point of reference for the entire relationship. The effect was the bounding-off of the contractual relation from the more extensive and boundless relationships that surround it.[19]

15 Kennedy, "Form and Substance," 1730 (the list appears there). See also Atiyah, *Rise and Fall*, 405, 435; Ibbetson, *Historical Introduction*, 221–42; Duncan Kennedy, "From the Will Theory to the Principle of Private Autonomy: Lon Fuller's 'Consideration and Form,'" *Columbia Law Review* 100, no.94 (2000): 115; Roscoe Pound, "The Role of the Will in Law," *Harvard Law Review* 68 (1954), 4–7; Samuel Williston, "Freedom of Contract," *Cornell Law Quarterly* 6 (1921): 370–1; John P. Dawson, "Economic Duress: An Essay in Perspective," *Michigan Law Review* 45, no.3 (1947): 253–90.

16 Christopher T. Wonnell, "The Abstract Character of Contract Law," *Connecticut Law Review* 22 (1990): 438. See also Lawrence M. Friedman, *Contract Law in America: A Social and Economic Case Study* (Madison, WI: University of Wisconsin Press, 1965), 20; Atiyah, *Rise and Fall*, 402; Donal Nolan, "The Classical Legacy and Modern English Contract Law," *Modern Law Review* 59 (1996): 614–15.

17 Atiyah, *Rise and Fall*, 400; John T. Nockleby, "Tortious Interference with Contractual Relations in the Nineteenth Century: The Transformation of Property, Contract, and Tort," *Harvard Law Review* 93, no.7 (1980): 1510–39; Grant Gilmore, *The Death of Contract* (Columbus: Ohio State University Press, 1974), 6–8; Gordon, "Britton v. Turner," 208.

18 The executory model of contract – the paradigm case of the will theory – was tied with the idea of a thing created by will. The introduction of rules of set-off between parties strengthened reification by pointing to the "net" sum representing the value of the contract-as-thing, Ibbetson, *Historical Introduction*, 216–17.

19 On contract's "limitedness" or "bordered relationship," see Arthur Alle Leff, "Contract as Thing," *American University Law Review* 19, no. 2 (1970): 131–57; Nolan, "The Classical Legacy," 604.

The free choice of the parties was almost beyond challenge. Contractual rights were conceived as absolute, and thus a person was not accountable for the reasons for her contractual choices. The approach was also reflected in a severe attitude to changed circumstances between formation and the time of performance: very little scope was allowed for adjustment of the parties' rights and duties.[20]

The flipside of the absoluteness of contractual rights was the idea that no duty arises before a binding contract comes into being, again explained in terms of the intentional basis of contract.[21] The absence of precontractual duties and the absoluteness of contractual rights focused the contractual outlook on the moment of formation as the crucial point in contract, both contributing to and emanating from contract's reification.

In the classical era a narrow formulation of excuses held sway. This narrow formulation suffers from a potential internal contradiction, for the ideal of the absolutely free will seems to justify a liberal interpretation of excuses if these represent cases of defective assent, or unfree will. The formulation of excuses, however, was in line with the commitments of individualism as historians describe them.[22] Indeed, and more broadly, historians have repeatedly explained logical incoherencies in the classical model's commitment to the abstraction of free will by viewing them as victories of the commitment to the ideal market over the subjectivist legacy embedded in the will theory.[23]

20 Atiyah, *Rise and Fall*, 405–54; Gilmore, *Death of Contract*, 14–15. For an account of the philosophical justification for dismissing subjective motives, hence supporting the absoluteness of contractual rights, see Alan Brudner, *The Unity of the Common Law*, 2nd ed. (Oxford: Oxford University Press, 2013), Chapter 4.

21 Kennedy, *Rise and Fall*, 227–8; Kennedy, "Form and Substance," 1778–1685, Gilmore, *Death of Contract*, 14.

22 Some accounts explain the tie between narrow excuses and individualism in terms of the intertwining of freedom in contract with the ideal market. Thomas L. Haskell, "Capitalism and the Origins of the Humanitarian Sensibility, Part 2," in *The Antislavery Debate: Capitalism and Abolitionism as a Problem in Historical Interpretation*, ed. Thomas Bender (Berkeley and Los Angeles, CA: University of California Press, 1992), 136–60; Dawson, "Economic Duress," 266; Atiyah, *Rise and Fall*, 402–3. Others refer to the basic individualistic position which seeks to enlarge the sphere in which a person may act in a self-interested fashion. The contraction of the initial liability in contract (its limitation to intention) leaves greater areas for people to behave in a self-interested fashion, but liberal rules of excuse oblige the promise to share the losses of the promisor who is unable to perform. Kennedy, "Form and Substance," 1735. Narrow excuses were also part of the limited sphere for pre-contractual duties and reinforced the idea of absolute contractual rights, for excuses were a route into subjective motivations undermining the objective fact of an agreement. Finally, a narrow formulation of excuses was part of the reluctance to concretize.

23 Robert B. Seidman, "Contract Law, the Free Market, and State Intervention: A Jurisprudential Perspective," *Journal of Economic Issues* 7, no. 4 (1973): 55 –7; Friedman, *Contract Law in America*, 22: "the law of contract was the legal reflection of that market and naturally took on its characteristics"; Atiyah, *Rise and Fall*, 435–7. Atiyah argues that

The picture of the market is at the heart of historians' assessments of the classical legacy in contract. The same is true for the image of the human agent acting through contract in the market. I now turn to examine those constructs of liberal thought as contracts histories have described them. While the themes are all too familiar from work on liberalism in general, the manner in which contract law has been read with them merits emphasis.

The Promising Individual in the Market

> [E]very branch of doctrine must rely tacitly if not explicitly upon some picture of the forms of human association that are right and realistic in the areas of social life with which it deals.[24]

Contract law assumed the economic sphere of trade as its typical context. The picture of the market emerging from contracts histories is part of the history of separate spheres, elemental to atomistic individualism.

Separate spheres denote a compartmentalized view of the world, a separation of "forms of human association" and more generally human experience into identifiable areas answering to distinct logics and

the model was based on the free market bargaining process; Melvin A. Eisenberg, "Why There Is No Law of Relational Contracts," *Northwestern University Law Review* 94, no. 3 (2000): 808: "classical contract law rejected principles of unfairness, which typically ... have little application to contracts made between strangers on perfect markets."

One major tension in the model was between "freedom" and enforcement, explained in terms of the model's ultimate commitment to market security. For commentary see for instance. Betty Mensch, "Freedom of Contract as Ideology," *Stanford Law Review* 33, no. 75 (1981): 753–72; Mark Pettit Jr., "Freedom, Freedom of Contract, and the 'Rise and Fall'," *Boston University Law Review* 79 (1999): 263 –354; R.B. Ferguson, "Commercial Expectations and the Guarantee of the Law: Sales Transactions in Mid-Nineteenth Century England," in *Essays in the History of English Law*, eds. G.R. Rubin and David Sugarman (Abingdon: Professional, 1984), 192–208.

Another tension was between the notion of "will" and objectivism adopted by courts, likewise explained in terms of law's promotion of market rationality. Explanations vary somewhat. For instance, Atiyah, *Rise and Fall*, 459–60, offers as explanation the avoidance of factual inquiries and mistakes; Morton J. Horwitz, *The Transformation of American Law 1780–1860* (Cambridge, MA: Harvard University Press, 1977), 26, suggests promotion of uniformity and predictability; Gilmore, *Death of Contract*, 44–5, suggests imposition of absolute liability in contract and limiting the range of excuses; Kennedy, *Rise and Fall*, 239–40 explains objectivism as the limitation of judicial policing of contract through this pseudo-scientific measure of protecting reliance. Swain, wary of critical history in general and seeking a doctrinalist emphasis, does not commit to a broad ideological effort, and highlights complexity, but still suggests that important deviations from a real "inquiry into the mind of the parties" are explicable by commercial needs and a judicial interest in promoting economic entrepreneurship. Swain, *The Law of Contract 1670–1870*, 192, Chapters 8 and 12.

24 Roberto Mangabeira Unger, *The Critical Legal Studies Movement* (Cambridge, MA: Harvard University Press, 1986).

exemplifying typical patterns of relationships. Most familiarly, separate spheres entailed a distinction between state, or politics, and civil society, that is, "public" and "private" life. The state/civil society distinction was associated with the rise of the idea of a self-regulating market which began with a premise of a sphere in which the state was somehow uninvolved.[25]

Within the private sphere, a second separation was made between economic and family life (often, and confusingly, discussed through public (market) and private (home)). That separation, variously formulated as market versus home, economy versus family, exchange versus gift, and so forth, imports with it a basic contrast in both norms of conduct and structure: rational, calculative, self-interested action, based on abstract freedom and formal equality in the former, are contrasted with altruistic, fluid, compassionate action in an often more dependent and hierarchical context, in the latter.

Historians of the Victorian era, particularly feminists and market critics, have long attended to separate spheres both as ideology – as a tenet of liberal thought, and as a sociological reality – as a structural element of the capitalist social order. Max Weber famously propounded an understanding of the rise of capitalism as an evolutionary story of separation between family and economic activity.[26] The story, with a controversial starting point periodized to various eras from the thirteenth to the nineteenth centuries,[27] describes the shedding of obligations that stood in the way of rationalization. Zygmunt Bauman recounts the basic plotline: the rise of modern society was a "melting of solids." The dense tissue of social obligations was undone, leaving "the whole complex network of social relations unstuck." Through this process, the economy was progressively untied from its traditional political, ethical, and cultural entanglements.[28] Feminist

25 Karl Polanyi, *The Great Transformation* (Boston, MA: Beacon Press, 1967), 71. On the state/civil society separation see also Frances E. Olsen, "The Family and the Market: A Study of Ideology and Legal Reform," *Harvard Law Review* 96, no. 7 (1983): 1514; G.R. Searle, *Morality and the Market in Victorian Britain* (Oxford: Clarendon, 1998), Chapter 11; Joseph William Singer, "Legal Realism Now," *California Law Review* 76, no. 2 (1988): 477–82.

26 Max Weber, *Economy and Society: An Outline of Interpretive Sociology*, eds. Guenther Roth and Claus Wittich (Berkeley, CA: University of California Press, 1978), Chapter 4; Alan Macfarlane, *The Origins of English Individualism* (Cambridge: Cambridge University Press, 1978), 50–1.

27 For a review of the various positions see Macfarlane, *The Origins of English Individualism*, Chapters 2 and conclusion. Macfarlane himself argues that English capitalism, including private ownership of land, mobile labor, rational accounting, a profit motive, and a separation between "family and farm," dates at least as far back as the thirteenth century. The latest periodization should probably be credited to Polanyi, *The Great Transformation*.

28 Zygmunt Bauman, *Liquid Modernity* (Oxford: Blackwell, 2000), 4. On the melting of solids, see also Marshall Berman, *All that Is Solid Melts into Air: The Experience of Modernity* (New York: Simon & Schuster, 1982), itself echoing Karl Marx and Frederick Engels, *The Communist Manifesto* (1848).

histories have spent more energy on the emerging role of the domestic sphere to which women were increasingly confined, construed in opposition to the economic. The story recounts a sharp dichotomy reaching its zenith in the nineteenth century between the feminine home and the male workaday world. The separated spheres were defined one against the other, with the home assuming significance for its difference from, and compensation for, the market, and vice versa.[29]

As a sociological account, the separation of spheres suffers from descriptive limitations that have seriously diluted, if not debunked it.[30] Multiple histories of the Victorian era speak to differences in the experience and practice of separations, explicable by differing personal and social circumstances such as occupations, classes, and geographical areas. However, questions on the sway of separate spheres as an ideological construct integral to liberalism, rather than sociological account, have been less systematic and remain marginalized in the context of contracts. The following chapters contribute to a reassessment. At this point, however, I want to

29 E.g. Walter E. Houghton, *The Victorian Frame of Mind, 1830–1870* (New Haven, CT: Yale University Press, 1957); Olsen, "The Family and the Market"; Catherine Gallagher, *The Industrial Reformation of English Fiction: Social Discourse and Narrative Form 1832–1867* (Chicago, IL: University of Chicago Press, 1985), 121–6; Leonore Davidoff and Catherine Hall, *Family Fortunes: Men and Women of the English Middle Class, 1780–1850* (Chicago, IL: University of Chicago Press, 1987); Nancy Armstrong, *Desire and Domestic Fiction: A Political History of the Novel* (New York: Oxford University Press, 1987); Lynda Nead, *Myths of Sexuality: Representations of Women in Victorian Britain* (Malden, MA: Blackwell, 1988); John Tosh, *A Man's Place: Masculinity and the Middle-Class Home in Victorian England* (New Haven, CT: Yale University Press, 1999); Talia Schaffer, *Romance's Rival: Familiar Marriage in Victorian Fiction* (New York: Oxford University Press, 2016). Shaffer suggests that a picture in which separate spheres originated in women's own advocacy.

30 For instance, Mary Poovey addresses the complexities of the disaggregation of spheres. The negotiation of sphere boundaries, she argues, was full of fissures that resulted not only from the uneven relationship between discourse and institutional practice, but also from the historical indebtedness of spheres to older ones from which they emerge. Mary Poovey, *Making a Social Body* (Chicago, IL: University of Chicago Press, 1995). Marcel Mauss criticized the modern Western conception of economic exchange based on material utility with evidence from "archaic" societies. In those societies, he argued, the modern conception is nowhere to be found, and the concepts that "it pleases us to contrast," like liberty and obligation, generosity and self-interest, are in one melting pot. Modern society, too, is not as rational as it imagines, Mauss suggested; we too would do well to put our concepts back into the melting pot. Marcel Mauss, *The Gift*, trans. W. D. Halls (New York: W.W. Norton & Company, 2000). While market critics have investigated the social realities of the economy, feminist histories have done much to establish women's active role in the market; for a review of some this work see Wendy S. Jones, *Consensual Fictions: Women, Liberalism, and the English Novel*, 2nd ed. (Toronto: University of Toronto Press, 2004), Chapter 1. See also Robert B. Shoemaker, *Gender in English Society: 1650–1850: The Emergence of Separate Spheres?* (New York: Longman, 1998), for a review of debates, and argument about both the limited implications of separations and the continuities with earlier eras.

clarify the relation of separate spheres to contract law as established by histories.

Historians often suggest that classical contract thought both assumed and reinforced the ideology of separate spheres. The model of contract, centered as it was on the primacy of the individual will as the source of obligation, as opposed to the will of the community, grounded the private/public distinction. The private/public distinction ran through every level of doctrine,[31] and was significantly grounded in the centerpiece of contract law, the doctrine of consideration. The basic question raised by the doctrine was deceptively simple: what promises will the law of contract enforce? Whatever the answers were, argues Roy Kreitner, the very question had already succeeded in achieving a crucial conceptual goal: promise, understood as an individually created, self-imposed obligation, became the sole source of contractual duties.[32] The realm of exchange was the realm of individual action, from which the community was excluded.

Another important feature of classical contract law was its attention to the formation of contract over its content. The role of contract law in its classical formulation was to ensure that it enforced free transactions, not police their content; the nineteenth-century development of intricate rules of formation and their centrality for contract thinking obscured the role of societally-imposed obligations in contractual contexts in favor of individually-chosen ones.[33]

The idea of individual choice freed from social policing as a necessary and sufficient principle assumed a promisor who did not require society in order to become a meaningfully choosing person. This individual has been described by Lukes as an abstract one: at stake is a self pictured abstractly as given, with given interests, wants, purposes, needs. The crucial point is that the relevant features of individuals, which determine the ends that social arrangements are held to fulfill (whether these features are called instincts, faculties, needs, desires, or rights), are assumed as given independent of social context.[34] Being self-sufficient, the promisor of classical

31 Kennedy, "From Will Theory," 107. For the historical evolution of this idea, see Kennedy, *Rise and Fall*; Seidman, "A Jurisprudential Perspective," 554–6.

32 Kreitner, *Calculating Promise*, Chapter 1. The conceptual place of promise was discussed above, notes 10–14 and accompanying text.

33 Kreitner, *Calculating Promise*; Atiyah similarly notes how consent was increasingly sought and found by courts inclined to impose liability. Atiyah, *Rise and Fall*, 455–6.

34 See Lukes, *Individualism*, 73–8. The critique of givenness as a vision of self-sufficiency is well established. See for instance Charles Taylor, *Philosophy and the Human Sciences: Philosophical Papers 2* (Cambridge: Cambridge University Press, 1985), 189–90. As Taylor argues, the assumption is that individuals can develop their human capacities, be they rationality, or becoming a fully responsible and autonomous beings, independently of society.

contract knew her own interest best. She did not, at least not by definition, owe any duties except those she first chose to owe to her promisee. She preceded society in terms of significance and conceptual structure.[35] Self-sufficiency bears a close relation to the opposition between self and society in which the social is pictured as a threat to individual development, a form of thought that reinforced the normative attractiveness of the private/public distinction.

The second distinction within separate-spheres ideology – family/market – was embedded in a reluctance, as Roberto Unger called it, to allow contract law to intrude upon the world of family and friendship and destroy their communal quality.[36] One example is the distinction between contract and gift, with gift (or, in classical thought, any unbargained-for promise), like status, left outside the contractual boundary. Whereas the nonenforcement of gratuitous promises had a long history in case law, classical thinkers turned it into "the cornerstone of the contractual edifice." The boundary line not only protected the world of family, but more crucially traced the lines of rationality: unreciprocated transfers raise the specter of economically irrational social transactions which the legal vision of the capitalist market denied.[37]

Another formulation of the discursive constitution of separate spheres in law is the opposition between what Unger calls principles and counter-principles. Classical contract doctrine expressed as one of its dominant principles the freedom to contract, or to choose one's contractual partners. Doctrinal developments that undermined freedom to contract in order to

35 For the epistemological shifts enabling this outlook, see Craig Muldrew, *The Economy of Obligation: The Culture of Credit and Social Relations in Early Modern England* (Basingstoke: Palgrave Macmillan, 1998), 328–32.

36 Unger, *Critical Legal Studies Movement*, 62–6. This stark formulation has since been adjusted, in contemporary if not strictly historical terms. Jill Hasday makes the subtler point that law does not stay clear of economic exchange in intimate relationships, but rather denotes intimacy by regulating and restricting the exchange of economic resources within them. The basic impulse in law to distinguish spheres, however, remains put. Jill Hasday, "Intimacy and Economic Exchange," *Harvard Law Review* 119, no. 2 (2005): 491–530.

37 Kreitner, *Calculating Promises*, 34, 91; see also Atiyah, *Rise and Fall*, 451–2. Atiyah explains that liberality or beneficence (which are the grounds for a gift) were considered a good cause but not sufficient consideration. However, he does not discuss the constitutive effect on views of the market emerging from this distinction, but rather seems to think that consideration was gradually stripped of any important role in contract law. Note that leaving gifts outside contract did not entail only a conceptual separation between market and nonmarket relationships, but one that made family and friends inferior contestants in fact when they happened to compete with market creditors. See W. R. Cornish and G. de N. Clark, *Law and Society in England 1750–1950* (London: Sweet & Maxwell, 1989), 207–8.

protect communal aspects of social life were counterprinciples.[38] Principles and counterprinciples, then, relate to background assumptions about different kinds of human association, the former acknowledging nothing but self-interest, the latter taking into account reciprocal loyalty, support, and dependence. Counterprinciples were understood in their oppositional stance to principles, and were formulated as ad hoc qualifications to them; they were not allowed to undermine the basic conceptual structure expressed in the dominant principles, but rather worked from the outside as it were, to limit their application. Maintaining the dominance of principles as the essence of contract and treating the areas subjected to counterprinciples as anomalies or somehow less contractual, grounded the idea of different models of association for different spheres of life; they reinforced the distinction between the economic and the intimate, market and family.

The distinction between the family and the market, like the one between state and civil society, was also an investment in a vision of a particular person: as Kreitner describes her, when contracting the individual is calculating and calculable, a person with a market consciousness. The formulation of classical contract theory supported this vision.[39] The presocial individual was the basic unit of thought, on top of which a specific rationality informing the behavior of that person in the market was added, both with the aid of a separate-spheres imaginary.

The two levels of separation assumed in contract law formulated a rigorous version of the capitalist market domain. While the separation between public and private spheres conceptualized it as a free realm of private interaction, the one between economic and noneconomic private relationships

38 Hence the discouragement of contract in family and friendship settings. For instance, norms of interpretation reversed the presumption of intent to be legally bound in family and friendship contexts. Unger, *Critical Legal Studies Movement,* 62. The doctrine of intent to create a legal obligation was a nineteenth-century innovation, which, as Simpson argued, explained in terms of the will theory the absence of contractual liability for domestic and social arrangements. Simpson, "Innovation," 189. Peter Goodrich traces the separation of the sphere of friendship from contract to an old separation of jurisdiction between religious and secular law. Ecclesiastical case law placed friendship (including domestic relations) within the jurisdiction of the church, giving primacy to patriarchal control – an effective Alsatia, as Goodrich calls it. Peter Goodrich, "Friends in High Places: Amity and Agreement in Alsatia," 1 *International Journal of Law in Context* 1 (2005): 41–59. Goodrich emphasizes the domestic, yet the underlying point to note is the effect of such active rationalizations of separations on the image of the market.

39 Kreitner, *Calculating Promises,* 228–35. Note that Kreitner distinguishes theory from case law. For an argument distinguishing legal ideology from judicial discourse in the English context see R.B. Ferguson, "The Horwitz Thesis and Common Law Discourse In England," *Oxford Journal of Legal Studies* 3, no. 1 (1983): 34–58. See also Swain, *The Law of Contract 1670–1870* for the argument that case law was not consistently shaped by theory.

rendered it rational. Contract law marginalized relations that were not individually chosen and shaped, and relations not adhering to a strict rationality and rigid allocation of rights and duties, sustaining a liberal view of compartmentalized social life. That view involved an idealized contracting party characterized by extreme atomism. The parties envisioned in contract need not discuss or agree on ends or values; they could achieve complex interdependence in production and consumption without acknowledging any interdependence as moral beings.[40]

Narrative Strand 2: Stability in Contract's Meaning, Or the Otherness of Status and Collectivism

Contracts histories have long acknowledged that classical contract law was never a clean analytical structure nor an exclusive ideological construct. This part reviews histories of classical law's Others: status and collectivism, the two "social" alternatives to classical law's individualism.

Histories of contract's Others, while diverse in many ways, establish these two interrelated points of agreement. *Undisputed Point #2*: the conceptual alternatives to classical contract in the Victorian era were, predominantly, status and collectivism. *Undisputed Point #3*: in the nineteenth century these alternatives did not represent alternative meanings *of* contract but rather alternatives *to* contract; hence they did not challenge contract's meaning.

The consensus I trace here may be less obvious to readers than that treated in the previous part; it emerges from a complex field of historical inquiry usually understood as revealing the fall or failure of the classical legacy rather than its solidification. To make things more complex still, historians have treated status and collectivism both as external and as internal critiques of contract. The following discussion clarifies how the consensus nonetheless emerges. If the two points above are conceded by historians, that is, if status and collectivism were the two conceptual alternatives to classical contract, and did not challenge its meaning during the nineteenth century, histories speaking to these points effectively identify one kind of individualism in contract – for the alternatives were something other than individualism – and allow that that individualism was the only thing considered contractual in the nineteenth century, at least in its latter part, after the classical construct had been firmly established. Together, these points confirm the conceptual link between contract and atomistic individualism and generate an account of stability in contract's meaning.

40 See Kennedy, "Form and Substance," 1767–71.

Status and Contract

From Status to Contract

The classical model of contract, recall, established a distinction between status and contract. Contract represented a set of freely chosen self-imposed obligations of abstract individuals, unlike status which represented obligations imposed without an individual's consent. Kennedy explains the change in the operation of status categories in contract law: first, status came to exist as the opposite of rights in the abstract rather than the medium for the organization of rights in the particular; second, the elements composing particular statuses were fragmented and dispersed rather than treated as elements of operative wholes.[41] Both of these developments, Kennedy argues, were influenced by and appeared to confirm Maine's generalization of a movement from status to contract.[42]

Indeed, the analytical distinction in legal thought between status and contract often emerges from histories as an echo of a wider sociopolitical implication. While Kennedy points to the communal commitments erased by the rejection of status in law (a position that, as I argue in Chapter 5, underplays gender hierarchies), contract's meaning as not-status is often understood by historians as part of the Victorians' search for an alternative system that would erase traditional hierarchies,[43] the readiest mode, as Albert Venn Dicey put it, of "abolishing a whole body of antiquated institutions."[44] Maine's aphorism invoked contract as a proxy for the refined and progressive essence of liberal modernity.

Status Still Here

The story of the classical model's triumph has been challenged by histories that identify status categories as operative sources for contractual practice and for the common law at the high Victorian era. While hardly acknowledged conceptually, according to these histories status remained a challenge to the Victorian idea of contract.

41 Kennedy, *Rise and Fall*, 186–94. See also Singer, "Legal Realism Now," 477–82 for a discussion of classical thought's emergence in opposition to status, which became an abnormality.

42 Henry Sumner Maine, *Ancient Law: Its Connection with the Early History of Society and Its Relation to Modern Ideas* (New York: Henry Holt, 1906), 165.

43 Pound, "End of Law 2," 209–10.

44 A.V. Dicey, *Lectures on the Relation Between Law and Public Opinion in England During the Nineteenth Century*, 2nd ed (London: Macmillan, 1962), 151. See also Amy Dru Stanley, *From Bondage to Contract: Wage Labor, Marriage, and the Market in the Age of Slave Emancipation* (New York: Cambridge University Press, 1998), 1 (discussing William Graham Sumner's similar understanding in the American context).

Histories of credit contracts – contracts central to the socioeconomic developments of the era, show their entanglement in hierarchic relations. Margot Finn describes the experience of personal credit contracts in England from the onset of the industrial and consumer revolutions to the outbreak of World War I, and argues that the autonomous individual model did not gain prominence and coexisted with the model of the social individual, who gained rights and responsibilities by virtue of her status and connections. Finn shows, for instance, how both tradesmen and courts confirmed differences in the social-hierarchical position of debtors in the way they handled and responded to credit contracts, and how gender identities played a role in contractual exchange. Finn's review of county court litigation reveals that judges urged the continual need to moderate legal obligations by equitable considerations, most notably those of gender and class, rather than promoting a transition from status to contract.[45] Erika Rappaport similarly depicts consumer credit's cultural role and its entanglement with social positions, both class and gender, defying the supposed rationality of the market.[46]

Employment contracts were another site in which status came into play. The history of labor reveals this point from two complementary angles, speaking to the two meanings of status, as state-controlled relations and as social ascription. One angle is the rapid rise of labor regulation by the state. As John Orth argues, while the reconceptualization of labor in terms of contract, completed by the mid-nineteenth century, was a major factor in the reorientation of the common law as a whole in the direction of contract, it was no sooner established than it began to be undermined.[47] Historians suggest that the new priority accorded to property and contract in Victorian England was qualified, as far as labor contracts were concerned, by a continuing role for status-based forms of regulation.[48]

Another angle is revisionist labor histories which question even a moment's victory of contract in its Victorian meaning. Coercive elements of labor contracts undermine stories of freedom even as a matter of simple legal formality, that is, quite beyond the compulsion embedded in economic inequality, which today we tend to see as mostly acceptable, partly

45 Margot Finn, *The Character of Credit: Personal Debt in English Culture, 1740–1914* (Cambridge: Cambridge University Press, 2003).

46 Erika Rappaport, "'A Husband and His Wife's Dresses': Consumer Credit and the Debtor Family in England, 1864–1914," in *The Sex of Things: Gender and Consumption in Historical Perspective*, eds. Victoria de Grazia and Ellen Furlough, (Berkeley, CA: University of California Press, 1996): 163–87.

47 John V. Orth, "Contract and the Common Law," in *The State and Freedom of Contract*, ed. Harry N. Scheiber (Stanford, CA: Stanford University Press, 1998), 62–5. But see Simon Deakin, "Legal Origin, Juridical Form and Industrialization in Historical Perspective: The Case of the Employment Contract and the Joint-Stock Company," *Socio-Economic Review* 7, no. 1 (2009): 35-65, for the argument that in mid-century there was still no general category of contract of employment.

48 Ibid. See also Gordon, "*Britton v. Turner.*"

by ignoring its formal legal basis. Robert Steinfeld's history of wage labor, for instance, reveals that employment contracts could not be terminated at will by workers, and that employers could enforce contracts with criminal sanctions, a centuries-old practice which was revived and redefined more severely at the same time that regulation of the labor market regarding contractual terms (like wage setting) was eliminated. The modern regime of Victorian contract in the context of labor was inseparable from the fact that workers refusing to perform their agreements could find themselves imprisoned at hard labor. Marc Steinberg has recently described the regime of master and servant law consolidated by mid-century as a distinctly modern "hybrid of status and contract" leaving workers unfree in service.[49] The elimination of most criminal sanctions in late century was entangled with forms of regulation which Orth and others discuss (relevant to the rise of "collectivism" as well, to which I turn in a moment).[50] In between these two moves, the notion of individually-determined contractual relations on terms of abstract formal equality disappears. As Melanie Williams suggests in a literary-based critique, power disparities alone render the move from status to contract in the realm of labor a myth (which, she complains, contracts histories have not done enough to dispel).[51]

The legal treatment of promises of marriage has also been challenged as a site of abstract contract principles answering to the classical formulation. Ginger S. Frost, for instance, disputes the understanding of breach of promise of marriage cases as extreme sites of the triumph of individualism and abstraction in contract. Instead, she argues, these actions demonstrated that despite formalistic contractual language, judges brought social, gender- and class-aware values, to bear on contractual issues.[52] The promise

49 Marc W. Steinberg, *England's Great Transformation: Law, Labor and the Industrial Revolution* (Chicago, IL: The University of Chicago Press, 2016), 44.

50 Robert J. Steinfeld, *Coercion, Contract, and Free Labor in the Nineteenth Century* (Cambridge: Cambridge University Press 2001). But see Steinberg's argument, set against Polanyi's thesis of double movement, that labor was made not more but rather less embedded in consequence. Steinberg, *England's Great Transformation*, Chapter 7.

51 Melanie L. Williams, "Coercion and the Labour Contract – Revisiting Glasbrook Brothers and the Political Fiction of Lewis Jones," *International Journal of Law in Context* 8, no. 1 (2012): 1–25.

52 Ginger S. Frost, *Promises Broken: Courtship, Class, and Gender in Victorian England* (Charlottesville: University of Virginia Press, 1995). For an example in a different vein see Peter Goodrich, "The Posthumous Life of the Postal Rule: Requiem and Revival of *Adams v. Lindell*," in *Feminist Perspectives on Contract Law*, eds. Linda Mulcahy and Sally Wheeler (London: Glasshouse Press 2005): 75–90. Goodrich argues that the postal rule, sometimes seen as the marker of the rise of the will theory and modern contract as based on mutuality of consent, was in fact not a doctrine of abstract equality, but a rule of equity originating in ecclesiastical law on promises of marriage, and predicated on differences between offeror and offeree in "status, place, gender and expectation." Ibid., 85. See also Peter Goodrich, *Oedipus Lex: Psycholanalysis, History, Law* (Berkeley, CA: University of California Press, 1995), Chapter 7.

of marriage, at once marginal and central to a contractual social order, is a revealing site. In Chapter 5 I return to it to examine more closely how status and liberal ideals interacted structurally. (Chapter 5 also discusses historical work that examines the debate on marriage itself as a contract, and feminist attacks, famous among them Mill's *The Subjection of Women* (1869), on the unequal and unchosen content of that contract, which looked more like status. As I explain there, one of the interesting moves of classical contract theorists was to exclude marriage from the category of contract, implicitly conceding these critiques.)

More broadly, feminist history argues that the basis of classical contract was historically premised on women's subordination and a specifically male imaginary of the contracting individual. Thus Pateman's work ties between the intellectual history of social contract philosophy and contracts in everyday life, to claim that contract could not possibly signal equality for women given the embedded assumption of sexual access to their bodies at the basis of civil liberties in modern Western thought.[53]

Such diverse histories, pointing to social locations and social roles as relevant and operative sources for contract practice and law, expose that status had never disappeared and remained a social alternative to the atomism of the classical model. What are the implications for the history of contract's meaning? Three points are worth observing.

First, no alternative individualist meaning of contract can be glimpsed here, only a "return" or possibly a newly-couched formulation of status, understood as an alternative to the liberal model. Finn's work is a possible exception. Many of the findings in support of her model of the "social individual" that competed with the more radical model of autonomy, could in fact speak to a relational, nonatomistic yet liberal view of contract. While Finn tends to emphasize the continuing force of statuses in her discussion, the direction she charts informs my effort in Part I to set apart different kinds of sociality and to highlight the Victorian liberal interest in relationality in contract, as well as my effort in Part II to re-examine the relation of liberalism and statuses beyond notions of opposition and competition.[54]

Second, accounts often reinforce the classical meaning in their tendency to describe status in terms of an "obstacle" to contractual enforcement or more broadly to contract's liberal hegemony.

Finally and importantly, histories often intimate that despite status's persistence, the meaning of contract as not-status was triumphant; the classical model of contract proved conceptually resilient to status-based definitions. For the most part, status was not discursively, analytically, or theoretically acknowledged as part of what contract was, although it

53 Pateman, *The Sexual Contract*, 4.
54 Finn, *Character of Credit*.

influenced contractual relations and informed legal responses. As my discussion of collectivism below clarifies, the issue often goes beyond a distance between books and action, theory and practice, or ideology and reality. It reaches deeper, for all of these levels could and did accommodate status – only not as part of liberal *contract*. My concern is with what could and what could not, according to dominant histories, be considered contractual in liberal thinking. Once the classical idea of contract took hold, its alternatives became and remained, according to contracts histories, external to its meaning; as such, they strengthened that meaning even as they critiqued its normative appeal and eroded its practical significance.

Collectivism and Contract

Collectivism, unlike status, is considered part of the "Age of Contract" and the story of contracts' modernization, rather than a rejected past. Individualism and collectivism are customarily identified as the two ideological currents that influenced modern contract, itself repeatedly portrayed in terms of their contest.

The general tension between individualism and collectivism is a persistent point in analyses of contracts on two levels: historical, and conceptual. As a matter of historical account, the story of the rise and fall[55] is a dominant narrative of the Victorian era, and accounts of contracts converse with it. When collectivism is analyzed as a historical trend it generally denotes historical attempts dating from mid-century onward to mitigate the unwanted effects of the unrestrained pursuit of self-interest, whether as part of a radical or a liberal political program. Indeed, given its often-liberal turn, the term "collectivism" is confusing. In using it I trace a common practice in contracts histories. However, "collectivism" is also useful as a reminder that in all versions it denotes determinations of the scope of contractual rights and obligations through a *collective* effort represented in state institutions (courts included). Radical or liberal, in the pursuit of its goals in contract collectivism, according to contracts histories, reacted to individualism and functioned as a palliative rather than a full-fledged alternative. References to "collectivism" in histories do not generally point to a consistent program despite the positive ideals of egalitarianism and the advancement of positive freedom they identify with it.

But references to collectivism do not denote only a historical development, but also a conceptual possibility, a possible route of action existing from the start within classical contract doctrine.[56]

55 Individualism-collectivism, laissez-faire-protectionism, industrial revolution-consumer revolution, individual-based-corporate-based economy, and so forth.

56 Examples below. To get a sense of the dominance of this argument, see Brudner, *Unity of the Common Law*.

The first subsection below synthesizes accounts of collectivism as a historical trend to consider its assessed impact on classical contract. I briefly revisit the tenets of classical law reviewed earlier to clarify how they changed under the collectivist impact. The next subsection then discusses the limited influence of collectivism on the legal conceptualization of contract, to which histories speak. Finally, I discuss collectivism as a conceptual possibility developed by the internal critique of classical contract. My overall aim is to show how histories of collectivism, both as historical trend and as an internal conceptual possibility, in fact confirm the relation of contract and atomistic individualism in the nineteenth century.

Collectivism as Historical Trend

Unlike invocations of "individualism" in contracts which can be more or less related to identifiable commitments, "collectivism" of the late nineteenth century is treated more diversely by historians; its uses in history invoke radical and liberal programs as well as isolated and conceptually hazy trends. This section concentrates on changes in law associated with collectivism which together loosely added up to a more welfarist legal regime. Accounts treating collectivism as a historical trend and focused on these changes generally rely on the story in which individualism first rose to prominence, and then (even if almost immediately) was eroded by collectivism.

IMPACT

No alternative theory of contract was formulated in the nineteenth century. The impact of collectivism on contracts was to be found in case law and in legislative activity.[57] But contract law's commitment to individualism was more than a lack of textbook theory. The collectivist outlook, histories show, worked against a backdrop conceptualization of contract's meaning the plausibility of which it hardly disputed. This complaint remains remarkably pertinent, as Linda Mulcahy observes: "the neo-classical model has favoured a pragmatic approach to the failings of classicalism and lacks a rigorous unifying conceptual structure."[58]

57 Atiyah, *Rise and Fall*, 764, 773; see also the discussion of collectivism's impact below.

58 Linda Mulcahy, "The Limitations of Love and Altruism: Feminist Perspectives on Contract Law," in Mulcahy and Wheeler, *Feminist Perspectives on Contract Law*, 7.

CONCEPTUAL TENDENCIES IN CONTRACT LAW: INDIVIDUAL WILL STILL HERE

The core of contract in law remained a highly abstract description of promissory relations. However, legislative activity began to apply special rules to types of ordinary contracts (labor, corporate, consumer, etc.) on an ever-increasing scale. These were becoming specialized bodies of law for legal thinkers, areas in which the parties' rights and duties were understood as determined by state law, not by contract.[59]

Contract itself remained reified in legal thought as a "thing" created by the parties, available for analysis in isolation. The important difference within contract law was an increasing willingness to forgo the assumption of equality (or acquiescence in inequality), or on another formulation, to forgo the assumption that parties were under all circumstances the best arbiters of their own interest, which in classical thought was uncontested.[60] Instead, there was an increasing willingness to protect the weaker party in the relationship from her own creation and to prevent injustice between parties. The relative power position of the parties vis-à-vis one another gradually became part of the relevant social context of contract. In addition, judicial inquiry began to consider post-formation circumstances to prevent abuses that emanate from strict adherence to literal contractual content.[61] The effect of concerns about interparty justice and equality was a relaxation in the absoluteness of contractual rights: terms of contracts became more susceptible to judicial adjustment.[62] As David Ibbetson notes, however, "[t]hese circumstances were never linked together as a general principle."[63]

Protection of precontractual reliance also became more acceptable, mitigating the atomistic view that hardly acknowledged precontractual duties. Cases, however, were confused and, as Atiyah puts it, "bogged down in a mass of technicalities ... and anyhow did not adequately reflect the essential point that justifiable reliance depended on a much wider set of factors."[64] What seemed clearer was an increase in reliance-based liabilities under tort law, that is, under something perceived as other than contract.[65]

A similar trend toward interparty justice and equality was found in a liberalization of excuses.[66]

Attending to a party's weakness was a potential acknowledgment of relational interdependencies. The collectivist outlook on contract, however,

59 Atiyah, *Rise and Fall*, Chapter 21.

60 Pound, "Role of the Will," 11–12.

61 Scrutiny of motivations also became more acceptable, but this development belongs largely to the twentieth century.

62 Atiyah, *Rise and Fall*, 736–7.

63 Ibbetson, *Historical Introduction*, 258.

64 Atiyah, *Rise and Fall*, 772.

65 Ibid., 772–4.

66 Gilmore, *Death of Contract*, 80–1; Ibbetson, *Historical Introduction*, 252.

was hardly able to accommodate contract to its own insights; histories suggest that the parties' interdependence was acknowledged only to the extent that one had a power to overbear the other, whether prior to the contract's formation, using her preexisting advantages, or after formation, relying on her contractual ones.

Parties' relational conditioning more broadly was relevant only in terms of their power contest within the antagonistic contractual relation. The changes in the approach to contract were, in other words, inward-looking: they represented an effort to make contract fairer as between the contracting parties, an effort beginning with their chosen content. A corollary point is that these changes did not undermine contract's reification. The core remained the individual choices that created the contract. The liberalization that resulted in parties empowered or weakened by the state – achieving something less or more than they had ostensibly intended – was rationalized against that core; both the consensual idea and the attendant independence of parties were maintained as cornerstones. In fact, the whole process can be seen as an attempt to restore to weaker parties the independence they appeared to have risked, to reinstate classical thought's ideal image of competitive equality, and to deliver on contract's promise of enabling each individual to assert herself.[67] The result was a limited conceptual change in contract's meaning, conceded by historians virtually without exception. I return to this point in a moment.

THE PROMISING INDIVIDUAL IN THE MARKET

The historical story of the rise of collectivism is linked with the suggestion that atomism was no longer a plausible account of the social structure; with the establishment of the bureaucratic state and the rise of corporations, atomism lost its hold. This development, however, could not be seen from within contract law; it did not so much affect the meaning of contract in law, or the way individuals came to owe duties under it, as it diminished contract's appeal and practical importance. The image of individually-chosen relationships was displaced in legal thought by a structure of organizations, with individual duties increasingly assigned through legislation applicable to individuals' relations with organizations.[68] Where contract was thought to exist, the idea of control through choice held sway (with greater support at the fringes); where choice was out of control – when third parties and public interest were offended by it – contract was thought to be displaced altogether by state collective effort.

67 Harry N. Scheiber, "Economic Liberty and the Modern State" in Schieber, *The State and Freedom of Contract*, 123–4. As Scheiber argues, interventions were justified as necessary for bringing social realities into line with the theoretical premises of freedom of contract. See further discussion below.

68 See Atiyah, *Rise and Fall*, 724.

A limited appreciation of individuals' sociality within contract law was observable in courts' increasing willingness to consider a party's weakness relative to her partner. However, by and large, when contracting, a person was assumed to be manifesting a (more or less successful) attempt at independent generation of economic plans according to her own (more or less well-founded) perception of self-interest. All that could be done was to add patches that would help the promising individual achieve that goal.

The ideal market in which individuals contracted thus remained a conceptually distinct sphere, but one acknowledged as less than perfect. Outside support for market failures, and for uninformed and weak parties, became an acknowledged need. The outside was the state; in other words, the conceptual separation on the level of state and civil society remained intact, a significant point for historians' evaluation of the collectivist outlook on contract, to which I now turn.

ASSESSING THE LIMITS OF THE COLLECTIVIST IMPACT

Histories that view collectivism as a historical trend imply that it carried limited importance for the meaning of liberal contract in the nineteenth century. Nineteenth-century collectivism represents a specific stage in the historical attack on classical contract law. The important point about this stage is its reactive quality, widely acknowledged by historians. The content of the collectivist attack was the inappropriateness of the regime governed by the ideal of freedom of contract. The drama of the "fall of contract" was not a dispute about the meaning of contract in its classical formulation but rather about contract's desirability or workability. Collectivism acquiesced in the classical view of contract, and moved to narrow its scope; or, on another reading, moved to remedy its failures in fact. Critique at that historical point left aside the possibility that the legal regime in force did not, or did not necessarily, correspond to that required by the abstraction of free contract, and instead emphasized that freedom of contract was pernicious.[69]

The story of collectivism's limited impact on the legal conceptualization of contract appears in multiple histories. Lawrence Friedman, for example, explains the external quality of the collectivist impact as a characteristic of contract law, directly related to its coextension with the free market ideal. Contract law, argues Friedman, sought to provide legal support for the residue of economic behavior left unregulated – that is, for the free market. Accordingly, it was busy defining its own boundaries – what kind of transactions were and were not contractual. A residual category, contract law was

69 Duncan Kennedy, "Distributive and Paternalist Motives in Contract and Tort Law, with Special Reference to Compulsory Terms and Unequal Bargaining Power," *Maryland Law Review* 41, no. 4 (1982): 563–658.

expanded and narrowed primarily through a process of inclusion and exclusion. By definition, therefore, no revolution could take place within it. The most dramatic changes impacting the significance of contract law in modern life, Friedman claims, came about not through internal developments but through developments in public policy which robbed contract of its subject matter.[70] This analysis has been confirmed over and over.[71] The process in essence left the classical paradigm intact, and compelled, as Unger has argued, "all other modes of thought to define themselves negatively, by contrast to it."[72] Collectivism, historians suggest, largely failed to replace the classical view of contract; the dominant outlook influencing reform approached contract from the outside, addressing a variety of its unwanted effects. Whether collectivism's normative content was liberal or radical, its approach was external to contract.

The same point emerges by examining the opposition between state and civil society. According to the classical view contract was something belonging to civil society, a private sphere of action. The welfare state (or steps toward it) – the achievement of collectivism – did not challenge the opposition between state and civil society.[73] Rather, collectivism represented a redefinition of state roles: the state now had in addition to its role of legalizing private interaction, a redistributive function and a responsibility to protect individuals against severe adversity. Because the opposition between state and civil society with regard to the source of obligations remained intact – no "private/public flip"[74] had been performed as yet in legal thought – the controversy between individualism and collectivism within contract could be framed in terms of "non-intervention" and "intervention." The subject of (non)intervention remained the same idea of contract, the debate turning on the role of the state with regard to it, most significantly with regard to inequalities in fact in contractual relations.[75]

Collectivism brought about changes in doctrine and in the scope of applicability of general contract law. While, as the next subsection explains,

70 Friedman, *Contract Law in America*, 21–4.

71 E.g. Atiyah, *Rise and Fall*, 714; Farnsworth, "The Past of Promise," 604; James Gordley, "Contract, Property, and the Will: The Civil Law and Common Law Tradition" in Scheiber, *The State and Freedom of Contract*, 85–6.

72 Unger, *Critical Legal Studies Movement*, 58. For additional accounts of the continued dominance of the classical formulation of contract, see Brudner, *Unity of the Common Law*, 164; Nolan, "The Classical Legacy," 614–15; Kennedy, "From Will Theory," 162–3; Scheiber, "Economic Liberty,"124; Pettit, "Freedom of Contract"; Ibbetson, *Historical Introduction*, 245; Atiyah, *Rise and Fall*, 686; Hugh Collins, *The Law of Contract*, 2nd ed. (Austin, TX: Weidenfeld and Nicolson, 1993), 5–6.

73 Olsen, "The Family and the Market," 1516.

74 Kennedy, "From Will Theory" (coining the term).

75 The discourse of interventionism versus noninterventionism itself functioned rhetorically to preserve the centrality of private ordering as the contractual paradigm. See Kreitner, *Calculating Promises*, 164.

little prevented collectivists from achieving the same results from "within" contract and replacing the classical conceptual apparatus, the Victorian collectivist conceptual apparatus continued to work against the essence of contract; its moves were perceived as interference with it. Changes were superimposed by a source understood as foreign to contract and otherwise worked only at contract's periphery, neutralized within the terminology of the will theory.

This point emerges repeatedly from historical accounts of contract but it is too often submerged under the governing theme of the "fall of contract." Viewed from the perspective of contract's meaning, however, histories of nineteenth-century collectivism are better seen as accounts of contract's victory. That it has been lost in the seams of historical narratives is a consequence of a specific analytic focus. The rise-and-fall narrative implicitly suggests that the meaning of contract is not in itself very significant; what is significant is its fate in the world. This analytic position seems to be the legacy of legal realism and the resonance of the sociology of law handed down from Eugen Ehrlich. Ehrlich criticized the juristic focus on unchanging legal propositions and argued that the focus inhibits appreciation of actual changes in law properly understood.[76] While contract maintained a stable meaning into the twentieth century, the legal world around it changed, arising in a different "social law," in Ehrlich's terms. This changing perception is the main thrust of the histories of nineteenth-century collectivism and contract.

But to disregard the external quality of the collectivist wave and the significant stability of the meaning of contract, as those emerge from contracts histories, is to miss a whole analytic focus, important both as a matter of the concept of contract's own history and in terms of its continued influence. It is through meaning that the ubiquitous human practice of contracting was understood, experienced, lived, and transformed.

Collectivism as Conceptual Alternative: Internal Critique

Collectivism appears in contracts histories not just as a historical trend, but also as a conceptual alternative that internal critiques of the classical model found within the model itself. Identifying collectivism as a conceptual possibility available within classical contract doctrine represents a second stage in the historical attack on the model.[77] This twentieth-century development arguably rendered obsolete the earlier debate, since the social or collective principle that Victorian opponents put forward as an

76 Eugen Ehrlich, *Fundamental Principles of the Sociology of Law* (Cambridge, MA: Harvard University Press, 1936), 397.

77 Kennedy, "Distributive and Paternalist Motives."

alternative to contract turns out to have been established within contract from the start.

Internal critique is primarily the work of legal realism and Critical Legal Studies which have foreclosed on the deductive aspirations and logical coherence of the classical model. Internal critique is woven into this chapter: it is internal critique, for example, that points to the contradiction between will and coercion in classical contract law; it is likewise internal critique that links contract law with a specific vision of the market, rather than with any abstract concept of freedom.

Internal critique showed that the link between contract and individualism did not lie in the basic ideals which contract supposedly protected – individual will, freedom, or choice – but more concretely in choices within doctrine that could, conceptually, go the other way (the collectivist way) just as well. The critique thus left any account of the relation of these ideals to atomistic individualism a matter of ideological bias only; that relation was not inherent in them but rather depended on the specific way in which they were put to use in law. The private/public distinction turned out to be groundless, as contract law was shown to be a principle of social order. Contract never represented a presocial order, and, as a principle social order was not inevitably oriented to atomism.[78]

But all of this was not available for Victorian jurists. Internal critique is an intellectual move that history finds only in the twentieth century. Contract's ability to encompass collectivist concerns within its paradigmatic core, historians argue, was not entertained by thinkers of the nineteenth century.[79]

When internal critique arrived, it confirmed the basic association of contract and atomism. Paradoxically, it might have strengthened it, for in showing the association to be contingent and unnecessary, internal critique found contract to contain not just gray areas, but an antagonistic ideological possibility, perhaps too oppositional to be openly endorsed.

Narrative Strand 3: Hegemony of Contract's Meaning, Or Atomism as Culture

I have so far focused on three points that tie together into a single assumption: contract's persistent tie with atomism as a specific liberal vision, confirmed even when historians turned their attention to the significance of status and collectivism. This part turns to the fourth undisputed point. *Undisputed Point #4*: The individualism of contract law was of broad cultural

78 Kennedy, "From Will Theory," 175–94; Brudner, *Unity of the Common Law*.

79 Kennedy's histories of legal thought speak to this point; see e.g. Kennedy, "From Will Theory," 175–94.

resonance, falling in line with economic, political, and ideological currents of the Victorian era.

I use the term "culture" loosely to refer to these currents; any more precise a use would fail to capture the diversity of references in contracts histories. My use aims to capture a simple commonality: references all invoke social sites, systems, and processes of meaning-making considered in some recognizable sense nonlegal. The relations of all of these to law is a matter of debate: law may be reflective of, a product of, constitutive of, or part of those other sites, systems, and processes, with more or less emphasis on the unique mechanisms through which law establishes and transforms meaning in relation to nonlegal sites. Historical accounts of classical law embody diverse theoretical approaches to these issues, involving differing attention to the broader cultural terrain. The important point for my purposes is the emergent sense that contract's atomism enjoyed a broad cultural resonance. Histories portray, often with few words, a continuous and smooth cultural landscape, a virtually hegemonic idea of contract, at least for Victorian liberals.

The consensus here is possibly the least obvious one; this part aims to clarify it and so complete the argument about histories' solidification of the assumption of a single historical meaning of contract. It is least obvious because, while some well-known histories have centralized the cultural context in their accounts of the individualism of classical law, many others have resisted these assessments from a variety of theoretical positions. This part shows, however, that resistances to context have not significantly challenged the sense of continuity between legal and nonlegal culture, from which the atomism of contract law emerges as a phenomenon entirely consonant with a broader cultural history. Explorations of collectivism in broader culture, in the meantime, add a layer of explanation to collectivism's perceived failure to reconcepualize contract; they thus support the same sense of continuity between the atomistic meaning of contract and Victorian culture at large.

Individualism Around Contract

At the background of historical analyses of contracts lies a picture of broadly economic, political, and ideological shifts in the nineteenth century. The broader context has been mostly elaborated by historians who consider it part of the explanation of classical contract law, but the picture is not only their work. While, as an explanation for legal developments, atomistic individualism is contested, as a general backdrop it is almost undisputed. I pause on controversies among historians concerning the relation between the broader context and contract law; controversies deal with questions of causality, periodization, and internal contradiction in law. They interest me not just in themselves but because they reveal the points of consensus; even historians who attribute legal developments largely to other grounds or are otherwise reluctant to move too quickly between law and nonlegal culture, view atomistic individualism as classical contract law's receptive cultural soil.

Context

At least since Dicey's Harvard lectures, the story of contract law's continuity with cultural mores has been something of a common wisdom. "Nowhere," proclaimed Dicey, "have changes in popular convictions or wishes found anything like such rapid and immediate expression in alterations of the law as they have in Great Britain during the nineteenth century, and more especially during the last half thereof."[80] Dicey identified three main currents of public opinion: the first third of the nineteenth century Dicey named the period of Old Toryism or legislative quiescence; the second third of the century, the period of individualism in public opinion; the last third, the period of collectivism.

The period of individualism, Dicey argued, was in fact "Benthamism of common sense"[81] rather than strict dogma, which under the name of liberalism became the main factor in the development of English law. Dicey articulated the terms of this position. While presumably only an idealist articulation which neither he nor anyone else thought was exclusively or coherently at work in English culture, it was this version he took care to expound: Benthamite liberals looked upon humanity as separate persons, each of whom must by her own efforts work out her happiness and well-being. They held that the prosperity of a community means nothing more than the prosperity or welfare of the whole, or of the majority of its members. On Dicey's account, from 1832 onward the supremacy of individualism was for many years incontestable and patent; conservatives were as much imbued with individualism as were Whigs or liberals. From Benthamite principles, English individualists had in practice deduced a corollary: that the law ought to extend the sphere and enforce the obligation of contract; this was conceived as an extension of individual liberty, for contract itself was understood as an expression of individual wishes.

An affirmation of the tie between developments in contract law and the expansion of contractual freedom, on the one hand, and individualism in culture, on the other, is famously found in Atiyah's classic, *The Rise and Fall of Freedom of Contract*.[82] Atiyah refers to individualism rooted in or given

80 Dicey, *Law and Public Opinion*, 7.

81 Ibid., 170.

82 Atiyah, *The Rise and Fall*; see also P.S. Atiyah, *An Introduction to The Law of Contract*, 5th ed. (Oxford: Clarendon, 1995), Chapter 1. Atiyah also criticizes Dicey's historical account, Atiyah, *Rise and Fall*, 231–7, 326, 479. The controversy, however, centers on the role of

impetus primarily by utilitarianism and classical political economy, and emphasizes the relation of legal ideas to economic thought, although he does argue that individualism was asserted as a moral value throughout the nineteenth century. The new individualistic ideas of the utilitarians and political economists came to have a pronounced effect on the law from 1830, with the idea of freedom of contract seizing hold of legal thought.[83] The basic premise, again, was that individuals knew their own interests best, and were concerned with maximizing their wealth or happiness. In the economic sphere, the emphasis was on the role of the choosing individual at the center of the free market. Other historians have likewise identified atomistic doctrines and mores echoed in contract law.[84]

Roscoe Pound's account of individualism and classical contract began interestingly with atomism outside contract but not outside the law – with the conception of justice at common law. Pound described the evolution from antiquity of the idea of the end, or purpose, of law, and saw the culmination of the process in the nineteenth-century "thoroughly individualist" theory of law.[85] The theory rested on the conception of justice as the securing of maximum individual self-assertion, with law having the purely negative function of removing obstacles to self-assertion. Utilitarianism arrived, according to Pound, when individualist ideas were already firmly fixed, and in fact took its (unnecessary) individualist turn from the earlier individualist tradition, reinforced by classical economics and post-French Revolution politics. This conception of justice, suggested Pound, led to an exaggerated importance of property and contract, a preference for private

government, while Dicey and Atiyah share much in common concerning the legal view of contract. Morton Horwitz's classic thesis links the change in contract thought in the nineteenth century to the rise of the market economy and to the service of commercial interests. Horwitz concentrates on American law, but attributes the change to England as well. Horwitz, *The Transformation of American Law*, Chapter 5.

83 Atiyah, *Rise and Fall*, 368–9. For the problematics of periodization, see note 4 above.

84 E.g., Gilmore, *Death of Contract*, 96, who views the rise and fall of the general theory of contract and of laissez-faire economics as "remote reflections of the transition from nineteenth century individualism to the welfare state and beyond," but also offers "specifically legal ... factors," like the distrust of the civil jury; Williston, "Freedom of Contract," 366, who connects, on the one hand, freedom of contract and various doctrines of individual freedom, and, on the other hand, the social philosophy that called for the greatest individual freedom and development. Peter Gabel and Jay Feinman also argue that classical law in the United States was an ideological apparatus that must be grasped in the socioeconomic context that it legitimated. Gabel and Feinman make explicit the idea of a legal "translation" of broader cultural dynamics when they argue that lawyers "associated themselves emotionally and intellectually with the new socioeconomic order and expressed in their professional activities the individualistic nature of the new system of human relationships". Jay Feinman and Peter Gabel, "Contract Law as Ideology," in *The Politics of Law: A Progressive Critique* 3rd ed., ed., David Kairys (New York: Basic, 1998), 501.

85 Pound, "End of Law 2," 204.

over public right, and an antagonism toward legislation.[86] Individualism at the common law, on this account, influenced both ideology outside the law and the area of contract law.

Challenges to the Historical Narrative

The story of the period of individualism in culture and its relation to classical law has been repeatedly challenged. What requires emphasis here is how the challenges end up reinforcing, or at least leaving undisputed, the sense of a cultural background of atomism.

THE CHALLENGE OF CAUSALITY

One important challenge has been to the causal explanation behind the cultural story. James Gordley argues that the will theories of contract arose as a response to an intellectual crisis within the legal discipline, namely the fall of the Aristotelian philosophical tradition. However, Gordley concedes that the will theory corresponded with, and even gave credibility to, prevalent individualistic ideas.[87] Philip Hamburger also argues that economic liberalism played a very limited role in shaping contract theory. Consensus theory specifically, he suggests, was selectively adopted by common lawyers from natural law and civilian ideas, and was gradually assimilated into common law. Hamburger agrees, however, that economic liberalism was compatible with the English version of contract theory and may have encouraged it and made it appealing.[88]

To the extent that the story of atomism as culture is a liberal functionalist history, critical history has challenged it by allowing a measure of autonomy to legal thought itself, thus complicating causal explanations and making room for law's indeterminacy. Duncan Kennedy's history of classical legal thought focuses on the internal structures of legal consciousness, viewed as a device mediating the contradictions of experience. What contradictions? Most broadly, the conflicting pull, and relevance, of individualism and altruism, autonomy and community, or, as Robert Gordon puts it elsewhere, "the fundamental contradiction between the needs for fusion and for individuality."[89] While Kennedy veers away from the "back-

86 See Roscoe Pound, "The End of Law as Developed in Juristic Thought (Part 1)," *Harvard Law Review* 27, no. 7 (1914): 605–28; Pound, "End of Law 2," 201–25; Roscoe Pound, "Liberty of Contract," *Yale Law Journal* 18, no. 7 (1909): 454–87.

87 Gordley, "Contract, Property," 83. See also James Gordley, *The Philosophical Origins of Modern Contract Doctrine* (Oxford: Clarendon, 1991).

88 Philip A. Hamburger, "The Development of the Nineteenth-Century Consensus Theory of Contract," *Law and History Review* 7, no. 2 (1989): 241–329.

89 Robert W. Gordon, "Critical Legal Histories," *Stanford Law Review* 36, nos. 1 and 2 (1984): 114.

ground" story,[90] his focus on the conceptual structures of legal consciousness offers highly elaborate accounts of historical human experience as played out in legal thought, accounts both of the individualism established at the core of contract law, and of its conceptual (altruist) alternative. The individualism of classical contract, it turns out, represented a contingent arrangement of the pieces of a contradictory existence. The point to note is that the account remains silent about the possibility of other arrangements of experience enacted in history. And so, one is left primarily with a sense of the conceptual pieces which were available for arrangement in historical consciousness, among them one ideal arrangement of individualism.

THE CHALLENGE OF PERIODIZATION

The problem of causality is also related to objections centered on periodization. Those essentially argue that it is a misunderstanding to represent the changes in nineteenth-century contract law – particularly the executory contract model at its base – as new. Thus Brian Simpson explained the change in the nineteenth century primarily in the production of systematic treatises relying on Continental writers who assimilated Roman sources. John Baker too finds the executory model in earlier periods; Hamburger points to the early roots of consensus theory; and Ibbetson says that the idea of contractual liability rooted in voluntary intentional acts had been familiar to common lawyers for at least "half a millennium." In a recent contribution Warren Swain centralizes the decline of the jury, which made legal doctrine more prominent as it had to cover newly opened gaps, but the principles themselves were not new; indeed, he argues, the old roots of assent undergirded its centralization in the nineteenth century.[91]

And yet, these histories little contest the suggestion that the formulation of contract law and its rising importance as the center of private law in the nineteenth century bore the marks of atomism, and some expressly concede it.[92] Swain is probably the outlier here. Pointing to various

90 He only commits incidentally to not denying the importance of "ideologies like laissez-faire, nor of concrete economic interests," Kennedy, *Rise and Fall*, 2.

91 A.W.B. Simpson, "The Horwitz Thesis and the History of Contracts," *Chicago Law Review* 46, no. 3 (1979): 533–601; J.H. Baker, "Book Review of *The Rise and Fall of Freedom of Contract* by P.S. Atiyah," *Modern Law Review* 43, no. 4 (1980): 467–9; Hamburger, "Consensus Theory of Contract,"; Ibbetson, *Historical Introduction*, 232; Swain, *The Law of Contract 1670–1870.*

92 The rejection of executory contract and will theories as a nineteenth- or late eighteenth-century transformation was elaborated by Simpson in his critique of the Horwitz thesis. Simpson did not, however, discuss the relation of culture to the reception of, perhaps, older ideas in this period, and their formulation under the will theory of contract.

motivations and tendencies of legal actors, he ends not so much by offering an alternative account as by resisting any firm or broad conclusions on "the relationship between law and society," and more broadly by refusing historical discussion of law's cultural or ideological resonances.[93]

THE CHALLENGE OF CONTRADICTION/COMPLEXITY

Cornish's and Clark's critique is of a different kind, one returning to internal contradictions in law. They emphasize the underplayed principles of nineteenth-century equity rules, which offered a competing ideology to the common law's individualism. Chancery evolved a view of contract which emphasized dependence and took a broader view of the contractual relationship, seeking to encourage trust and fairness in bargains and to protect the weak and unfortunate. This outlook was associated with the older world of status – with landed property and familial alliance. The authors admit, however, that equity's outlook did not pose a threat to the hegemony of common law individualism, which, again, was everywhere apparent: it was only toward the end of the century that any serious challenge was made to the "ideals on which the greatest nation of the nineteenth century had been built," and therefore it was only then that equity had to be sharply curtailed.[94]

* * *

The golden age of contract in law, historians suggest, was in line with, if not a result of, nineteenth-century individualism. Whether a historical continuity, coincidence, or innovation, the atomism of classical contract law emerges from dominant contracts histories as a legal construct tuned to nineteenth-century culture in general.

Simpson, "The Horwitz Thesis," 601–503; Simpson, "Innovation," 247–78; From Simpson's review of Atiyah's *Rise and Fall*, it appears he would not deny the relation of a culture of individualism to contract law, at least in terms of emphasis, and he agreed that "philanthropy" or paternalism eroded the significance of private contract. A.W.B. Simpson, "Contract: The Twitching Corpse," in *Legal Theory and Legal History: Essays on the Common Law* (London: Hambledon Press, 1987), 332. Maitland and Montague confirmed the general argument of "nothing new" in claiming that in nineteenth-century contract law, "more [had] been done to codify existing law than to introduce new principles." They suggested, however, that contract law gained in importance by a vast expansion of business. Frederic W. Maitland and Francis C. Montague, *A Sketch of English Legal History*, ed. James F. Colby (New York: G.P. Putnam's Sons, 1915), Chapter 8, 182. Ibbeston agreed that the greater depth and weight given to the idea of the will was a nineteenth-century novelty. Ibbetson, *Historical Introduction*.

93 Swain, *The Law of Contract 1670–1870*, 281.

94 Cornish and Clark, *Law and Society in England*, 226.

Collectivism Around Contract

Historians who view collectivism as a historical trend associate it with broader changes in the political, economic, and ideological scene. This subsection reviews some accounts, and then considers how they contain within them explanations for the collectivist failure to reconceive contract despite the transformative effects collectivism had on nineteenth-century law as a whole. My purpose is neither to provide a comprehensive account of available explanations nor to evaluate them; rather, I am again interested in narrative implications: my aim is to offer a sense that the collectivist failure to reconceive contract is a phenomenon which, like atomism, emerges from histories as something rooted in the deep currents of the nineteenth century, reinforcing the story of contract law's continuity with broader mores.

Dicey identified roughly the last third of the nineteenth century as the period of collectivism in public opinion. As he described it, the period was characterized by intellectual attacks on individualism, a waning belief in general maxims, and underlying conditions that stressed collective action and diminished the importance of individual effort. The practical corollary of the rise of collectivism was a demand for restrictions on freedom of contract. Unequal bargaining power and problems of monopoly and externalities called for paternalistic intervention in contractual freedom.[95]

Atiyah similarly locates the beginnings of the collectivist trend in contract law in the last third of the nineteenth century, and elaborates on many of Dicey's underlying factors. According to Atiyah, the trend was largely attributable to the rise of a consumer society with a prospering working class, the growth of corporations, the expansion of democracy, and the establishment of a vast governmental bureaucracy. All of these were correlated with conceptual changes. Conceptions of positive freedom, a more benevolent meaning of the state following the Reform Act of 1867, shifting ideas of responsibility (from individuals to their social environment), and the egalitarian ideal – all made the classical model seem less and less adequate. Attempts were accordingly made to restore concrete equality or to provide a substitute at the expense of abstract freedom of contract.[96]

But historians all concede that the processes were external to contract. Why were they so? Why did contract retain its link to atomism? Prominent in analyses of the effects of collectivism on contract law is an argument that "real" collectivism in contract appeared only in the twentieth century.[97] Until then, collectivist influences did not provide an alternative reading of

95 Dicey, *Law and Public Opinion.*

96 Atiyah, *Rise and Fall,* 582–6, 627–33. See also Pound, "Role of the Will," 14–15.

97 Ibbetson, *Historical Introduction,* Chapter 13, argues that real collectivism arrived only toward the end of the twentieth century, and only then an argument emerged that perhaps principles of substantive fairness underlay contractual liability; Cornish and Clark, *Law and Society in England,* 112–13, argue for the liberal turn and individual-based

social relations; individualism reigned supreme. Collectivism's proponents did make efforts, according to some historians, to articulate philosophical and economic underpinnings.[98] But by and large those who took an interest in social issues, historians observe, were in search of ways of adapting and conditioning the known world of private property and free contract and were at least suspicious of any dramatic breach with that present. Collectivism is sometimes even reduced to a form of apologetics. On some versions at stake was little more than capitalist apologetics.[99]

Furthermore, Cornish and Clark read the Judicature Acts of 1873–1875 which merged the common law courts with the court of Chancery, as the triumph of individualistic common law principles over the competing values of equity, and the next seventy-five years or so as the unequivocal ideological control of common law ideas in contract adjudication. They suggest that case law was consolidating its individualist ideology precisely because of the sensed threat of a collectivist government expressing itself through legislation. On this account, collectivist legislation was not part of the general rules governing contract, at least not until the mid-twentieth century.[100] It thus failed to transform contract and even prompted its consolidation.

An encompassing explanation lies in the broader context of the conflict. The critique of individualism in contract law was closely associated with the critique of the capitalist economy. Collectivism was a reaction to the market, and contract in this larger picture was but one aspect. Rather than redefine it, collectivism placed limits on contract as part of the greater protective effort. Within this process, the almost automatic assumption that contract "belonged" to atomistic individualism remained intact.[101]

commitments of collectivism, with Marxian influences awaiting another twenty to thirty years; Scheiber, "Economic Liberty,"125, notes the involvement of English liberals in important "interventionist" legislation; Richard A Epstein, "Contracts Small and Contract Large: Contract Law Through the Lens of Laissez-Faire," in *The Fall and Rise of Freedom of Contract*, ed. F.H. Buckley (Durham, NC: Duke University Press, 1999), 25–60, claims that nineteenth-century collectivist changes were not inconsistent with laissez-faire; Eric A. Posner, "The Decline of Formality in Contract Law," in Buckley, *The Fall and Rise of Freedom of Contract*, 61–77, supports Epstein's analysis.

98 E.g., Cornish and Clark, *Law and Society in England*. Cornish and Clark reject the view of collectivism as an un-theorized sentiment, as expressed by Dicey. Polanyi, too, famously viewed collectivism as a spontaneous and varied response to the rise of the market, see below.

99 Searle, *Morality and the Market*, Chapter 11.

100 See Cornish and Clark, *Law and Society in England*, 200–26.

101 Polanyi argued that "[t]he great variety of forms in which the 'collectivist' countermovement appeared was not due to any preference for socialism or nationalism on the part of concerted interests, but exclusively to the broader range of the vital social interests affected by the expanding market mechanism." Polanyi, *The Great Transformation*, 145. The idea of a broader conflict in which contract is but a proxy for the larger question of a social order also seems to fit with Dicey's and Atiyah's accounts.

The stability of contract's conceptualization in dominant legal discourse, these various accounts suggest, sprang from Victorian collectivism itself. Taken together with the broad consensus about atomistic individualism in culture, contract law appears to have been, quite simply, part of a sweeping cultural wave.

* * *

Histories show that classical contract was imbricated with atomism (*Undisputed Point #1*), that the social alternatives were two collectivized options, status and collectivism (*Undisputed Point #2*), which remained external possibilities, and ideological antagonists, until well into the twentieth century if not ever since (*Undisputed Point #3*), and suggest, or do not emphatically dispute, that law's version of individualism in contracts was in tandem with the individualism of its age (*Undisputed Point #4*). And the concord of opinion here, or at least lack of disagreement, is so overwhelming in a field of heated discussion that you would imagine it is either a certainty or a triviality, but it is neither. Atomism in contracts, though emerging from histories as virtually hegemonic, was in fact just a version – one possible interpretation – of promissory relations in liberal thinking. Its dramatic opposition (or otherwise total collapse) with status is likewise a questionable assumption.

Part I

From Status

Foreword

Forms of Sociality

Status is a form of sociality. It is therefore not atypical for theorists of relationality to tie status with non-status relationships under the same organizing theme of persons-in-social-relations. Take for instance Jennifer Nedelsky's insight in *Law's Relations*: "The self is relational because human beings become who they are – their identities, their capacities, their desires – through the relationships in which they participate. These include intimate relationships with parents and lovers, more distant relationships with teachers and employers, and social structural relationships, such as gender, economic relations, and forms of governmental power."[1] As I noted in the Introduction, Ian Macneil made a similar move in relational contract theory when he argued for "a great range of nonpromissory exchange-projectors" and kept the list open and fluid with unspecified "internalizations": "Custom, status, habit and other internalizations, command in hierarchical structures, and expectations created by the dynamics of any status quo."[2]

In historical contracts scholarship, Margot Finn's work is a close analogue to Nedelsky's claims. As noted in Chapter 1, Finn's history of credit recovers the "social individual" as a conceptualization coexisting with the autonomous individual, a claim which complicates and challenges models of contractual freedom that attend too consistently to the genealogy of personal autonomy. The social individual, Finn explains, is a person who gains rights and responsibilities by virtue of his status and connections

1 Jennifer Nedelsky, *Law's Relations: A Relational Theory of Self, Autonomy, and Law* (Oxford: Oxford University Press, 2011), 4. See also Catriona Mackenzie and Natalie Stoljar, "Introduction: Autonomy Refigured," in *Relational Autonomy: Feminist Perspectives on Autonomy, Agency, and the Social Self*, eds. Catriona Mackenzie and Natalie Stoljar (Oxford: Oxford University Press, 2000), 4 ("the focus of relational approaches is to analyze the implications of the intersubjective and social dimensions of selfhood and identity ...").

2 Ian R. Macneil, *The New Social Contract: An Inquiry Into Modern Contractual Relations* (New Haven, CT: Yale University Press, 1980), 8.

rather than by virtue of his autonomous identity alone.[3] Like Nedelsky, Finn refers both to "connections" which were sometimes finely grained, and to "status."[4]

Such insights are analytically valid both as a matter of current perspectives on sociality and as a matter of historical observation on the ongoing power of various social entanglements, among them the status hierarchies of gender, class, and nationality, in late modernity. However, within this book's interest in the history of Victorian liberalism in contracts, status should be set apart from forms of sociality defined, at least ideationally, by being non-status. My focus will be relationality in the sense of interpersonal relationships.

Relationality was a form of sociality framed not as a matter of social structure and ascription, but rather as immediate and individualized. Individualization implied getting away from ascriptive social categories like class. It also meant that reference points should not be households or other kinship units as they had been in earlier history, but natural persons. Immersion in interpersonal relationships was presumably more fluid than the status-constitution of relations, hence responsive to hopes of social mobility, in two senses: different in each setting, so that social predetermination would be less powerful; and susceptible to meaningful change without social backlash.

While I do not deny the interdependencies between relationality and status, setting them apart allows me to analytically isolate a particular historical effort, the benefits of which have long been recognized in the theory of social embeddedness. In his seminal article on the embeddedness of economic action in modern industrial societies, Mark Granovetter argued against "oversocialized conceptions of how society influences individual behavior" for being overly deterministic in the sense that "once we know the individual's social class or labor market sector, everything else in behavior is irrelevant." Most importantly, "ongoing social relations and structures are irrelevant"; the problem is "the relegation of the specifics of individual relations to a minor role in the overall conceptual scheme, epiphenomenal

3 Margot Finn, *The Character of Credit: Personal Debt in English Culture, 1740–1914* (Cambridge: Cambridge University Press, 2003).

4 Denise Lovett's dissertation on the construction of exchange in Victorian novels suggests that novelists represented the economy as socially embedded. She emphasizes the coexistence of ideas of status and free will in a manner resonating with Finn's broad claim, and places both within "the social context of the exchange and the exchanging subject." Denise M. Lovett, "Economic Exchange and the Discourse of Contract in the Victorian Novel 1846–1875" (PhD diss., University of Connecticut, 2011), 95.

See also Regenia Gagnier, *Individualism, Decadence and Globalization: On the Relationship of Part to Whole, 1859–1920* (Basingstoke: Palgrave Macmillan, 2010) for an account of models of individuals-in-relations of Victorian thinkers. Gagnier draws on both status and relational forms of sociality, discusses a variety, and calls for a dynamic account.

in comparison with enduring structures of normative role prescriptions ..."[5] Relationality captures concerns with these more dynamic and context-specific forms of embeddedness, and the care for individualized content.[6] While Granovetter's focus was the sociological analysis of economic behavior, his analytic insight is no less important for the way that relationality was historically serviceable within and for liberal thinking, particularly in contracts.

I avoid much usage of "embeddedness" and refer instead to sociality or social constitution so as to highlight the deep-reaching stakes of relationality. At least since Karl Polanyi, the concept of embeddedness calls up images of resistance to the disembedded market that already admits it as a powerful option, whereas at least some of the relational visions I explore were involved less in a negative reaction to such a reality (a point I revert to below) or to such a theoretical delineation,[7] than in a *positive* effort to describe a world that moved beyond status.[8] At stake was an elaborate economic and social outlook premised on relational sociality, a primary phenomenon. Nonetheless, Granovetter's insights carry theoretical significance for the distinctions I want to emphasize. Marking relationality as a distinct kind of sociality, and turning it into an important locus of meaning, were the features of a specific style of liberalism in history.

(Non)implications

The three chapters in this part argue for the dominance of relationality in novelistic representations of contracts as a liberal effort which gained meaning by being not status. However, I want to clarify upfront that understanding liberalism as a historical effort to get away from status often assumes unjustified implications in historical analyses.

One unwarranted implication is to see the liberal turn away from statuses as an attempt to eliminate them; on this understanding, with the rise of liberalism, status hierarchies which loomed large in English history – as noted I will be looking at gender, class and nationalism – became unacceptable. As a matter of historical record, and as this study too confirms,

5 Mark Granovetter, "Economic Action and Social Structure: The Problem of Embeddedness," *American Journal of Sociology* 91, no. 3, (1985): 486. Granovetter argued that oversocialized conceptions were ultimately as atomistic as the undersocialized conceptions of market atomism that they criticized.

6 Ibid.

7 Gaskell's *Ruth*, discussed in Chapter 3, is an exception on this point.

8 Karl Polanyi, *The Great Transformation* (Boston, MA: Beacon Press, 1967). See also Zelizer's discussion of the debate about "embeddedness" and her suggestion to concentrate sociological analysis on the way that "personal relations ... constitute economic activity." Viviana Zelizer, "How I Became a Relational Economic Sociologist and What Does That Mean?," *Politics & Society* 40, no. 2 (2012): 145–74.

such an account of liberalism would be false. While this part is devoted to exploring the alternative of relationality and highlights its attraction as not status, it should not be read as recounting a historical vision which sought to make statuses disappear. This point, however, does not in itself affirm the alternative and widespread insight that liberalism simply perpetuated "dominant interests of gender, class, race and nation."[9] Instead, the implication of the liberal problematization of statuses was that they were reinterpreted: they had lost their moral and conceptual generative capacities as cultural attention shifted to other sources of order, particularly relationality. The next part (*With Status*) accordingly develops new terms that account for the patterned manner in which liberalism both sustained and altered status hierarchies by reinterpreting them.

Relationality was also an alternative to atomistic individualism, and here comes in another unwarranted implication of reading liberalism as a turn away from status, namely, liberalism's association with atomism in contracts. Atomistic individualism, with its celebratory abstractionist and universalist tones, is too often framed as the almost logical result of the liberal revolt from statuses (even if one assumes that it was not a genuine revolt but rather a thinly veiled universalist formalism), as if the effort to construe (even disingenuously) a non-status order immediately pushed the liberally-minded from a status sociality to no sociality at all, no solids left. This is precisely the problem that Granovetter recognized in moves between undersocialized and oversoicalized accounts of sociality.[10] Again, historically that is untrue. As David Kaufmann argues, "the 'liberal tradition' is only a tradition in that its participants try to solve similar problems, not ... because the solutions are the same."[11] No single solution was mandated by the liberal problematization of statuses. The cultural diffusion of the realist novel suggests that nothing could be less true than assuming atomism as the default form of the revolt from statuses. Relationality, I argue, lay at the core of the effort to forge a shared sense of social reality that was not status-based.

Reading Relationality

This part examines a range of novelistic engagements with contracts. It begins, in Chapter 2, with displeasured representations of the status sociality of contracts in Thackeray and Trollope, leading to idealized visions

9 David Wayne Thomas, *Cultivating Victorians: Liberal Culture and the Aesthetic* (Philadelphia, PA: University of Pennsylvania Press, 2004), ix. As discussed in Part II, Thomas is critical toward this historical assessment and develops an affirmative account.

10 Granovetter, "The Problem of Embeddedness," 481–510.

11 David Kaufmann, *The Business of Common Life: Novels and Classical Economics Between Revolution and Reform* (Baltimore, MD: Johns Hopkins University Press, 1995), viii.

which both authors never pretended to realize in their narratives: on the one hand, the social order as one large sentimental family; on the other, the social order as separate spheres, with the market as a locus of economic rationality. Chapters 3 and 4 examine relational constructions of contracts and the market located between these two extreme idealizations. Chapters 3 and 4 proceed in conversation with the two broadest tropes in histories of Victorian contracts: contract as abstraction, and contract as freedom. A picture of liberalism as an effort to instate relational sociality in lieu of statuses emerges from this account. Relationality functioned as a liberal trope arming authors and readers with tools to frame multiple kinds of cultural concerns.

The last three decades have seen mounting theories of relational liberalism which can be broken down twice: they rely on different schools of thought, and they converse with different implications of non-relational individualism.[12] However, in drawing on a number of different novels, I cannot and do not argue for a philosophically coherent version of relationality in any of these senses. Rather, I trace the astounding variety of cultural concerns, from national cohesion, through gender expectations (which are important in my analysis, but by no means controlled exclusively the Victorian relational imagination, contra tendencies to feminize relationality), to self-fulfillment, that novels explored with and through the assumption that relational sociality was the predominant model of the Victorian capitalist social order.

Relationality, while not a matter of a specific philosophical version, *is* important in the abstract. This part is concerned with the persistence of the relational outlook which was meaningful in its individualizing tendencies. I am interested in relationality's persistence as a principled vision, beyond the concrete implications of different relational contexts, such as specific employment or friendly relations, that theorists following Viviana Zelizer explore, even as such implications emerge in the details of analysis.[13] Indeed, when relationality is emphasized over specific contexts as a principle of social ordering, as I argue it was, processes of contextual differentiation are at some points put under pressure. As we shall see, relationality was often a resistance, more or less successful, to efforts of differentiations (Zelizer's "relational work"), for instance between intimate and professional contexts.

That relationality, as a persistent conceptual framework of the capitalist order, has been written out or marginalized in the histories of Victorian contract, the par excellence legal structure of formal relationships, is a mistake that needs correcting.

12 For a review see Mackenzie and Stoljar, "Autonomy Refigured."

13 Zelizer, "How I Became a Relational Economic Sociologist."

When readers emphasize relationality in novels, they often read it as a romantic resistance to the market. From such a perspective, the claims I make in this part might be read as an embedding resistance to a dismebedding narrative found in contracts histories. Yet, even as my account does not align with dominant histories of Victorian liberalism in contracts, it does not suggest resistance to the capitalist order. The liberal commitments underlying relational constructions of contracts were not consistently geared to resist that order and this book is not geared to repeating the Polanyian "double movement" of disembedding and embedding at the level of scholarship. My effort throughout will be to show that the relational vision of the market and of market actors in novels was very often an alluring form of support for capitalism, though not the support that contracts histories collectively might lead us to expect. The support for capitalism channeled through visions of relational sociality is in line with what Martijn Konings describes as affective responses. To connect to a social order in modernity, and specifically to modern capitalism, was not to conceive its injunctions, particularly of economic experience, as remote, abstract, or formally rational, but to experience their relation to the complexity of personal networks, a "connectivity" as Konings calls it – the web, as Victorians imagined it.[14]

14 Martijn Konings, *The Emotional Logic of Capitalism: What Progressives Have Missed* (Stanford, CA: Stanford University Press, 2015).

Chapter 2

Credit and the Market

Vanity Fair and *The Way We Live Now*

> [F]or there to even be a discipline called "economics," a discipline that concerns itself first and foremost with how individuals seek the most advantageous arrangement for the exchange of shoes for potatoes, or cloth for spears, it must assume that the exchange of such goods need have nothing to do with war, passion, adventure, mystery, sex, or death.[1]

Victorian liberalism in contracts shared, according to current historical accounts, the same assumption. As David Graeber explains, the assumption at stake is that of separate spheres, "a division between different spheres of human behavior" which has become part of our common sense.[2] Indeed, as Graeber observes, the very idea that there is something called an "economy" was historically new.[3] This chapter is not about economics as discipline, but rather about the emergence of the economy, which is a question for different disciplines and cultural productions of the nineteenth century, not least law and literature. The history of the cultural construction of the economy which gave us the notion of the modern market, is one historians have been writing.

In Chapter 1 I examined the connection that historians identify between nineteenth-century liberal constructions of contract and separate spheres, particularly the view of the market as a realm of economic rationality. I suggested that that view requires rethinking not only as a sociological account – where it has been fundamentally undermined – but as a matter of *ideological* commitment within historical liberal thought on contract. Historians engaged directly with economics as a genre already invite the rethinking. Claudia Klaver's history of the rise of economics, for instance, speaks to ideological complexity. Klaver argues that the social and cultural

1 David Graeber, *Debt: The First 5,000 Years* (New York: Melville House Publishing, 2012), 32–3.

2 Ibid., 33.

3 Ibid., 44 (referring to Adam Smith).

authority of classical political economy depended on political and rhetorical forms; those forms exhibited a tradeoff between popularity among readers, and the construction of the economic domain as an autonomous set of concerns and laws. To slightly shift to my focus, Klaver shows how different texts that were all historically committed to a joint ideological project, created different levels of independence for the economic domain.[4] What would it mean to think about the history of contract as a complexity of positions, dependent on a variety of discursive mediations, all liberally-minded, but differently construing contract, and hence the market (or economy)?

This chapter tackles the question of the economy's disembeddedness – as cultural construct – in its relation to contracts in William Thackeray's *Vanity Fair* (1847), and Anthony Trollope's *The Way We Live Now* (1875).[5] My alternating readings suggest how contract, and specifically the credit contract often taken as the paradigm instrument of the Victorian market economy, was paradoxically construed as an obstacle to the vision of a rational market, linking economic relations instead precisely to "war, passion, adventure, mystery, sex, [and] death," most often as those emerged not from subjective processes but from the status imperatives of class, gender and nationality. The ideology of a dismebedded economy was finally articulated in *The Way We Live Now* as a never-materialized alternative, this while *Vanity Fair* preferred a vision of the social whole inflected by intersubjective intimacy. Both novels developed their idealized visions, which were never realized in their plots, within a liberal effort to get away from a crude rule of statuses, foremost class. They represent two polar conceptual alternatives for the social order, located at the two ends of high Victorianism: the social as metaphoric family, and the social as separate spheres. The next chapters add more readings to the conversation, to argue that from the perspective of contracts both ends remained ideologically marginal. One implication is a challenge to the history linking contract to the ideals of a rational market, and realist literature to either support of or romantic resistance to that conceptualization. The overall picture made up a liberal vision lying in between *Vanity Fair*'s idealized all-around relationality, and *The Way We Live Now*'s hope of economic rationality. On this vision, a contract was primarily an individualized relationship. The economy was constituted by relationships which were often suffocating, routinely disciplining, yet both inescapable descriptively, and attractive normatively, for the liberal effort to institute alternatives to status.

4 Claudia C. Klaver, *A/Moral Economics: Classical Political Economy and Cultural Authority in Nineteenth-Century England* (Columbus, OH: Ohio State University Press, 2003).

5 All references are to William Makepeace Thackeray, *Vanity Fair: A Novel Without a Hero* (New York: Barnes & Noble Classics, 2003); Anthony Trollope, *The Way We Live Now*, ed. Frank Kermode (Harmondsworth: Penguin Books, 1994).

Vanity Fair and *The Way We Live Now*

The discussion that follows alternates between *Vanity Fair* and *The Way We Live Now*. The similarity in their satirical projects has received critical attention before.[6] My readings focus on a central axis in both: credit-based efforts to gain social capital by two parallel protagonists, *Vanity Fair*'s Becky Sharp and *The Way We Live Now*'s Augustus Melmotte, to offer a number of insights.

First, to the already familiar status categories of class and gender in contract, the analysis adds ethnicity and nationality. Contracts histories have all but ignored this element of cultural specificity, which goes against the grain of universalist abstraction and market globalization. With the exception of Irene Tucker's work on contract and nationalism,[7] the extensive engagement of historians of liberalism with nationalism and racial identities, which recovers their inextricability, seems to have left little impact on Victorian contracts histories despite its immense potential. Imperial rule was particularly relevant to national identity through the self/other dialectics it involved. Karnua Mantena's work on the culturalist paradigm of late Victorian imperialism, for instance, focuses on Maine's work, and particularly his status-to-contract formulation. The opposition, she shows, underlay an emergent view of foundational differences between peoples which transformed practices of imperial rule. While Mantena concentrates on Maine's account of status, that is, his "traditional societies," the other side of the same coin that awaits further development is the role of contract as a nationalist, or more loosely an exclusionary, nation-sensitive construct.[8] While Part I ultimately moves on to non-status sociality, I also hope to reopen the conversation on that front by pointing to the almost taken-for-granted association between the paradigm market tool – the contract of credit, and a specifically English and often xenophobic cultural identity in these two novels. If, as Patrick Brantlinger argues (paraphrasing Žižek), modern British history occurs on credit, that occurrence

6 And so Alain Jumeau suggests the title "*The Way We Live Now*, or, Trollope in Vanity Fair," *Cahiers Victoriens et Eduardiens* 58 (2003): 57–70.

7 Irene Tucker, *A Probable State: The Novel, the Contract, and the Jews* (Chicago, IL: University of Chicago Press, 2000).

8 Karuna Mantena, *Alibis of Empire: Henry Maine and the Ends of Liberal Imperialism* (Princeton, NJ: Princeton University Press, 2010). Mantena offers a corrective to claims that British imperialism was premised on universalist liberal assumptions. Yet accounts of universalism too point to a nationalist bias. See for instance Uday Singh Mehta, *Liberalism and Empire: A Study in Nineteenth-Century British Liberal Thought*, 2nd ed. (Chicago, IL: University of Chicago Press, 1999), for an argument about the national (or at least European) bias of self-proclaimed universalist liberal thought of major liberal theorists, Mehta also points to that bias in social contract philosophy. See also the literature review in Lauren M.E. Goodlad, "Liberalism and Literature," in *The Oxford Handbook of Victorian Literary Culture*, ed. Juliet John (Oxford: Oxford University Press, 2016), Chapter 5.

was inseparable from nation formation.[9] That Victorian cultural products, not least the novel which, since Benedict Anderson, has been repeatedly identified as key to the formation of the modern nation-state,[10] should link directly Englishness with credit seems almost inevitable. On one level, within a rapidly expanding capitalist economy, credit was a dominant form of concretizing nationalism for social experience on the inside as it were, as war, conquest and international relations did on the outside.

Second, the exclusionary impulse associated with contract through these forms of sociality speaks to a difference between credit and money, or more precisely between credit contracts and other access to cash. *Vanity Fair* and *The Way We Live Now* both spent considerable energy to explore the social differentiations between otherwise similar lifestyles and appearances, according to their background finance.

Third, *Vanity Fair* and *The Way We Live Now* differed in the critical stance they took toward the status-soicality of the credit contract, explicable in terms of their separate historical moments. *Vanity Fair* was morally oriented, and offered an ethically-inflected relational alternative to statuses which idealized the nuclear family as a model for the social order at large. *The Way We Live Now* was epistemologically oriented. Its alternative to statuses encouraged a separate-spheres view in which relationality was part of the private sphere of intimate relations, while the market was modeled as a distinct realm of economic rationality which, while tellingly hard to narrate – and *The Way We Live Now* never did narrate it, was missing from *Vanity Fair*, thirty years earlier. *The Way We Live Now*'s position iterated an ideological ideal in line with atomistic individualism recovered by contracts histories, but could not see how *contract*, of all things, would be the tool to that end.

Contract and Social Identity

A brief reminder: Becky Sharp is the daughter of a frustrated, drunk and indebted English artist, and a young French opera singer (or dancer, as later suggested), both dead before the story begins. Destined to the role of governess, Becky is determined to reach higher by all means, foremost her sexuality. The plot, set around the years of Waterloo and English imperial adventures, centralizes credit as an all-embracing condition of existence, and more crucially of spatial and social expansion, in the hypocritical world of social masking it calls Vanity Fair.

9 Patrick Brantlinger, *Fictions of State: Culture and Credit in Britain 1694–1994* (Ithaca, NY: Cornell University Press, 1996), 1. I am paraphrasing Brantlinger, who focuses primarily on public finance, and claims that realist novels privatized the public debt (Chapter 4). But this only confirms Žižek's original meaning in the quotation Brantlinger uses, that the future defines retroactively the meaning of present acts.

10 Benedict Anderson, *Imagined Communities: Reflections on the Origin and Spread of Nationalism* (London: Verso, 1991).

Augustus Melmotte is a financier of unsure origins which drive his obsessive efforts, parallel to Becky's, to gain social standing.[11] The plot of financial collapse, often associated with the financial crisis of 1873, draws on English-American interactions to explore the working of credit represented as the basic infrastructure of the social world.

Becky and Melmotte identify social openings for themselves in English materialism. These characters recognize that traditional class and ethnic prejudices deny their social inclusion, but see that, with the rise of the middle-class ethic of monetary measurement as independent indicator of social value, money encourages compromise. At stake was a lingering historical process in which, as E.P. Thompson put it, aristocratic influence remained formidable long into the century.[12] Indeed, revisionist history goes further to argue that landed aristocracy retained pre-eminence in social and political hierarchies throughout the high Victorian era.[13] That influence was in constitutive tension with capitalist values; this was "an uneasy mixture of rivalry and mutual dependence."[14] As monetary evaluation gained dominance, the system of old prestige (or, as Victorians often preferred, Old Corruption) faced a twofold threat: first, many privileged social members were in fact poor, therefore undeserving of their social superiority in a money-society; second, with money as the main form of social capital, wealthy outsiders threatened to penetrate the sphere of social privilege. Becky and Melmotte ambitiously rely on this historical change, of inclusive potential, to gain a place in the English world, but for different reasons make the same mistake of relying on credit.

Becky uses credit by default. She begins by seeking ready money through "husband-hunting" (21), the one career open to her. She fails with high income Jos. She marries Rawdon Crawley secretly, and so to her frustration is unable to accept a more financially secure offer from his father. The marriage to Rawdon relies on his rich aunt's, Miss Crawley's, "avowed contempt for birth" and "daring liberal opinions" (150). Miss Crawley

11 At the outset he declares himself an Englishman recently returned to his home country (30). This is occasionally falsified, for example when Melmotte's confusion with respect to the English system of titles and property is attributed to "men born and bred out of England," (184) or when Lord Alfred assures Melmotte that he need not be an Englishman to become a baronet (194). Melmotte experiences himself as a no-one, "[b]rought into the world in a gutter, without father or mother" (494). After his death, the general opinion is that Melmotte's father was an Irishman turned New York coiner. His wife is not English, and Jewish. His daughter is not his wife's, and rumored to have been born in New York or Paris.

12 E.P. Thompson, *The Peculiarities of the English* (London: the Socialist Register, 1965).

13 W.D. Rubinstein, *Capitalism, Culture and Decline in Britain, 1750–1990* (London: Routledge, 1993). See also the review of literature in Henry Staten, "Is *Middlemarch* Ahistorical?," *PMLA* 115, no. 5 (2000): 991–1005.

14 Paul Delany, *Literature, Money and the Market: From Trollope to Amis* (Basingstoke: Palgrave Macmillan, 2002), 9.

appears to encourage Becky: "I adore all impudent matches ... I wish some great man would run away with you, my dear" (104–5). But Crawley has her limits: "Rawdon married – Rebecca – governess – nobody – Get out of my house, you fool, you idiot" (160) she screams at the unfortunate bearer of evil news, and disinherits her nephew and his new wife. With cash beyond her reach, credit appears to Becky just "as good as money" (435) in breaking social hierarchy. She assumes that upper-class lifestyle and manner is the goal, and credit becomes a way of life as she joins Rawdon in the art of "how to live well on nothing a year" (title to Chapter 36).

> Rawdon, with roars of laughter, related a dozen amusing anecdotes of his duns, and Rebecca's adroit treatment of them. He vowed with a great oath that there was no woman in Europe who could talk a creditor over as she could. Almost immediately after their marriage, her practice had begun, and her husband found the immense value of such a wife. They had credit in plenty, but they had bills also in abundance, and laboured under a scarcity of ready money. Did these debt-difficulties affect Rawdon's good spirits? No. Everybody in Vanity Fair must have remarked how well those live who are comfortably and thoroughly in debt: how they deny themselves nothing; how jolly and easy they are in their minds. Rawdon and his wife had the very best apartments at the inn at Brighton; the landlord, as he brought in the first dish, bowed before them as to his greatest customers: and Rawdon abused the dinners and wine with an audacity which no grandee in the land could surpass.
>
> (212)

Becky's debts are indiscriminating: from the poorest washerwoman, through her personal companion Briggs whom she ruins, to aristocratic patrons, she talks all into financing her efforts to inhabit "fashion."

Melmotte's use of credit is more complex because *The Way We Live Now* relies on his character as metaphor for finance itself. Melmotte's ambitious goal is not just to penetrate fashion, but to become society's ultimate source of value, represented in a distinctive maneuver: replacing the sign of every value – money, with his promises. Melmotte wants to be the omnipotent source through which the society of *The Way We Live Now* mediates value, a scheme rehearsed in transactions introducing promises when money is expected.

> "If your banker is pressing you, refer him to me," Mr Melmotte had said. As for many years past we have exchanged paper instead of actual money for our commodities, so now it seemed that, under the new Melmotte regime, an exchange of words was to suffice.
>
> (346)

The narrator sketches a process of departure from the idea of "actual money" (precious metal): it was replaced by paper (fiat money), then by promises. It is not simply that Melmotte defers payment of "actual" money, but that a new means of payment is at stake: that promises *are* a new money. This invokes the problematic of representation in capitalism which has been central to cultural histories at least since Jean-Christophe Agnew's work.[15] However, I want to emphasize a different point – the plot's dichotomous assumptions about money and contractual credit, which begin by staging Melmotte's credit-based strategy.

Melmotte's use of credit as money is underlined by tracing a gradual replacement of all other assets, which slowly disappear from visibility, leaving only the promises in circulation. Symbolic episodes clarify the process. Thus, Dolly owes Felix £1,000; Felix wants to buy shares with the money; Dolly asks Melmotte to advance £1,000 on account of the Pickering property debt to Felix, and Felix asks Melmotte to use the money to buy shares; Melmotte simply agrees. Money, property and shares all remain with Melmotte; everybody else must do with his promises. These episodes encapsulate the structure of the entire railway project in which Melmottian promises replace economic value.[16] With his promises treated as money, the initial rumor that Melmotte "could make money dear or cheap as he pleased" (31) becomes a meaningful foretelling.

Credit circumscribes him, with the railway credit at one end, the Pickering estate debt on the other. In the interim lies an endless chain of credit in which Melmotte no longer knows "what he owned, or what he owed" (561). Promises to marry and not to marry his daughter interact with the work of credit as Melmotte ties all to his goal of social success.

The initial plot rationale for both Becky and Melmotte is a marginality which is not only class- or gender-determined, but a deep foreignness: everything French in *Vanity Fair*, everything alien and particularly the kicking ex-colony America, in *The Way We Live Now.*

Becky's low-class and French origins are provocative in two convergent senses: to adopt Hobsbawm's terms, as *system* France as Revolution signals a democratic liberty which threatens the privilege that demeans Becky's humble English origins. Then again, France as *power (state)* is at war with England at the height of the novel, and remains its classic foe throughout.[17] Both senses tie into anti-French sentiments in popular English nationalism. Becky's use of French (language) as a weapon against English oppressors,

15 Jean-Christophe Agnew, *Worlds Apart: The Market and the Theater in Anglo-American Thought, 1550–1750* (Cambridge: Cambridge University Press, 1986). For a more recent account see for instance Mary Poovey, *Genres of the Credit Economy: Mediating Value in Eighteenth- and Nineteenth-Century Britain* (Chicago, IL: University of Chicago Press, 2008).

16 Details below.

17 Eric J. Hobsbawm, *The Age of Revolution 1789–1848* (New York: Vintage Books 1996), 76.

from the conservative headmistress Miss Pinkerton to the Ladies of Gaunt, signals the nationalist origins of her exclusion.

Melmotte's unsure origins invoke, first, an abstract English xenophobia and racism which flourished in this era of imperial expansion and migration. Associated with Jews, Irish, French, just the Continent, and Americans, Melmotte is unlocatable so as to invoke the sentiment of suspicion of the alien as such. This plot-based point is also iterated at an artistic level: criticism has been debating the possible originals, both historical and literary, for Melmotte, registering the same problem of slippery identity.[18] Second, structurally Melmotte is part of the novel's preoccupation with the English-American love-hate complex, manifest in plots of betrothals and commerce across the Atlantic merged around his character and expanding by his agency.[19] The railway project that Melmotte both symbolizes and is symbolized by, begins with an American-English tie. Paul Montague takes his money out of England to his American uncle. The uncle had been an Englishman, had gone to California "and had there become an American" (50). Paul returns to England dissatisfied with America, but he cannot undo the tie and get his money out of the California farm. Instead, he ends up with a promissory deed and is made partner in his uncle's enterprise with the American Fisker. The partnership intensifies when Fisker arrives in England and turns Paul into the unwilling intendant of the "British interests" in a new railway company established to build a line between the U.S. and Mexico; Fisker soon recruits Melmotte to attract public investment, in a plotline gesturing at the massive investment in international railway networks in this era, one that Hobsbawm described as a "combination of romanticism, enterprise and finance," which involved "[r]ockets of self intoxication" as well as "robber barons."[20]

At the same time that Becky and Melmotte appear foreign, their foreignness is unsure, and both vacillate between admission and denial. Their threat lies in that space of insecurity, which seems to speak directly to Homi Bhabha's suggestion that "the problem of outside/inside must always itself be a process of hybridity, incorporating new people in relation to the body politic ..."[21] The problematic of the not-surely-English protagonist is

18 For a short review of these debates see Delany, *Literature, Money and the Market*, 26–7.

19 For an account of Trollope's interest and opinions concerning the English/American relationship see Frank Kermode, *Introduction to Trollope, The Way We Live Now*, vii, xv–xvi; D.M. Alexander, "Trollope's Cosmopolitanism," *Trollopian* 2, no. 1 (1947): 3–10; Helen K. Heinman, *Three Victorians in the New World* (American University Studies Series No. 4: English Language and Literature, 1992), vol. 106, 240–5. See also Annette Van, "Ambivalent Speculations: America as England's Future in *The Way We Live Now*," *Victorian Structures of Feeling* 39, no. 1, (2005): 75–96.

20 Eric J. Hobsbawm, *The Age of Capital 1848–1875* (Harmondsworth: Penguin Books 1979), 57.

21 Homi K. Bhabha, ed., *Nation and Narration* (New York: Routledge 1990), 4.

extenuated by their refusal to play by the English rules of gender and class. Becky angrily revolts against expectations of innocent femininity which her inverse image Amelia performs, and rejects in full consciousness both sentimentality and virtuousness: "I'm no angel" (12). She likewise refuses to accept her class destiny as governess. Thackeray holds up her socially-informed position with a certain admiration for a while, but finally lets it deteriorate into banal corruption – a point I revisit below. Melmotte for his part violates norms of gentility and normative upper-class masculinity. Unlike Becky, who has been raised and educated in English institutions and appreciates the violations of social roles that she commits, Melmotte is only half aware of his: "[H]e scolded earls and snubbed dukes, and yet did it in a manner which showed how proud he was of connecting himself with their social pre-eminence, and how ignorant of the manner in which such pre-eminence affects English gentlemen generally. The more arrogant he became the more vulgar he was ..." (416). These additional transgressions of norms by Becky and Melmotte are tied up with the question of national identity. As Lynda Nead argues, such transgressions were perceived as a threat not only to the stability of internal class relations but also to national and imperial security, for English international pre-eminence was believed to depend on a stable domestic base.[22]

Both Becky and Melmotte turn to credit. The problem explored in both novels, which I examine in detail, is that credit cannot replace money: neither functionally, as Becky attempts, nor more fundamentally as a source of value, as Melmotte hopes. Instead, both novels represent credit as precisely the instrument of social discipline and exclusion that Becky and Melmotte paradoxically try to overcome by using it. In consequence, while Becky and Melmotte reach very high, touching paradigmatic forms of social capital: royalty and parliament, they end up, after a credit whirlpool which sweeps everyone around them, outside the English social belonging they covet. For Becky, the "far-off shining cliffs of England were impassable" (632); the same sentiment in Melmotte leads to nothing less than suicide.

Credit vs. Money

Vanity Fair and *The Way We Live Now* both explicitly satirized English materialism, and particularly the havoc that the pursuit of money can wreak on value systems. From this perspective, they both sided with classical social and economic thought which views money as a rationalizer and leveler of complex meaning. From Marx onwards, money's theorization as colorless,

22 Lynda Nead, *Myths of Sexuality: Representations of Women in Victorian Britain* (Malden, MA: Blackwell, 1988), 91.

homogenous, fungible, reductionist, a universal equivalent – the measure of value of all things, implies a radical ability to flatten social structures and meanings. On this view, Viviana Zelizer explains, the fundamental revolutionary power of money came from its complete indifference to values.[23] With money "we do not ask what and how, but how much"; in consequence, Simmel says, "the quantitative differences of money ownership imply the most considerable qualitative differences for the owner."[24] The effect, often decried as dehumanizing and corrupting, is also potentially democratizing when read against restrictive statuses, as Becky and Melmotte recognize. After all, money appears to "give equal rights to the most contradictory tendencies in life"[25] Indifference to values is also indifference to hierarchic values. Moreover, implicit in Simmel's observations above – not asking "what and how" – is a forgetfulness of *history*: how you came to have money, what is behind your moneyed position, is obliterated.[26] Temporal forgetfulness, not just the present and ongoing reduction of incommensurabilities to the ultimate commensurate, is how money does the work of social leveling on which Becky and Melmotte count.

The classical view of money as radical leveler becomes contested as a matter of everyday experience, where money operates and is used differently in different social contexts, and since Zelizer's work, as a matter of theory as well. Money, Zelizer claims, is constrained and shaped by social specifications of different uses, social designations of users, allocation systems applied to different monies, structures of control of monies, and links between sources and particular uses. The "culturalists" in monetary debates, Zelizer among them, submit that money's ability to obliterate all differentiations except the quantity of money itself, is determined by the social and cultural contexts of money. Nigel Dodd summarizes, "culture influences what money actually *does*."[27] The debate between the classical and culturalist positions is revealing in reading *Vanity Fair* and *The Way We Live Now*.

Becky and Melmotte see that English privilege makes compromises with money, in line with the classical view. The rule of universal equivalence, however, does not work smoothly with borrowed money. This is Becky's initial mistake: she sees that upper classes are poor yet maintain social

23 Viviana A. Zelizer, *Economic Lives: How Culture Shapes the Economy* (Princeton, NJ: Princeton University Press, 2011), 94.

24 Georg Simmel, *The Philosophy of Money*, trans. Tom Bottomore and David Frisby, ed. David Frisby, 3rd ed. (New York: Routledge, 2004), 260–1.

25 Ibid., 445.

26 This simple denial might relate to a broader philosophical insight: Noam Yuran's theory of money takes the denial of history – in the sense of socially-determined drives – to be the very essence of money. Noam Yuran, *What Money Wants: An Economy of Desire* (Stanford, CA: Stanford University Press, 2014).

27 Nigel Dodd, *The Social Life of Money* (Princeton, NJ: Princeton University Press, 2014), 269.

privilege by using credit. She expects the other side of the coin to work too: climbers should be able to *enter* privilege through credit just as privilege uses credit not to fall. Becky counts on the functionality of available funds and fails to understand the contractual systematics: Credit's origins can be traced to a variety of social relations which can be differentiated to maintain social distinctions. Contracts do everything that the culturalist view poses, and in fact resist the obliteration of history required for the plan of social climbing to work. The Victorian experience of knowledge generated through credit systems was pervasive, as legal players also observed; "The system of inquiry and knowledge in a town," one judge testified, "which has ... been got up by these men who enforce the debts ... is astonishing. They know practically everybody in the town, and they talk to one another, and they know exactly who is to be trusted and to what extent, in a way that without this system never would have been possible."[28]

Tucker's work suggests ways to read the relation between contract law and liberalism precisely in contract's role in negotiating historicity, by which she means contingent cultural specificity, not least by assuming the readability of speech acts performed in a specific language and context in contract. A contract, in other words, is a cultural tool which acknowledges contingencies of time and place.[29] *Vanity Fair*'s assumptions about contract confirm Tucker's insights from a different direction: they link contract to history through the narrativity that it invites. The structure of a contract implies an ongoing relationship between creditor and debtor which tells the story of money's channeling, and so colors money. Rather than the forefront of money-rational capitalism, the credit system functions as resistance, undoing the potential erosion of nonpecuniary social distinctions.

Becky's "practice" of credit is first represented as a form of English imperialism: she and Rawdon are the style of "English adventurers who have subsequently invaded the continent, and swindled all the capitals of Europe ..." (359). Their rendezvous, which leaves creditors violently cursing "against the English nation" (360), ends with Becky using her immunity to imprisonment for debt as married (covered) woman, to return to England and compromise with Rawdon's creditors. Put otherwise, Becky capitalizes, literally and metaphorically, on every benefit she in fact ridicules, of the English and of submissive femininity. The same maneuver repeats itself in escalating social circles. Becky advances on credit until even her worst social enemies "succumbed before" her (497). The meaning of credit, however, becomes more complex as Becky's debts are subjected to the closer scrutiny of realist everyday detail within English borders.

28 Select Committee on Debtors (Imprisonment), Report, HC 1909–239, q. 2249 q 3163 (Bompas J.). And see more generally Margot Finn, *The Character of Credit: Personal Debt in English Culture, 1740–1914* (Cambridge: Cambridge University Press, 2003).

29 Tucker, *A Probable State.*

The central and revealing failure of Becky's strategy is Lord Steyne's patronage, the main source of her credit. Becky's tie with Steyne secures a stream of credit, but its form violates every possible norm of gender, class and Englishness as nationality. She has switched roles of household provider with Rawdon: "He was Colonel Crawley no more. He was Mrs. Crawley's husband" (370). She has violated norms of sexuality – or rather, in openly practicing the role of concubine, outed what can only be practiced through denials. She has breached class lines and reached for "the great Lord" (368), soon after she encouraged Rawdon to be patient: "You can't shoot me into society … Remember, my dear, that I was but a governess," (365). She has inflected the English with French promiscuity. Steyne himself represents French violence which translates into familial brutality, and Becky formally unleashes it. These violations are all registered in the loans Becky obtains, each coming with a string of social knowledge. Unlike other money, which in *Vanity Fair* does not have a certificate of origin, as Simmel put it,[30] money obtained through credit does. The ongoing ties that Becky's credit reveals, with their violations of status norms, offer the social world something to operate on, and secures her downfall.

The narrator insists on the distance between Becky's borrowed money and ready money for social position: "there were times when she believed herself to be a fine lady and forgot that there was no money in the chest at home – duns round the gate, tradesmen to coax and wheedle – no ground to walk upon, in a word" (467). The importance of the concrete background of contract for this outlook cannot be overemphasized: The problem for Becky is not debt as such. There is a historical distinction to be drawn between credit in general, seen as morally tainted and bordering on criminality, and cash, seen as intrinsically moral. This cultural distinction, Graeber explains, was the consequence of the legalization of interest and the consequent criminalization of debt, which changed the history of credit and is key to modern capitalism.[31] But *Vanity Fair* reveals a more nuanced point about the contractual basis of credit. Becky's problem is the particular rationale of *her* contracts, rooted in Steyne's patronage. As Becky observes, everyone is in debt; when debt is the focus it is hard to understand why Becky's indebted but otherwise high-class-compatible style should be less successful than others'. From the perspective of monetary theory too Becky's expectation to succeed does seem to have a "ground to walk upon." As Dodd notes, the increasingly widely accepted theory that all money is debt; from this perspective the material world around Becky looks even less differentiated; for anyone with money, there is someone, or

30 Simmel, *The Philosophy of Money*, 387.
31 Graeber, *Debt*, Chapter 11.

perhaps everyone, in debt. And yet, money as debt means a generalized, socialized obligation that, Dodd emphasizes, should be distinguished from contractual obligation.[32] Contracts have implications that do not arise otherwise, and that distinguish money raised through a credit contract from money otherwise available. In *Vanity Fair* contracts facilitate constructed social knowledge.[33] And so the credit contract turns out to be an obstacle to a rational market economy. *Vanity Fair* cannot be reduced to a critique of capitalism in which credit is an extension of money.[34] Such readings replicate Becky's mistake.

The implications are ruinous for Becky. She assumes that lifestyle – which can be bought with money however obtained – is what matters, but her contracts surround her with signs of inferiority. Credit providers understand the implications of the contracts from the start: "I shame to say, she would not have got credit had they not believed her to be guilty" (437). The social knowledge generated by credit reflects back on Becky's ability to treat it as a safe zone, which is just what Melmotte means when he says, "the nature of credit, how strong it is – as the air – to buoy you up; how slight it is – as a mere vapour – when roughly touched" (312). Becky's plan could not have worked with the kind of credit she had. "[T]o be so near, and to lose all" (539), grieves Becky, not realizing, for all her cleverness, that she was never very near.

When Becky is outside England again after her English credit collapse, her life, still dependent on credit, is represented in abstraction as a form of vagabond bohemianism. The confident imperialism of the opening troops of English debtors has been replaced with unrooted "alternations of splendour and misery" (637), but the narrative treatment of this stage resembles the opening: an account of sweeping moves in Europe condensed in a few short paragraphs, standing in opposition to the social rootedness and social knowledge generated by credit inside England. The formal contrast in the narrative treatment of Becky's credit outside and inside England, and its

32 Dodd, *The Social Life of Money*, 93.

33 This view of contract resonates with Keith Hart's account of digital money as a form of collective memory which conveys information about users that "anonymous" money does not. Ibid., 344–8.

34 Armour Craig, for instance, suggests that "[t]he ghostly paradigm upon which human nature plays in *Vanity Fair* is the credit economy that in Thackeray's own lifetime finally developed from a money economy." G. Armour Craig, "On the Style of *Vanity Fair*" in *Twentieth Century Interpretations of* Vanity Fair: *A Collection of Critical Essays*, ed. Michael G. Sundell (Englewood Cliffs, NJ: Prentice-Hall, 1969), 66. See also John Vernon, *Money and Fiction: Literary Realism in the Nineteenth and Early Twentieth Centuries* (Ithaca, NY: Cornell University Press, 1984), 68–9.

For a general discussion of the failure of market critics (particularly from the Marxist tradition) to distinguish between cash and credit see Finn, *The Character of Credit*, Introduction.

explicit relation to the physical and metaphoric question of national borders, reaffirms the meaning of contract in the plot.

If Becky's contracts reveal her violations, with Melmotte the logic which contrasts credit to money operates from the inside as it were, in terms of an almost technical error at the heart of his scheme. Recall that Melmotte seeks to penetrate the social center by letting his promises circulate as money. Like Becky's conflation of money as social debt and credit as private (contractual) debt, Melmotte wants to conflate public and private debt, literally by expanding his debts to the entire public – to "everybody" – a favorite trope in *The Way We Live Now.*[35] The scheme's predestined failure lies in its very structure: money's ability to act as the sign of every value depends on its exogeneity to the social relations it affects; the obliteration of history is crucial. Melmotte's promises cannot serve that purpose.

To be successful money, Melmotte's promises cannot convey meaning which disturbs their work as a sign of every value. Melmotte intuitively recognizes this prerequisite: He repeatedly denies that history matters and insists that his promises are all alike. When he fails to pay for the aristocratic Pickering estate, Longestaffe's lawyer appeals to him: "We are not asking for payment of a commercial debt … but for the price of a considerable property which you have purchased." For Melmotte's promises to become money, however, the pecuniary element must obliterate the concrete relation behind it, and so "Mr Melmotte had suggested that the characteristics of the money were the same, let the sum in question have become due how it might" (560). Ironically, Melmotte belies his own claim of universal equivalence: He wants to buy the Pickering estate precisely because it is a symbol of deep-rooted high-ranking Englishness. His effort is perhaps most meaningful against the historical fact that in this period new men of wealth seldom purchased land on any significant scale;[36] purchasing land, in other words, reflected a significant historical struggle for political change. The property virtually embodies history, and the contract to pay for it registers Melmotte's ambition as an outsider, and the violation involved in the transfer of property to him.

The land transfer finally fails, but the span of the plot is a long interval in which attempts to transfer the property to Melmotte include a lease in his favor, invitations to the even grander country house of the Longestaffe family – the "secular temple" of aristocracy,[37] Georgiana Longestaffe's stay with the Melmottes, and Melmotte actually getting hold of the property.

35 "[I]n *The Way We Live Now* … 'everybody' seems to be the main actor, motivator and object of almost every aspect of the novel." Ayelet Ben-Yishai, "Trollope and the Law," in *The Cambridge Companion to Anthony Trollope* eds. Carolyn Dever and Lisa Niles, (Cambridge: Cambridge University Press, 2011), 163.

36 Rubinstein, *Capitalism, Culture and Decline in Britain*, 147–8, 159–60.

37 Delany, *Literature, Money and the Market*, 20.

This elongated in-between state allows an exploration of the problematic that Melmotte's foreignness presents. Rather than some abstract promise to pay money, the Pickering property promise has socially-concrete meaning and so becomes a major plot hinge despite its disproportion to the general circulation of credit in Melmotte's story. The property is the formal meeting point between Melmotte and aristocracy which rules his rise and fall: it is causally linked to Melmotte's ability to enter exclusive social circles and to raise unspoken amounts of credit, and to his collapse: Dolly Longestaffe's investigation into Melmotte's too-early hold of the property becomes the source of rumors which cause his social failure, and the entire credit meltdown.

The formal structure of Melmotte's failure to obtain the coveted estate relies on the impossibility of replacing money with promises. At the heart of the credit scheme Trollope planted a seemingly simple device of forgery: Dolly refuses to sign the deeds transferring the property to Melmotte, and so Melmotte, who has already leveraged the property both socially and financially, forges Dolly's signature. Read at face value, this is nothing but corruption, analogous to the gradual exposure of moral depravity in Becky's story, to which I turn in a moment. However, as a matter of the novel's deep logic, the forgery is not corruption but rather the logical end of Melmotte's centrifugal movement in which all assets attach to him. The narrator's comment that "money was the very breath of Melmotte's nostrils, and therefore his breath was taken for money" (268) is more than irony from this perspective: if his word can replace any value in the plot, surely it can do so here. The episode is Melmotte's ultimate symbolic attempt to turn himself into money's source. Driven to this logical end, we find a short circuit in his system. We have here word replacing value, but in this case word is given to none else than its speaker. Since Melmotte can only make promises to drive the circulation of value, his self-referential act, emptied from the relational qualities of promise in a formal denial of history and context, must lead to collapse. Therefore, when the transfer deeds evaporate, the whole Melmottian system of credit disappears with them.

Like Becky, Melmotte's reliance on promises is a doomed plan. While *Vanity Fair* worked with the concrete relations of Becky's credit to assess her failure, *The Way We Live Now* examined the logical incoherence of the analogy between promises and money, which relied on the same assumptions developed in *Vanity Fair*. The money-thing obliterates concrete social histories while promissory relations do the opposite. Obliteration allows the exponential growth of value seemingly from nowhere. As in Marx's M-C-M (money exchanged for commodity exchanged for money of greater sum) formula, where money begets more money, so here the narrative move of spiral social climbing seems to equally deny a foundation except the fact of climbing itself, which becomes known through social circulation, as money's principle of growth becomes known through economic circulation.[38] The success of protagonists assumes a velocity with every contact with social circles (think for instance of Becky's move from humble merchants to low aristocracy, then up the scale with increasing velocity). The movement, mirroring the logic of money, is checked because credit does not answer to the principle of obliteration. Promises in *The Way We Live Now* signal social existence, and particularly exclusionary impulses. Not only do promises channel money in a manner revealing the history of status norm-violations, but the very attempt to treat them like money – driven to its logical end – indicates a non-Englishness.[39]

38 For a discussion of absence as the core of the theory of money see Yuran, *What Money Wants.*

39 *The Way We Live Now* iterates the same logic in the plot of the Beargarden club IOUs. The story signals the slowly-disappearing social world represented by the English upper-class-male club, a process told through the treatment of IOUs: their non-transferable, socially-specific quality is questioned in interactions mistakenly treating IOUs as money.

The club is threatened by Felix when he pays Fisker – a foreigner, with members' IOUs: "Sir Felix .... should have understood that he was not entitled to pay a stranger with documents which, by tacit contract, were held to be good among themselves" (81). While Fisker is happy to play by the club's rules and postpone payment, the members insist that he must be paid on the spot, understanding individual debts between them as collective responsibility to the outer world, in a symbolic construction of IOUs as socially-circumscribed transactions. Felix does not relent. When Paul loses money to Miles in a game, Felix urges Paul to buy Miles' IOUs and pay Miles with them, because Miles never repays them. Miles reacts indignantly: "On what principle of justice could Sir Felix come between him and another man?" (191). The non-transferable quality of IOUs again stands to differentiate them from the abstract idea of money, to Felix's frustration. Nidderdale preempts Felix's complaint by frankly stating the principle at work here:

> [I]t isn't very nice for a fellow to play when he knows he can't pay; but I don't know that it's worse than getting drunk like Dolly Longestaffe, or quarrelling with everybody as Grasslough does – or trying to marry some poor devil of a girl merely because she's got money [as Felix does]. I believe in living in glass houses, but I don't believe in throwing stones.
>
> (174)

Club IOUs are part of a glass house: an entire set of norms of a social circle. Treating them as money obliterates this concreteness and so defies that entire set.

The club's fall comes with Vossner's critical defection. This defection by a non-Englishman marks the initial problem of letting him in. After the defection, "[t]he Beargarden had been opened again with difficulty ... Nor could even this be done without rigid laws as to the payment of ready money" (567). The new insistence on ready money signals the descent of a social system, and the club soon closes. Flatfleece then fails to collect the debts sold to him in a symbolic reassertion of their quality as specific social relations, and as such – non-transferable, non-translatable, and now no longer viable. As Denise Lovett puts it, the IOUs plot tells us that "an apparently 'free' or unregulated market in fact is highly dependent on a stable set of transparent systems of representation." The IOUs disappear with the club's social setting. Denise M. Lovett, "Economic Exchange and the Discourse of Contract in the Victorian Novel 1846–1875" (PhD diss., University of Connecticut, 2011), 276.

Melmotte's promise to pay for English aristocratic land contains the key to his problematic. Differentiating debts he wanted others to treat like undifferentiated money, and denying his own doing through the wonderfully symbolic moment of forgery, Melmotte's maneuvers underline the novel's deep assumptions about the social roots of contract. Credit contracts in particular are not simple market instruments. Just as *Vanity Fair* cannot be convincingly read as a critique of capitalism in which credit and money work together, so in *The Way We Live Now* the problem of promises cannot be reduced to a process of abstraction – a growing distance between the origin of value and its derivatives. At stake is a radical alteration in the source of value; credit represents an alternative logic to the monetary one, not an abstraction from it.[40] For a similar reason, Trollope cannot be said to deny all differentiations between forms of credit[41]; he at least differentiated contractual from collectively-backed credit. Finally, *The Way We Live Now* (like *Vanity Fair*, again), is not simply another staging of the battle between land and money – or aristocratic and bourgeoisie-capitalist value;[42] it is not merely, to use Bourdieu's terms, about a struggle over the principle of social domination,[43] but an investigation of the credit contract's role in making that historical struggle deeply complex, and possibly irresolvably so.

The Alternative: Sphere Making

Vanity Fair and *The Way We Live Now* both rely on the contrast with money to represent credit and more broadly promises as relations sustaining class, gender and nationalist forms of sociality and exclusion. The critical impulse of both novelists drove them to seek alternatives, but here they diverged. Thackeray worried about the relational failures of his protagonist debtor – Becky, in moral terms. Trollope turned from the protagonist debtor – Melmotte, to the lending public, to investigate the production of knowledge that drives the circulation of credit – here used more abstractly as trust in economic transactions, both contractual credit and investments,

40 For an argument that the problem of credit in *The Way We Live Now* is premised on abstraction see for example Nathan K. Hensley, "Mister Trollope, Lady Credit and *The Way We Live Now*," in *The Politics of Gender in Anthony Trollope's Novels: New Readings for the Twenty-First Century*, eds. Margaret Markwick et al. (Farnham, England: Ashgate, 2009), 147–60.

41 Poovey, *Genres of the Credit Economy*, 400–4. From this perspective, Trollope sided with views developed in economics more than Poovey acknowledges.

42 Brantlinger, *Culture and Credit in Britain*, 171; Vernon, *Money and Fiction*, 43–5; Nicola Lacey, "Gamblers and Gentlefolks: Money, Law and Status in Trollope's England," accessed February, 2016, doi:10.2139/ssrn.2745378.

43 Pierre Bourdieu, *Distinction: A Social Critique of the Judgement of Taste*, trans. Richard Nice (London: Routledge & Kegan Paul, 1984), 251.

and worried about its unsoundness, a concern framed in epistemological terms. The following discussion examines these alternatives. At first blush they might appear like mirror images, reflecting the respective parts of the home/market dichotomy. However, they were incompatible: the moral thrust of *Vanity Fair* modeled the social world on a sentimental relational ideal which appears naïve and ideologically obsolete when compared with the epistemological basis *The Way We Live Now. The Way We Live Now* invoked a separate-spheres outlook in which intersubjective relationality is relegated to the private home, while the ideal market proceeds on economic rationality as a matter of neutralized knowledge.

Vanity Fair represents the credit contract's sociological role as a force sustaining status norms – and operating in opposition to colorless money, but it cannot justify Becky's fall in terms of these norms. After all, the novel's energy is spent showing that at the highest social statuses "too was Vanity" (495); if the overwhelming effort is to expose an all-around moral vacuity, Becky might fall, but the sense that she also *deserves* to fall lies elsewhere. The failures that justify the fall are relational, rather than status ones. Relationality in *Vanity Fair* represents an alternative ideal for contract as much as outside it. Becky's fall occurs at the point where relational violations reach an extreme; violations trigger a change in the narrative disposition toward Becky, to support a sense of moral appropriateness where before all was equally vain.

Becky betrays everyone, but her greatest failures are at the heart of the hearth: as mother and wife. She is emotionally alienated from her son, who is set in the text against her intensifying attachment to Steyne: "'Don't agitate your feelings by going to look for him,' said Lord Steyne sardonically. 'Bah!' replied the other [Becky] … 'he'll cry himself to sleep'; and they fell to talking about the opera" (370). As Becky rejects her son for Steyne, her fall materializes: "The cook looked at the housemaid, the housemaid looked knowingly at the footman – the awful kitchen inquisition which sits in judgement in every house and knows everything – sat on Rebecca at that moment" (436). Narratively, the boy's presence as a psychologically significant character removes the humor and brilliance of Becky's maneuvers, and leaves only banal desperation, "sneering, with green scornful eyes" (446).

Becky's other failure is toward Rawdon, who "[i]n the midst of these intrigues and fine parties and wise and brilliant personages … felt himself more and more isolated every day" (624), and for whom her "contempt … grew greater every day" (514). While climbing up Becky makes "a purse for herself" (516) without telling Rawdon. As Steyne's demands become more exclusive, Becky's son and her companion are thrown out of the house, but Rawdon proves more difficult. By this point Rawdon too is but an obstacle to Becky's plans, and once again the narrative voice loses its layers of complexity in favor of banal moral panic: "[Rawdon] did not see the face opposite to him, haggard, weary, and terrible" (518). To relational failures the narrator is unforgiving, all humor and double meaning gone. Charlotte Brontë described the impulse as "sentiment jealously hidden, but genuine, which extracts the venom from that formidable Thackeray."[44] Narrative changes reveal the sentiment.

Becky's relational failures as mother and wife are the formal flipside of the prostitution that drives her stream of credit. Although the sexual details of the Steyne affair remain playfully doubted throughout ("What had happened? Was she guilty or not?" (526)), Becky's failures as wife and mother confirm their meaning nonetheless. These failures are among the very few certainties in the novel. *Vanity Fair*'s account of the society of vanity relies on the playfulness of masks, that is, on the space of interpretation and uncertainty of social appearances, but Becky's maternal and wifely roles are outside that space. It is Lady Jane, suddenly revealed as an independent character in saving Rawdon, who insists that no innocence can be assumed in a woman who "never loved her dear little boy" (540).

Thackeray's removal of Becky's relationships with her son and husband from the space of social interpretation explains why Becky's link to prostitution does not seem to complicate her guilt. *A priori*, it could: failures of emotional attachment paradoxically make Becky an icon of psychological victimhood; from this perspective her self-representation in overly sentimental terms like "poor orphan" are layered, not merely cynical. In the next chapter I examine Gaskell's efforts to resurrect a poor orphan from the guilt of female fallenness. And yet, by denying layered meaning from Becky's maternal and marital relations, the novel opts for moral corruption and rejects a more complex reading of her guilt. Tropes of maternity and domesticity would later become the flag of feminist attacks on the social treatment of even acknowledged prostitutes. Such positions allowed for a transition of fallen women back into normativity, contra more familiar mythologies of an inevitable downward trajectory.[45] Becky's failures undermine the potential of reform and of moral defense even among less censorious circles.

Resistance to reading Becky as victim also lies in the comedic twist whereby Steyne assumes throughout that Rawdon is his contracting party, implicitly willing to prostitute his wife for a stream of credit, when in fact Becky is self-prostituting and managing this elemental contract too by herself, outwitting men even here.

44 Brontë is quoted in A.E. Dyson, "*Vanity Fair*: An Irony Against Heroes," in *Twentieth Century Interpretations of* Vanity Fair*: A Collection of Critical Essays*, ed. Michael G. Sundell (Englewood Cliffs, NJ: Prentice-Hall, 1969).

45 Nina Attwood, *The Prostitute's Body: Rewriting Prostitution in Victorian Britain* (Toronto: Toronto University Press, 2011), Introduction and Chapter 3; see also Nead, *Myths of Sexuality*, Chapter 5.

The same failures that typify Becky's familial relations extend to her contracts, all of which suffer from a basic lack of empathy; the closer a person and the more elaborate and intimate the relationship, the more Becky sees her as mere pecuniary source.

The height of Becky's moral corruption and the moment of inevitable fall returns to the formalities of credit. Steyne and Becky cooperate in Rawdon's imprisonment for debt to keep him away. Rawdon, recall, is the formal debtor of all of Becky's credit, and is therefore in constant risk of legal enforcement. This move exceeds the familiar Victorian male complaint that wives got their husbands in trouble by extravagant spending; imprisonment for Becky becomes the planned benefit, rather than unavoidable downside of credit. When Rawdon returns to find Becky with Steyne and to discover her hidden treasures he says: "You might have spared me a hundred pounds, Becky, out of all this – I have always shared with you." (526). As Tillotson argued, Rawdon points to the real problem.[46] It lies away from the question of sexual promiscuity on the one hand, and from the extremity of Becky's action – which exceeds realism – on the other; Thackeray locates the problem in the delicate relationship of two people, consisting of finely-tuned small gestures. The framing, suddenly invoking everyday sharing which has hardly been the focus of narrative and lies outside the dramatic effect of the discovery scene of blazing lights, diamonds, fight and blood, has the effect of highlighting an individualized relationship of trust as an alternative context to the many breaches of status and adventurous satire in Becky's transactions. As Andrew Miller observes, "the category of the ideal, though evacuated of specific content by [Thackeray's] satire, nonetheless maintains power over him."[47]

If the home as a sentimental relational alternative to status is *Vanity Fair*'s ideological choice – gestured but never materialized in any of its subplots, with *The Way We Live Now* intimate intersubjectivity is not a model beyond the family, while the market as a locus of economic rationality is the never-materialized hope. The main site of investigation is the railway plot. To see how the hope of a rational market emerges requires an examination of the failures of investors. The railway plot is often understood, following Trollope himself, as a critique of the age's "commercial profligacy,"[48] yet

46 Kathleen Tillotson, "*Vanity Fair*," in Sundell, *Twentieth Century Interpretations of* Vanity Fair, 40–54.

47 Andrew Miller, *Novels Behind Glass: Commodity Culture and Victorian Narrative* (Cambridge: Cambridge University Press, 1995), 37.

48 Anthony Trollope, *An Autobiography* (New York: Dodd, Mead & Company, 1905) (1883), Chapter 20; see discussion in Deborah Denenholz Morse, "The Way He Thought Then: Modernity and the Retreat of the Public Liberal in Anthony Trollope's *The Way We Live Now*, 1873," in *BRANCH: Britain, Representation and Nineteenth-Century History*, ed. Dino Franco Felluga (Extension of Romanticism and Victorianism on the Net) (2014).

profligacy turns out to be a specific social problem: the qualities of the English as irrational economic players.

The plot begins with American rational economic plans: Fisker expects that American/English competition would heighten share value. At the outset, the railway too is examined in economic terms. The reader learns that there is no paid-up capital, that the railway is unnecessary, and that it may never be built. These are easily comprehensible points which carry an air of verifiability. After the clear introduction, as the company's English presence becomes important – both in the plot and as a structural principle of financial expansion pulling together separate plot strands – the textual treatment becomes obscure. Melmotte grows secretive about the railway. The problematic, first elaborated openly, is made more and more opaque, the railway progress and the share allocations in the public company less and less clear. The motion culminates in the *Evening Pulpit* article which is "in nothing more remarkable than in this – that it left on the mind of its reader no impression of any decided opinion about the railway" (229). Like the unknown sexual details in *Vanity Fair*, a motion toward unknowing is central to the plot. As Tara McGann argues, the reader is placed, like the fictional investing public, in an unsure position.[49] With no decided opinion about the railway, why and how is the public investing?

An elaborate answer is found not in the railway story, but instead in the market for tickets for Melmotte's dinner party. The logic of the railway share trade, having been obscured, is dislocatingly elaborated in the ticket-trade subplot which functions as a mock market trading in social desires. Trollope obscured the nature of credit in railway shares, but he is concrete and detailed in Georgiana Longestaffe's adventure with tickets. Outcast Georgiana buys her way back into a desired milieu by trading tickets for the party with her friend Julia. This little story links a market-like world of exchange with the social aspirations at its heart, and closely tracks the rise and fall of exchange value. Julia first promises to entertain Georgiana – specifically, to chaperon Georgiana at Melmotte's party, to take her as a visitor for three days, and to have one party at her house during this time (observe the contract-like specification of undertakings) – in return for dinner tickets because "so greatly had the Melmottes risen in general appreciation" (344); she then agrees to raise the price and entertain Georgiana's Jewish fiancé as well, because the ticket value continues to rise with Melmotte's popularity; finally Julia finds that she had given her pricey promises for nothing, because the fall in ticket value – following the fall in social faith in Melmotte – made her tickets worthless, a worthlessness concretized in the novel through Julia's failure to meet the royal dinner guests.

49 Tara McGann, "Literary Realism in the Wake of Business Cycle Theory: *The Way We Live Now* (1875)," in *Victorian Literature and Finance*, ed. Francis O'Gorman (Oxford: Oxford University Press, 2007), 133–56.

The formal dislocation of railway shares to dinner tickets explains trade in terms of a particular social logic. Investors extending credit to Melmotte's are, like Julia, interested in a quintessentially English social capital. The dinner event concretizes that capital: mixing with social superiors, meeting symbols of English culture, royalty foremost, and appropriating English inherited land. The dislocation of trade clarifies the continual reinstatement of national boundaries in what is supposedly a tale of capitalist globalization.[50] The movement is herd-like and explicitly uninterested in Melmotte's financials, the underlying suggestion being that Melmotte's financial rise has nothing to do with economic solidity. The ironic rendering of the Melmottian project insists on the fact/social-process opposition: "Mr. Melmotte was indeed so great a reality, such a *fact* in the commercial world of London, that it was no longer possible for such a one as Montague to refuse to *believe* in the scheme" (74; my emphases). With facts present, belief is mandated in line with the basic epistemological formula, but, an ironic narrator implies, Melmotte rises on the non-factual. Investments are driven by processes of social interaction in contrast to verifiable knowledge.

The ideological turn of the novel lies in two elements: first, in drawing a contrast between socially constructed value and real value anchored in economic facts. Insisting on the contrast between facts and social process, the novel strives to untie what Mary Poovey identifies as a tension inscribed in the modern fact, between that which is isolated from context and immune to assumptions, theory and interest, and that which cannot be isolated.[51] English "profligacy" lies in failing to untie the two. Perhaps the clearest symbolic moment occurs when Melmotte reaches the height of his career, in his first (and last) appearance in parliament, where he wants to speak:

> Melmotte listened … in the course of the debate … a question arose about the value of money, of exchange, and of the conversion of shillings into francs and dollars. About this Melmotte really did *know* something … It seemed to him that a gentleman whom he knew very well in the City – and who had maliciously stayed away from his dinner – one Mr Brown … understood nothing at all of what he was saying … [A] statement had been made … containing, as Melmotte thought, a fundamental error in finance; and he longed to set the matter right. At any rate, he desired to show the House that Mr Brown did not know what he was talking about – because Mr Brown had not come to his dinner.
>
> (529–30, my emphasis)

50 Hence Goodlad's claim about breached borders goes too far. Lauren M.E. Goodlad, "*The Eustace Diamonds* and 'The Great Parliamentary Bore,'" in *The Politics of Gender in Anthony Trollope's Novels*, eds. Margaret Markwick et al. (Farnham: Ashgate, 2009), 101–2.

51 Mary Poovey, *A History of the Modern Fact: Problems of Knowledge in the Sciences of Wealth and Society* (Chicago, IL: University of Chicago Press, 1998).

The attempt ends catastrophically. Melmotte's courage slips away under the intimidating presence of statesmen and House members; when corrected on formal forms of address he loses the gist of his argument. Melmotte is subjected here to norms of English upper-class masculinity. Ben Griffin describes the efforts that politicians made to appear gentlemanly in the House of Commons; in legitimizing the governing classes, the House actively disciplined members – as is done to Melmotte in this scene – to classed masculine standards which included not just conduct, but also dress, deportment and demeanor.[52] Observe the logic of the episode: a question of finance is at stake, described as a matter of knowledge, and so of error. The question, however, is transformed in the social space of parliament and becomes something worth talking about because – and only because – it relates to social injuries, hierarchies, and rules of conduct. The question of knowledge disappears completely – hence Melmotte is unable to pronounce it – and is displaced by social-status norms. The scene performs in small scale the move of the novel as a whole: constructing the distinction between the economic and the social.

Trollope's project of separating economic factuality from social processes was complicated by a contradiction haunting the question of representations of value in general, and his work specifically. Observing Trollope's obsession with the distinction between facts and social processes – or empirical vs. communal fact making – Ayelet Ben-Yishai suggests that Trollope spoke foremost to the inextricability of these modes, importantly because facts in Trollope's novels are only known because the *social* convention is that "facts supplied by the novel are always true."[53] Facts in the novel, in other words, depend on a strictly social process. In *The Way We Live Now*, moreover, the facts about the railway are gestured but never fully divulged, making the social process of gauging them all the clearer, and exerting an apparent pressure on the facts/social-process contrast. *Apparent*, because this pressure actually serves the contrast: it speaks to a historically-successful process of generic differentiation. Trollope's gesture at facts was articulated within a realist novel, a genre that elevated itself as art by relying on a vision different from the "rock of facts," as Trollope insisted.[54] In my Introduction I noted the novel's reliance on the place of fiction as a distinct mode, existing between facts and deception. The increasing distancing of fiction from fact is closely examined in Poovey's *Genres of the*

52 Ben Griffin, *The Politics of Gender in Victorian Britain: Masculinity, Political Culture and the Struggle for Women's Rights* (Cambridge: Cambridge University Press, 2012), Chapter 6. Langford argues that English parliamentary debates were known for their conversational, informal nature. Against this account, the social quality of this scene becomes more pronounced. Paul Langford, *Englishness Identified* (Oxford: Oxford University Press, 2000), 206–7.

53 Ben-Yishai, "Trollope and the Law," 126.

54 Trollope, *An Autobiography*, 117–18.

Credit Economy. Poovey traces the generic division of labor in which literature became a way to talk about the economy distinct from economics; she describes a historical process in which literature's value was found in the connotative capacity of language, rather than its ability to denote or refer, and discussing literature became a problem of interpretation, in contrast to economics' privileging of information and reference. Readers experienced the novel as "realistic" through a highly articulated mode of literary formalism. At first blush, the result appears to have been, as Poovey claims, that novels, and Trollope specifically, reminded readers of the social component of mutual belief inherent in all forms of credit, while economics denied it.[55] However, there was more than competing outlooks on the economy at stake. The division of labor between genres was an obsessive concern with the fact/social-process problematic. That obsession created the very distinction and gave it life, precisely the thing required for the view of the economy as a distinct domain to emerge.

The second ideological element in *The Way We Live Now* lies in representing the specific dynamics of social investment in the novel as problematic. Readers know that they are, first because the initial facts about the railway's disutility are neither verified nor repudiated, so as to underline not knowing. Within the railway board, the failure to know is an explicit point of critique:

> At the regular meeting of the board, which never sat for above half an hour, two or three papers were read by Miles Grendall. Melmotte himself would speak a few slow words, intended to be cheery, and always indicative of triumph, and then everybody would agree to everything, somebody would sign something, and the "board" for that day would be over.
>
> (171)

Each director understands his nomination outside the question of the railway, as opportunity for Melmotte's personal and social favors, hence the inverted commas: "board." The ironic rendering of board scenes turns comical as directors' silence becomes a new form of discourse: "Lord Alfred bowed down to the table and muttered something which was intended to convey most absolute confidence. 'Hear, hear,' said Mr Cohenlupe" (284). The single rebellion in the board, of Paul, is for other directors but a sign of incompetence, for he fails to appreciate the social dynamics at hand. The representation insists on the social process which fails to know what is talked about – just the problem that haunts public investment.

55 Poovey, *Genres of the Credit Economy*, 400–1.

Crucial to the critique of investment is its feminization. The ticket mock market is not just a detailed mini-example, but one run by women. Set against Trollope's complex treatment of gender, feminization always demands attention. It is particularly telling when used through a mock market because, as Nancy Henry notes, while Victorian women could do little else under formal law, they could be and were investors in financial markets, an activity that attracted mixed views.[56] Trollope could represent women in the stock exchange, but opted for a stereotyped scene in which women are irrational social players, reliant on his tendency to naturalize gendered divisions.[57] Trollope's incoherent insistence on the irrationality of women was most clearly evident in *An Autobiography*. His mother, Frances Trollope, was a model of literary industriousness and economic success which Trollope followed, and he often spoke of her in admiration, yet he also insisted that she was "neither clear-sighted nor accurate; and in her attempts to describe morals, manners, and *even facts*, was unable to avoid the pitfalls of exaggeration." Or again: "Whatever she saw she judged, *as most women do*, from her own standing-point."[58] In this line of thought women simply cannot avoid drawing on the wrong resources to make decisions. Frances Trollope may have succeeded inexplicably on her son's account, but Trollope quickly reduced Georgiana and Julia to ridicule. While Julia's mistakes are concretized in the worthlessness of the dinner, Georgiana herself loses value in the marriage market until her elopement out of the novel. The one formally rational female figure at the close of the railway plot is Marie Melmotte. Melmotte trafficked his daughter throughout the plot; Marie gradually reacts to the pressures of commodification, paradoxically by becoming more rational and disenchanted than the men trading in her. At that point she is clearly unsuitable for England, and so Trollope sent her across the Atlantic with Fisker. The women who model economic transactions in England are notable for their social logic.

Audrey Jaffe argues that Victorian novels distinguished the figure of the illegitimate speculator from the legitimate investor not through types of actions, but through a structure of feelings and attitudes toward money, a point confirmed by the sense of emotional control or its lack in *The Way We Live Now's* representations, as when Marie is marked by not over-

56 Nancy Henry, "'Ladies Do It?': Victorian Women Investors in Fact and Fiction," in *Victorian Literature and Finance*, ed. Francis O'Gorman (Oxford: Oxford University Press, 2007), 111–32.

57 Poovey, *Genres of the Credit Economy*, 401.

58 Trollope, *Autobiography*, 28, 21 (my emphases). For further discussion see Anat Rosenberg, "Power in Numbers: Commodity Fetishes and Facts Between Trollope and Law," in *The Edinburgh Companion to Anthony Trollope*, eds. Frederik Van Dam et al. (forthcoming).

feeling. The implication, argues Jaffe, was to make the rise of the stock market a safe one for virtually everyone except the over-feeling few. That, as I have argued, Trollope devoted impossible efforts to tell apart economic facts and social processes, and to condemn economic decisions premised on the latter, shared the same ideological implication of carving ways to invest safely. However, the epistemological appeal, which Jaffe observes but does not centralize, was fundamental. After all, appealing strictly to a structure of feeling to condemn an excess of feeling would be to undermine the very project.[59] Jaffe's work aligns with Anna Kornbluh's work in *Realizing Capital*, which traces the displacement of concerns with the fictitiousness of economic value onto a psychic economy, where subjectivity grounds capital. Kornbluh argues that Victorians learned to live with the fact of no facts, that is, with knowing that capital values were imaginary, and solved the problem by turning inwards as a substitute ground.[60] However, as I argue below, Trollope spoke to the difficulty of this turn, seeking solid epistemological assurance with all his might.[61]

Not knowing is shown to undermine value in *The Way We Live Now*, a point represented strikingly in not knowing Melmotte himself. Readers are made to experience their own unknowing through a perceptible change in narrative treatment that Kornbluh describes as a shift from satire to a more conventional realism.[62] The crucial moment is the dinner party: The defection of guests, signified as tickets (then shares) losing value, cracks Melmotte's confidence and the narrator uses the crack to change perspective, from here on with increasing intensity. Accounts of Melmotte's sunk heart, anxiety, confusion, loneliness, his assessment of his own conduct and that of others, his wavering resolution to "fight like a man," his past crimes, past life, hopes, ambitions, all begin to be divulged with omniscience. Melmotte is seen alone behind doors, which had been closed to readers until then. The loss of value turns out to be based in Melmotte himself. If Becky's closer narrative treatment in *Vanity Fair* is negative, Melmotte's is sympathetic, intended to unsettle his inhumanness, but formally achieves the same result: with Becky, censure emphasized her unappreciated failures; with Melmotte, empathy works to reveal the public's – and readers' – failure, their not knowing. For, as I discuss in more detail in Chapter 4, one *fact* about the novel as social artifact, is a complex ("realist") rendering of individual psychology, on which

59 Audrey Jaffe, "Trollope in the Stock Market: Irrational Exuberance and *The Prime Minister*," *Victorian Studies* 45, no. 1 (2002): 43–64.

60 Anna Kornbluh, *Realizing Capital: Financial and Psychic Economies in Victorian Form* (New York: Fordham University Press, 2014).

61 Kornbluh suggests as much in observing Trollope's ironic conclusion. Ibid., Chapter 15.

62 Ibid.

readers' sense of security in understanding – and hence evaluating – plot turns, depended.[63]

* * *

As a matter of sociological perception in both *Vanity Fair* and *The Way We Live Now*, credit was fully entangled in status so as to check the rise of a rational market economy and undo its effects. These novels challenge the historical association of contract with that economy. In one sense, their positions are not unfamiliar. Craig Muldrew's work on early modern credit vividly reveals that the sociality of credit was long taken for granted; until the eighteenth century, when this system began to give way, there was no separating between financial transactions and social relations – all exchange was social exchange. However, the other side of the coin is the too-familiar description of late modernity as bureaucratic, abstract, calculable and utilitarian.[64] Here lies the ideal of the market which Victorian liberalism in contract supposedly fostered. Only it often did not. Social history has been arguing for a while now that Victorian credit too was socially constituted, and has complicated the story of a demarcated economic sphere. Margot Finn's work, discussed in Chapter 1, frames the insight as a matter of a coexistence of competing views of individuals: as autonomous and as social persons. James Carrier's work explains the implications of debt circulation, that "living on nothing" which troubled *Vanity Fair* and *The Way We Live Now*, as a mark of the specifically social character of the credit relation.[65] *Vanity Fair* and *The Way We Live Now* offered sophisticated conceptual views of credit, rooted in its dependence on contract as a form of social knowledge-formation. They revealed how the logic of credit, understood in contrast to the classical view of money, repeatedly undermined the obliteration of history which the rationality of the market signaled for its supporters and opponents alike.

As a matter of ideological aspiration, both novels sought alternatives to crude status sociality. Thackeray's "sentiment" as Brontë described it, was a wish for a world modeled on an idealized home: an all-around relational web of sentiment. Unlike other explorations of relationality in contracts that I discuss in the next chapters, relationality in *Vanity Fair* was less a factual condition of existence to be negotiated, than a moral route-not-taken by the society of vanity. Vanity was the distance between self and

63 As Kornbluh says, Trollope sought here psychological grounds for the economy, ibid., Chapter 15. However, the success of his move depended on subjectivity being the hard coin – if we are to use economic language – of the novel. As I argue below, subjectivity could not be generalized outside the sphere of intimacy for Trollope.

64 Craig Muldrew, *The Economy of Obligation: The Culture of Credit and Social Relations in Early Modern England* (Basingstoke: Palgrave Macmillan, 1998), 7.

65 James G. Carrier, *Gifts and Commodities: Exchange and Western Capitalism Since 1700* (New York: Routledge, 1995), 92–3.

others: "This, dear friends and companions, is my amiable object – to walk with you through the Fair, to examine the shops and the shows there; and that we should all come home after the flare, and the noise, and the gaiety, and be perfectly miserable in private" (182). As Nicholas Dames argues, Thackeray explored the mixed condition of modern solitude, an aloneness in the midst of a multitude.[66] The alternative to solitude, a condition both morally degrading and emotionally painful, was intersubjectivity, an idealized form of relationality as unmediated openness and trust between selves. *Vanity Fair*'s many oppositions, all equally morally vacuous, "prosperous and famous, or poor and disappointed" (597), "Thriftless" and "Thrifty" (434–5), debtors and creditors, pointed to the persistent absence of intersubjective ties, which would eliminate the distance between the self and the world. Becky was only the best alienated character of many.[67] *Vanity Fair* is truly a novel without a hero as its subtitle claimed; its sentimentality was the direct consequence of the absence of heroism, which spoke to an absent ideal: To be heroic, the self requires relations of empathetic holism with others.[68]

Almost thirty years later, Trollope painted a satire evocative of *Vanity Fair*'s world in many ways; the parallels are striking. However, the question of intersubjectivity was relegated to families and marriage rather than made an ideological model for all social interaction. The novel invested in marriages which resolved memorable love triangles – Roger-Hetta-Paul, Hurtle-Paul-Hetta, Crumb-Ruby-Felix – in a manner iterating the Englishness of the novel's *Now.*[69] The losers in triangles had a joint problem: they did not live up to the distinctly nineteenth-century union of English love realized in the plot.[70] Meanwhile, the market's unrealized ideal

66 Nicholas Dames, Introduction to, *Vanity Fair: A Novel Without a Hero,* by William Makepeace Thackeray, xiii, xvi. New York: Barnes & Noble Classics, 2003.

67 Readerly indetermination between problematic options presented throughout the novel operates as part of the novel's critique of social value systems by turning the reader into an active participant searching for moral alternatives. Juliet McMaster, *Thackeray: The Major Novels* (Toronto: University of Toronto Press, 1971), 38 ("[Thackeray's novels are] also *about,* and in no superficial way, our response to these characters ...."); see also Wolfgang Iser, *The Implied Reader: Patterns of Communication in Prose Fiction from Bunyan to Beckett* (Baltimore, MD: Johns Hopkins University Press, 1974), Chapter 5 (arguing that *Vanity Fair* marks the transition to readerly participation in the realist novel).

68 I use "empathy" advisedly, to mark a distinction from the more formal notion of sympathy. Sympathy is more closely related to the relationality I explore in the next two chapters, which is also aligned with realist literary form. For the distinction see Rae Greiner, "Thinking of Me Thinking of You: Sympathy Versus Empathy in the Realist Novel," *Victorian Studies* 53, no. 3 (2011): 417–26.

69 There are additional triangles in *The Way We Live Now,* for example, Felix-Marie-Nidderdale, Brehgert-Georgiana-Betherbolt. They do not share the same plot structure in which one person loves another who loves a third, but do share other elements, particularly exclusions from Englishness.

70 Which was also class-compatible, more on which in Chapter 5.

was a realm characterized by economic rationality. *The Way We Live Now* called for something it could not realize narratively – could not imagine concretely, and surely not with contracts. The "psychic economy" as Kornbluh calls it, that resolved love problems in the novel,[71] did not provide an answer to market problems where something more solid was sought. The basis of the market had to be an account of knowing rather than a moral choice, an outlook that denied its own ideological turn.

The ideals of family and market in *The Way We Live Now* were nationalist in a sense missing from *Vanity Fair. Vanity Fair* aspired an ideal intersubjectivity which, because unrealized, could seem radically universal. *The Way We Live Now*'s realization of romantic unions exposed its nationalist limits as foreigners were rejected. The unions reflected the English-bred sensibility that characters like Melmotte lacked. Rational economic transactions, meanwhile, were unrealized for the English, but actively denied for the Americans in the last moment: All American characters slip to criminally. That a nationalist sentiment remained so dominant even in moments of strict idealism suggests that not all statuses posed the same problem: class was the most troubling category and target of satire, nationalism hardly, with gender somewhere in between, understood as a category requiring attention, but, at least with Trollope, without certainty that it was a contingent and unwarranted social construct.

The shift from *Vanity Fair to The Way We Live Now* is one that we might read directly through developments in economic thought. Gordon Bigelow traces the rise of neoclassical economics through a crisis set between the 1850s and the 1870s, the period lying between these two novels. It was only at the close of this period that Stanley Jevons proposed to change the title "political economy" to "economics." The turn was positivistic and empirically oriented, rather than politically and ethically inflected. Far from imperialistic, claims Bigelow, economic theorists actually conceded to the romantic critique of their field. They receded to describing market behavior alone, and claimed to withdraw from politics and more broadly from "culture," in a move that ultimately was triumphant in forming the economy as a distinct field, while centralizing the figure of the individual as an autonomous locus of desire.[72] Trollope's efforts to differentiate sources of desire (were investors driven by social processes of popularity, or by rational assessments of economic facts?) appear at first blush to be at odds with this picture and aligned more easily with classical economics' notion of real value, yet his move can be read as a cruder version of the effort to demarcate the market and exclude social relations from it. Bigelow's

71 Kornbluh, *Realizing Capital*, 112.

72 Gordon Bigelow, *Fiction, Famine and the Rise of Economics in Victorian Britain and Ireland* (Cambridge: Cambridge University Press, 2003).

argument complicates claims of a generic opposition by arguing that the change in economics actually conceded much to literature, and sheds light on *The Way We Live Now's* efforts, where a compromise and cooperation between these genres seems to be confirmed. The question is, how typical was this apparent agreement on the idea of the rational market, and how romantic was the critique of market imperialism, when read from the perspective of contract and promise in realist literature? As the next chapters show, the solution of liberally-oriented novels to pressures to imagine a contractual society often lay somewhere between *Vanity Fair* and *The Way We Live Now*. Relationality became a favored focus of promissory representations in the effort to shake statuses off. It was far from a sentimental morality as in *Vanity Fair*, and was often treated as a matter of fact – just like economic facts in *The Way We Live Now*. But it was also far from a rational economic pursuit in a demarcated market that *The Way We Live Now* aspired. Neither rational nor demarcated, relationality was a figure for the social at large. Novels' figure of the individual was insistently relational and dependent. It challenged ideas of market rationality, and no less those of the expressive autonomy of individuals, in contracts. If realism finally lent support to these figures, the effect had less to do with articulating such assumptions about individuality or the market, and more to do with inspiring and backing all kinds of liberal renegotiations of status hierarchies.

Chapter 3

Contract and Abstraction(?)

Agency in *Ruth* and *Bleak House*

The previous chapter ended with two idealized visions of the market. To begin exploring liberal visions which lay between the poles they represented, this chapter engages with the question of abstraction, a major theme in histories of liberalism in contracts, as Chapter 1 recounted.

To get away from status, the option of abstracting persons from social contexts was conceptually attractive; indeed it often appears as the logical implication of the social/individual opposition in liberal thinking. Historians have found that abstraction captured the core of atomistic individualism in contracts. As seen in Chapter 1, this view transpired in reification of the contractual relation as a bounded-off zone of rights and duties, in tendencies to exclude motivation, context, and pre- and post-execution circumstances from the analysis of contractual rights and duties, and in various other iterations of isolated agency, supporting a view of a rational market.

Abstraction was part of a more engrossing topos of modern practices of detachment, that is, of attempting to transcend partiality, interests and context, which preoccupied Victorians. As Amanda Anderson explains, detachment involved philosophical questions about whether procedures of analytic distance produced reliable forms of knowledge or valuable forms of art; psychological and cultural questions about whether individuals are capable of transcending their interests, pasts and racial heritage; and moral and political questions about whether forms of cultivated detachment promise the wellbeing or overall progress of individuals, communities, or nations.[1] The various historical analyses of liberalism in contracts suggest to us that concerns with abstraction involved all three kinds of questions. Abstraction in contracts was foremost a political project. It promoted a market-based order, but would not have gained the traction it did as a distributive scheme had it not tapped hopes of promoting progress by getting away from status. The political project of abstraction in contracts

1 Amanda Anderson, *The Powers of Distance* (Princeton, NJ: Princeton University Press, 2001), 4–5.

could only work if you assumed that transcendence of interests and more broadly of social context was both possible – at least as a regulative ideal, and meaningful, and if you were willing to treat the analysis as tending to produce knowledge about what contracting persons wanted, chose, and did. Epistemological aspirations were needed if the normative implications were to resonate in an age of empiricism.

The project of abstraction was ridden with tensions and insecurities that Victorian literary realism was positioned to explore. A genre premised on concretization, while often aspiring to totalizing accounts of the social world through omniscient narration, to universal moral recommendation, and to objective intellectual insight, realist novels depended on abstraction and its negation at once. Narrowing the focus to contracts, and particularly to the problem of promissory agency, I engage the question of abstraction in two mid-century novels, Elizabeth Gaskell's *Ruth* and Charles Dickens' *Bleak House*, both published in book form in 1853.[2] Both novels represented efforts to imagine what abstraction from social context would mean concretely. As oxymoronic as the idea of concertizing abstraction sounds, this chapter shows that such efforts were often productive.

A number of interrelated claims emerge from my readings. First, I observe a dramatic recoil from abstraction in these novels, a deep discomfort which resonates with histories like Anderson's, but is missing from histories of liberalism in contracts. *Ruth* and *Bleak House* explored the meaning of abstraction in contracts from different perspectives. In *Ruth* abstraction was treated literally, as a possible state of existence – considered dangerous. *Ruth's* exploration was set within a particular concern with female sexuality. In *Bleak House* abstraction was examined as a moral choice rather than factual condition, emerging in an (im)moral economy. The exploration here was more ambitious in scope, aimed at social panorama and targeting a host of social problems. Both novels recoiled from abstraction while having to differentiate their own formal modes from the abstractions they condemned. Such recoils from abstraction can be read as critiques of atomistic individualism; more interestingly however, they build toward an alternative liberal outlook, which leads to the second claim of this chapter.

Recoils from abstraction did not fall back on status-sociality, but instead favored relationality. Relationality was a socialized liberal outlook removed from atomistic individualism as well as from status; both Gaskell and Dickens developed it in efforts to identify and address the social problems their novels explored. The project of relational liberalism was uneasy. With

2 All references are to Elizabeth Gaskell, *Ruth*, ed. Alan Shelton (Oxford: Oxford University Press, 1985); Charles Dickens, *Bleak House*, ed. Nicola Bradbury (New York: Penguin Books, 2003).

Gaskell, a writer whose religiosity inflected her work, we can see clearly how uncertain the liberal imagination was: the historical effort of operationalizing in narratives immanent liberal solutions to problems of social order was in tension with a transcendent morality. Dickens was not plagued by the same uncertainty with immanence when he made relationality a moral and aesthetic principle. And yet, the complexity of his art and the demands it made on readers reveal with equal force that relational liberalism had to be actively constructed, indeed belabored. Such intense historical efforts to create a relational version of liberalism underline both the sense of historical novelty under which authors operated as they sought alternatives to statuses, and the centrality which relationality assumed, a centrality lost on accounts of abstraction in contracts histories.

A final and related claim is that the centrality of relationality in both *Ruth* and *Bleak House* implied a vision of the economy as relationally constituted. Indeed, the capitalist economy was made *attractive* through relationality, a point I explore in detail in *Bleak House.* Implicit support for the market lay in the assumption that it was susceptible, rather than resistant to, sociality. This was a liberalism which gave the market a rich resonance. As I elaborate in Chapter 4, the resonance was not romantic; it was often more concerned with suffocation than self-fulfillment.

Abstraction and Economy in Gaskell's *Ruth*

Ruth was written and received as an effort to arouse sympathy for the so-called fallen woman.[3] The novel's heroine, the orphaned Ruth Hilton, gives birth to an illegitimate child after her wealthy seducer Bellingham deserts her. Left without relatives or work, having been dismissed from her job as a seamstress, she is taken in by the Dissenting minister Benson and his sister. Ruth piously repents her past, and eventually gives her life to nurse Bellingham during a fever epidemic.

Ruth's fall is the consequence of two continuous processes: One is a detachment of economic from relational concerns – a staging of a disembedded economy, which is in direct dialogue with the danger of prostitution, understood as money without love. The second process is Ruth's detachment from social meanings – a staging of the abstract individual, which is a consequence of her symbolic slide to prostitution. Ruth is rehabilitated by being socialized into shared meanings, which teach her not only about female sexual purity, but that materiality without relational meaning is dangerous and must be avoided. This insight was fundamental to the novel's perspective on the economy.

3 Fallen from virtue, through sexual transgression.

The following discussion begins with the problem of the disembedded economy and its relation to prostitution, which, I argue, is the novel's encompassing concern. I then turn to Ruth's seduction to examine closely the novel's critique of abstraction and the way it is implicated with promissory agency. I finally examine how Ruth is rehabilitated as an agent, and how she (and the nation) are saved from prostitution. The overall move upholds the liberal fascination with individual agency, while socializing contracts and the market in relationships.

Disembedded Economy and Prostitution

In Chapter 2 I observed two idealized visions of the economy: *The Way We Live Now* envisioned the economy in terms of separate spheres, where the market is a locus of instrumental, factually-informed rationality, while *Vanity Fair* called for an all-around family-like order. *Ruth* contains explicit resistance to pressures toward a rational economy, which appear to resonate more closely with *Vanity Fair*; indeed *The Pilgrim's Progress*, from which Thackeray took his title, features in *Ruth* as idealized education.[4] However, the novel's resistance is far from an all-encompassing sentimentality matched by a general satire of vanity in the *Vanity Fair* style. When Gaskell narrated scenes in which economic concerns are inseparable from emotive ones and resisted market rationality, she was engaged in a more particular project, that of preventing Ruth's prostitution. While the novel does not construe an ideally familial social order, it insists that stripping economic concerns from emotive relational contexts is a dangerous endeavor.

Understood as a marketization of female sexuality, the risk of prostitution appears in *Ruth* as money without love. The novel narrates its heroine's fall as a process that begins before Ruth even meets Bellingham. The process and its reversal depend on the respective detachment and then reconnection of relational and economic concerns, a motif that runs through the novel.

Ruth's pre-Bellingham fall includes three milestones narrated in quick succession; they speak to a dramatic detachment of the economic from the relational and particularly from the emotive, leading to Ruth's secluded existence outside social meanings, and setting the conditions for Bellingham to come along and seduce her.

The first mark of fall is Ruth's loss of family. She is born to an economically struggling family – a sick mother and failing father: "His crops failed; his horses died; his barn took fire" (36). The implications of economic difficulty, however, are only felt when Ruth's mother dies, for until then her

4 Ruth defends the old servant Thomas by recalling him reading to her Bunyan's work (Chapter 4).

father, secure in his love, is immune: "all worldly misfortunes seemed as nothing to him" (36). And Ruth too is immune, basked in an atmosphere of "peace and encouragement" (36). The mother's death turns economic trouble into catastrophe, which the father cannot handle once deprived of relational support, and he dies soon afterwards. Ruth is left alone, with economic difficulty suddenly assuming independent meaning.

Here enters the second mark of fall, in a scene of debt collection:

> After his death, the creditors were the chief people who appeared to take any interest in the affairs; and it seemed strange to Ruth to see people, whom she scarcely knew, examining and touching all that she had been accustomed to consider as precious and sacred.
>
> (37)

Creditor instrumentalism in this scene robs the materiality around Ruth of meaning. "Strange" is a precise choice of term; phrases of pain or outrage, which one might have expected, would point to a replacement of one meaning by another; "strange" holds meaning at bay, speaking to a sudden senselessness imposed on Ruth.

The third scene in this sequence is Ruth's guardianship, which turns from Ruth's surroundings to Ruth herself, to commodify her and rob her very being of meaning.

Ruth's guardian is the flourishing maltster of Skelton, a man of duty whose moment in the novel is worth quoting at length:

> He was a sensible, hard-headed man of the world; having a very fair proportion of conscience as consciences go; indeed, perhaps more than many people; for he had some ideas of duty extending to the circle beyond his own family; and did not, as some would have done, decline acting altogether, but speedily summoned the creditors, examined into the accounts, sold up the farming-stock, and discharged all the debts; paid about £80 into the Skelton bank for a week, while he inquired for a situation or apprenticeship of some kind for poor heart-broken Ruth; heard of Mrs Mason's; arranged all with her in two short conversations; drove over for Ruth in his gig; waited while she and the old servant packed up her clothes; and grew very impatient while she ran, with her eyes streaming with tears, round the garden, tearing off in a passion of love whole boughs of favourite China and damask roses, late flowering against the casement-window of what had been her mother's room.
>
> (38)

This is how Ruth ends up in the alienating dressmakers' establishment, to which I turn in a moment. Gaskell highlighted the offhanded analogy between Ruth and her father's debts, both handled by the guardian with an efficient and relationally-empty standard. The guardian, never mentioned by name, is a figure of remoteness. His impatience with an aberrant object (incidentally, Ruth) exhibiting emotional responses inconsistent with his idea of the job is almost an overemphasis of the problem. Impatience is then followed by lectures on "economy and self-reliance" (38), from which Ruth is little able to "profit," being grief-stricken.

The guardian's reductionism of Ruth is experienced even before it is understood, through that one long sentence leaving the reader breathless at its end. The sentence replicates the guardian's manner of collapsing together assets, debts, and a young woman, all part of a single to-do list, satisfactorily performed. The part of the list dealing with Ruth begins with one clause between two semicolons: "paid about £80 … while he inquired for a situation … for poor heart-broken Ruth." The clause enacts the same analogy suggested by the whole structure: £80 in the bank are juxtaposed with Ruth. This is the only mention of an amount, explicitly attaching monetary value to Ruth which marks her reduction. Its about-ness ("paid *about* £80") speaks to careless commodification, a social neglect. The guardian episode in its entirety consists of only two paragraphs, the first beginning with the creditors, the second already continuing into the first night at the dressmaker's house. The mismatch between form and content – brief episode, huge crisis – textually performs Ruth's neglect.

These market instrumentalities prostitute Ruth before she knows it. In case readers miss the point, Gaskell let the same logic inflect the dressmaker's place. One important scene is Ruth's deportation to the street on Sundays, which pushes her into Bellingham's arms. Mrs Mason exercises a "pinching economy" (34):

> On Sundays she chose to conclude that all her apprentices had friends … Accordingly, no dinner was cooked … no fires were lighted in any rooms to which they had access. On this morning they breakfasted in Mrs Mason's own parlour, after which the room was closed against them through the day by some understood, though unspoken prohibition.
>
> (34)

As Ruth was positively monetized by her guardian, so she is negatively monetized by an employer who saves money literally on her body. These scenes build toward the danger of prostitution within a setting familiar to middle-class Victorians. Gaskell's implicit link between her heroine and prostitutes relied not only on the abstract claim of commodification, but on a common stereotype: the girl seduced, pregnant and abandoned, ending as prostitute. The expectation is given expression later in the novel as one character speculating on Ruth's fate says "Why, ma'am, what could become of her? Not that I know exactly – only one knows they can but go from bad to worse, poor creatures!" (321) As Judith Walkowitz showed in a classic study of Victorian prostitution, that picture in fact fitted only a small minority of prostitutes.[5] Gaskell relied on a stereotype which could link the fallenness actually narrated in the novel with a broader critique of marketization, through the trope of prostitution.

What kind of problem did marketization represent? One clear concern was feminist. *Ruth* can be read through Carole Pateman's analysis of the sexual contract.[6] Pateman's is a critique which delves deep both historically and philosophically in linking the market with women's domination by men. She begins with social contract theories as the dominant liberal philosophical tradition of the modern state, to resurrect their principle of female subordination, but also shows how they carry over into modern contractual relations – from political fiction to actual exchanges in everyday life. On Pateman's account, civil freedoms in modern political theories of the social contract presuppose men's domination over women, and particularly men's orderly access to women's bodies. The contract between prostitute and client, she claims, upholds men's rights of domination in the public domain; it is, in other words, thoroughly political, symptomatic of the conditions of a social and economic order much broader than that contract's subject matter. Pateman's work illuminates *Ruth's* fear of marketization and its link to Ruth's fall through promissory junctions; as I show in a moment, the novel moves from the risk of prostitution to the damming promises with which Bellingham traps Ruth, in a manner that resonates with Pateman's argument about a slide from the conceptual assumption of sexual subordination to its everyday manifestations in contracts. Late Victorian feminists likewise sounded claims about sexual enslavement by contract, as Susan Kent recounts, invoking the marriage contract and linking it to prostitution. In a reality of material dependence, feminists argued, marriage was legalized prostitution, and like it was a contract carrying every form of corruption denied by idealizations of domesticity and womanhood. Prostitution itself was but a consequence of women's structured subservience.[7]

And yet for Gaskell the problem was remediable, rather than inherent in the social order as feminist arguments often suggested. Pateman insists on a conceptual dependence between contract and women's subordination as

5 Judith R. Walkowitz, *Prostitution and Victorian Society: Women, Class and the State* (Cambridge: Cambridge University Press, 1980), 18.

6 Carole Pateman, *The Sexual Contract* (Stanford, CA: Stanford University Press, 1988).

7 Susan Kingsley Kent, *Sex and Suffrage in Britain 1860–1914* (Princeton, NJ: Princeton University Press, 1987), Chapters 2, 3. See also Walkowitz, *Prostitution and Victorian Society*. (For classical contract theorists marriage was not a contract, a point I address in Chapter 5.)

a political principle, yet Gaskell assumed that an appropriate socialization could reverse the trend; she aligned with a familiar Victorian sentiment which ultimately sought a liberal venue into respectability. To see the limits of Gaskell's position vis-à-vis radical feminist perspectives which succeeded her, Victorian middle-class concerns with prostitution should be recalled.

In Victorian middle-class circles prostitution stood almost inversely to Pateman's suggestion, and hardly resonated with feminist claims that would become prevalent in the late Victorian era. Rather than recognize prostitution as manifesting a principle of social order built literally on the backs of women, many Victorians feared that prostitution undermined order. Prostitution was the ultimate female transgression which gestured at a general problem of national morality. It stood for moral degeneration, threatening to Christianity and bourgeoisie property alike. As Lynda Nead argues, prostitution was regarded as a metasystem which could lead to political and economic crisis, and destroy the nation and empire. One way to negotiate fears, important in *Ruth*, was to frame prostitutes as social victims ("poor creatures") rather than threatening Others, and attempt to accommodate them within normative discourses of femininity and morality. Such responses found particular favor with religious writers, but also resonated with social reformers, journalists, and physicians, among others.[8] The anxiety around prostitution was all the worse since the trajectory of fall, and prostitution's boundaries, were unclear. The question of boundaries generated heated debates which Foucault recognized as part of the Victorian multiplication of discourses on sexuality.[9] When Gaskell resisted the trajectory of fall she could tap into a broad set of concerns, not all of them by any means feminist or even ultimately women-centered. The novel repeatedly implies that economic concerns either have emotive contexts, or are inherently dangerous, but the danger is not just or even centrally to women, but to the health of the nation at large. Gaskell only just managed to save Ruth and reverse the trajectory, by a great effort to which the novel is devoted.

Fall Without Agency

The dramatic turning point in Ruth's life is cast as a moment of formal agency through the use of promises: Bellingham promises love and money, and she accepts his promises – and so "falls." Having invoked the question of agency, Gaskell worked hard to deny that Ruth is an agent in these

8 Lynda Nead, *Myths of Sexuality: Representations of Women in Victorian Britain* (Malden, MA: Basil Blackwell, 1988), Chapters. 3–5.

9 Michel Foucault, *The History of Sexuality: An Introduction (vol. 1)*, trans. Robert Hurley (Harmondsworth: Penguin Books, 1978).

scenes, so as to refute her responsibly for the fall. She then spent equal efforts on articulating the conditions through which Ruth gains agency which allows her, by the end of the novel, to reject another set of promises that Bellingham makes years later, and to end her life martyr-style.

At the heart of the rehabilitating project lay the problem of abstraction. *Ruth* criticized abstraction by treating it not as an analytical position, but literally as a descriptive possibility, a possible way of existence in the world in isolation from human relationships. The novel's fundamental assumption is that relationships ground access to interpretive tools without which choices are meaningless. Choice cannot occur in isolation – as the abstractions of atomistic individualism in contracts, taken literally, would have it. Staking a claim for a relational determinism, Gaskell suggested that if choice is the ground for freedom and responsibility, it can proceed only with recourse to communal interpretive contexts achieved through relationships. With this assumption, *Ruth* proceeds by sketching an abstract heroine, in a state of isolation from social meanings – hence not morally responsible for wrong choices.

To see how Gaskell problematized abstraction, recall that there is a single guiding light throughout *Ruth's* plot, underlining the novel's class and gender subversiveness as well as sexual prudence: Bellingham must be rejected. Ruth's ability to do so, dramatized in promissory junctions in which Bellingham makes offers that she can seemingly accept or reject, is the question thrown open.

Bellingham's promises of love[10] meet a vulnerable Ruth, after the quick slide we have seen into a commodified vacuum of meanings. Ruth is in a state of perfect isolation: no family ties, no friends, no institutional belonging, no acquired knowledge of social rules nor understanding of convention. "How strange it is," wonders Ruth on the verge of her fall, "that I should feel as if this ... walk [with Bellingham] were, somehow, not exactly wrong, but yet as if it were not right. Why can it be?" (41) Virtually no habitus, Ruth is almost the abstract individual personified, able to draw only on internal processes. This position is an inherent weakness when faced with human interaction like promise. She is drawn to Bellingham because her "loving disposition, continually sending forth fibres in search of nutriment, found no other object for regard ... to compensate for the want of natural ties" (39); Anderson argues that Gaskell was positing unthinking sympathy as an ethical ideal which grounds purity, set against rational instrumental calculation.[11] Ruth, however, is not an unthinking

10 Yoko Hatano argues that Bellingham's first promise of love and a home for Ruth is analogous to a promise of marriage. Yoko Hatano, "Evangelicalism in *Ruth*," *Modern Language Review* 95, no. 3 (2000): 637. The last promise, discussed later, is expressly so.

11 Amanda Anderson, *Tainted Souls and Painted Faces: The Rhetoric of Fallenness in Victorian Culture* (Baltimore, MD: Cornell University Press, 1993).

character, but rather a person thinking outside social context. She reads Bellingham out of his social context too, drawing him and their relationship into her internal world, unable to give it conventional meaning: "a thing [their relationship] which was, as far as reason and knowledge (*her* knowledge) went, so innocent ..." (40; Gaskell's emphasis).

To Bellingham's proffered love Gaskell adds money, in keeping with the novel's fear of prostitution. Bellingham orders tea for Ruth who, having been dismissed from the dressmaker's workshop and offered Bellingham's love, had just agreed to go to London with him; having made the order, he leaves her to bring the carriage. At this point Ruth decides to consult Thomas and Mary, the old family servants who mistrust Bellingham. She then perceives the landlord at the door:

> [S]he feared that he would not let her quit the house without paying. She thought that she would leave a note for Mr. Bellingham, saying where she had gone and how she had left the house in debt, for (like a child) all dilemmas appeared of equal magnitude to her; and the difficulty of passing the landlord ... and of giving him an explanation of the circumstances ... appeared insuperable, and as awkward, and fraught with inconvenience, as far more serious situations ... Her energy left her.
>
> (60–1)

Like a child, Ruth lacks social knowledge which would bring proportion to a triviality. She waits for Bellingham in symbolic consideration of his undertaking to pay the tea debt, and he then prevails and takes her to London. The triviality of the debt in both monetary and cultural terms – the most banal of everyday scenes – which leads to social ruin, signals cheapness.

Margot Finn argues that Ruth is led to her ruin by a false understanding of personal and credit relations.[12] While at the level of immediate content Ruth is indeed mistaken, viewed from the perspective of the novel's deep structure Ruth's understanding is not false; it is reflective of her secluded existence. Both reason and knowledge, the text suggests in a moment reminiscent of Charles Taylor's critique of atomism,[13] are not decontextualized capabilities; absent the social networks within which they obtain recognizable form, reason and knowledge do not ground promissory agency. The novel's manifesto on behalf of fallen women relies on this carefully constructed conceptualization of agency.

12 Margot C. Finn, *The Character of Credit: Personal Debt in English Culture, 1740–1914* (Cambridge: Cambridge University Press, 2003), 39–40.

13 See discussion in Chapter 1 under "The Promising Individual in the Market."

To reverse the trend, Gaskell socializes Ruth. Educated into interpersonal and communal meanings, first by trauma and then by embrace, Ruth learns to suspect disembedded materialism and is finally able to reverse her promissory subjection by saying NO.

Rehabilitation and Relational Economy

Ruth's reversal of the fall is narrated as a series of rejections of material benefits unaccompanied by emotive ties. Ruth is explicit about the problematics of detaching economic from emotive concerns as soon as she begins to reverse her fate, rejecting the £50 that Mrs. Bellingham sent her when she took her son away:

> "I have a strong feeling against taking it. While he," said she, deeply blushing, and letting her large white lids drop down and veil her eyes, "loved me, he gave me many things – my watch – oh, many things; and I took them from him gladly and thankfully because he loved me … I thought of them as signs of love. … This money seems – oh, Miss Benson – it seems as if he could comfort me, for being forsaken, by money."
>
> (126–7)

The white dropping eyelids over a blushing face clarify why readers have been impatient with Ruth's representation; Gaskell opted for angelic imagery in looks, in voice, in gestures, in content. The angelic denial of the prostitute came with a rejection of everything sexual, a process extenuated by placing Ruth in a family of asexual characters. (Observe the contrast with Jemima Bradshaw: More human (while less pretty), more sexualized, and standing for an outspoken feminist liberation of women, Jemima nonetheless can do all that because she conforms to norms of sexual purity.) And these representations escalate. Here is Ruth's response to a gift from Bradshaw:

> "What right had he to send it me?" asked Ruth, still in her quiet voice. … "There are people to whom I love to feel that I owe gratitude … but I cannot see why a person whom I do not know should lay me under an obligation."
>
> (156)

Bradshaw's motives are patronizing rather than strictly sexual and seem to apply indifferently to men and women, yet his position in relation to Ruth has everything to do with sexuality: Bradshaw stands for the still unrealized threat of condemning her sexual transgression. Ruth's discomfort, much greater than Benson's, who is also patronized by Bradshaw, speaks to the relation of Bradshaw's material benefits to her symbolic prostitution. While the gift/contract theoretical axis here is interesting in itself, the novel's predominant effort glosses over it as it collapses varied representations under the overarching concern with materialism detached from relationships.

In such episodes Gaskell had Ruth working almost too hard, uttering positions modeled on Christian mythologies to the point of denying material existence (and, again and concurrently, bodily experience). When these positions are read within the problem of prostitution, however, *Ruth's* resistance to both the discourse and occurrence of disembedded material exchanges, and its assertion of the significance of a relational economy, becomes clear. Prostitution's deep connections with a broader order that Pateman describes as patriarchal capitalism, and that middleclass Victorians feared as loss of any order, led to a critique of the possibility of a disembedded market.

The process of reversal comes to the test when Bellingham reappears to again promise love and money. The love is now missing not on Bellingham's part, but on Ruth's: "I do not love you" (302). Ruth's recognition of the absence allows a triumphant reversal of her first promissory choice. If in the first promissory scene she was moved into a humbled "do tell me what I must do!" (58), now she moves to dominance with "Listen to me!" (299). While in the first encounter Ruth remained physically put and Bellingham left, in the second she initiates the departure: "'You have humbled me enough, sir. I shall leave you now'. She turned away resolutely" (301). In the first promise Ruth uttered a low and hesitating "yes," and leaned on Bellingham's arm on the way to her fall. In the second promise she stands "very erect" (303) and acknowledges her substantial agency: "You shall have nothing to do with my boy, by my consent, much less by my agency" (303), on her way to martyrdom. The rejection is structured to contrast the initial acceptance, signaling a move from a diminished to a robust agency.

Power disparities are not the marker of difference; Ruth is still vulnerable in economic, social, even in symbolically physical terms (finally dead). If initially she was secluded from any supportive networks, now she is living humbly under a false identity and in danger of exposure as Bellingham quickly realizes. Ruth's dramatic agency cannot be explained away in terms of her improved place within socioeconomic hierarchies. Critiques of socioeconomic differentials were not foreign to the novel, which stages a gender and class gap between Ruth and Bellingham, but they are secondary. The position that Gaskell developed, in other words, was not a form of welfarist critique of contracts, sensitive to power disparities in promissory contexts; it reached deeper. To overcome weakness is not to secure an empowered social position, as welfarism would urge. Primarily and fundamentally, Ruth developed agency by entering relationships which introduce her into social meanings. Processes of socialization enable revised knowledge and reason, finally revised emotions, which now make the still vulnerable Ruth a person whose decisions are worthy of respect: an agent. Gaskell thus offered a solution to a substantive and formal tension that Catherine Gallagher explores in industrial novels: how do you attribute agency to someone, while also acknowledging the determining force of social conditions?[14] The relational determinism that *Ruth* sketched carved a space between isolated agency on the one hand, and social structure on the other.

Bellingham's last promise is in the closing chapter. Ruth dies saving him, and he now proposes to take responsibility for Leonard's financial needs in a final symbolic reduction of Ruth to money. The price has been raised since the tea debt, but the logic is consistent. Benson rejects: "Every offer of service you have made, I reject in his [Leonard's] name, – and in her presence [the dead Ruth in the bed]" (454). Benson actually and metaphorically slams the door at the offer (454), a gesture contrasted with Ruth's lack of energy in the first instance ("[h]er energy left her").

Relational socialization, which ensures that Ruth finally makes the right choice, was an interim route lying between atomistic individualism with its radical abstractions, on the one hand, and collectivist critiques of social structure, on the other. With its middle grounds for "moral freedom" as Gallagher calls it,[15] social collectivist solutions were not on *Ruth's* agenda. Complaints about Gaskell's failure to tackle gender oppression have therefore been forthcoming. Stacey Gottlieb, for instance, argues that Gaskell insists on the primacy of the individual as the locus of amelioration, as opposed to large-scale adjustments of the social order; Jaffe claims that despite the social root of Ruth's problem Gaskell offers a solution in the form of individual sympathy; and Deirdre d'Albertis observes that the novel's title itself speaks to representing a problem of reform in terms of individual lives and character development.[16] Gaskell's biography, Anderson argues, explains her interest in "resolutely individualistic and improvisatory charity ... in keeping with the tenets of her Unitarian milieu."[17] The novel's liberalism, in other words, is hard to dispute. Yet its terms merit attention for it was an exercise in individualism without individualist abstraction which the public/private tension in itself does not clarify.

14 Catherine Gallagher, *The Industrial Reformation of English Fiction: Social Discourse and Narrative Form 1832–1867* (Chicago, IL: University of Chicago Press, 1985).

15 Ibid., Chapter 3.

16 Stacey Gottlieb, "'And God Will Teach Her': Consciousness and Character in *Ruth* and *Aurora Leigh*," *Victorian Institute Journal* 24 (1996): 57–85; Audrey Jaffe, "Under Cover of Sympathy: Ressentiment in Gaskell's *Ruth*," *Victorian Literature and Culture* 21 (1993): 51–65; Deirdre d'Albertis, *Dissembling Fictions: Elizabeth Gaskell and the Victorian Social Text* (New York: Palgrave Macmillan, 1997), 74.

17 Anderson, *Tainted Souls and Painted Faces*, 108.

Ruth's logic revealed the fear that abstractions *from* the social (Ruth abstracted from social meanings) and *of* the social (Ruth viewed abstractly as a social problem and therefore condemned; Ruth saved through collective social solutions) would end up converging, and undermine agency. Ruth's socialization, in consequence, is a process of accumulating concrete interpersonal relationships. The socialized construction of promissory agency in *Ruth* was not a denial of individualistic ideological commitments; rather, it represented a problematization of atomistic individualism from within liberalism, reliant on relationality as route to social meaning.

A Troubled Liberalism

To reject abstraction and uphold socialization as the basis of agency, when social responses to female sexuality were the obvious source of difficulty, was a questionable route. To pursue it Gaskell had to differentiate *kinds* of socialization, and insist that the public (readers) evaluating fallen women required recourse to sets of meanings to do so, just as Ruth required them to make choices. Gaskell turned from the individual choosing person in the plot to her readers, to offer them alternative social readings of fallenness. The novel stages a battle of moralities, grounding the sense that it was, as Jaffe put it, "a moral tale" at a marked distance from realism.[18] The turn to readers allowed Gaskell to deepen not only her treatment of fallenness, but also at the same time to escape the problem of the novel itself as abstraction, by bringing to the fore its relational characteristics, reliant on its dialogue with readers.

Ruth's characters as well as readers were offered two alterative frameworks. One was Victorian domesticity with its sexual policing of women, which also found resonance in stern Calvinism represented as having lost spiritual authority. This set of attitudes, crystalized as a common morality, is described as worldly. The other framework was Evangelical Dissenting theology, with its own sexual puritanism. Historians often point to the combined religious and secular influences on Victorian middle-class gender ideology.[19] In Gaskell, however, tensions rather than combined power assume center stage as spirituality remains only with her favored theology. Written in the 1850s, when the religious revival of the late eighteenth- and early nineteenth centuries was waning, and, as Leonore Davidoff and Catherine Hall argued, domestic ideology no longer depended on Christian framings,[20] *Ruth* relied on the alternative

18 Audrey Jaffe, "Cranford and Ruth," in *The Cambridge Companion to Elizabeth Gaskell*, ed. Jill L. Matus (Cambridge: Cambridge University Press, 2007), 47.

19 See Chapters 1 and 4.

20 Leonore Davidoff and Catherine Hall, *Family Fortunes: Men and Women of the English Middle Class, 1780–1850* (Chicago, IL: University of Chicago Press, 1987), Chapter 3.

approaches that the worldly and the Dissenting Christian potentially embodied toward fallenness and redemption. For Gaskell, where worldly ideology treated fallen women and their illegitimate children unforgivingly, and turned sexual misconduct into a reality of punishment, Christianity (properly interpreted), which likewise recognized Ruth's sexual conduct as sinful, offered salvation achieved by looking "to God, rather than to man's opinion" (121), and taking a "stand with Christ against the world" (351).

The battle of moralities was turned into an operative plot element through the Bensons' lie about Ruth's past, which set in motion the narrative of secret revelation. The narrative logic that promises that revelation will eventually come, keeps up the question of alternative interpretations of Ruth's life, expected to have consequences in plot resolution. Paradoxically, the alternative worldly and religious moralities that Gaskell offered were epitomized most clearly not in Ruth's life but rather in the different deaths available to her: suicide of an outcast woman – which Benson duly arrives to prevent, or sacrificial death at the end of a (short) life of Christian humility – which is finally her lot.

The battle of moralities in *Ruth* implied to readers that any form of freedom and responsibility, not least the freedom and responsibility to evaluate a woman's conduct, depended on socialization, and should not be naturalized. From this perspective, the novel was more radical than might appear. Critics often point to the novel's conservatism in sacrificing its heroine. Jaffe, for instance, complains that "the force of [...] details [mitigating Ruth's responsibility] is countered by the story's reproduction of the familiar cultural narrative in which sexual transgression results in the woman's punishment."[21] However, the novel positioned readers themselves as choosers of moral frameworks which it denaturalized; readerly response *to* the sacrifice, in other words, was part of the message.[22] Responses were mixed from the start; alongside book burners were also those who with Charlotte Brontë complained to Gaskell, "Why should she die?"[23] To the extent that readers feel frustrated at the need to sacrifice Ruth, the novel's efforts to redeem her might be more successful than many critics concede.

And yet, *Ruth's* effectiveness in redeeming its heroine depended on treating its version of Christianity as one social system of meaning on a battlefield with others. This immanent, essentially sociological understanding of religion clashes with the novel's religiosity. *Ruth* is a religious novel not only in representing religious characters, in narrating religious practice and

21 Jaffe, "*Cranford* and *Ruth*," 54. See also Anderson, *Tainted Souls and Painted Faces*, 131. Jaffe argues that Gaskell finally relies on social harshness as providential tool.

22 Jennifer M. Stolpa, "What's in a Name? Echoes of Biblical Women in Elizabeth Gaskell's *Ruth*," *Gaskell Society Journal* 18 (2004): 50–64.

23 Cited in Ian Ward, *Sex, Crime and Literature in Victorian England* (Oxford: Hart Publishing, 2014), 115.

theological controversies, in relying on Christian imagery of self-sacrifice, in incorporating biblical allusions, and in placing narrative authority behind Christian doctrine – much of which we can find in other novels too, often in secularized ethics building on older Christian theologies – but fundamentally in that God is a literary character driving plot turns, large and small. Ruth, for instance, does not see Bellingham after his desertion because "[i]t was one of those prayers which God is too merciful to grant" (93). Or again, "God works in His own way" (101), the narrator explains another turn. Or indeed, "The low-breathed sentences which she [Ruth] spoke into the ear of the sufferer and the dying carried them upwards to God" (391). This transcendental logic is at odds with the battle between systems of meaning, in which religion battles with other interpretive schemes on the immanent plane of socialization. To borrow Bruno Latour's theoretical terminology, there is a tension in the novel between speaking about religion, and speaking religiously, which remains unresolved and is devastating to one of the two.[24] Criticism like Gallagher's has examined Gaskell's difficulties in reconciling changing Unitarian beliefs between determinism and free will, with other forms of social criticism;[25] in *Ruth*, however, we see also the problem of immanence on which Gaskell's relational solution to questions of agency depended. The novel either failed to redeem its fallen woman, or if it did, by advocating the "correct" form of socialization, the moral authority behind it remained compromised.

And so, *Ruth* emerges as a compromised novel at the core: either its plot cannot uphold its own claims about agency (or its lack) through socialization, or it does not retain its religiosity as a transcendental framework. This problem was fundamental to *Ruth's* wavering popularity; it remains one of Gaskell's least popular works. The incongruity between socialization and transcendence compromised the novel far beyond the back and forth between radicalism and conservatism.

Critical discontent on this front too is revealing. A common line of critique argues that the novel's depiction of unworldly martyrdom by a self-abandoning heroine ultimately left more typical cases of fallen women unredeemed.[26] But precisely this problem registers the unsure experience

24 Bruno Latour, *The Making of Law: An Ethnography of the Conseil d'État*, trans. Marina Brilman and Alain Pottage (Cambridge: Polity Press Cambridge, 2010), viii–ix.

25 Gallagher, *Industrial Reformation of English Fiction.*

26 E.g., Hatano, "Evangelicalism in *Ruth*," 637, argues that Gaskell's categorization of Ruth corresponds to Magdalenalism thus differentiating Ruth from "other" prostitutes; Jaffe, "Under Cover of Sympathy," 61–5, argues that Ruth's claim on readers' sympathy has less to do with the insupportability of the idea of fallenness than with her status as not really fallen; Monica Correa Fryckstedt, *Elizabeth Gaskell's* Mary Barton *and* Ruth*: A Challenge to Christian England* (Uppsala: Uppsala University, 1982), 164–5 argues that Ruth's not entirely convincing characterization was a concession made by Gaskell in order for the novel to be accepted.

of immanent liberal solutions, the unresolved tension in *Ruth* between transcendentalism and socialization as a basis for agency: Gaskell explored an immanent basis of agency in relationships, but at the last moment turned to Christian martyrdom. Boyd Hilton describes the sharp break with Evangelical pessimistic conceptions of experience in terms of temptation, danger, trial and retribution, and their replacement with a progressive optimism and trust in individual citizens around mid-century.[27] Although he actually demonstrates the break in Gaskell's work, *Ruth* shows that there was no clear break. Gaskell was continually playing with, but not sure about society as an immanent supplier of meaning for action.

The remedy of relational socialization, set against abstraction, illuminates a liberally-leaning search for individual agency and for an economic imagination which would align with sentiments of reform. For all its tensions, the novel developed an elaborate position distinct from atomistic individualism, from sentimentalism, and from radicalism at once.

Abstraction and Immorality in *Bleak House*

Bleak House, like *Ruth*, had a problem of fallenness and illegitimacy at its core. Esther Summerson, one of the novel's two narrators, is the illegitimate daughter of Lady Dedlock, a story that unfolds as various characters pursue the mystery through the novel's hundreds of pages. Yet I want to take advantage of *Bleak House's* ambitious scope and examine the question of abstraction and market relations from a different perspective, to get at the breadth and depth of novelistic problematizations of abstraction and their distance from market rationality. (I return to Esther's story in Chapter 5.) I begin with the novel's other major plot strand which, as Kieran Dolin notes, many readers felt was in competition with Esther's mystery of illegitimacy:[28] the famed critique of the court of Chancery in the Jarndyce suit, which just like Esther's mystery proliferates through the novel.

Critics also offer various explanations on the level of Gaskell's aesthetics. For instance, Tatsuhiro Ohno, "The Structure of *Ruth*: Is the Heroine's Martyrdom Inconsistent with the Plot?," *Gaskell Society Journal* 18 (2004): 16–36 is a formal-structural analysis of Ruth which supports the claim that Ruth's martyrdom was necessary in terms of the novel's structure; Susan Morgan, "Gaskell's Heroines and the Power of Time," *Pacific Coast Philology* 18 (1983): 43–51, explains Ruth's death outside Gaskell's declared social purpose. For contemporaneous criticisms of Ruth's characterization and martyr death see Elizabeth K. Helsinger et al., *The Woman Question* vol. 3 (Manchester: Manchester University Press, 1983), Chapter 4.

27 Boyd Hilton, "Moral Disciplines," in *Liberty and Authority in Victorian Britain*, ed. Peter Mandler (Oxford: Oxford University Press, 2006), 224–46.

28 Kieran Dolin, *Fiction and the Law: Legal Discourse in Victorian and Modernist Literature* (Cambridge: Cambridge University Press, 2009). For a view of the two plots as a separation of spheres rather than a fault see Virginia Blain, "Double Vision and the Double Standard in *Bleak House*: A Feminist Perspective," *Literature and History* 11, no. 1: (1985): 31–46.

Bleak House's plot resists summary, a point that will become part of my argument about the novel. However, it is worth recalling some lines: The court case at the heart of the novel, *Jarndyce and Jarndyce*, is an inheritance suit in which generations of litigants are involved. Esther, who will eventually discover her descent, comes to live with John Jarndyce, one of the litigants, in his house (Bleak House) as companion to one of his two court wards. The debtors and creditors I soon examine are connected with Jarndyce either directly or indirectly in pursuit of the mystery of Esther's birth (or often, more precisely, in pursuit of her mother's – Lady Dedlock's – secrets). Credit chains, we shall see, create formal links between the court and the illegitimacy plots. The suit ends when an original will is discovered, but at that point the funds in dispute have all been used up in lawyers' fees. *Jarndyce and Jarndyce* has kept *Bleak House* famous among lawyers to this day, and in its own time was considered an influential call for legal reform.

Bleak House's attack on Chancery is part of a broader problem of abstraction in the novel: The moral imperative is to never abstract. I begin by explaining the novel's criticism of abstraction, which has received vast critical attention. I then observe that the market – as system – is not the focus of critique, and wonder why. Through a reading of the credit web in the novel vis-à-vis the legal systems of the court and the police, I argue that Dickens individualized the market, which therefore never appeared as a system, in contrast to state systems. While *Ruth's* liberalism lay in its search for relational individual agency, which represented a twist on the liberal individual/social divide, *Bleak House* ultimately lent support to the liberal market/state divide, in which the market appears more attractive. Paradoxically and again contra much history of liberalism in contracts, the market appeared more attractive not because it was rational and demarcated, but rather because it was relationally socialized, and could therefore be more easily transformed when compared with state systems.

Connexion

> What connexion can there be, between the place in Lincolnshire, the house in town, the Mercury in powder, and the whereabout of Jo the outlaw with the broom … What connexion can there have been between many people in the innumerable histories of this world, who, from opposite sides of great gulfs, have, nevertheless, been very curiously brought together!
>
> (256)

The connection that *is* is *Bleak House's* unifying constituent, both an aesthetic principle of form and a moral principle in content. The novel relies on a bewildering multiplicity of subplots, characters, contexts, themes, and social problems, which move from illegitimacy and the legal system in all directions: sanitary reform, urban slums, philanthropic inefficacy, imperial expansion, parliamentary corruption, illiteracy, economic inequality – exhibited not least through the novel's length, which, as Caroline Levine argues, was necessary for the networked vision it developed[29] – yet which converges into a coherent plot. Connections within the novel's complexities become gradually visible, finally expressed in a significant overlap and coordination between *Bleak House's* two contrasted narrators: Esther and her impersonal Other. As J. Hillis Miller observes, the novel's characters themselves assume throughout that there must be an intelligible connection and explanation to the seeming chaos around them.[30] Diverse experiences must make sense within a single plot before the novel is over. With this claim to connection *Bleak House* staged an elaborate attack on abstraction understood, I argue, as attempts at conceptual, operational, and ultimately moral separateness – attempts, that is, to a legitimate isolation of a concern from immediate surroundings, a process lawyers readily recognize. The novel belied separations between classes, spheres of experience, institutions, and persons, inflicting literary punishment on every attempt, and insisting that a sense of human immediacy, barred by no specialized language, professional logic, or moral denialism, will do.

While *Ruth* critically examined the possibility of abstraction as a factual state of affairs in which persons – character or reader – are detached from social meanings, with *Bleak House* the guiding assumption is that abstraction is impossible, for the world is an intricacy of interdependencies, just like the novel's form. The impossibility of abstraction in fact, turns every attempt to achieve it into a moral transgression: a choice to overlook relevant meanings. Forster's complaint clarifies the difference between *Ruth's* and *Bleak House's* recoils from abstraction: Dickens' characters are not just up against facts, Forster argued, they are up against the author's theory of morality.[31] In *Ruth*, heroine and readers need recourse to social meanings, which the novel supplies; in *Bleak House* they always already have them, and abstractions are therefore themselves forms of (im)morality which the novel condemns.

Dickens' web of "connexions" was so elaborate that J. Hillis Miller could claim that it defied its own project. In a deconstructive reading, Miller argued that Dickens subsumed the contextual specificity he wanted to guard under a systemic operation which was itself a form of abstraction: a

29 Caroline Levine, "Narrative Networks: *Bleak House* and the Affordances of Form," *Novel* 42, no. 3 (2009): 517–23.

30 J. Hillis Miller, *Charles Dickens: The World of His Novels* (Cambridge, MA: Harvard University Press, 1958), Chapter 6.

31 Ibid., 59.

system (interpretive system) was forced on particulars.[32] Miller's argument, first made in 1971, set a dominant critical agenda in *Bleak House* studies[33] with readers arguing with and against him about the implications of the novel's obsession with connections and its critique of abstracted systems. Within this critical context, Gordon Bigelow's reading of the problem of connection and disconnection in *Bleak House* places Dickens "at the center of nineteenth century economic discourse."[34] Dickens, claims Bigelow in an insightful reading, was responding to the danger that the system of total exchange would produce chaotic circulation and a final instability of value, experienced in economic crises. The court of Chancery is for Bigelow the central model in the novel of such a total system and the dangers it posits to life. Chancery develops an internal language which sustains its systemic existence (in the novel's famed statement, "The one great principle of the English law is, to make business for itself" (621)), while ruining those who depend on it, closed to their claims of meaning and value. The court, in other words, overlooks crucial connections. The oddity of the thing is, as the character of Skimpole to whom I soon turn would say, that no representation of formal market operations appears in Bigelow's account. At stake is a symbolic vocabulary, which Bigelow describes as a meeting between philology and political economy; in Bigelow's analysis the market can be read as a semiotic system, and the anxieties that it generated can therefore be represented in fictional nonmarket systems – and were indeed represented and explored through none else than the fictional court of Chancery.

In what follows I take seriously this absence of the market which Bigelow's analysis reveals vividly, and which is indeed significant in *Bleak House*. The absence of the market is especially curious since the novel seems to keep inviting readings vis-à-vis political economy. For all its panoramic ambitions, there is no stock market in *Bleak House*, nor much by way of businessmen, merchants, or the Trollopian city discussed in the previous chapter. At the same time, wealth creation and transfer through inheritance of old – the world of status – are represented as catastrophically collapsing, stuck with the miserable Chancery litigants whose generational history is destined to disappear, and formally explodes into lawyers' fees by the end of the novel. You might fairly wonder where and how this novel of ambitious panorama deals with mechanisms of resource allocation. One answer is the web of credit contracts which spreads throughout the novel.

32 J. Hillis Miller, "Interpretation in *Bleak House*," in J. Hillis Miller, *Victorian Subjects* (London: Harvester Wheatsheaf, 1990), 179–99.

33 For a discussion see Bruce Robbins, "Telescopic Philanthropy: Professionalism and Responsibility in *Bleak House*," in *Nation and Narration*, ed., Homi K. Bhabha (London: Routledge, 1990), 213–30.

34 Gordon Bigelow, *Fiction, Famine and the Rise of Economics in Victorian Britain and Ireland* (Cambridge: Cambridge University Press, 2003), 103.

Even the Jarndyce case ending in "costs" is in fact a reference to credit contracts, between clients and lawyers; Dickens indicated that credit replaces the system of inheritance, yet the critical focus on the self-perpetuating quality of the court as system has obscured this point. My reading focuses on the web of credit which, for reasons I explore, does not *feel* like a system and therefore has not been on critics' priorities as they read Dickens with Victorian political-economic debates.

I begin with a reading of the web of credit in terms of the novel's interest in "connexion." I show how Dickens' critique of abstraction informed his treatment of credit. The critique of abstraction grounded a relational view of contract, which undermined an understanding of the web as a system, and resisted a systemic treatment of contractual conduct. This in turn leads me in the last part of the discussion back to the question of the market's absence, which makes it plausible to look at the court of Chancery as a market model. I argue that the moral economy that Dickens posited in consequence of his critique of abstraction is precisely the reason that the web of credit does not appear like a system, or, to put this more forcefully, *dis*appears, dispersing into individualized moments. This outlook stands in direct opposition to the state order examined in *Bleak House* through the court, and no less through the police with the all-times-favorite Detective Bucket. The novel's liberal turn finally depends on this opposition between state and market, from which the credit web emerges as a principle of organization susceptible to positive moral imperative, paradoxically because on Dickens' account it is relational in ways that state systems find hard to adopt.

Promissory Morality and the Problem of Abstraction

Harold Skimpole, *Bleak House's* most notorious debtor, appears at first sight to be a thematic engagement with credit as a reified relation. The theme, we might assume, is the problem of Victorian debt which pervades Dickens' novels and is often tied, partly in consequence of Dickens' own advocacy, to his personal biography. Skimpole's flatness seems to be the pure type at its best, with all the attendant comic relief. It invites thematic readings: The purest form of a flat character, Forster argued, is constructed around a single idea or quality.[35] With Skimpole, his indebtedness consumes his being; it seems to urge the assumption that *Bleak House* engaged in a polemic about it. Put otherwise, at first sight Skimpole seems to gesture at a systemic phenomenon. However, the deep problematic at stake is not contract nor the credit economy, but rather an immorality of abstraction from social relations which pervades the novel. Credit, in other words,

35 E.M. Forster, *Aspects of the Novel* (New York: Harcourt, 1927), 67.

gestures at the problem of "connexion" which haunts *Bleak House*. While credit is therefore dissolved into a broader theme, it is uniquely placed to solve it, as I will later argue.

Jarndyce introduces Skimpole to his wards as a perfect child. He is a "little bright creature, with ... a sweet voice, and ... a perfect charm in him" (89). Skimpole confesses to "two of the oddest infirmities in the world: one was, that he had no idea of time; the other, that he had no idea of money" (90). "[F]or heaven's sake," he pleads, "having Harold Skimpole, a confiding child, petitioning you, the world, an agglomeration of practical people of business habits, to let him live and admire the human family, do it somehow or other, like good souls, and suffer him to ride his rocking horse!" (91). Shortly after his introduction, Skimpole's infirmities assume practical meaning: He is arrested for debt, and calls Richard and Esther to the rescue with their small savings. From then on, Skimpole's theories and their corresponding material implications are introduced with increasing intensity, until even Esther is angered, and Jarndyce lets go of this peculiar object of charity.

Skimpole's appeal, both comical and intellectual, depends on his power of reasoning. At the most immediate level, his discourse turns around familiar oppositions: altruism/egoism, performance/breach, rationality/irrationality. His parasitism becomes a useful social function: "I almost feel as if you ought to be grateful to me, for giving you the opportunity of enjoying the luxury of generosity ... I may have been born to be a benefactor to you" (91), he says to Esther and Richard. Similarly, he altruistically sells Jo to Bucket:

> [T]his active police officer and intelligent man has acquired, in the exercise of his art, a strong faith in money; he finds it useful to him, and he makes it very useful to society. Shall I shake that faith in Bucket [by refusing the offered payment], because I want it myself; ... shall I possibly paralyse Bucket, in his next detective operation?
>
> (934)

With the same vigor, Skimpole inverts creditor claims:

> "Now my dear doctor, it is quite a delusion on your part to suppose that you attend me for nothing. I am overwhelming you with money – in my expansive intentions – if you only knew it!" And really (he said) he meant it to that degree, that he thought it much the same as doing it. If he had had those bits of metal or thin paper to which mankind attached so much importance, to put in the doctor's hand, he would have put them ... Not having them, he substituted the will for the deed ... [I]t appeared to him that it was the same as coin, and cancelled the obligation.
>
> (240)

Skimpole also explains his difference from a creditor who might propose that he too should only intend, rather than perform, his part of the contract:

> [P]ray let us reason like intellectual beings [said Skimpole to a butcher] ... You had got the lamb, and I have not got the money. You couldn't really mean the lamb without sending it, whereas I can, and do, really mean the money without paying it!
>
> (241)

The butcher took legal proceedings, "[b]ut, in that," says Skimpole, "he was influenced by passion; not by reason" (241). The ability of logic to subvert moral intuitions makes Dickens' joke work. To paraphrase Stephen Greenblatt's comment in another context, what is unsettling is the experience of Skimpole's assertions – the sense that they are at once irrefutable logical propositions and humbug designed to conceal rapacity.[36]

By this point, however, a second level of meaning informing Skimpole's reversals becomes clear: Skimpole presents a process of increasing distance from material reality as a successful culmination. He is asked for something which is really nothing ("metal or thin paper"); he means to give it, but he does not have it; and so he should be rationally lawsuit-proof. A set of denials of the relation between representation and reality – money representing value materialized in daily life, intention referring to objects with social implications, rationality representing real people who want those objects – points back to Skimpole's ego as a sole reality.

Having emptied the idea of responsibility of content, Skimpole is able to abstract himself from his worldly affairs altogether. When his landlord takes his furniture in collection of unpaid rent Skimpole muses:

> [T]he oddity of the thing is ... that my chairs and tables were not paid for, and yet my landlord walks off with them as composedly as possible. Now, that seems droll! ... The chair and table merchant never engaged to pay my landlord my rent. Why should my landlord quarrel with him?
>
> (284)

Skimpole's removal from his contracts creates a direct relationship (and quarrel) between his creditors, negating the meaning of his obligations.

The problem with Skimpole is not his breaches of contract but the abstracting move at their root. Skimpole's intentions, in which his ultra-subjectivist will theory figures, are not an issue, although the well-versed

36 Stephen Greenblatt, "Invisible Bullets: Renaissance Authority and Its Subversion," in *Glyph. Johns Hopkins Textual Studies* 8, ed. Walter Benn Michaels (Baltimore, MD: Johns Hopkins University Press, 1981), 40, 52.

mockery of the theory is anecdotally appealing,[37] but a reflection of his social disengagement, the object of *Bleak House*'s concern. Appropriately, the heart of the Skimpole problematic lies in his complicity in the two greatest social ills in *Bleak House*: the neglected poor (selling Jo to Bucket), and the neglecting legal system (selling Richard to Vholes). These are the two most painful operations of abstraction in the novel, each exhibiting a structural refusal to respond to interdependencies, spanning suffering and doomed to failure in consequence. Engaging in material realities while failing to acknowledge and act on material implications, Skimpole is conductive to the spread of evil in the novel.

Skimpole's problematic in terms of the immorality of abstraction develops through his contrast with George Rouncewell. Another failing debtor, George borrowed money from the usurious Smallweed. The deal is peculiar in a Dickensian fashion: one term is that George is entitled to a pipe with every interest payment, and George admits that "it's not for the value of it ... It was a fancy to get it out of you [Smallweed]" (346). But the joke is on George. The pipe-right ridicules his attempt to counteract power; he is overwhelmed when Tulkinghorn and Smallweed use his debt to get hold of Hawdon's letter in pursuit of Lady Dedlock's secret. The narrator remarks, "[W]hether there are ... two more simple and unaccustomed children, in all the Smallweedy affairs of life [than George and his guarantor Bagnet]" – may very well be doubted. (544). Yet, George is never anything but wholly good. His contrast with Skimpole merits attention because their debts are so carefully structured on similar terms. Dickens encouraged the question: Why is George's childishness as debtor more forgivable than Skimpole's? Why are his unpayable debts, which like Skimpole's lead to expanding misery, less condemnable?

The logic remains consistent: George reverses Skimpole's abstractions. Dickens' visual powers underline the contrast: George is in touch with life, his sunburnt face and arms having "been used to a pretty rough life" (341), as the abstracted Skimpole is delicate and "not at all like the manner or appearance of a man who had advanced in life, by the usual road of years, cares, and experiences" (89); while Skimpole's movement is light and bright, George's "step too is measured and heavy" (341). George is attached to earth in its concreteness; his immediate environment leaves physical marks on his body, a figurative image of direct involvement. George's involvement means he not only wants to pay, but ties repayment to daily efforts. The money he owns is recognized as contextualized value: something that could make him "steady" in life; that makes him fragile vis-à-vis Smallweed; that grounds his guarantors' wellbeing.

37 Anecdotally at most, for a subjectivist version of the will theory never took significant hold in England, as we have seen.

George's lender, Smallweed, claims contractual rights delegitimized in *Bleak House* within the same moral economy. The narrator's animosity spills over itself: "a horny-skinned, two-legged, money-getting species of spider, who spun webs to catch unwary flies, and retired into holes until they were entrapped. The name of this old pagan's God was Compound Interest. He lived for it, married it, died of it" (332–3). The problem is not the usuriousness of the loans, despite the provocative language;[38] it is the social disengagement they signal. Uninvolved Smallweed retires into holes awaiting his victims; not mixing with life, the Smallweeds are almost dead: the family presides in a solitary street, "closely bricked on all sides like a tomb" (332); the entire family is constituted of old people; their monkey-like appearance ties them to prehistory; the Smallweeds do not live: Smallweed never goes out nor occupies himself.

If Skimpole rhetorically denies the value of the money he borrows, Smallweed denies the value of anything but the money he is owed. Both fail, from the two sides of the credit contract, to admit their contracts' relation to the demands of involvement in everyday life. In *Bleak House's* web of interdependencies, if you attempt to abstract yourself your harms spread uncontrollably through contractual vessels, in content as in form; socially involved characters struggle to stop the spread. George actively places himself at the junctions of his creditor's effects, seeking to minimize their spread; his failure is almost beside the point.[39] The same moral economy applies to other failing debtors: Richard Carstone, Jobling and Hawdon, who occupy interim positions between Skimpole and George on the scale of appropriate involvement, and other creditors like Jarndyce and Vholes.

The web of credit urges the principle that could reverse Skimpole's absurdities. It is not a philosophically sophisticated account of rationality, altruism, or contractual performance, but a remarkably earthly commitment: direct involvement in daily toils – a work ethic. Anderson shows Dickens' fears that detachment corrodes moral character.[40] When examined as a thematic concern carried forward through contractual representations, it becomes clear that these fears, which stirred Dickens away from radical critique, carry capitalist substantive content which could not sit well with Victorian radicalism. Evaluating debt relations in *Bleak*

38 The loans, note, were probably not illegal. There are not enough details in *Bleak House* on the Smallweed loans to verify this point, but two indications may be helpful: one is Tulkinghorn's confidence of the legal right of Smallweed. The other is the fact that in the early 1850s usury laws were on their way to final repeal which came into force in 1854. This question can be left unanswered for the problem of illegality is marginal within *Bleak House*'s moral framework.

39 For a view of George as morally culpable see C.R.B. Dunlop, "Debtors and Creditors in Dickens' Fiction," *Dickens Studies Annual* 19 (1990): 36, 38–9.

40 Anderson, *The Powers of Distance*, Chapter 2.

House is about norms of industrious involvement; disengagement from the almost tiring meaning of the everyday are condemning in this novel. Kathleen Blake thus aligns – or realigns – Dickens with the political economists from which he had been too easily severed. Gallagher too explores the shared premises of Dickens and political economy. She points to Dickens' subscription, along with most Victorians, to the proposition that value derives from labor, and his need to justify the contribution of his own occupation to the wealth of the nation. With the capitalist work ethic in view, it should be obvious that the novel's recoil from abstraction need not be read as antagonistic to Victorian liberalism.[41] The work ethic, however, should be understood within a more general pull away from abstraction and toward involvement, otherwise we might fairly wonder why some work addicts, like the Smalleweeds, stand condemned.[42] Blame and praise in *Bleak House* are allocated according to characters' responsiveness to immediate demands on their efforts. One cannot skip stages and overlook web links; a controlling image in *Bleak House* is therefore its opposition between far and near-reaching. Those who look only at distant plights – Mrs. Jellyby's "Telescopic Philanthropy," like those who withdraw into holes, are moral failures. This is what Bruce Robbins calls a "politics of presence."[43] *Bleak House's* eccentric characters, Skimpole among them, are from this perspective a formal expression of their thematic failure to become involved: failing to become involved within the plot, eccentrics never become "real."[44]

Observe in passing how this politics of presence is also a politics of localism. *Bleak House's* resistance to global concerns has often been noted. Daniel Hack argues that the novel's ethics of proximity stopped at the nation's borders; the domestic is not just the home, but, in the linguae franca of international relations, the nation, and any attempt to look

41 Kathleen Blake, "*Bleak House*, Political Economy, Victorian Studies," *Victorian Literature and Culture* 25, no. 1 (1997): 1–21; Catherine Gallagher, *The Body Economic: Life, Dearth, and Sensation in Political Economy and the Victorian Novel* (Princeton, NJ: Princeton University Press, 2006), Chapter 3. The work theme has been widely observed. George H. Ford comments on its salience in *Bleak House*, claiming, as Blake later argues, that *Bleak House* has more consistently to do with earnestness or the lack of it than with the satire of Chancery. Alexander Welsh, *The City of Dickens* (Oxford: Oxford University Press, 1971), 76 (Welsh cites Ford and agrees). See also Robbins, "Telescopic Philanthropy."

42 Blake notes that the Smalleweeds too are committed to work, and seems to settle this contradiction within *Bleak House's* support of the work ethic with the suggestion that "Dickens is no doctrinaire." Blake, "*Bleak House*," 15.

43 Robbins, "Telescopic Philanthropy," 215.

44 Gary Watt argues for the significance of stirring, or constant movement, for *Bleak House's* moral outlook. It is worth observing that failures of involvement in the text are closely tied with a sense of freeze, from which the impression of caricaturized characters, as well as moral censure, emerge. Gary Watt, *Equity Stirring: The Story of Justice Beyond Law* (Oxford: Hart Publishing, 2009), 183–91.

beyond it receives censure.[45] In Chapter 2 I suggested that nationalism was a hierarchy less problematic for novelistic liberal projects; in *Bleak House* too, explicit attacks on social hierarchies as forms of abstraction did not problematize national consciousness but on the contrary, consolidated it.

When abstraction occurs (inside the nation), we might have a perfectly consistent logic, like Skimpole's, but it is a closed logic, without referential meaning. This problem resonates with what Bigelow recognizes, following Barthes, as "metonymic confusion" whereby signifiers circulate but do not signify. However, Dickens sees here a moral problem, a *refusal* to acknowledge meaning – or value, which backlashes inevitably, a consequence of the fact of interdependence – or connexions – which Dickens at once created and claimed to have found.

Relationality and the Undoing of System

Bleak House's recoil from abstraction overturns the notion, so familiar from the perspective of legal contract, of treating like cases alike. Condemning abstraction as an illegitimate claim to dissociation in a world of interdependencies, Dickens was able to contrast similarly failing debtors and see analogies between apparently contrasted positions of debtors and creditors, reading their conduct within surrounding relational frameworks. By placing moral demands of direct involvement on its characters, at the level of contract the novel ends up with alternative readings of familiar things, to slightly alter (does it?) Dickens own description of his art.[46]

The novel's reversal of familiar meanings points to a way out of Hillis Miller's claim that *Bleak House* imposed an elaborate interpretive scheme on particulars, and was therefore ultimately problematic in its critique of assimilative systems. Because it challenged familiar meanings, not least of promissory agency which lay at the heart of an emergent market order, readers were compelled to critically assess and frame their own understandings. This is an experience of political agency, born out by the novel's intricacies of interdependence in a web in which choice – like the devil – is in the details. In the tension between individual agency and systemic pull, therefore, *Bleak House* was able to land on the individualizing side.

The individualizing tendencies of *Bleak House's* moral economy aligned with its work ethic. The novel performed an artistic labor through excruciating attention to concrete detail analogous to the labor it asked of its characters in their everyday lives, and of systems in their immediate surroundings, and so also placed its own style of abstraction at a distance

45 Daniel Hack, "Close Reading at a Distance: The African Americanization of *Bleak House*," *Critical Inquiry* 34, no. 4 (2008): 729–53.

46 Preface to *Bleak House*, 7 ("In Bleak House, I have purposely dwelt upon the romantic side of familiar things").

from the lazy abstraction it condemned. Gary Watt suggests that *Bleak House* calls for responsibility in interpretation which Hillis Miller's analysis overlooks, ironically promoting too formalistic an interpretation which is the evil of assimilative systems.[47] Miller did in fact observe that the novel freed itself from the guilt of creating a system by reminding the reader that it was itself (just) an act of interpretation, leaving individual agency at the margins, in the hands of the interpreter-reader.[48] Exercising responsibility in interpretation is another level of labor, this time demanded of readers. Just as characters are required to exercise contextual moral judgments which make similar contractual behaviors stand at opposite moral ends, so readers are asked to do the same. Miller noted as much: the narrators' reports, he said, "can only be understood by means of a further interpretation – the reader's."[49]

The question is how the system operates: The novel's critique of abstraction is successful not because it is no system at all, but because it is a system that operates on individual decisions. This is where Dickens aligned with ideological accounts of the market as a source of order and hope at once, to which I now turn.

The Market as Non-System

How is it that the web of credit – the most formal economic axis in *Bleak House*, and one entangled with the concerns of economic collapse of its time, does not come across as a system at all in a novel famously worried about systems – and on some critical accounts, the market system foremost? Because Dickens did not give the credit web a center, and instead represented the choice between abstraction and responsiveness as a matter of individualized moral decisions. The web of credit is the opposite of state – or organized society, represented in law – both court and police.

Since D.A. Miller's Foucauldian analysis of *Bleak House*, it has become a critical commonplace to recognize two forms of legal power in the novel: the court, and the police. Impersonal and anonymous law, argues D.A Miller, is contrasted in *Bleak House* with law enforcement, personified in Detective Bucket (gesturing at the detective branch of the Metropolitan Police that had been recently reformed). While the Jarndyce suit proliferates uncontrollably through society and through the novel, Bucket ties up loose ends to provide a coherent narrative. Indeed, the police seems to operate on a non-abstracting mode, in direct contrast to the court, and so to earn its status as plot resolver. The legal system is culpable of detachment, of developing a closed and abstract logic. The police offers a compelling

47 Watt, *Equity Stirring*, 171.
48 Miller, "Interpretation in *Bleak House*," 198.
49 Ibid., 181.

alternative, both on the level of content and in satisfaction of narrative desire, because it reverses the trend. As Miller notes, the police is represented by a human face while the Jarndyce suit by generations of nameless suitors, lawyers and judges. Bucket is successful because he is non-abstract, adapting himself to the surroundings he investigates, rather than impose a standard oblivious to their embedded meanings in the fashion of the court. Bucket reaches out to all milieus at their own environments, rather than sit like Chancery "at the very heart of the fog" (14), deaf to nonlegal language. In each of his encounters Bucket is able to communicate on the terms of his interlocutors. "Time and place cannot bind Mr Bucket" (803), importantly because he is not limited to a fixed frame of mind into which he translates everything around him. Bucket's success within the plot and as its formal resolver depends on his non-abstract quality.

Yet, D.A. Miller also argues that the containment of power represented by the detective story in *Bleak House* serves an ideological function within the law rather than against it, offering a compelling institutional alternative to the court which finally reconciles readers (subjects) to a totalizing power.[50] This position has sparked critical arguments on various fronts, some of which are concerned with the assumption that readers were drawn in by Bucket, and that he successfully contains the social problems raised by the novel (to be fair, Miller too did not argue for a fully successful containment). I concur with Lauren Goodlad that Bucket does not contain nor resolves the novel's overarching social ills, particularly that of poverty. As Hillis Miller reminds us, he does not even save Lady Dedlock.[51] Bucket, furthermore, cannot be trusted. As Goodlad argues, "Bucket polices for the status quo," serving an unholy alliance between aristocratic and bourgeois interests.[52] Readers were explicitly warned not to trust Bucket: "He is in the friendliest condition towards his species ... free with his money, affable in his manners, innocent in his conversation – but, through the placid stream of his life, there glides an under-current of forefinger" (803). Bucket's complex omnipresence prefigures almost uncannily Walter Benjamin's argument that in the police's formless involvement in everyday life the separation of lawmaking and law-preserving violence is suspended, making the police an especially troubling institution of modern life.[53] And *Bleak House* urged readers to see the problem. To the extent readers *are* charmed by Bucket, still, to be a form of disciplinary power as Miller claims he is, it

50 D.A. Miller, *The Novel and the Police* (Berkeley, CA: University of California Press, 1989), Chapter 3.

51 Miller, "Interpretation in *Bleak House*," 187.

52 Lauren M.E. Goodlad, *Victorian Literature and the Victorian State: Character and Governance in a Liberal Society* (Baltimore, MD: Johns Hopkins University Press, 2003), 101.

53 Walter Benjamin, "Critique of Violence," in Walter Benjamin, *Walter Benjamin: Selected Writings, Volume 1: 1913–1926*, eds. Marcus Paul Bullock and Michael W. Jennings (Cambridge, MA: Belknap Press, 1999), 236–52.

must be the case that his non-abstract, involved mode is misleading: a disguise or superficiality, a form of "manipulative action" as Robbins calls it.[54]

And so, neither the court nor the police are set up in *Bleak House* as attractive modes of social order. The reason is not the divide between humanist and antihumanist processes, where agency is absent or unlocatable in the latter;[55] such an account would tend to set the court apart from Bucket, or otherwise would have to argue too strongly that Bucket is fully depersonalized. The reason is rooted elsewhere: both the court and the police have a center; they are modes of order emanating from the state (and frequently the aristocratic control of its operations which resonates with premodernity but, as Bucket exemplifies, does not disappear with modern bureaucracy). On Dickens' account both therefore embody the threat of abstraction as a systematic tendency, for the enabling moment of abstraction is a distance between the generator of meaning and meaning's subjects. In a formal legal order, whether its power to generate meaning – and value – radiates from the heart of the fog, in the case of Chancery, or from an omnipresent Bucket with a face (or forefinger), there is a locus to which power can be traced and which is formally distanced from the order's subjects. This quality is just what the credit web does *not* have, or at least: that is what Dickens suggested can be absented from the credit web. The spread of troubling meaning through the web, whether Tulkinghorn's evil pursuit, Smallweed's avarice or else, is a problem of morality which can be fixed, the novel implies, through an accumulation of individual choices which opt for involvement rather than abstraction. Making right choices is not even hard, for the novel's attention to surrounding details means that it is easier to observe immediacies than to abstract from them; abstracting characters therefore tend to be as shrewd as they are cruel, while the morally worthy are typically simple. The continuously in-touch movement advocated in *Bleak House*, "concentric gradualism" as Robbins describes it,[56] flattens the relation between source and object of meaning. Moreover, and crucially, in the credit web there is no single "originary center"[57] but many, a multiplicity of local decisions of individuals, hence the cumulative picture ultimately denies a center and a directionality.

The historical moment was apt for such a vision, as Robbins recounts: it was in the same era that the meaning of "responsibility" underwent an ethical shift and came to inhere in individuals rather than relations of accountability (in which, for instance, a servant is not responsible).[58]

54 Robbins, "Telescopic Philanthropy," 225.
55 Ibid.
56 Ibid., 215.
57 Ibid.
58 Ibid., 219.

Dickens asked responsible individuals to take account of their immediate relationships, compensating for this shift away from status with a vision of interdependence, which became an individualized moral imperative. The buildup of multiple decisions by individuals into a system is therefore less threating, unlike systems with centers: unlike the state. That the credit web is a system, a principle of order, can be glimpsed from the structure of the web which effectively links the novel's multiple plots; contract is as dispersed and proliferating through society and through the novel as other essential plot elements. Yet, the systemic quality tends to disappear under individualized cases. When readers are encouraged to evaluate each case on its own, through relational contexts, without a center, the disappearance gains momentum. The market, in other words, emerges as a principle of alternative order to both the court and the police, one susceptible to relationality as a moral imperative, and therefore much more hopeful, or, at the very least, not systematically threatening. Here lies the final element of *Bleak House's* liberal turn.

Read this way, *Bleak House* might appear suspiciously close to the most radical articulations of free market capitalism. Milton Friedman, to take the paradigmatic spokesman, based his vision in *Capitalism and Freedom* on the idea of dispersing power: "Viewed as a means to the end of political freedom, economic arrangements are important because of their effect on the concentration or dispersion of power."[59] The distinction between centralized and dispersed power is key to market defenses;[60] it sets a premise more fundamental than any argument you might build on it, by immobilizing the search for systemic elements. Still, the conclusions that follow from the claim of dispersed power do matter, and begin to explain why *Bleak House*'s liberalism can hardly be read as version of laissez faire. For Friedman the ultimate project is checks on government: "The kind of economic organization that provides economic freedom directly, namely, competitive capitalism, also promotes political freedom because it separates economic power from political power and in this way enables the one to offset the other."[61] Dickens was differently positioned, far less certain that no good could come from centralized institutions, and resistant to the very project of demarcating systems. As Goodlad argues, Dickens' liberalism, like that of other progressive authors, was caught up in a candid if paradoxical enterprise of "imagining a modern governing agency that would be rational, all-embracing and efficient, but also anti-bureaucratic, personalized and

59 Milton Friedman, *Capitalism and Freedom* 4th ed. (Chicago, IL: University of Chicago Press, 2002), 9.

60 See also F.A. Hayek, "The Use of Knowledge in Society," *The American Economic Review* 35, no. 4 (1945): 521: "Competition… means decentralized planning by many separate persons."

61 Friedman, *Capitalism and Freedom*, 9.

liberatory."[62] In that project we see resistances to atomization at odds with laissez faire, and *Bleak House* is a good case in point. Preference for the market in *Bleak House* was neither a consequence of a direct faith in the market – we see enough rapaciousness in the web of credit for instance, nor a consequence of a decided position against state governance, where Dickens was on the search for workable solutions. Instead, it was the novel's suspicion of abstraction that rendered the market structurally more responsive than the state to the moral imperative of involvement. The novel's form, engaged in "connexions" of multiple details, operated on the same principle of the credit web, working through dispersed interrelations. For that reason, Esther, who emerges bottom-up from within webs of relations, and who recognizes her dependence on them, rather than the impersonal narrator whose omniscience is centralized, top-down, finally has the last word.[63] Dickens' implicit upholding of the market against the state was thus a consequence of his way of imagining and narrating the moral critique of abstraction.

Bleak House upheld the modern market economy by resisting, rather than supporting, its demarcation, a position speaking to complexities in liberalism that research of the last two decades has been examining. While Marxist criticism was faulting liberal thought for its failure to heed the dramatic interdependencies involved in the capitalist division of labor, novelists were giving these interdependencies the best of their attention, treating them as inescapable elements of modern life without romanticizing them. Relational accounts of the economy were about negotiating forms of agency different from status, but did not necessitate the abstractions familiar to us from contracts histories; indeed those abstractions were less readily available to the Victorian imagination which worked with the past of status, not with the neoliberal future. That such resistances did not easily align with atomistic individualism in contracts, and particularly with its vision of a rational economy, did not imply, however, rejections of the capitalist order, as Gaskell's and Dickens' relational economies made clear.

62 Goodlad, *Victorian Literature and the Victorian State*, xii.

63 A second reason for Esther's triumph is the impersonal narrator's association with status, a point I explore in Chapter 5.

Chapter 4

Contract and Freedom(?)

Constrained Existence in *Middlemarch* and *The Mayor of Casterbridge*

The previous chapter examined styles of relational liberalism in contracts and the socialized market they envisioned, by probing the project of abstraction. In this chapter I turn to another persistent theme of contracts histories, namely, the ideological association of liberal contract with freedom. The novels read in this chapter, George Eliot's *Middlemarch* of 1871, Thomas Hardy's *The Mayor of Casterbridge* of 1886,[1] complete my analyses in Chapter 3 on a number of levels.

First, here too I examine a significant divergence from atomistic individualism in contracts. The novels discussed here represent contract as constraint, and so reveal a mood at virtual opposition to the celebratory tones of contract as freedom. The nineteenth century was from early on preoccupied with philosophies of freedom, will and volition, and attendant questions of determinism and necessity, all of these within tensions between religious and secular worldviews. The question in what sense a person was free to contract, or in what sense her promise represented a willed obligation, found different responses, metaphysical, psychological and sociological. My discussion touches these debates, yet I am less interested in conceptualizing different theoretical positions, an intellectual project that has received justifiably vast attention, than in highlighting an association between contract and constraint which was focused on *relationality*. While *Ruth* and *Bleak House* were involved in a mid-century project of imposing on readers the significance of relationality for individual agency and for the morality of choice, with *Middlemarch* and *The Mayor of Casterbridge* the effort was to clarify the constraints involved in the inescapability of "connexions," and to explore the delimiting implications of living in a web of relationships. Rather than extensions of the individual – ways to improve and expand her scope of self-determination, promises were

1 All references are to Thomas Hardy, *The Mayor of Casterbridge*, ed. Dale Kramer (Oxford: Oxford University Press, 1998); George Eliot, *Middlemarch: A Study of Provincial Life*, ed. David Carroll (Oxford: Oxford University Press, 1996).

fictionalized as figures for her points of break, anxiety, and limitation. No romanticism remains, if one was ever imagined. The cultural consciousness that these novels imply, the mood they adopted, are significant from the perspective of contracts histories because, as we have seen in Chapter 1, while historians do not collectively insist on a single philosophical meaning of freedom and related concepts, they do collectively suggest that contract became culturally prominent because it signaled them in some sense.

Read through the lens of contracts histories, one explanation for the opposition to the contract-freedom trope could be the rise of collectivism in the closing decades of the nineteenth century. As discussed in Chapter 1, collectivism is often interpreted as a response to the excesses of atomism, particularly as it implicated power disparities in contracts. The wary mood toward promises at stake here would seem in line with the collectivist critical mood. Hardy in particular shared radical political sentiments. Yet the concerns I elaborate were not aligned with the emphases traced by contracts histories: neither power disparities nor a search for alternatives *to* contract occupied the center of *Middlemarch* and *The Mayor of Casterbridge*; the question is not collective solutions. Instead we see an investigation of terms of existence which Raymond Williams described in both Eliot and Hardy as registrations of a creative disturbance, records of struggles of an unprecedented time.[2] Both novels investigated a world predominated by individualized relationships as a new kind of world. They therefore deepen my argument that the relational sociality of contract and the market had a deep and far ranging, while not consistently enthusiastic, resonance.

Second, *Middlemarch* and *The Mayor of Casterbridge* reveal complex dialogues with the concerns explored, respectively, in *Bleak House* and *Ruth*. *Middlemarch* was capacious in its social representation and shared with *Bleak House* the ambition of the web imagery. But Eliot turned on its head Dickens' main point, namely, comprehensible "connexions". Instead, the web in Eliot is an entanglement which cannot be grasped wholly. Contract and promise are for her key sites expressive of the modern limitations embedded in capitalist society. While Dickens made room for the capitalist market by virtue of its openness to relational sociality, Eliot incorporated popular political-economic advice about economic prudence into the terms of meaningful existence in the web of constraints.

In *The Mayor of Casterbridge* the problem of contractual agency was framed as a misguided masculine performance. If Gaskell's protagonist has to struggle with expectations from women, and experiences a fall and rise, Hardy's protagonist, Michael Henchard, pays the price that contract's masculinity imposed on men, and, with Hardy's bleaker outlook,

2 Raymond Williams, *The English Novel from Dickens to Lawrence* (London: Hogarth Press, 1984), 85.

experiences a rise and fall. Taken together, *Ruth* and *The Mayor of Casterbridge* deepen the conceptual implications of gender that feminist histories of contracts have recovered. Gaskell's *Ruth* began with a gender-informed relational vision to model the market at large, while Hardy captured the masculine side of contracts not as power but as constraint, an outlook that remains to be engaged in contracts histories beyond issues of marriage. Both underlined, if with inverse moods, the relationality of contracts.

Ultimately both *Middlemarch* and *The Mayor of Casterbridge* accounted for the capitalist social order as a negotiation of relationally-constrained lives, Hardy, as I will argue in conclusion, with much more skepticism than Eliot.

Suffocation and Economy in *Middlemarch*

Middlemarch's was an ambitious liberal project, drawing together, complicating and extending many of the concerns I have so far discussed. The broadest achievement that will occupy me is a non-naïve and therefore deeply divided liberal consciousness. That consciousness was able at once to invest the capitalist order with meaning by hallowing the efforts it demanded, and to maintain a critical distance from its own investment by acknowledging the suffocations that living in the capitalist order implied. This is a legacy still experienced today, in lives at once fully implicated in the existing order and second-guessing our own implication, hoping that critical awareness is more a reformist than a docile energy.

The web metaphor appears in *Middlemarch* as the implication of moving away from status into an appreciation of multitudinous (as Eliot put it) discrete relationships. The Eliotian web, I will argue, is not a structure, in contrast with the Dickensian one; indeed structures were for Eliot imagined projections of a status-based worldview which induces blindness and misunderstanding. The alternative, appropriate to modern living and Eliot's realism, is a constant negotiation of inescapable interdependencies, appearing as obstacles and barring a holistic vision. The consciousness that goes along with this picture is of suffocation: as characters begin to move away from status-consciousness and appreciate interdependencies, they not only experience illimitable and unforeseen pressures, but the constant risk of submitting themselves to others and being annihilated. To maintain the liberal tenet central to *Middlemarch*, of differences between individuals, characters need to negotiate the dependence between self and other and reach compromises without obliterating the self or her other, in a dynamic process of relational becoming. The novel's striking tool featuring in the process of becoming is the practice of economy – the famed learning "what everything costs" (762).

Middlemarch's complex liberalism was reliant on promises. Promises' attraction as narrative mechanisms speaks to their conceptual role as par excellence cases of relational interdependence, with all the suffocation involved. Read this way, Eliot hardly saw contracts as reflecting a social order based on consent, as Dermont Coleman suggests. She instead treated promissory obligations as inescapable in the order of her time, and fictionalized them to seek coping mechanisms, in the hope of attaining, as Coleman puts it, higher moral considerations.[3]

One point about *Middlemarch's* wary framing of promises bears emphasis upfront: legal effectiveness is not the point; contracts and unenforceable promises, reciprocal and nonreciprocal alike are collapsed under a single framework concerned with a common problematic. Catharine Frank observes the role of wills – legal testamentary instruments – in *Middlemarch*, as tools exerting dramatic pressure on the plot by forming within it a world to which testators attempt to submit their successors.[4] This effect resonates with the work of promises in the text, which likewise involve submissions, yet Frank suggests that it is the legal effectiveness of wills which sets them apart from Eliot's idea of justice. The incessant interest in promises in *Middlemarch* reveals that the problem of submission through instruments of will exceeds the sphere of formal legal power, and speaks to a more fundamental sense of peril in an interdependent society. The problem that Frank attributes to legal enforceability seems to be instead the effect of the disturbance of death which disables relationality as a moderating force, precisely the force central in promises.

The association of promise and contract with constraints rather than freedom, and the turn to economy to handle the suffocations they implied, marks a profound instance of a relational liberalism which is not romantically resistant to the capitalist order but rather resolved to find antidotes to the interdependencies that the order generates *within* the order's economic language. As characters learn to economize they depart from practicalities; economizing assumes the depth of existential questions which preoccupied Eliot. However, the gap that Eliot herself opened up in insisting that she was dealing with the "unhistoric" stuff of life and yet that she was dealing with deep meaning was huge, and she kept upfront the fear that her tools of mediation were inadequate.

The following discussion begins by expounding the web in *Middlemarch* as a move from status to relationships. I then examine the novel's treatment of existence in the web in terms of suffocation, and its attendant turn to economy, all driven by promissory pressures.

3 Dermont Coleman, *George Eliot and Money: Economics, Ethics and Literature* (Cambridge: Cambridge University Press, 2014), 41. Coleman refers to a consent-based order in Herbert Spencer's sense.

4 Cathrine O. Frank, *Law, Literature, and the Transmission of Culture in England, 1837–1925* (Farnham: Ashgate, 2010), Chapter 2.

The Web: From Status to Relational Obstacles

Gillian Beer describes the web as a metaphor and metaphoric form found everywhere in Victorian writing, common among scientists, philosophers, poets and novelists.[5] Novelistic uses, however, were diversified in ways relevant for this chapter. Dickens used the web metaphor only once and almost incidentally in *Bleak House*, yet as I argued in Chapter 3, the web functioned as a structural basis for his narrative, its logic the ground of "connexions." In *Middlemarch* Eliot centralized the metaphoric use of the web, yet the moral imperative of responsiveness to connections under which Dickens belabored appears in reverse, as characters all too eager to respond are hindered through failures of understanding. Williams described the difference as network vs. web: Dickens' image connects while Eliot's disturbs and obscures.[6]

In what follows I read *Middlemarch's* outlook by engaging three stories, those of Lydgate, Dorothea, and Fred, where the fictionalization of promises is pivotal to the unfolding of the plot. Fred is less central than the first two who are often viewed as the novel's parallel centers, two variations on a single motif of chastening youthful ambition;[7] his story is almost inverse; for that reason, the commonalities are revealing of concerns that exceed the disciplinary notion of chastening.

Brief reminder: Tertius Lydgate is an ambitious surgeon and new arrival to the provincial Middlemarch who marries Rosamond Vincy, daughter of Middlemarch manufacturer and mayor. Lydgate's ambitions clash with his wife's and the Middlemarch community; he quickly contracts debt and in consequence becomes implicated with the corruption of the town's banker and his wife's uncle, Nicholas Bulstrode, whose fortune was built on an illegitimate inheritance. The pious Dorothea Brooke lives on her uncle's estate at the rural outskirts of Middlemarch, which she is expected to inherit. Dorothea constantly conceives redistributive plans for bettering the lives of poor tenants, which remain unheeded. She marries the Reverend Edward Casaubon, a middle-aged scholar and estate owner, but her hopes to find new horizons are disappointed and she finds herself imprisoned in marriage. At Casaubon's deathbed she almost commits to an open-ended promise he asks for, but is saved by the bell of death. Dorothea eventually marries Casaubon's younger cousin Will Ladislaw, thus operationalizing Casaubon's will which disinherits her. Fred Vincy, Rosamond's

5 Gillian Beer, *Darwin's Plots: Evolutionary Narrative in Darwin, George Eliot and Nineteenth-Century Fiction*, 2nd ed. (Cambridge: Cambridge University Press, 2004), 155–6.

6 Williams, *The English Novel*, 88. He actually argued that *Middlemarch* was more connected than Eliot's other novels, the society more integrated, yet conceded that there too Eliot dealt with restrictions.

7 E.g., Catherine Gallagher, *The Body Economic: Life, Death, and Sensation in Political Economy and the Victorian Novel* (Princeton, NJ: Princeton University Press, 2006), 132.

brother, expects to inherit from his uncle Featherstone and marry his beloved Mary Garth. His road to happiness is strewn with trouble as reckless debts, unpayable when disinheritance materializes, subvert his plans and undermine his standing with the Garths. Shaken by failure, Fred is eventually offered employment by Mary's father, buys the Featherstone estate, and marries Mary. Observe at the outset how these plots are crucially entangled with promises, and how, furthermore, promises are set up in constitutive relations with inheritance, as trouble in the transfer of wealth through inheritance assumes its meaning in promissory contexts, a concern we have also seen in *Bleak House*.

Lydgate, Dorothea and Fred are all eager to engage with the world around them; however, socially-inscribed dispositions disable them from appreciating immediate realities. Lydgate, of aristocratic background, "walked by hereditary habit" (327) and expects life to rearrange itself around his engagement to Rosamond; short of ready money to furnish a new house, he borrows money, signs a bill of sale on his furniture as security to a creditor, and continues to run a household on credit. Fred, the son of a new bourgeois, notices that his father "himself had expensive Middlemarch habits … while mamma had those running accounts with tradespeople, which give the cheerful sense of getting everything one wants without any question of payment" (216), and lives "according to family habits and traditions" (216).[8] He complacently asks Mr. Garth to guarantee a gambling debt. Dorothea marries under imaginative preconceptions about the higher goals she might serve as a scholar's wife. Dorothea's consciousness, and particularly her asceticism, is a function of a life unencumbered by material concerns. Unlike Lydgate's and Fred's positive relation to material convenience, with Dorothea we see a negative one springing from the same source. While the three protagonists cherish idols considered unusual in their surroundings: Dorothea with her religiosity and ascetic egalitarianism, Fred with his unrelenting love for the ungenteel Mary, Lydgate with his modern science, their decisions are inescapably conditioned by social background, "[f]or there is no creature," the narrator assures us in generalizing from Dorothea, "whose inward being is so strong that it is not greatly determined by what lies outside it" (784–5).

8 The familial self-reflex with which Fred starts out is figuratively encapsulated in the story of Featherstone's inheritance. When Fred's hopes to inherit Featherstone are disappointed, Fred's mother protests: "I call it a robbery: it was like giving him the land, to promise it; and what is promising, if making everybody believe is not promising?" (322). Mrs Vincy's complaint takes a two-step detour only to arrive at the initial point of self-reflex: the general belief becomes a promise, the promise becomes property, and property cannot be taken away; the Vincy inclinations become almost a material reality. Mrs. Vincy's resort to a promise marks the problem, for in *Middlemarch* promise depends on adjustment to relational constraints, missing from the Vincy expectations.

The novel's unfolding of these dispositions is entangled with the important point of estrangement from popular advice on economic prudence. Lydgate's upbringing means that "it had never occurred to him to devise a plan for getting half-crowns … Money had never been a motive to him" (167–8). The Vincy children "had no standard of economy" (216). The echo of Dickens' Skimpole ("no idea of money") is obscured because what features in Dickens as moral rapacity is explained by Eliot as socially-induced blindness. Finally, Dorothea's Puritan energy threatens to turn her into a wife who "might awaken you some fine morning with a new scheme for the application of her income which would interfere with political economy" (9). Indeed, her misconceived attraction to Casaubon is itself a consequence of frustrated economic plans: "his elevating thought lifted her above her annoyance at being twitted with her ignorance of political economy, that never-explained science which was thrust as an extinguisher over all her lights" (17).

Eliot set her protagonists against the sociality of statuses, from hereon to begin a process of adjustment to otherness within the web, handled with the aid of economy. If society "emerges as a monolith of oppression"[9] in *Middlemarch*, that is because of its role as the bearer of status-encoded behavior and responses, framed now as both petty and shallow. Eliot's principle of agency requires individual action beyond class-conditioned reflexes, or, as she more often puts it, "habits." Elain Hadley recovers just this effort in her work on political liberalism of the period. The effort, she claims, was to develop cognitive practices often described as "habits of thought," which would be differently marked from non-individualized reflexive habits.[10] Eliot's protagonists are marked structurally by undergoing a process of change, rather than substantively by aligning with favored moral stances. As individual differences enter characters' frame, they begin a process of becoming through a struggle to refigure understanding.

To exceed their status-informed consciousness, Eliot's characters must give up the idea of coherence. The web of *Middlemarch* is incomprehensible as a totality and as a structure. While the genealogies in the novel are elaborate and connect its many characters and plots,[11] there is no coherent framework, just a move, often arbitrary, lacking an organizing logic, from one connection to the next. As the finale memorably says, "the fragment of a life, however typical, is not the sample of an even web" (779). This was a final insistence on the principle of narration in which every generalization

9 Elizabeth Langland, *Nobody's Angels: Middle-Class Women and Domestic Ideology in Victorian Culture* (Ithaca, NY: Cornell University Press 1995), 196.

10 Elaine Hadley, *Living Liberalism: Practical Citizenship in Mid-Victorian Britain* (Chicago, IL: University of Chicago Press, 2010).

11 For an overview see Kathleen Blake, ed., *Approaches to Teaching Eliot's* Middlemarch (New York: The Modern Language Association of America, 1990), Appendix 2.

made is soon undermined,[12] and every character's presupposition belied. Comprehension is only of one's own limitations, an openness rooted in humility.

Status-informed consciousness is a generator of misinterpretations in *Middlemarch*, most obvious in the interim stages of plots of adjustment, when protagonists begin to acknowledge concrete otherness yet the pull of preconceptions still applies. Lydgate, for instance, turns to new forms of idealization. As Rosamond reveals ideas of her own about debt, he begins to see her as a different kind of creature so that he might still accept her: "[I]t was inevitable that in that excusing mood he should think of her as if she were an *animal of another and feebler species*" (628; my emphasis). Henry Staten argues that Rosamond is but a mirror of Lydgate's own class tastes, and therefore she sinks him.[13] However, the problem becomes interesting when Eliot lets Lydgate move beyond the initial class reflex toward a consciousness of interdependence, while leaving Rosamond frozen behind. At the interim point of dim awareness, Lydgate's career, like his wife, is reconceptualized too ideally: "[B]y the bedside of patients the direct external calls on his judgment and sympathies brought the added impulse needed to draw him out of *himself*" (628; my emphasis). Lydgate's idealized separations between professional, intimate and economic experience quickly collapse. As Suzanne Graver observes, his failures occur with attempts at these kinds of private/public, feminine/masculine separations.[14] The collapse reveals Lydgate's misreading of web realities; despite the moral attractiveness of his selfless treatment of patients, he has not freed himself of preconceptions which blind him to the full implications of concrete interdependencies. Assumptions about sphere-separations ally with attempts at holistic structures, but the web subsumes all spheres[15] in its demands for an alternative consciousness.

The interim stages in plots of adjustment speak to both the power and faults of socially-inscribed readings of reality. While hard to let go, attempts at coherent accounts of reality turn out to be, in the novel's famed

12 On these reversals see Catherine Gallagher, "George Eliot: Immanent Victorian," *Representations* 90, no. 1 (2005): 61–74. Gallagher explains the gap between the general and the particular in the opposing impulses toward reference (referring to people in the world) and toward realization (resembling people in the world); that fictional persons do not conform to types, Gallagher claims, drives the desire for fiction. See also Elizabeth Deeds Ermarth, "Negotiating *Middlemarch*," in Middlemarch *in the Twenty First Century*, ed. Karen Chase (Oxford: Oxford University Press, 2010), 107–32.

13 Henry Staten, *Spirit Becomes Matter: The Brontes, George Eliot, Nietzsche* (Edinburgh: Edinburgh University Press, 2014), 121.

14 Suzanne Graver, "'Incarnate History': The Feminisms of *Middlemarch*," in Blake, *Approaches to Teaching Eliot's* Middlemarch, 69.

15 I adapt this phrase (with concurrence) from Jeffrey J. Franklin, "Anthony Trollope Meets Pierre Bourdieu: The Conversion of Capital as Plot in the Mid-Victorian British Novel," *Victorian Literature and Culture* 31, no. 2, (2003): 510.

pier-glass parable, a problem of egoism, while reality is unstructured, "minutely and multitudinously scratched in all directions" (248). Observe that egoism in Eliot's parable, as in her plot, is itself a consequence of status: The pier glass, in which "scratches will seem to arrange themselves in a fine series of concentric circles," is "made to be rubbed by a housemaid." The mistake of seeing a pattern where there is none crucially begins with the distance generated by class hierarchy. Overcoming status biases leaves you with no direction. The reality of multitudinous scratches has the authority of "the serene light of science" shed by an "eminent philosopher" who is also a "friend [...]" (248), but the scientific reading too, observe, is undermined by Eliot's symbolic choices: the "light" of science is a parallel to the light of the candle which creates the illusion of concentricity, and stands the same risk of being eventually discovered as mere illusion. At Eliot's historical moment, a grappling in the dark, one step at a time, is all there is. The web urges a principle of careful moves, each negotiating interpersonal differences with persons on whom you depend. Characters are right to engage in denial because opening up to dependencies exposes them fully to constraints. In what follows I pay more sustained attention to the terms of negotiation.

Negotiating the Web: Dependence and Difference

Beer draws out connections between the web metaphor and Darwin's work, and points to a passage in *The Origin of the Species* which is particularly important here:

> It is interesting to contemplate an entangled bank, clothed with many plants of many kinds, with birds singing on the bushes, with various insects flitting about, and with worms crawling through the damp earth, and to reflect that these elaborately constructed forms, so *different* from each other, and *dependent* on each other in so complex a manner ....[16]
>
> (my emphasis)

This imagery – incredibly widespread as Regenia Gagnier shows in her work on conceptions of individualism[17] – provided a way of seeing. It replaced the categories of social status with intricacies too complex to claim holistic views, and crucially, at once interdependent and different. Far from optimistic visions that political-economic models and later evolutionary

16 Charles Darwin, *On the Origin of Species by Means of Natural Selection, or the Preservation of Favoured Races in the Struggle for Life* 1st ed. (London: John Murray, 1859), Chapter 14.

17 Regenia Gagnier, *Individualism, Decadence and Globalization: On the Relationship of Part to Whole*, 1859–1920 (Basingstoke: Palgrave Macmillan, 2010).

biology associated with this complexity, whereby the ever increasing differentiation resulting from the modern division of labor signaled progress,[18] *Middlemarch* relied on promises to explore the unhappy implications of dependence and difference in the web.

> "It will be treating me as if I were a child. Promise that you will leave the subject to me." … and thus the discussion ended with his promising Rosamond, and not with her promising him. In fact, she had been determined not to promise … She meant to go out riding again … and she did go on the next opportunity of her husband's absence.
>
> (549)

Promissory struggles are the symbolic locus of Lydgate's and Rosamond's quickly deteriorating marriage. When Rosamond rides again Lydgate realizes that what he sees as "[h]is superior knowledge" is "set aside on every practical question" (549). The loss of Rosamond's baby, which Lydgate attributes to horse-riding and Rosamond insists was inevitable irrespectively, clarifies how unbridgeable the gap is, as contestation dominates over a common grief. The pattern repeats itself. When Lydgate wants to let their house Rosamond revokes his instructions to the auctioneer. Lydgate is again painfully amazed but she does not see his point:

> "It cannot be good to act rashly … Promise me that you will not go to him [auctioneer] for a few weeks, or without telling me." Lydgate gave a short laugh. "I think it is I who should exact a promise that you will do nothing without telling me."
>
> (620–1)

Lydgate's bitterness signals a new awareness of difference between him and Rosamond within a structure of mutual dependence. The marital unit, that "terribly inflexible relation" (621), is the par excellence case of interdependence in which irreconcilable difference yields suffocation. Daniel Malachuk suggests that marriage is a prime location of Eliot's development of a liberalism influenced by republican traditions of civic virtue, and particularly the notion of sociable individuals.[19] Marriage, however, is but an extreme form of a persistent condition of dependence within difference, fundamental to Eliot's resort to promises in the novel.

Dependence within difference is a broad theme in *Middlemarch* scholarship, most extensively explored through work on sympathy, central to the

18 For an account see ibid., Chapter 1.

19 Daniel S. Malachuk, "George Eliot's Liberalism," in *A Companion to George Eliot*, eds. Amanda Anderson and Harry E. Shaw (Oxford: Wiley-Blackwell 2013), 370–84.

novel's content as well as to Eliot's own understanding of novels' ethical significance. Understood as form no less than content, sympathy points to relationality, premised on mutual dependencies, as a formal process undergirding literary realism. Rae Greiner, for instance, explains sympathy as a way of underwriting reality as a product of fellow feeling. The realist novel, she claims, prompts a particular imaginative experience: an intellectual and affective engagement which does not demand emotional identification but rather a "going along with" the mentalities of others – a term she derives from Adam Smith, whose *Theory of Moral Sentiments* is central to theories of sympathy in Victorian realism.[20] At once contextually minute and an abstract principle, sympathy is "the medium in which [microscopic transactions of exchange] take place."[21] Sympathy thus depends on relationality, ultimately enabling an integration into society by imagining worlds one does not inhabit.[22]

Greiner notes not only the role of interdependence but also the role of *difference* within the web of relations when she observes that sympathy does not deny individual separateness. Jean-Cristophe Agnew's reading of Adam Smith's concept of sympathy insists that difference was the crucial impulse in historical terms. "Fellow feeling was … a mark of immense distance that separated individual minds …,"[23] hence the need for *imaginative* experience. Mutual sympathy, Agnew goes on, "sprang, paradoxically, out of realization of mutual inaccessibility."[24] Inaccessibility is the dominating experience of difference in the misery between Lydgate and Rosamond, and for all its pain, was integral to Eliot's liberal outlook.

A short detour to cultural histories of late modern selfhood should allow us to recall the centrality of difference for liberal thinking more broadly and to clarify the specifics of Eliot's vision. As Charles Taylor tells the history of selfhood in *Sources of the Self*, in the late eighteenth century the idea of differences between individuals gained prominence. That individuals were different was nothing new, but now difference was no longer an

20 Rae Greiner, *Sympathetic Realism in Nineteenth-Century British Fiction* (Baltimore, MD: Johns Hopkins University Press, 2012).

21 Ibid., 30. The bracketed words are from Ian Duncan, *Scott's Shadow: The Novel in Romantic Edinburgh* (Princeton, NJ: Princeton University Press, 2007), part of a discussion of the real in Adam Smith.

22 Ablow argues for a significant continuity between realist form and idealized families, a claim speaking to the relationality (idealized relationality) of the form from a different perspective. Rachel Ablow, *The Marriage of Minds: Reading Sympathy in the Victorian Marriage Plot* (Stanford, CA: Stanford University Press, 2007).

23 Jean-Chrisophe Agnew, *Worlds Apart: The Market and the Theater in Anglo-American Thought, 1550–1750* (Cambridge: Cambridge University Press, 1986), 178. Kornbluh similarly emphasizes the self-interested projection involved in Smithian sympathy. Anna Kornbluh, *Realizing Capital: Financial and Psychic Economies in Victorian Form* (New York: Fordham University Press, 2014), 83.

24 Agnew, *Worlds Apart*, 179.

unimportant variation on the same basic human nature; rather, each person's originality became crucial for how she ought to live: a moral source. The importance of originality or uniqueness, together with the ideals based on disengaged reason, became the heart of modern identity.[25] Dror Wahrman confirms a similar historical turn through a diversified cultural investigation. On his account, toward the end of the eighteenth century something akin to a cultural revolution took place in England. Invoked into shape at the demise of the American war, a new regime of identity, or understanding of the self, emerged. Under the new regime identity came to mean that quintessential uniqueness that separates a person from all others, a regime of "*individual identity*." The new perception replaced abruptly the "ancien régime of identity" based on "*intersubjective identicality*" which was in place during most of the eighteenth century. The *ancien régime* was outward, or socially turned, more concerned with what persons had in common; *ancien régime* identity was determined by a matrix of social relations.[26] These claims are in line with George Simmel, who identifies two kinds, or stages, of historical individualism in modernity. The nineteenth century was a second stage (after an earlier focus on the individual/collectivity tension), with an individualism that ponders the differences between individuals and their qualitative peculiarities.[27]

The rise of difference has also specifically literary histories, centered on characterization, that Deidre Lynch has called "the business of inner meaning."[28] The famous anchor for histories here is Ian Watt's classical study which associated the rise of the novel with the individualist emphasis on

25 Charles Taylor, *Sources of the Self: The Making of Modern Identity* (Cambridge: Cambridge University Press, 1989), *passim*, 375. See also Mauss's account of the historical emergence of the concept of the indivisible innate self in a long process reaching its peak toward the end of the eighteenth century. Marcel Mauss, "A Category of the Human Mind: The Notion of Person; the Notion of Self," in *The Category of the Person: Anthropology, Philosophy, History*, eds. Michael Carruthers *et al.* (Cambridge: Cambridge University Press, 1985), 1–25. See generally Roy Porter, ed., *Rewriting the Self: Histories from the Renaissance to the Present* (London: Routledge, 1997), for discussions of the historical emergence of modern selfhood.

26 Wahrman, *The Making of the Modern Self*, 88.

27 Georg Simmel, *The Philosophy of Money*, 3rd ed., trans. Tom Bottomore and David Frisby, ed. David Frisby, 3rd ed. (New York: Routledge, 2004), 362–3. See also Niklas Luhmann, *Love as Passion: The Codification of Intimacy*, trans. Jeremy Gaines and Doris L. Jones (Cambridge, MA: Harvard University Press, 1986) for a similar periodization. And see Richard Sennett, *The Fall of Public Man: On the Social Psychology of Capitalism* (New York: Vintage Books, 1978). Sennett argues that the belief in immanent facts in the nineteenth century, representing the second stage of secularization after the first stage of eighteenth-century belief in transcendental Nature, explains the emphasis on difference between individual personalities, which was taken to be the very basis of social existence.

28 Deidre Shauna Lynch, *The Economy of Character: Novels, Market Culture, and the Business of Inner Meaning* (Chicago, IL: University of Chicago Press, 1998).

inner subjectivity.[29] As Lynch reminds us, the psychological depth of fictional characters is not simply an instance of novels giving literary form to ideologies, but rather a historical locus of action at which readers defined themselves relationally. On her analysis the pressure was on consumers to mark themselves as competent readers within an emerging mass commercial culture.[30] Audrey Jaffe highlights a different pressure, that of statistical thinking which drew readers into a finely-tuned analysis of averages and divergences from them, to construe the locus of identity. *Middlemarch,* she says, epitomizes that construction of nineteenth century character.[31] Nancy Armstrong articulates the argument most broadly when she claims that the history of the novel and the history of the modern subject – who has interiority in excess of the social position (but, Jaffe would add, is only meaningful in reference to an average), are one and the same.[32]

Eliot's interest in the negotiation of differences between persons confirms the emphases of these histories. However, her no less intensive interest in interdependence as an ensuing consciousness, and the crucial assumption that individuals are not given but rather in a constant state of *becoming* through relationships, "altering with the double change of self and beholder" (88), offered a unique perspective. The self, on Eliot's account, is not a stable innate core, as Wharman insists in describing the modern regime of individual identity. To extend the many criticisms of the history of the innate self,[33] one might describe Eliotian selfhood by drawing on the old and new together, as "intersubjective identity." The self develops by being socially turned and outwardly oriented, yet its outwardness is oriented to individualized relationships rather than status-based social relations.

29 Ian Watt, *The Rise of the Novel: Studies in Defoe, Richardson and Fielding* (Berkeley, CA: University of California Press, 1957). Lynch challenges his periodization and effectively offers a literary parallel to the cultural histories of selfhood just discussed; on her account, characterization understood as the representation of subjectivity only emerged from the 1770s, whereas earlier novels relied on types.

30 Lynch, *The Economy of Character.*

31 Audrey Jaffe, *The Affective Life of the Average Man: The Victorian Novel and the Stock-Market Graph* (Columbus, OH: Ohio State University Press, 2010), Chapter 1. Jaffe does argue that the common self is the consumer who wants what others want. Ibid., 39–40.

32 Nancy Armstrong, *How Novels Think: The Limits of British Individualism From 1719–1900* (New York: Columbia University Press, 2005).

33 E.g., Kate Flint addresses Taylor's argument (supra note 25 and accompanying text), and suggests that women's work problematizes the history of a stable idea of innate selfhood, posing a more social (gendered) model. Kate Flint, "'As a Rule, I Does Not Mean I': Personal Identity and the Victorian Woman Poet," in Porter, *Rewriting the Self,* 156–66. Lynda Nead likewise discusses social space as an active part rather than passive backdrop to the formation of identity. Lynda Nead, "Mapping the Self: Gender, Space and Modernity in Mid-Victorian London," in Porter, *Rewriting the Self,* 167–85.

While intersubjective identity is a socially-turned vision of selfhood, it is not the kind of social vision that leftist criticism would espouse. Daniel Cottom, for instance, argues that representations of discrete relationships are not truly social but rather the mark of individuality discovered or evolved through experience.[34] In this exaltation of individuality, Cottom claims, liberal intellectuals – Eliot among them – were providing a metaphysics for the basic middle-class theory of economic and social practice. The intensive attention Eliot paid to the difficulty of isolating the individual is for Cottom a measure of the demand that the individual appear to be real and the real basis of all understanding, and so Eliot came close to the abstract ideal of individuality.[35] As discussed in Chapter 1, historical assessments of Victorian liberalism in contracts repeatedly point to the conceptual association between promise and the abstract ideal of individuality, and clarify its significance: The image of the abstract individual who was a rational market player did not represent a form of naïve blindness but rather an ambitious normative vision serviceable in a reorientation of social structures toward market paradigms.

While I concur with Cottom that Eliot was seeking to move beyond class, or more broadly status, the particular style of liberalism that she espoused cannot be collapsed with ideals of abstract individuality.[36] This is clearest when *Middlemarch's* promissory representations are examined; relying on promises as paradigms for countering dependence within difference, rather than expressing a predetermined innate self, Eliot elaborated a dynamic of becoming that was thoroughly socialized, but not in class or similarly broad ascriptive structures; the web was a socialization in relationships, a vision that requires historicization within the complexities of liberalism, rather than external critiques.

Alex Woloch's *The One vs. The Many* reveals the deep-reaching implications of relational becoming on the level of narrative structure. The "character system" in Woloch's terms is the overall structure of a novel (or any narrative) in which attention is asymmetrically allocated among different characters, each character occupying a *space* which frames the interaction between the implied individual and the overall narrative form.

34 Watt already articulated the claim that the obsession with relationships was a consequence of individualism, although his argument was also that relationships compensated for the undermining of status cohesions, "offering the individual a more conscious and selective pattern of social life." Watt, *Rise of the Novel*, 177

35 Daniel Cottom, *Social Figures: George Eliot, Social History, and Literary Representation* (Minneapolis, MN: University of Minnesota Press, 1987).

36 See also Bigelow's argument that Eliot's intersubjective vision was resistant to atomistic individualism developed in neoclassical economics, particularly Jevons'. Gordon Bigelow, "The Cost of Everything in *Middlemarch*," in *Economic Women: Essays on Desire and Dispossession in Nineteenth-Century British Culture*, eds. Lana L. Dalley and Jill Rappoport (Columbus, OH: Ohio State University Press, 2013), 97–109.

If characters do not always gain relationships in the plot, their character spaces, belonging to a single narrative structure, inevitably do. Characters depend on one another; in particular, the celebrated interior depth of novelistic characterization requires the distortions of its absence in minor characters. Woloch goes on to argue for the social meaning of the form, invoking two central concerns of the high era of realism: democracy and capitalism. With respect to both, the fact of representation of minor characters registers a dual sentiment: a pull toward inclusiveness, evident by the very appearance of multiplicity and social expansiveness in literary representation, and the failures of democracy and of capitalism, perhaps not just accepted but also reinforced by the existence of minor-ness, and by the distortions it produces for non-protagonists; on Woloch's account minor characters are ultimately the proletariat of the novel. To (mildly) apply Woloch's theory to his own work, observe that his attention to system, and so to novels' distributive schemes, leaves less theorized what is perhaps his central argument, namely that "the realist novel is structurally destabilized not by too many details … but by *too many people*."[37] To become distributive systems, novels rely on the interdependencies of character spaces; these interdependencies are irreducible to a single repeated form but rather are endlessly variable, made of dynamic interactions, and so "the fictional individual gets elaborated in numerous ways."[38] This basis of character systems resonates with the vision of individuality in Eliot as a process of multiple interdependencies. Woloch's theory, in other words, reveals not just the way that literary form became homologous with large-scale social conditions of inequality in capitalism, but also how it performed a particular liberal ideology of individuality. This performance is possibly more radical than that of content, because on the level of the form the process of relational becoming does not leave behind even minor characters, who are left behind ("flat" or "undeveloped") in content.

Eliot's vision of selfhood as a dynamic becoming led to a concern that dominates *Middlemarch*: relational pressures might lead to annihilation of the self (again, concerns with minor-ness in terms of Woloch's theory seem to capture the point) no less than status-induced blindness which annihilates individual concreteness. Promises were uniquely placed to examine the problem of relational annihilation for they raised the classical liberal concern with voluntary submission, whereby persons, supposedly no longer constrained by statuses, gave up freedom through acts of will, precisely those acts supposed to represent the rule of freedom.

The classical Victorian articulation of the liberal concern with voluntary submission was in J.S. Mill's *On Liberty*. Mill justified legal and popular

37 Alex Woloch, *The One vs. the Many: Minor Characters and the Space of the Protagonist in the Novel* (Princeton, NJ: Princeton University Press, 2003), 19 (Woloch's emphasis).

38 Ibid., 177.

objections to the contract of slavery, the paradigm of voluntary submission: "The principle of freedom cannot require that he should be free not to be free" he argued, for such freedom defeats its own purpose.[39] His objection to the contract of slavery gave rise to generations of debate about paternalism; political and legal philosophy continues to debate whether Mill failed in sustaining his principle of self-sovereignty when he supported the social overriding of voluntary commitments which he himself described as concerning only the individual. However, framing the problem in terms of the classic antagonism between the social and the individual is hardly helpful in *Middlemarch* which concerns itself with the more nuanced second part of Mill's position: the inescapable submissions involved in everyday contexts, within the "less marked vicissitudes which are constantly shifting the boundaries of social intercourse" (88). Mill recognized that the logic of freely agreeing to not be free had a "far wider application" than slavery. Yet, he said, "a limit is everywhere set … by the necessities of life, which continually require, not indeed that we should resign our freedom, but that we should consent to this and the other limitation of it."[40] *Middlemarch* interrogated precisely such necessities of life, making mundane limitations on freedom far more central than the principle of liberty itself in its fictional world. While Mill moved on to ask about the liberty to retract from contracts, Eliot worried about the inescapability of living with them. In the struggle to articulate terms of action exceeding statuses, the fear was that there were no significant spaces for freedom. Eliot's liberalism constituted the relational subject whose achievement was rooted in compromise, attained first by the management of personal economies. The turn to economy to overcome suffocation and find meaning was at once bold and insecure, as I now turn to argue.

Compromise and Economic Wisdom

The final stage in the adjustment stories of *Middlemarch's* protagonists is figuratively tied with the final stage of the promissory stories, in which promissory obligation overwhelms each.

Lydgate bends to ask Bulstrode for a loan, and in an exasperating circumstantial twist involving him in Raffles' suspected murder, he brings his marriage and career to a near-breaking-point from which they never fully recover. With this over-straining of narrative causality, contractual debt has forced constraints on Lydgate not just practically but as a matter of perception. By all accounts "a successful man" (782) the narrator assures us, Lydgate nonetheless spent his life considering himself a failure.

39 John Stuart Mill, *On Liberty* (London: Penguin Books, 1974) (1859), 173.
40 Ibid.

Fred's debt too shakes him into full awakening. Remorse bites when he faces Mary's parents, in a moment of intersubjectivity:

> [W]e are most of us brought up in the notion that the highest motive for not doing a wrong is something irrespective of the beings who would suffer the wrong. But at this moment he [Fred] suddenly saw himself as a pitiful rascal who was robbing two women of their savings. (234)

The meaning of Fred's debt is now tied with concrete otherness. The reversal of self-reflex, which in Lydgate's case ends in sad disappointment, in Fred's story leads to salvation. Failure need not be the final experience; Eliot's emphasis instead was on the new awareness forced by the route of promissory obstacles.

Lydgate's and Fred's contracted debts place demands on their consciousness which begin and end with economy. Lydgate, who began with disregard for small economies realizes that he should learn to count half-crowns. Compared to Rosamond, Lydgate is dynamic, willing to shed "habits" and deal with an unknown as if it is, indeed, unknown: "Having been roused to discern consequences which he had never been in the habit of tracing, he was preparing to act on this discernment with some of the rigour (by no means all) that he would have applied in pursuing experiment" (554). Lydgate's efforts to readjust bespeak a romantic version of popular household economy, whereby economizing is a route to material and spiritual independence which would reduce suffocation in the web.

The formal route that Lydgate seeks is Smilean self-help: "To secure independence," preached Samuel Smiles in his best seller, "the practice of simple economy is all that is necessary. Economy requires neither superior courage nor eminent virtue; it is satisfied with ordinary energy, and the capacity of average minds."[41] Lydgate is determined to stop the "wonderful ... amount of money [that] slips away" in their housekeeping (610), a measure he indeed views as simple. His frustration is that indebtedness entangles him in "abject calculations" and makes him needy, as Smiles warned his readers' lack of economy would. As Coleman notes, thrift was a requirement that underlay secular and religious manifestations of classical political economy alike, and was central to all its popularizers.[42] But Lydgate only understands how urgent economy is for him when there is no way out, for learning to economize comes with learning to understand Rosamond, no less of an experiment, and much less obliging.

41 Samuel Smiles, *Self-Help: National and Individual* (Cambridge: Cambridge University Press, 1859), 195, http://dl4a.org/uploads/pdf/Samuel%20Smiles%20-%20Self-Help%20-%20National%20and%20Individual.pdf

42 Coleman, *George Eliot and Money*, 34.

Rosamond operates with a different economic consciousness, and counters Lydgate's thrifty ideas with two alternative economic plans: that Lydgate should ask his relatives for help, and that he should enlarge his practice by compromising his professional principles and indulging Middlemarch preferences, like sending out medicines. Lydgate dismisses her suggestions: "That is not the question between us" (611). It is just the question of course. Lydgate, once conscious of relational constraints, wants economy that would minimize them, while Rosamond remains obstinately committed to class practices; she proposes matching economic plans that take for granted social dependence in the traditional sense of status sociality, with always-deferred economizing, and with social ascription determining action.

Fred gets to learn in time. He socializes into the Garth style of careful economies, his initiation involving disliked "desk-work" needed for him "to understand the accounts and get the values into [his] head" (531). Fred learns to "be remarkably prudent, and save money every year" (778). The learning wins him the Featherstone estate that could not be gained through inheritance, and he is eventually successful as a "theoretic and practical" farmer, publishing "work on the 'Cultivation of Green Crops and the Economy of Cattle-Feeding'" (779). Fred does accounts only as a stepping stone from which to rise above the paradigmatic bourgeoisie desk upward to Eliot's espoused intellectual labor, and outward to romanticized agricultural labor. Fred and Lydgate learn, like average people, to think about money carefully so that they can be free from "money-craving" (609) – and so not think about money, as Smiles urged: "[Economy] does not make money an idol, but regards it as a useful agent;"[43] this would free them to self-realization, denied to Lydgate but achieved by Fred who is saved from being "a curate in debt for horse-hire and cambric pocket-handkerchiefs," that is, from the suffocation of social-status dependencies which must also lead to the wrong profession.

In a reversal of Lydgate's trajectory, flowing from inability to economize, Fred's economizing, described by Garth as soul saving (531), wins for him aspired love and career of the kind that Lydgate had lost. The importance of inverse trajectories is pressed on readers when Fred observes their "strange reversal of attitudes" (632). Fred could well enter Smiles' endless lists of exemplary men, while Lydgate lives to regret that he never could.

Economizing is recognized by Lydgate and Fred as a procedural way out of a conundrum that Franco Moretti finds in Eliot's work: He argues that Eliot espoused the Weberian paradigm that opposed "vocation" as a depersonalized sphere to "everyday life" and maintained that one must be sacrificed to the other.[44] In invoking the advice of Smiles, "[t]he mid-

43 Smiles, *Self-Help*.

44 Franco Moretti, *The Way of the World: The Bildungsroman in European Culture* (New York: Verso, 2000), 216–21.

Victorian embodiment of … respect for self-command at a practical and daily level,"[45] Eliot sought ways of reconciling the daily with the vocational. Lydgate and Fred practice economy, or want to practice it, so as to avoid sacrifice and become ideal persons of political economy whose labor is properly a source of value, not just economic but spiritual.

But Eliot was far from certain that economic advice could carry the weight of re-hallowing life without the aid of an overt religious ethic,[46] possibly even in opposition to Christianity's too-strict demands;[47] she heeded the advice without the celebratory tones. The boldness of her effort came to the test in Dorothea's plot. As with Lydgate and Fred, here too Eliot led Dorothea at the last stage of her adjustment story toward economizing. However, gendered oppositions disrupted the trajectory which appears pretty simple, even reductive, with Lydgate and Fred. Dorothea's story exposed both the role of economizing at the heart of *Middlemarch's* liberal vision, and Eliot's insecurity that it worked. To see how, we should follow through the breakdown of the pattern whereby promissory obligation reveals relational suffocations – and economizing signals relief.

While the promissory stories of Fred and Lydgate drive their process of adjustment from the start, with Dorothea the promise appears at a late stage, representing a high point in the difficult acknowledgement of her distance from Casaubon's "centre of self" (198). Casaubon's demand arrives when Dorothea is at once as involved in his work as she had hoped, and conscious of its futility. The problem is not the force of a promise to the dead as sometimes argued[48] but rather the lived process of Dorothea's relational becoming; the literary device of empty promise shifts attention from its content to Dorothea's problem. She has come to appreciate her difference from Casaubon concretely as confinement, but still finds it difficult to part with her devotional ideals. Casaubon's death is not the end of the process. To finally refuse requires placing the promise on a level with those of Fred and Lydgate, a nontrivial feat that Eliot achieved through Casaubon's will.

Postmortem, the deathbed promise obtains unimagined content: Dorothea assumed that Casaubon wanted to engage her in his scholarship, but the codicil tells her that Casaubon worried about Will. Conditioning her inheritance on not marrying Will, the codicil forces a shift of focus from an elevated devotion of efforts that characterized Dorothea's

45 John R. Reed, *Victorian Will* (Columbus, OH: Ohio University Press, 1989), 10.

46 On Eliot's implicit alliance with a Christian pattern of renunciation as freedom see ibid., Chapter 15.

47 As Blumberg suggests in her reading of mid-century novels. Ilana M. Blumberg, *Victorian Sacrifice: Ethics and Economics in Mid-Century Novels* (Columbus, OH: Ohio State University Press, 2013).

48 E.g., Melissa J. Ganz, "Binding the Will: George Eliot and the Practice of Promising," *ELH* 75, no. 3 (2008): 565–602.

misconceived marriage, to a personalized place for money. Eliot reduced Dorothea's drama to the banality of her male protagonists, locating the problem of relational suffocation at the level of economy. She was explicit about her move: Lydgate's debts, representing "small solicitations of circumstance" (736), like Fred's "miserably small" debts (111), are "a commoner history of perdition than any single momentous bargain" (736). As Henry James summarized Lydgate's story, "It is a tragedy based on unpaid butchers' bills, and the urgent need for small economies."[49] The novel's meaning develops through small economies, and so Dorothea gets there too.

Dorothea's promissory plot ends not when Casaubon dies but when she remarries. In uniting with Will, Dorothea effectively refuses at last the promise requested by Casaubon, bringing to a pitch her process of adjustment. In consequence, she is not just resigned but astoundingly excited to embrace the threat of the codicil and become a woman who learns what everything costs. On the surface, Dorothea's economizing is one with Fred's and Lydgate's: she finally says NO to Casaubon and so reduces the implications of relational suffocation. Dorothea's economizing brings her story to level with Fred and Lydgate as persons who understand what it means to truly be *in* the world, finally comprehending constraints implied by interdependence within difference and working through them. Dorothea's other-worldliness is definitively overcome.[50]

However, Dorothea's move does not work well because her way of being *in* the world shrinks her existence. She gives up the position of benevolent patron of social justice to become an economizing person. Critics have offered various explanations for her choice. Dorothea's union with Will might, for instance, be consistent within Kantian ethics, or be read as a turn away from Christian asceticism which requires extreme self-denial toward middle grounds.[51] The novel itself suggests Dorothea had little choice because gender oppression undermined her subversive economics. At the opening of the novel Brooke dismisses Dorothea's economic plans because "Young ladies don't understand political economy" (16). As Anna Kornbluh shows, the novel took pains to contrast her expansive vision with Smithian political economy.[52] Dorothea's schemes clearly posed a challenge to classical political economy and had therefore been consistently thwarted

49 Patrick Swinden, ed., *George Eliot, Middlemarch: A Casebook* (London: Macmillan, 1972), 60, 65 (citing Henry James, *Galaxy*, March 1873).

50 As Gallagher notes, Dorothea also achieves embodiment. Gallagher, "George Eliot: Immanent Victorian."

51 Respectively, Coleman, *George Eliot and Money*; Blumberg, *Victorian Sacrifice*, Chapter 3 (I am adapting Blumberg's claims with regard to *Adam Bede*).

52 Kornbluh, *Realizing Capital*, Chapter 3. See also Coleman's suggestion that the theory would require that investments of the kind she proposes should command an increase in rent, Coleman, *George Eliot and Money*, 96.

by the men around her before and after Casaubon. In desperation she tries to study directly the dismal science, only to find that she cannot:

> She sat down in the library before her particular little heap of books on political economy … trying to get light as to the best way of spending money so as not to injure one's neighbors, or – what comes to the same thing – so as to do them the most good … Unhappily her mind slipped off it for a whole hour; and at the end she found herself reading sentences twice over with an intense consciousness of many things, but not of any one thing contained in the text. This was hopeless.
> (756)

By this point male oppression has led to complete alienation: Dorothea lacks access to language that would frame her ideas; the sentences stir. She is at a loss when Will appears on the scene which ends with their union in the immortal "and I will learn what everything costs" (762). Dorothea endorses personal economizing as a way out of the gendered constraints which made her economic ideas inoperable and finally inaccessible even to herself.[53]

These explanations clarify Dorothea's turn from public to private, but do not capture the reason that the turn fails to work; after all, *Middlemarch*, like other novels, repeated the privatizing maneuver incessantly in its search for existential meaning in everyday life. What undermines the coherence of Dorothea's story is not the replacement of private for public in itself, but rather that Dorothea's embrace of the private relies on turning *to* economizing, rather than recognizing economizing as a procedure leading to greater things. Economizing *is* her union with Will: it is consummated in learning what everything costs, in a moment that confirms in the extreme Nancy Henry's argument that for Eliot all relationships are also economic relationships.[54] Economizing becomes an end in itself, replacing rather than enabling benevolence. This structure unsettles the logic of economizing, and more broadly of the private-public dialectic whereby private deeds of duty make the world go round, espoused in the plots of Fred and Lydgate.

The difficulty of moving *to* rather than *from* economizing explains why Dorothea's and Will's union is a famously anticlimactic scene which has exasperated generations of readers. Eliot had built toward it throughout

53 As Andrew Miller points out, economizing, and cutting down on dresses, is also a way out of another gendered constraint, that of avoiding a commodified subjectivity which threatened women. Andrew Miller, *Novels Behind Glass: Commodity Culture and Victorian Narrative* (Cambridge University Press, 1995), Chapter 6.

54 Nancy Henry, "George Eliot and Finance" in Anderson and Shaw, *A Companion to George Eliot*, 330.

the novel, but in frustrating the basic logic of her plot she halted the sexual and emotional excitement that should have offered a sense of closure, and no thunderbolts in the background could recharge the scene. Kornbluh sees the thunderbolts as part of an artifice which calls attention to the problematic of Dorothea's compromise.[55] The point is not the compromise in itself, but the way it signals a subversion of a logic otherwise informing the plot, whereby you compromise to attain something better. Economizing becomes not a solution to suffocation but part of the problem. This was a failure of closure. *Middlemarch's* finale was a second attempt to achieve it.

In the novel's famed ending, Dorothea achieves effects which are "incalculably diffusive" (785): in the last moment, with a rhetorical trick rather than narrated detail, Eliot wanted to free her female protagonist too from calculation for the greater good by virtue of economizing; she replaced the romanticized commitment to always calculate made in the union scene, with incalculability. Yet, success here depends on quick forgetfulness: incalculability was part of a finale that finalizes almost nothing, as Hillis Miller observes,[56] not even rhetorically. Just before Dorothea's incalculability, Eliot confirmed that it was the consequence of her being "absorbed into the life of another" (783); she invoked again status oppressions – a point I examine further in the next chapter, and so undermined Dorothea's turn to private economy as meaningful. For all her efforts, with Dorothea Eliot seemed unable to close the gap between "small economies" and existential meaningfulness. Dorothea's achievements remain equivocal.

Kornbluh concludes that *Middlemarch's* equivocations sounded a warning about the fatality of the burgeoning capitalist economy.[57] The sounding of warning, however, is also often a way of living in peace with what you should resist with might, as Dorothea once wanted to. Eliot's socialized capitalist order of relational dependencies offered a "diffusive" sense of hope that you could embrace without thereby being the fool who does not realize all the suffocations involved. As Martijn Konings says, "[c]apitalist socialization involves productive admixtures of hope and disappointment, illusion and disillusion."[58] Kornbluh acutely studies Eliot's use of parabasis – moments in which the narrator stands beside the text to comment on it, as a formal performance of the irony of the novel's own alliances with capitalist solutions. Yet this "standing beside" enables *Middlemarch.* To exist unrevolutionarily – and successfully – within the capitalist order without being naïve is the paradoxical consciousness that haunts many still.

55 Kornbluh, *Realizing Capital*, 87.

56 J. Hillis Miller, "A Conclusion in Which Almost Nothing is Concluded: *Middlemarch's* Finale," in Chase, *Middlemarch in the Twenty First Century*, 133–56.

57 She is concerned specifically with financial capitalism.

58 Martijn Konings, *The Emotional Logic of Capitalism: What Progressives Have Missed* (Stanford, CA: Stanford University Press, 2015), 62.

Limiting Masculinity in *The Mayor of Casterbridge*

Eliot's interest in suffocations, Williams argued, bespoke the beginnings of what we still call a modern consciousness. Fifteen years later Hardy was more clearly there. He was far more apprehensive than Eliot and lacked confidence in the possibility of liberation,[59] an outlook I want to examine through the problem of masculinity in contracts.

When contracts historians think about the patriarchal dimensions of modern contract law, the focus is often the place of women in political and economic life. Feminist contracts histories explore the broad spectrum of contracts involving female sexuality directly, from marriage to prostitution. From the perspective of contract as a general category, there have been two main focal points: the doctrinal logic of coverture, which denied married women's contractual capacity, and the ideology of separate spheres, which confined women to the domestic sphere, delimiting the imagination of their relevant contractual agency(ies) while the market was elaborated in contradistinction. The center of concern and debate in its broadest articulation is that the very notion of freedom to enter contracts is masculine because, as Carol Pateman argues, the individual is a patriarchal category.[60] It has become a critical commonplace to associate paradigms of abstract rationality, autonomy, and competitive action in liberal theory generally, and more specifically in contracts, with male prerogatives: "[A] correlation between the characteristics of masculinity and the ethos and philosophy of classical legal doctrine has been central to feminist engagements with the law."[61] Feminist histories have been struggling uphill in two directions, often in apparent tension but in fact fully complementary: to read women back into history and recover the limits of formal legal and ideological discourses in historical realities, and yet to reconstruct and explain the sources of women's disempowerment.

I have discussed some of the implications of contracts' masculinity for women in the previous chapter and return to them in Chapter 5, but in this chapter I want to look at what it meant for men by reading Hardy's *The Mayor of Casterbridge*. The novel's remarkable achievement is not merely in recognizing the centrality of masculinity in contracts, but in problematizing it as an operative model in the world of modern capitalism. Published at the outskirts of high Victorianism and located at the margins of realism, Hardy's tale, I argue, examined the masculinity of contracts as itself a form of unrealistic constraint, a ruinous imperative underwriting the novel's structure of tragedy.

59 Williams, *The English Novel*, 88.

60 Carole Pateman, *The Sexual Contract* (Stanford, CA: Stanford University Press, 1988).

61 Linda Mulcahy, "The Limitations of Love and Altruism – Feminist Perspectives on Contract Law," in *Feminist Perspectives on Contract Law*, eds. Linda Mulcahy and Sally Wheel (London: Glasshouse Press, 2005), 1.

Brief reminder: *The Mayor of Casterbridge* was part of Hardy's Wessex series. The novel opens with Michael Henchard selling his wife Sue and their daughter Elizabeth-Jane in a rural fair, under rum intoxication. When Henchard wakes up the next morning his wife and child are gone. After months of futile search he settles in the rural town of Casterbridge. Sue and her daughter arrive in Casterbridge nineteen years later to discover that Henchard is the town's mayor and a prominent hay and corn merchant. On the same day the Scottish Donald Fafrae too arrives. Henchard befriends and hires Farfrae to manage his business, and remarries Sue. While Casterbridge begins to experience industrialization, things deteriorate for Henchard on all fronts. Sensing his disadvantage with Farfrae, Henchard drives him out and eventually loses all positions to him: Farfrae opens a successful competing business while Henchard's business fails and is eventually bought by Farfrae, together with Henchard's house and his furniture; Farfrae also becomes the town's mayor, and marries Hanchard's old lover Lucetta. Concurrently, Sue dies and Henchard discovers that his daughter too had died young and that Elizabeth is the daughter of Sue's buyer; he drives Elizabeth out too, and comes to miss her. Lucetta dies after her past with Henchard is discovered. Elizabeth, whom Henchard only just wins back, marries Farfrae, and Henchard dies a poor outcast.

My reading of the novel proceeds through a number of arguments. First I examine the opening scene of wife sale. The sale stands in temporal and stylistic distance from the rest of the narrative which plots Henchard's downfall, yet foretells it not just causally but symbolically, for the problem throughout is the performance of masculinity in capitalism. Hardy's plotting of wife sale, I argue, invoked the theme of masculinity in contracts in the starkest way possible, while also already hinting at the necessary victimization of men.

I then turn to the downfall plot, in which Farfrae appears as Henchard's foil – a projection of Henchard without the rigid masculine debasement. A crucial starting point that becomes clear only with Farfrae in view, is that Henchard is caught up in a masculinity that he does not fully own, a compulsory masculinity (a concept I explain in a moment), which the novel underlines and motivates by giving Henchard an aberrant sexuality. Possibly a homosexual, Henchard is driven to exhibit masculine excesses that secure his downfall. In particular, the excesses implicate his promissory discourse and conduct. Enacting a formally strict version of atomistic individualism, Henchard insists on will and choice in disregard of constraints, while his foil exhibits the exact opposite sensibility; Farfrae is particularly sensitive to relational concerns, and so thrives in the industrializing setting of the novel while Henchard becomes increasingly detached from it. Farfrae represents a refined version of modern rationality, which rejects atomism in favor of relational sociality. Hardy, however, was hardly impressed with the historical change hence, I will argue in conclusion, the tragic form.

I use "compulsory masculinity" to gesture at the way *The Mayor of Casterbridge* represents Henchard's performance of an atomistic contractual logic as an unchosen, historically constituted imperative which he recognizes from a distance, as it were. Far from having a protagonist embodying the normative ideal of masculinity naturally, the ideal is exposed as ideological and socially mandated, demanding a performance forced on the body as much as on social interaction. The term of course invokes Adrienne Rich's work,[62] helpful here not only for the theory of identities as enforced norms which might work to the detriment of their bearers, but also for a more specific reason that will be clear when I discuss Henchard's wife sale below.

Overall, the novel's treatment of contracts is important in a number of distinct senses. First, it provides a literary articulation of atomistic individualism in contracts as a construct gendered at the core. Second, it implies that the masculine identity at stake is a victimizing cultural imperative. This outlook compensates for a particular blindspot in contracts histories, which (unlike theory) have read the gender of contracts from the perspective of women's exclusions, and have too often left the positive content – contracts' inclusions, to nongendered readings. Finally, *The Mayor of Casterbridge* suggested that the failure of the male contractual identity is a consequence of contracts' relationality, which emerges as the determining factor for prosperity in an industrializing world. This point moves the debate about gender beyond the historical claim that contracts remained wedded to statuses, particularly gender, and opens up another angle on Victorian relational conceptualizations of contracts.

Wife Sale

The Mayor of Casterbridge's concern with the masculinity of contracts is flagged in the novel's brutal opening scene, in which Henchard auctions and sells Sue. The sale is the first and looming failure in the plot of Henchard's fall as well as an encapsulation of the fall's logic.

Wife sales were illegal,[63] and widely considered rare, yet, as E.P. Thompson argued in his classic study of the history of wife sales, at stake was a ritualized plebian practice. Thompson identified 176 "authentic cases" between 1800 and 1880, with a notable decline from mid-century.[64]

62 Adrienne Rich, "Compulsory Heterosexuality and Lesbian Existence," *Signs: Journal of Women in Culture and Society* 5, no. 4 (1980): 631–60.

63 For a discussion see Sandra Berns, "Women in English Legal History: Subject (almost), Object (irrevocably), Person (not quite)," *University of Tasmania Law Review* 12, no. 1 (1993): 37 n.31, 38; Julie C. Suk, "The Moral and Legal Consequences of Wife Selling in *The Mayor of Casterbridge*," in *Subversion and Sympathy: Gender, Law and the British Novel*, eds. Martha C. Nussbaum and Alison LaCroix, (New York: Oxford University Press, 2013), 27–47.

64 E.P. Thompson, *Customs in Common* (London: Penguin 1991), Chapter 7.

The data's relation to the volume of actual incidences remains contested, with some historians arguing that sales were marginal.[65] Controversy about the probability of the plot began soon after the novel's publication.[66] Hardy insisted in his preface to a later edition that he had based the narrative on a real event. The question of historical significance has been tied up with the controversy about the interpretation of wife sales, which carries implications for reading Hardy's fictionalization.

Thompson interpreted wife sales as a form of divorce for the poor, often with the consent of the wife. His reading met with scathing feminist critiques that he partly conceded in saying, "One cannot always be reiterating the elemental organisation of a society and its gender relations."[67] The controversy between Thompson and his feminist critics was but an instance of an ongoing debate between functional accounts which associate sales with divorce needs of the poor within an unobliging legal and economic context, and critical assessments of sales as marks of patriarchy.

Read against the controversy, I suggest that Hardy's representation emphasized patriarchy over functionalist explanations. As Thompson himself argued, while Hardy's novel was a "powerful influence" asserted against indifference to wife sales, it was too stereotyped in its representation to match the ritual process of divorce. The details of the ritual, explains Lawrence Stone, were designed to emphasize the final nature of the separation and ensure community legitimation to a prearranged agreement.[68] Hardy's scene was lacking just there. Ritualized features, including the memorable use of a halter, are missing from Sue's sale, and most crucially, there is no preplanning. The buyer is a stranger, Henchard impulsive, senseless from drinking, and Sue, far from an active participant, is a victim who has met with the threat of sale in the past, and when it finally materializes proves to be the archetype of objectified consciousness: "I dared not desert him when he had paid so much for me in good faith" (73), she reflects back on her sale.

Thompson assumed that Hardy relied on middle-class newspaper reports which framed sales as low-class brutality, hence the misrepresentation.[69] However, the effect runs too deep into the novel's logic to be dismissed at that: the masculine logic of Henchard's promises will animate his downfall. The sale is a narrative benchmark in line with Pateman's point: Hardy's scene is a graphic illustration of sexual subordination as the

65 For a conclusion that sales were insignificant see Lawrence Stone, *Road to Divorce: England 1530–1987* (New York: Oxford University Press, 1995), 148.

66 Shanta Dutta, "Hardy and his Mayor: A Gendering of Critical Response," *The Thomas Hardy Journal* 19, no. 2 (2003): 33–40, reviews the controversy.

67 Thompson, *Customs in Common*, 458.

68 Stone, *Road to Divorce*, 143–8.

69 Thompson, *Customs in Common*, 404–5; Suk, " Moral and Legal Consequences," 35–6.

core of contract.[70] As Elaine Showlater argued in an article which inaugurated the discussion of masculinity in *The Mayor of Casterbridge*, the sale expressed women's subjugation in capitalism. Yet, within the novel's overall structure the point was not women's predicament as such – indeed from Sue's perspective there's a case to be made for the sale's benefits – but rather the backlash on men.[71] The novel's opening scene is a narration of masculine excess that will prove victimizing for Henchard for its disregard of relational constraints.[72]

Henchard's conduct is notably crude, intended to unsettle readers:

> For my part I don't see why men who have got wives and don't want 'em, shouldn't get rid of 'em as these gipsy fellows do their old horses … Why shouldn't they put 'em up and sell 'em by auction to men who are in need of such articles? Hey? Why, begad, I'd sell mine this minute if anybody would buy her!
>
> (11)

The conversation continues with male evaluations of Sue which treat her as if she were indeed an old horse, not least the narrator himself who says that Sue "was by no means ill-favoured" (11). Julie Suk argues that the scene begins as chattel sale, but with Sue's cooperation becomes a divorce and remarriage, thus offering a complex and uncertain picture of the sale's meaning.[73] Sue's consent, however, is prompted by her rising despair as Henchard ignores her imploration to stop; the consent operates to underline her humiliation, "the harshness of the act just ended" (15) and the beginning of backlash.

Hardy created a scene of female humiliation through contract in which Henchard acts out of his senses. Regretful Henchard will soon take a vow of temperance for twenty-one years (his age at the sale), the implication being that he would not otherwise have acted as he did. However, Henchard's miserable, formally self-inflicted and perfectly sober downfall before the end of the set term, in which additional promissory junctions

70 See Pateman's discussion of its relation to slavery, Pateman, *The Sexual Contract*, 121. See also Ann Heilmann, "Marriage," in *Thomas Hardy in Context*, ed. Phillip Mallett (Cambridge: Cambridge University Press, 2013), 354. Heilmann argues that Sue is an extreme representation of marriage as sexual trafficking.

71 Elaine Showlater, "The Unmanning of the Mayor of Casterbridge," in *Critical Approaches to the Fiction of Thomas Hardy*, ed. Dale Kramer, (London: Palgrave Macmillan, 1979), 99–115.

72 This argument differs from emphases on familial relations, for example by Showlater, ibid., and Armstrong, *How Novels Think*, 98. My argument focuses on the demands of modern capitalism specifically. Henchard does not change to accommodate relationality, but instead turns to the other side of the same coin: from aggressive willfulness to annihilation.

73 Suk, "Moral and Legal Consequences."

play part, reveals a different implication: the compulsion is not alcohol but rather a standard of masculinity that Henchard performs too strictly, to his own detriment.

The sale is set apart from the downfall plot in time – nineteen years, and in style – narrated with more distance than is used afterwards in the novel. Without broaching the vexed question of omniscience in Hardy's work, it is worth observing that in the downfall plot the narration often aligns with characters' viewpoints, while the sale is narrated strictly from afar, perhaps the clearest case of what Hillis Miller has called a "superficiality of consciousness."[74] And yet, both Hardy's play with narrative duration and with style make the sale the causal and symbolic generator of the downfall plot.

The nineteen years after the sale are the rise of Henchard as merchant and mayor. As George Levine argues, these years are Henchard's assertion of the absolute power of his self.[75] Henchard moves from poor hay-trusser to the heart of middle-class gentlemanliness as if in a liberal fairytale gone wild. His brutal contractual gesture miraculously translates into the core requirement of Victorian normative masculinity: as I explain below, the requirement is achievement attained through energetic effort, a hard-attained self-mastery, formally gestured in Henchard's vow of temperance, itself in line with popular advice to the lower classes.[76] Hardy's ellipsis, however, belittles the significance of the prosperous years; the plot turns directly to the downfall, before the term of the vow is over, insisting that the masculinity of contract, brutal in its low-class articulation and attractive

74 On Miller's argument, Hardy's and his characters' self-awareness is always involved in their awareness of the world. As a result there is no recognition of the intrinsic quality of the mind; the habitual stance of the narrator is of detachment which sees events from above them or from a time long after they have happened. J. Hillis Miller, *Thomas Hardy: Distance and Desire* (Cambridge, MA: Harvard University Press, 1970). Miller relates Hardy's style to a late nineteenth-century scientific objectivism in which human significance was eroded.

For additional discussions of Hardy's omniscience see for example Linda Shires, "'And I Was Unaware': The Unknowing Omniscience of Hardy's Narrators," in *Thomas Hardy: Texts and Contexts*, ed. Phillip Mallett (Basingstoke: Palgrave Macmillan, 2002), 31–48. Shires argues that Hardy questioned omniscience even as he relied on it, and was content with moments of not knowing. See also Neil Powell, "Thomas Hardy's *The Mayor of Casterbridge*," in *British Writers Classics, Vol. 2*, ed. Jay Parini (New York: Charles Scribner's Sons, 2004), 183. Powell suggests that the novel's narration is "only patchily omniscient" for "we do not have a full interior sense of Henchard." Norman Page, *Thomas Hardy: The Novels* (New York: Palgrave, 2001), calls Hardy's narration observant rather than omniscient.

75 George Levine, *The Realistic Imagination: English Fiction from Frankenstein to Lady Chatterly* (Chicago, IL: University of Chicago Press, 1981), 243–6.

76 Eric J. Hobsbawm, *The Age of Revolution 1789–1848* (New York: Vintage Books, 1996), Chapter 11.

when performed as middle-class energy, is one and the same. Further ellipses of shorter periods maintain the connection between the sale and other narrative events. These allow for retrospective gap-filling, completing the dramatic effect of the contract.

When the sale is revealed it haunts all corners of Henchard's environment anew:

> The amends he [Henchard] had made in after life were lost sight of in the dramatic glare of the original act ... the act having lain as dead and buried ever since, the interspace of years was unperceived; and the black spot of his youth wore an aspect of a recent crime.
>
> (218)

Presentiation, explained Ian Macneil, "is a recognition that the course of the future is so unalterably bound by present conditions that the future has been brought effectively into the present so that it may be dealt with just as if it were in fact the present."[77] Macneil explained the role of promises in helping people presentiate – reduce future choices.[78] With Sue's sale contract, the novel dramatizes a reverse presentiation: It denies the crucial assumption of control through promises, which it marks as a masculine fallacy; instead, not only does the text stretch the future beyond the control of the promissory moment, it allows the future to redefine the meaning of the present, negating all but the future's backlash.[79]

Even before readers read on, the sale scene itself speaks to the paradoxical meaning of compulsory masculinity which victimizes men, supposedly the gainers of modern gender constructions. When Rich elaborated Kathleen Gough's characteristics of male power, under the characteristic entitled "*to use them [women] as objects in male transactions*" she listed a host of things, the first four of which were "use of women as 'gifts'; bride-price; pimping; arranged marriages."[80] Each of these arguably captures elements of a wife sale, but not fully its implications. Missing in all of these options is the husband's pain. A wife sale, for all its gender brutality, is always on some level also painful because all visions of marriage, including the most patriarchal, implicate also the husband's identity to conceptualize the marital relation; whether the implication emphasizes psychological, social or

77 Ian Macneil, "Contracts: Adjustment of Long-Term Economic Relations Under Classical, Neoclassical, and Relational Contract Law," *Northwestern University Law Review* 72, no. 6 (1978): 863.

78 Ian Macneil, "Restatement (Second) of Contracts and Presentiation," *Virginia Law Review* 60, no. 4 (1974): 592.

79 These add up to my discussion in the Introduction warning against too quick a collapse of the relational vision of contract emerging here with Macneil's relational contract theory.

80 Rich, "Compulsory Heterosexuality," 639.

theological elements of the union is less crucial than the simple point that a parting with your wife cannot be entirely a matter of indifference. Henchard too experiences pain, which is integral to the novel's plot. This complexity in the specific category of wife sales, different from other forms of trafficking women, serves the project of examining compulsory masculinity as victimization of the empowered contractor. The remainder of the plot will get in closer touch with the meaning of men's victimhood so as to close the distance between the opening scene of wife sale narrated from afar, and the nearer narration of downfall.

Wearing Masculinity Like a Costume

Henchard's deviant sexuality has long been observed by readers. He is not only a misogynist, as he openly confesses (78), he is also uninterested in sex with women: "I solemnly declare that philandering with womankind has neither been my vice nor my virtue" (79). On the other hand he is attracted to Farfrae. "[H]ow that fellow does draw me" (57) he says to himself, and soon to Farfrae: [W]hen a man takes my fancy he takes it strong" (65). Farfrae "could play upon him as on an instrument" (274). Possibly a repressed homosexual,[81] Henchard at least displays an open rejection of normative heterosexual drives, at a felt tension – or perhaps ancient alliance – with his physique which is mythically male. He is a "stern a piece of virility" (274), of "heavy frame, large features, and commanding voice" (34).

Henchard's attraction to Farfrae leads to his spontaneous confession of his secret past, and so makes him, on his own understanding, vulnerable. In a quick reversal he therefore turns the friendship into an all-fronts competition of manliness. The competition involves symbolic scenes linking it with Henchard's insecure sexual identity, including a comparing of erections (in the form of town entertainments)[82] on Henchard's part, and a wrestling match. When the match ends Henchard is unable to hurt Farfrae; instead he confesses his love: "no man ever loved another as I did thee at one time" (273–4), and is left without sense of manliness: "[s]o thoroughly subdued ... that he remained on the sacks in a crouching attitude, unusual for a man, and for such a man. Its womanliness sat tragically on [his] figure ..." (274). Henchard realizes that Farfrae's appreciation remains his driving force: "my heart is true to you still!" (286).

The Mayor of Casterbridge was written in years in which conceptions of masculinity, particularly as they emerged from domestic ideology, were under strain. While, as John Tosh observes, to say that the ideology was in

81 As Jones insists: Tod E. Jones, "Michael Henchard: Hardy's Male Homosexual," *Victorian Newsletter* 86 (1994): 9–13.

82 As Jones notes, ibid., 12.

crisis would be a wild exaggeration, it was under enough pressure to allow Hardy, himself uncomfortable with demands of masculinity, to use his protagonist's sexuality to challenge the masculine discourse of control.[83] Henchard's distance from normative sexuality pushes him to an over-strained performance of atomistic individualism's assumptions in contracts and becomes a predicament within an unobliging context.

Contracting Like a Man

Henchard seizes symbols of normative masculinity almost with despair, particularly acts of will. His vow is a first act of control through will. The nineteen years of ellipsis deny the effectiveness of this act and the scheme crashes. The marks of the fall are then represented in promissory overload, that is, a multitude or clash of contracts which typically involve assumptions that contract is a realm of control. Henchard attempts to tame chance with contractual rationality, and to treat contract as a circumscribed realm of formal rights and duties, and so iterates the idea of isolated human agency through contract. His performance marks a continuing crisis

The opening promissory overload in the downfall plot concerns Henchard's business. He had supplied bad corn "in his contracts" (37) and caused a severe shortage of food supplies in the town. He refuses to replace the grown flour, arguing that the risk passed on to his customers (38). His customers, he says, "must make allowances for the accidents of a large business … You must bear in mind that the weather just at the harvest of that corn was worse than we have known it for years" (38). Henchard's defense is a symbolic attempt to tame chance, in this case, natural forces; he speaks as if nature is digestible within the contractual allocation of risks. Observe that while such moments in the novel invoke directly the Victorian debate on determinism and chance,[84] Hardy's concern was ultimately elsewhere: Henchard ignores a more direct source of predicament, namely, the fury of his customers, and that move, we shall see, marks him apart from Farfrae whose inverse trajectory occurs under the same natural conditions. The scene of customer outrage is a public dinner in which social relations determine the sitting at the table; the setting speaks to the interdependencies of which Henchard should be sensible: his contracts are inseparable from the socio-political setting.

83 John Tosh, *A Man's Place: Masculinity and the Middle-Class Home in Victorian England* (New Haven, CT: Yale University Press, 1999), 160. On Hardy's relation to masculinity see Margaret R. Higonnet, "Hardy and His Critics: Gender in the Interstices," in *A Companion to Thomas Hardy*, ed. Keith Wilson (Malden, MA: Blackwell, 2009), 117–29; Elizabeth Langland, "Hardy and Masculinity," in Mallett, *Thomas Hardy in Context*, 374–83.

84 See e.g., Ian Hacking, "Nineteenth Century Cracks in the Concept of Determinism," *Journal of the History of Ideas* 44, no. 3(1983): 455–75.

Farfrae's position as foil begins here as he duly arrives to suggest a solution that saves Henchard. Farfrae performs a sensitive, relational and at the same time heterosexual masculinity, an alternative model to Henchard's, suited to the emergent capitalism depicted in the plot. Before I explain further the models of masculinity at stake, it is worth adding yet another example to the picture.

A second promissory overload concerns Farfrae's engagement as manager of Henchard's business. The contract contradicts a promise Henchard had already made to another candidate, Joshua Jopp. When Jopp arrives Henchard bluntly says that Farfrae is the new manager and explains he engaged him since Jopp had not kept their Thursday appointment. Jopp presents Henchard's letter which named Thursday or Saturday as the appointment days, but Henchard replies: "well, you are too late" (66) and denies that he engaged Jopp, arguing that the engagement was subject to an interview. Henchard uses formal contractual reasoning to explain away his responsibility for a promissory failure, leaping with no little legalistic intuition from one defense to another. However, once again this is not the end of the story: The rationalist imperative, which uses formalities to cover for Henchard's attraction to Farfrae, meets Jopp's bitterness which returns to haunt Henchard on several occasions. The peak is Jopp's exposure of Lucetta's secret letters which leads to her death; this undoes a redeeming moment for Henchard, for Henchard only just promised to keep her secret.[85]

It is important to see that Hardy was not moralizing about promise keeping; instead he underlined Henchard's failure to carve contractual behavior and discourse to contextual constraints. Henchard's impossible position begins with the contingent set of circumstances which brought Farfrae to him in the interim period between the letter to Jopp and Jopp's arrival, and its meaning is determined by relational responses, yet Henchard refuses to acknowledge this picture, claiming instead to master the situation through formalities.

Henchard's model of control converses with a set of expectations that might be described as the conventional model of Victorian middle-class masculinity. While working-class masculine identities tended to be multiple and local, historians claim more hegemony in the middle and upper classes, achieved through the consumption of common cultural products, among them attending the same educational institutions and reading the

85 Or maybe he meant the exposure, because the continued traffic in women, and the implicit relation established through Lucetta between him and Farfrae are more essential in his promises. For the argument that Henchard wanted the exposure see Deanna K. Kreisel, *Economic Woman: Demand, Gender, and Narrative Closure in Eliot and Hardy* (Toronto: University of Toronto Press, 2012), 170.

same periodicals and novels which both taught and authorized manliness.[86]

Demands of conventional masculinity issued most pressingly from the domestic sphere, a point that historians interested in complicating the public/private divide emphasize. As Tosh argues, the home as a privileged site of subjectivity in the Victorian era was integral to masculinity.[87] Ben Griffin highlights a curious starting point for many of the demands of masculinity in the public world: the Victorian obsession with the avoidance of marital discord in the home. At stake in masculinity, then, was Victorian domestic ideology. That ideology was made up of religious ideas which from the end of the eighteenth century converged with gender panic and a consequent hardening of gender identities.[88] The ideology's chief tool toward marital harmony was the subordination of women to their husbands.[89] The logic of subordination, which turned women into altruist caregivers, underwrote the independence of men.

Independence was the key attribute of manliness, to be acquired through competition with one's peers. Independence suggested autonomy of action and opinion, and implied a host of personal qualities which had to be actively cultivated through self-improvement and self-discipline, among them energetic self-assertion – an aggressive mastery contrasted with female self-denial, will, straightforwardness, and courage – whether of physical or of moral kind was one of many contested points, especially between Evangelical and non-religiously inflected versions of masculinity.[90]

The conventional view of masculinity contained internal contradictions and was necessarily fluid, but was also just one of a multiplicity of models or styles of masculinity, among them models of deviant desires which Henchard absolutely refuses to entertain whenever he can help it; in his acts of will, primarily in his contracts, he denies deviance. Henchard's contractual style performs conventional expectations to an extreme. He is blunt rather than just straightforward, so willful that others "wince" under him (114), overly energetic, and in utter denial of relational dependencies. These performances invoke the formalist logic of strict rights and obligations of atomism in contracts which proceeded analytically by disregarding dependencies, and its ideological discourse of independence and freedom through willful self-authorship that historians have recounted. Henchard's

86 Ben Griffin, *The Politics of Gender in Victorian Britain: Masculinity, Political Culture and the Struggle for Women's Rights* (Cambridge: Cambridge University Press, 2012), 168–74.

87 Tosh, *A Man's Place.*

88 On the hardening of identities, whereby cultural demands for unambiguous and consistent displays of feminine and masculine roles escalated, see Dror Wahrman, *The Making of the Modern Self: Identity and Culture in Eighteenth Century England* (New Haven, CT: Yale University Press, 2004).

89 Griffin, *The Politics of Gender*, Chapter 1.

90 Tosh, *A Man's Place*, Chapter 5.

insecure identity, however, motivates the narration of all of these as superficial rigidities belied by his real motivations. That Henchard does not naturally meet the conventional standard but rather performs it aligns with the theoretical claim in masculinity studies that hegemony, being a historical construct, is established at a collective level; as Connell explains, hegemonic masculinity embodies a "currently accepted" strategy.[91] Demands of masculinity exert power even when the activities they promote are unavailable to the men who consent to them, as Bradley Deane explains.[92] Henchard exemplifies just that.

The model that Henchard performs fails through a refusal to internalize constraints. Farfrae exhibits a different middle-class model, most closely resonating with the so-called New Man. Before I explain it further I want to examine additional contractual overloads and bring Farfrae into the picture. My claim will be that Farfrae's capitalist success is tied up with a vision of rationality which is in fact not new but old, more apologetic for capitalism than Henchard's, and therefore not espoused by Hardy.

Contracting Like a New Man

Henchard's breaking of the promise to Jopp is the making of a promise to Farfrae. The hiring scene beams with erotic impulse and a reversal of typical power structures. Henchard shows "the inelegance of one whose feelings are nipped and wishes defeated" (64) and admits, "I like thee well!" (64). When he hires Farfrae, on terms that he asks Farfrae himself to set, he insists on lodging him in his house.[93] Within this complete reversal of employer/employee disparities, of detached rationality, and of formality, Henchard nonetheless offers a formal contract "so as to be comfortable in our minds … [W]e will … settle terms in black-and-white if you like; though my word's my bond" (65). The gesture exposes a tension, inherent in conventional Victorian masculinity, between adaptations to the commercial age, which Henchard associates with a written contract, and traditional heroic and homosocial concepts of masculinity, which resonate in the proud and informal "my word's my bond."[94] Henchard commits to both, as if to solidify his manliness on all sides, but they are equally empty for Henchard's relation to Farfrae is governed by more passionate impulses; his vulnerability soon pushes him to competitive exhibitions of manliness, and so in disregard of his written and spoken word he dismisses Farfrae, who opens his own business.

91 R.W. Connell, *Masculinities* 2nd ed. (Berkeley, CA: University of California Press. 2005), 77.

92 Bradley Deane, *Masculinity and the New Imperialism: Rewriting Manhood in British Popular Literature, 1870–1914* (Cambridge: Cambridge University Press, 2014), 7.

93 As Showlater argued, the employment has the overtones of marriage. Showlater, "Unmanning," 106.

94 On the tension generally see Tosh, *A Man's Place*, 6–7.

While competing with Farfrae, Henchard insists repeatedly that he engages in "fair buying and selling" (113). However, his language of contractual rationality is set against a passionate relational enmity, with no-longer friendly town councilmen to warn him, each having "individually" (114) suffered under Henchard's hands, and with the angry Jopp as a "commercially unsafe" (184) colleague enlisted to do the buying and selling. Against all this relational trouble, Henchard suffers irrecoverable losses. The narrator contradicts Henchard's rationalist language, and describes his commerce as "mortal commercial combat" (116). James Eli Adams offers a historical explanation: he suggests that "the grain market could become an arena of masculine rivalry as fierce and nearly as destructive as a duel by sword" in "the years straddling the abolition of the Corn Laws in 1846, as well as the sometimes ferocious aggression informing the career of the self-made man."[95] However, Hardy's efforts were geared toward the symbolic failure of conventional masculinity in an emergent capitalism no less than toward a referential account.

Passions and interests appear in reverse in Henchard's "combat," as if to confirm his unsuitability to the capitalist world that Albert Hirschman found in early ideological arguments for capitalism.[96] As Hirschman argued, the world of economic self-interest became the basis of the modern social order in the wake of an intellectual fascination of elites with the possibility that the once-suspicious passion for wealth would overcome other passions which blinded men, among them lust for power and sexual lust. Capitalist interest in gain was framed as innocent and undangerous, The anticipated result was a civilizing effect whereby men become predictable, steadfast and methodical, that is, everything that Henchard, blinded by passionate jealousy and a desperate need for respect, is not. His commercial dealings breach the model of tamed passions, and create an unsustainable excess, a combat where commerce was to be associated with peace.[97]

The emerging world of the novel is of tamed passions, as critics often observe. David Musselwhite for instance argued that the novel depicted the over-coding and supplanting of an agrarian, rural, territorial regime represented by Henchard, by an imperial, centralized, impersonal administrative order of which Farfrae is master.[98] Farfrae's commercial success, argues

95 James Eli Adams, *A History of Victorian Literature* (Oxford: Wiley-Blackwell, 2009), 358.

96 Albert O. Hirschman, *The Passions and the Interests: Political Arguments for Capitalism Before Its Triumph* (Princeton, NJ: Princeton University Press, 1977).

97 Ibid., chap. 2.

98 David Musselwhite, *Social Transformations in Hardy's Tragic Novels: Megamachines and Phantasms* (Houndmills: Palgrave Macmillan, 2003), Chapter 3. See also Neil Powell, "Thomas Hardy's *The Mayor of Casterbridge*." Powell views Henchard as a figure for the rural world outmoded by the more egalitarian but duller modern world represented by Farfrae; and see the critical review of this line of criticism in Kreisel, *Economic Woman*, Chapter 4.

Joanna Devereux, "represents the triumph of the ordinary over the exceptional."[99] Farfrae brings commercial modernity characterized by rational measures: "[Henchard's] accounts were like a bramblewood when Mr. Farfrae came. He used to reckon his sacks by chalk strokes all in a row like garden-palings, measure his ricks by stretching with his arms, weigh his trusses by a lift, judge his hay by a chaw, and settle the price with a curse. But now this accomplished young man does it all by ciphering and mensuration" (107).

And yet, for all these rational measures, Farfrae's suitability for the new world lies in responding to *relational* concerns in contracts, in a reversal of Henchard's radical atomism and formalism. Farfrae refuses his first customer when the competition begins, explaining: "He was once my friend … and it's not for me to take business from him" (115). The same logic applies when the wheel has turned and Henchard is Farfrae's employee: in an inversion of his own early dismissal, Farfrae sentimentally refuses to discharge Henchard despite his disloyalty (241). Under the same weather conditions which cause losses to Henchard, Farfrae accumulates "a large heap of gold" (191) because he watches not the sky but rather the behavior of local farmers who shift between extremes of buying and selling.

Farfrae's determining quality is his mastery of the mutually informative relation between rationality and passion: "the curious double strands in Farfrae's thread of life – the commercial and the romantic – were very distinct at times. Like the colours in a variegated cord those contrasts could be seen intertwisted, yet not mingling." (161) Farfare wins the town's tradesmen with tearful romantic singing, but when Elizabeth expects romance to inform his life he frankly says, "it's well you feel a song for a few minutes and your eyes they get quite tearful; but you finish it, and … you don't' mind it or think of it again for a long while" (94). "[U]sually sedate" (106) he can nonetheless dance and fling in a costume in town celebrations, and for that very reason, also make a profit on the ball while Henchard's free alternative remains abandoned. Farfrae is a man whose taming of passions by interests, to return again to Hirschman, is remarkable. He is precisely Hirschman's account of the "'polished human type – more honest, reliable, orderly, and disciplined, as well as more friendly and helpful, ever ready to find solutions to conflicts."[100]

This pre-Victorian style of justification for capitalism appears to have found new resonance in the "New Man," a model of masculinity that was conceptualized as an alternative to the conventional model in the 1890s, but increasingly challenged it already from mid-century. As Tara

99 Joanna Devereux, *Patriarchy and Its Discontents: Sexual Politics in Selected Novels and Stories of Thomas Hardy* (London: Routledge, 2003), 52.

100 Albert O. Hirschman, "Rival Interpretations of Market Society: Civilizing, Destructive, or Feeble?," *Journal of Economic Literature* 20, no. 4 (1982): 1465.

Macdonald explains, the alternative model was premised on a more egalitarian conception of gender relations in which women were companions rather than subordinates. The New Man's manliness consisted in sensitivity and gentleness at odds with the ideals of professional competitiveness and aggression.[101] Farfrae, so much closer to this model – rather than compromisingly feminine as is sometimes argued,[102] need not opt for an aggressively demarcated and formally rational economic pursuit. As Hirschamn argued, the kind of predictability that a proper relation of passions to interests would foster in the early justification for capitalism would be a "web of interdependent relationships," making communities more cohesive.[103]

The style of modern rationality that Farfae represents consists in a humility of the will, an acknowledgement of its limits. As Mark Granovetter explains in discussing relational embeddedness, "What looks to the analyst like nonrational behavior may be quite sensible when situational constraints ... are fully appreciated."[104] Whenever Farfrae acknowledges situational, and specifically relational constraints, for their delimiting implications, he thereby wins over his fellows and expands his commercial success. The narrator offers his biblical equivalent: "Like Jacob in Padan-Aram, he would no sooner *humbly limit himself* to the ringstraked-and-spotted exceptions of trade than the ringstraked-and-spotted would multiply and prevail" (115). Farfrae's appeal is extremely powerful, a mastery achieved through "genial modesty" (97) that Henchard, compelled to be a man despite himself, fails to grasp. Henchard behaves as if freedom of will and the acknowledgement of constraints are two alternative routes – as if he can gain something from believing in his own free will – but as Weber once argued, in a setting of objective constraints no one can;[105] Farfrae, meanwhile, is rational in the strict sense of acknowledging constraints, most centrally relational contexts, and aligning means to ends accordingly.

Promises of the Better Man

While Henchard's masculine excesses appear increasingly clumsy, Farfrae's style makes him sexy in a mixture of capitalism and eroticism. The symbolic height is the scene of the modern horsedrill, a machine brought to town at

101 Tara MacDonald, *The New Man, Masculinity and Marriage in the Victorian Novel* (New York: Pickering & Chatto, 2015).

102 E.g., Kreisel, *Economic Woman.*

103 Hischman, *The Passions and the Interests,* 52.

104 Mark Granovetter, "Economic Action and Social Structure: The Problem of Embeddedness," *American Journal of Sociology* 91, no. 3 (1985): 506.

105 Max Weber, *Roscher and Knies: The Logical Problems of Historical Economics* trans., Guy Oakes (New York: The Free Press, 1975), 193–4.

Farfrae's recommendation that it would "revolutionise sowing" (169) – contra Henchard's ridicule. The symbol of industrialization is placed at the center of the Casterbridge market, and becomes the locus of Farfrae's heterosexual erotics. Lucetta's cherry-colored dress "alone rivalled it [the machine] in colour" (168). The machine is literally sexualized as Farfrae gets inside it singing, and the infatuated Lucetta responds with a gesture at reproduction: "The 'Lass of Gowrie' from inside a seed-drill – what a phenomenon!" (169). As Ruth Perry says, industrial technology always provided new metaphors for describing sexual behavior. The discourse of output and production aligned particularly well with heterosexuality.[106]

Lucetta herself lives in a house above the market that had been vacant because the mixture of market and intimacy did not appeal to potential residents. The new sexuality represented in the Lucetta-Farfrae attraction builds precisely on the back-and-forth between romance and exchange that Farfrae masters so well. The constant female gaze at the market functions as forbidden pleasure. Farfrae as New Man is uninhibited in crossing the line to the female side. Hardy shows him watching with Lucetta a market scene of contract negotiation where a laborer is pressured to take a job away from his "sweetheart" (162). Farfrae sheds tears just like Lucetta and then, easily translating the manifest gentleness into business, offers a competing contract to the laborer which would prevent the lovers' breakup. Lucetta is of course falling at his feet. When Farfrae's attention will later return to Elizabeth, this will again be represented as a gaze from "the corn-exchange door" (303).

Henchard's loss of Lucetta represents a culmination of contingencies ignited by his performance of masculine control in romantic promises, revealing a parallel to his business catastrophes.

The first promissory overload in romance comes with Sue's arrival. Henchard promises to remarry Sue and so breaks his conflicting promise to marry Lucetta. Performing yet again the outer layers of conventional masculinity, Henchard acknowledges the demand to willingly act on a sense of duty.[107] His declaration that his "first duty is to Susan" (79) frames his action as prioritization through rational assessment: his emphasis is not on the unwieldy constraints which lead him into conflicting promises – as happened with Jopp and Farfrae, but on the mastery involved in correctly prioritizing within them. Henchard's earlier promise to marry Lucetta was likewise a discourse of rational mastery over a conflicted situation; he proposed to her to take the lesser risk between living unmarried with compromised virtue, and getting married with the knowledge that Sue might return, a chance he assessed as "very slight" (79). Claiming mastery

106 Ruth Perry, *Novel Relations: The Transformation of Kinship in English Literature and Culture, 1748–1818* (Cambridge: Cambridge University Press, 2004), 243–4.

107 Griffin, *The Politics of Gender*, Chapter 6.

over and between two women who need to survive gendered scandals of his making, Henchard is caught up in the difficulties of his own sexual identity which led him first to sell Sue, and then to take a lover he never wanted. In both cases Henchard performs not just masculine rational assessment but its other side, of total female subordination, rather than relational companionship. His first communication with Sue in Casterbridge is a letter in which he includes without explanation five guineas, "and it may tacitly have said to her that he bought her back again" (69). He likewise attempts to end his relationship with Lucetta by sending her a check in the mail. Both commodified women return to ignite his fall.

Sue deceives Henchard about Elizabeth, a deceit consequential both before and after he finds out. Before he does, Henchard continues the logic of female subordination and makes Elizabeth promise not to see Farfrae, a promise that only steps up his losses that, the narrator suggests, could have been avoided through relational ties. After Henchard discovers the deceit he drives Elizabeth out (here too giving her money to replace commitment), and re-invites Farfrae's attentions, but at this point Lucetta too has arrived on the scene to take Elizabeth in. The result of all this effort of control is that Farfrae meets Lucetta.

The competition over Lucetta is an erotic triangle with a twist, for only one side appreciates that he is in competition with the other. Eve Sedgwick's analysis of erotic triangles suggested that the bonds between the two men rivals in these cases are no less potent than the man-woman ones; contra gender-neutral readings of triangles, Sedgwick claimed that they rely on the traffic in women to cement male-to-male homosocial bonds.[108] Her analysis holds true here, except that Henchard alone is at work on the bond. Henchard's repeat traffic in women is more about his obsession with Farfrae. His desperation drives him again to use contract as an isolated realm of formal security. He threatens to expose Lucetta's past if she does not promise to marry him. She promises, but uses the period of his secured silence to marry Farfrae. His reliance on contract as a mode of control turns on him again.

Observe that the problem that Hardy explored was not the unenforceability of the promises that Henchard uses. All of his trafficked women cooperate: Sue lived with her buyer, Elizabeth stops seeing Farfrae, and Lucetta considers her coerced promise binding and is driven to break it when she learns about Sue's sale. Legal force is not the problem, but a compulsory masculinity in contracts, misaligned with its surroundings.

Henchard's loss of Lucetta is tied up with the final collapse of his business in bankruptcy. Henchard could have avoided the bankruptcy at the last moment by borrowing money from Lucetta. Compelled by conventional

108 Eve Kosofsky Sedgwick, *Between Men: English Literature and Male Homosexual Desire* (New York: Columbia University Press, 1985).

masculinity to refuse, Henchard says, "I'm not the man to sponge on a woman" (209). As an alternative which fits hegemonic gender roles he asks Lucetta to give his largest creditor the impression that they will soon be married. That route is blocked, formally because she is already married to Farfrae, and symbolically because the scene is geared toward an explicit invocation of Henchard's masculine performance in contracts, and he must go wrong with every stringent reliance on its assumptions.

Showlater describes Henchard's fall as an unmanning in which he connects with his feminine side.[109] And yet, unlike the combination that Farfrae achieves, this is simply the other side of the same coin, and so not a real change: a radical conventional masculinity replaced by femininity as subordination: "He schooled himself to accept [Elizabeth's] will ... as absolute and unquestionable" (304). When Hardy combined romantic and business promises in the downfall plot, he used narrative form to reinforce not the turn from masculine to feminine, but rather Farfrae's strategy of "intertwisting" realms to successful effect.[110]

A few years after the publication of *The Passions and the Interests* Hirschman responded to readers who wanted to know what happened next in his narrative, when the nineteenth century wore on. He observed that the optimistic vision embedded in the view of capitalism as a driver of social peace through the rule of interests over passions, was not shared by the Victorians, who experienced the violence of industrialism at home. Optimism had to take more complex forms, and benevolent views of capitalism were recast in critical garb.[111] *The Mayor of Casterbridge* confirms the pessimistic mood. Fafrae is a suspicious character; his globalist capitalist consciousness represents a coldness increasingly revealed in his insensibility to the violence with which he does not simply defeat Henchard, but takes his life to himself – and Hardy did not flinch in exceeding realist narration to show it. The victory of Farfrae was uncontested and yet was set in a literary form of tragedy whereby a "man of character" becomes a sinking hero, a victim of imperatives he does not fully appreciate.

Levine argues that Henchard's tragic departure at the close of the novel finally asserts the power of his will: he chooses his own disaster. Henchard uses a legal will as an instrument of unilateral imposition on those left behind, but his willful assertion is total self-annihilation: "that no man remember me" (333), anticipating, as Levine says, "the worst they [society and nature] can do."[112] In the last moment Henchard achieves a

109 Showlater "Unmanning," 71, 114.

110 To an extent, this point falls in line with efforts like Kreisel's to read a dialectic; read this way, the figure of Farfrae is not simply Henchard's opposite but a figurative parallel to the synthesis achieved between Henchard and Elizabeth together, as masculine and feminine strategies. Kreisel, *Economic Woman.*

111 Hirschman, "Rival Interpretations."

112 Levine, *The Realistic Imagination,* 241.

reconciliation between acknowledging constraints and acting willfully, by operationalizing tragedy, the artistic form that Hardy found appropriate for an emergent capitalism.

At the closing of *The Mayor of Casterbridge*, when Hardy gave the upwardly-mobile Elizabeth a retrospective moment of control, often evaluated as a sign of liberal optimism,[113] the paragraph read more like a mocking echo of *Middlemarch* (my interventions in brackets):

> [T]he finer movements *[like Eliot's "subtle movements,"]* of her nature found scope in discovering to the narrow-lived ones around her the secret … of making limited opportunities *[just like the limited opportunities of Eliot's modern Theresa]* endurable; which she deemed to consist in the cunning enlargement *[like incalculable diffusiveness, but with a wink]*, by a species of microscopic treatment *[Eliot's microscopic lens]*, of those minute forms of satisfaction *[just as Eliot's invisible minute processes, but "satisfaction" sounding irony rather than sympathy – a consequence of the "cunning" and the overall context of "endurance" rather than achievement]* that offer themselves to everybody not in positive pain; which, thus handled, have much of the same inspiring effect upon life as wider interests cursorily embraced *[Eliot's theme of "unhistoric acts" which nonetheless achieve a greater good, ironized here by the equation which suggests that what makes small things, which are merely absences of positive pain, as inspiring as "wider interests" is not a real worthiness but a particular – and cunning – way of looking at them and abandoning greater goals]*.
>
> (334)

Already sharing the *fin de siècle* mood, Hardy was unable to reconcile his readers to what Armstrong describes as Victorian fiction's preference for partial gratification over threats to the social order.[114] He ended with Elizabeth's middle-class privileges, his last sentence a reminder that "happiness was but the occasional episode in a general drama of pain" (335).

* * *

This and the previous two chapters examined persistent tropes appearing in contracts histories – abstraction and freedom, to show how deep-reaching departures from them spoke to a relational sociality which required intensive effort, leaving older forms behind. Strikingly, the relational liberalism that these novels delineated, whether from an internal or external (Hardy) perspective, could consecrate the market precisely

113 Reed, *Victorian Will*, 352–3. Reed also quotes Hardy's own protests against being labeled a pessimist.

114 Armstrong, *How Novels Think*, 137.

because of the persistent sociality typifying modern capitalism. The role of promises at the heart of this vision challenges contracts historians to extend and complicate their accounts of Victorian liberalism in contracts.

What remains to be accounted for, however, is the persistence of statuses long after liberalism, relational and atomistic, had captured the Victorian social imagination. The next Part develops a new assessment.

Part II

With Status

Foreword

I have so far emphasized relational liberalism in contracts and the relational vision of the economy it implied, and argued that it assumed dominance as a conceptual alternative to status-sociality. The normative effort to get away from statuses which typified novels, likewise typified atomistic individualism, as histories of law recounted in Chapter 1 suggest. And yet, status hierarchies remained formidable, and remain still. Part II puts aside the tensions between relational and atomistic conceptualizations of contract in order to examine the terms of coexistence of liberal ideals – contract among them – and status hierarchies, which posed conceptual challenges for liberalism of any hue. The difficulty that interests me in Part II can in fact be stated more abstractly as the question of complexity, that is, the existence of apparently contradictory yet intertwined conceptual commitments in liberalism, that critical history has long recognized.

In 1961 Raymond Williams wrote: "we need quite different forms of analysis, which would enable us to recognize the important contradictions ... between different parts of the general process of change."[1] Looking back on Williams's call, it seems to have been an early articulation of the centrality that "complexity" would assume in studies of Victorian liberalism for the decades that followed his *Long Revolution*. The contradictions that troubled him have since joined a long list of complexity imagery which animates liberalism critique: tension, paradox, incoherence, indeterminacy, subversion – all abound. Williams's search for forms of analysis dealing with complexity might well qualify as the defining effort of liberalism critique. The existence of apparently irreconcilable commitments in liberalism has set the critical agenda for decades now. To mention additional problematic dualities beyond those invoked by status/contract: autonomy and dependence, abstraction and embodiment, objectivity and situatedness, freedom and subjection, optimism and bleakness, control and arbitrariness, reason and emotion, rationalism and enchantment – and the list continues with slight variations on themes, troubling critical thought.

1 Raymond Williams, *The Long Revolution* (London: Chatto and Windus, 1961), 294.

Complexity is not necessarily devastating. Studies of Victorian liberalism of this century appear distinctive in their efforts to explore new theoretical frameworks which salvage liberalism from devastating critique and instead develop the observation of complexity into nuanced accounts of its structures. In their move beyond suspicious hermeneutics they offer new ways of conceptualizing the coexistence of incongruities without downplaying the historical meaningfulness of either side of the dualities at hand. More or less inclined to reembrace liberalism, criticism has developed new responses to the anxiety that Williams captured.

I mentioned examples in previous chapters but they are worth repeating and putting together to get a sense of the research trajectory, without by any means attempting to cover the field, just to press the sense of its richness. Elaine Hadley's *Living Liberalism* (2010) recovers abstract embodiment as the form through which liberal ideals such as disinterestedness and reflection were practiced as a politics in embodied ways.[2] Lauren Goodlad's *Victorian Literature and the Victorian State* (2003) explores Victorian liberal governance beyond Foucauldian paradigms.[3] Goodlad recounts the efforts of progressive liberal thinkers to imagine a governing agency that would be rational, all-embracing, and efficient, but also anti-bureaucratic, personalized, and liberatory, a project enacted through shifting ideals of character. Amanda Anderson's *The Powers of Distance* (2001), explores forms of contending with the tension between objectivity and situatedness.[4] Anderson defends the liberal search for a distanced view not in terms of a successful impartiality, but rather as a self-aware aspirational effort continually facing its own limits.

A broad-ranging effort in scholarship on liberalism explores communal elements and the forms of their entanglement with liberal atomism – a description that might well fit the effort of Part I in this book. Regenia Gagnier's *Individualism, Decadence and Globalization* (2010), for instance, establishes a plurality of models for conceptualizing individuals-in-relations, which informed individualist Victorian thought. Her work highlights the liberal anxiety with the interdependence of the part and whole, and the availability of nonreductive responses.[5] Bruce Robbins's *Upward Mobility and the Common Good* (2007), uncovers the ties between individualist stories of mobility and welfarist concerns with redistribution.[6] David Wayne

2 Elaine Hadley, *Living Liberalism: Practical Citizenship in Mid-Victorian Britain* (Chicago, IL: University of Chicago Press, 2010).

3 Lauren M.E. Goodlad, *Victorian Literature and the Victorian State: Character and Governance in a Liberal Society* (Baltimore, MD: Johns Hopkins University Press, 2003).

4 Amanda Anderson, *The Powers of Distance: Cosmopolitanism and the Cultivation of Detachment* (Princeton, NJ: Princeton University Press, 2001).

5 Regenia Gagnier, *Individualism, Decadence and Globalization: On the Relationship of Part to Whole, 1859–1920* (Basingstoke: Palgrave Macmillan, 2010).

6 Bruce Robbins, *Upward Mobility and the Common Good: Toward a Literary History of the Welfare State* (Princeton, NJ: Princeton University Press, 2007).

Thomas's *Cultivating Victorians* (2004) is an affirmative account of self-reflective liberal agency which traces its influence on aesthetics. Thomas describes liberalism as a complex historical effort, irreducible to hegemony, to substantiate a regulative (for lawyers: procedural) rather than substantive ideal. In that context he insists that the embrace of the ethos of cultivation, despite its individualist turn, involved both individual-focused ideas of self-improvement and collectively-oriented social amelioration.[7]

These and other studies collectively reconceive complexity as inherent. As Goodlad summarizes the current state of the field, "[d]iscussing liberalism and its contradictions ... could involve an almost infinite parsing of tensions."[8] Complexity is challenging for easy assessments of liberalism as a normative program, assessments too suspicious but often also too enthusiastic, for liberal idealism cannot be revived.

Part II seeks theoretical terms for historical complexity in Chapter 5, and examines their aesthetic enactment in Chapter 6. To examine complexity I turn to two liminal sites. One is a specific promissory context, that of the promise of marriage. The promise was legally a contract in nineteenth-century England (and well into the twentieth century), yet existed uneasily in the grey zone between market and family, politics and intimacy, liberal ideals and status hierarchies, exerting pressure on the meaning of contract and raising cultural anxieties. The other liminal site is Emily Brontë's *Wuthering Heights* (1847). Emily Brontë's novel treaded uneasily between genres and explored the underside of normativity, and so elicited discomfort from its publication onwards.

The anxieties that liminality generates are always a reason for pause and an opportunity for understanding. The promise of marriage and *Wuthering Heights* represent two kinds of liminality that Victor Turner described as "liminal" and "liminoid."[9] In complex, modern societies "both types coexist in a sort of cultural pluralism"[10] and touch cultural experience, but, as Turner argued, tend to occupy different locations. Liminal phenomena tend to be collective, possibly concerned with "socio-cultural rhythms or

7 David Wayne Thomas, *Cultivating Victorians: Liberal Culture and the Aesthetic* (Philadelphia, PA: University of Pennsylvania Press, 2004).

Additional studies do not define themselves as studies of liberalism but speak to close themes. For instance, Ayelet Ben-Yishai's *Common Precedents: The Presentness of the Past in Victorian Law and Fiction* (New York: Oxford University Press, 2013), which explores the coexistence of communal and rational-positivist forms of knowing in the Victorian era; Talia Schaffer, *Romance's Rival: Familiar Marriage in Victorian Fiction* (New York: Oxford University Press, 2016), which explores the "familiar marriage" as a relational and communal alternative to the romantic model.

8 Lauren M.E. Goodlad, "Liberalism and Literature," in *The Oxford Handbook of Victorian Literary Culture*, ed. Juliet John (Oxford: Oxford University Press, 2016), 103–23.

9 Victor Turner, *From Ritual to Theatre: The Human Seriousness of Play* (New York: Performing Arts Journal Publications, 1982).

10 Ibid., 55.

with crises in social processes"[11] while liminoid phenomena are more typically individual products that might have "mass" effects. Furthermore, liminal phenomena tend to be integrated into the total social process whereas liminoid phenomena develop along the margins of central economic and political processes, more fragmentary in character; liminal phenomena appear like collective representations that reveal a common history even as they reverse quotidian representations, while liminoid phenomena tend to be more idiosyncratic, their symbols closer to the personal-psychological than to the objective-social typological pole; liminal phenomena tend to be ultimately eufunctional – they tend to make things work without much friction even when seeming inversive, while liminoid phenomena often belong with social critiques. Finally, the liminal is bound up with social membership while the liminoid is more like a commodity. Without drawing these distinctions too strongly, I invoke them to clarify the fruitfulness of the broad concept of liminality and my varying treatment of the promise of marriage and of *Wuthering Heights* in the chapters that follow. The liminal is a category that might well describe the promise of marriage as legal structure and social process with multiple participants, with novels representing it understood as part of that social process. The liminoid might well capture *Wuthering Heights* when treated, as I treat it here, as a troubling text. At the same time, the commonalities between the liminal and the liminoid as culturally-revealing phenomena, precisely in their uneasy locations, are crucial. Both sites examined in Part II were at once contentious and instructive about core concerns of liberalism.

In Chapter 5 I examine complexity in the promise of marriage, in both law and literature. The chapter focuses on the continuing power of statuses, particularly class and gender. The question is, how should statuses' persistence be read from the perspective of the history of liberalism? Debates among historians have oscillated between liberal and radical interpretations. At one pole the persistence of class and gender is treated as a matter of slow and difficult progress, at the other as the very essence of liberalism, an essence supported by discourses of choice and consent which paralyze critique.

The oscillation between these poles suggests that the problem of statuses is the area of liberal complexity most resistant to accounts that treat complexity as a viable historical phenomenon. One reason is the political resonance of the question of statuses: when social hierarchies are at stake, the need to identify who wins and who loses looms large. I discuss this problem at the close of Chapter 6 in terms of the theoretical assumption of the functionality of ideology. But perhaps Maine himself deserves some credit for this structure of debate. His dichotomism, as Karuna Mantena calls it,

11 Ibid., 54.

may have had more purchase than we like to acknowledge.[12] The heart of Chapter 5 is an effort to move beyond the dominant – and dichotomized – debate, by developing an account of the conceptual patterns through which liberal ideals and statuses became entangled, without either of them being emptied of real content. Those patterns functioned somewhat like cultural codes – embedded in culture while not coherently serviceable to any interest or normative program – and allow us ultimately to read liberalism as a historical reinterpretation of statuses, rather than either as their attempted elimination or as their covert preservation.

In Chapter 6 I closely read *Wuthering Heights*. Here I do not focus on the promise of marriage alone but on various promises that Emily Brontë explored; memorably, Heathcliff himself arrives as broken promises. Nor do I focus on the problem of statuses alone but more abstractly on the multiple tensions that plague liberalism. I treat the novel as a critical commentary on structures of liberal complexity, rather than as an historical example of those structures. My interest is in Brontë's effort to give aesthetic expression and impart to readers an aesthetic experience of the anguish that liberal complexity continues to cause, an anguish one can explain, as I try to do, but hardly impart through the medium of academic discourse.

At the close of Chapter 6 I discuss some implications of the structures of complexity examined in Part II for ideology critique.

12 Karuna Mantena, *Alibis of Empire: Henry Maine and the Ends of Liberal Imperialism* (Princeton, NJ: Princeton University Press, 2010), 83.

Chapter 5

Status-to-Contract Reassessed

The Victorian Promise of Marriage

This chapter focuses on the promise of marriage to examine the place of statuses in liberal thinking, the heart of complexity in the enduring status-to-contract. A moment's glance at the promise's history reveals that along with classically liberal ideals like contract – and love, a second ideal that one cannot overlook in treating Victorians' ideas of marriage – statuses, particularly class and gender, exerted formidable power.

Debates among historians about statuses' persistence along the liberal ideals of contract and love do not tend to conceptualize a viable entanglement, but rather to move between two alternative interpretations. At the liberally-inclined end, historians attribute the coexistence to the process of historical change and social reform, which is uneven, difficult, never perfect – yet progressively oriented. At the radically-inclined end, historians often conclude that liberalism is exposed in its true hierarchical colors, whether classed, patriarchal or else, from which it was never meant to detach, which were indeed its very heart.

The prevalence of the liberal/radical, progress/hierarchy binary has become almost an obstacle to understanding. Victorian liberalism was neither a progressive elimination of statuses – not even an *attempted* elimination, nor, on the other hand, a preservation of statuses that ultimately kept them in place. Viewed in its historical relation to statuses, Victorian liberalism, just at the moments that it was most consciously attempting to get away from statuses, is best understood as their new interpretation. As a new interpretation, liberalism, as manifested in law and novels, achieved two seemingly paradoxical results: On the one hand, it made statuses part of an acceptable order of things, and secured their persistence; on the other, it altered the cultural role of statuses by denying their function as both dominant explanations and goals of social relations, a duality often hard to reconcile. The overall picture is of a complexity we might think of as a *living liberalism.* My use of this term invokes Elaine Hadley's way of reading tensions usually considered contradictory as in fact constitutive of liberalism as a historically concrete form of thought,[1] but I also use "living" as an adjective rather than a verb, to gesture at historical realities that were not part of liberal self-descriptions and that have not been fully theorized as part of liberalism except by way of critique.

To account for the conceptual process that kept liberal ideals and statuses in a mutually-transformative coexistence, this chapter diverges methodologically from previous ones. I discuss not only contract as a liberal ideal but also the rise of an idealist celebration of romantic love as the foundation of families. Love has particular relevance to the promise of marriage – a relation enforced like a contract, while ideally motivated by love. As one Victorian commentator put it, "The poetry of love is now wedded to the trammels of the law. The offspring of this union is the action of breach of promise of marriage."[2]

To discuss the role of love I return to *Bleak House* and *Middlemarch*[3]; of the novels I have read so far, those two famously centralize the question of the love marriage of female protagonists, and reveal the liberal concern with status hierarchies in that context. In discussing contract, however, I turn back to legal histories. While my conclusions diverge from those offered by existing histories and hence function as a critique, somewhat similarly to previous chapters, I also rely here on findings of these histories concerning salient developments in the law of promise of marriage. Three considerations inform the methodology. First, no liberal site is more closely associated with contract than law, just as no liberal site is more closely associated with the romantic ideal than novels. While previous chapters strove to open up the accepted array of historical sources concerning contract, at this point I am interested in prompting a reevaluation at the accepted core of liberal thought, without taking issue with it. Second, I am less concerned here with the distinctions I have so far insisted on between atomistic and relational liberalism, than I am in the relation of either or both to the persistence, and indeed modernization and consolidation of statuses. Finally, I would like to expand the purview beyond a close discursive analysis and to observe mechanisms more encompassing than discourse, like developments in doctrine and litigation practice; existing histories collectively allow me to capture these broad processes. The move between close readings in texts, and analyses of broad processes, bring into view the structures they share in ways that would be otherwise difficult to grasp in their full significance, and open up routes for further investigation beyond the

1 Elaine Hadley, *Living Liberalism: Practical Citizenship in Mid-Victorian Britain* (Chicago, IL: University of Chicago Press, 2010).

2 Charles J, McColla, *Breach of Promise Its History and Social Considerations* (London: Pickering & Co., 1879), 35.

3 All references are to Charles Dickens, *Bleak House*, ed. Nicola Bradbury (New York: Penguin Books, 2003); George Eliot, *Middlemarch: A Study of Provincial Life*, ed. David Carroll (Oxford: Oxford University Press, 1996).

topic and materials of this chapter, which is modest in scope and intended to start a conversation.

The central possibility explored through this chapter's methodology is that the coexistence of liberal ideals and statuses was a conceptually-patterned one; that is, liberal ideals and statuses were fused together through conceptual patterns which repeatedly played out in Victorian liberal thought. The habituality of these patterns means that accounts of social struggle as well historical chaos are not enough in coming to terms with the entanglement of liberal ideals and statuses. These patterns, functioning somewhat like a cultural code – historically contingent, yet sticky through their embeddedness in culture, despite their limits for any interest, power or normative aspiration – shed explanatory light on the forms of persistence and strengthening of statuses in liberalism beyond the Victorian era.

One pattern I explore is *containment*: moves in which considerations of status were contained within the conceptual frameworks of contract and love, and, in consequence, reduced in magnitude, their effects and relevance redirected. A second is *withdrawal*; it gestures at a different conceptual setup: the application of the liberal framework (contract, love) was bordered and limited, leaving areas beyond it to forces of status – but the delimitation was construed as inconsequential, because liberal ideals retained relevance in areas now treated as the core of social relations; cultural energies were accordingly rechanneled.

A Liberal Problematization of Status

"Not many of us are so unobservant as not to perceive that in innumerable cases where old law fixed a man's social position irreversibly at his birth, modern law allows him to create it for himself by convention."[4] Maine's association of contract with progressive mobility, in opposition to status, remains unsurpassed. The further association of contractual mobility with the economy specifically, which contracts histories emphasize in describing Victorian liberalism as market-oriented, could also be glimpsed in Maine:

> It is certain that the science of Political Economy, the only department of moral inquiry which has made any considerable progress in our day, would fail to correspond with the facts of life if it were not true that Imperative Law had abandoned the largest part of the field which it once occupied and had left men to settle rules of conduct for themselves with a liberty never allowed to them till recently.[5]

4 Henry Sumner Maine, *Ancient Law: Its Connection with the Early History of Society and Its Relation to Modern Ideas* (New York: Henry Holt, 1906), 295.

5 Ibid., 296.

The distinction that Maine articulated, between laws made by individuals for themselves – through contract, and laws imposed by social authority, was key, as histories discussed in Chapter 1 argue, to a vision of an economy no longer driven by group identities and social roles. For holders of that view, statuses could not be operative sources for contractual rules, hence the articulation of rules around ideas of will and choice. Novels too, I have argued, relied on contract to explore alternatives to status-sociality. While relationally-inclined, novelistic conceptualizations of contract were nonetheless a challenge to statuses. In both law – as described by historians, and novels – as I have been reading them, the concept of contract is key to the liberal vision of the market at a remove from statuses.

The conceptual relation of love and the family mirrors that of contract and the market. Here too common historical wisdom identifies a process of material change accompanied by ideological shifts. The nuclear family, based on wife, husband and children, was a new familial structure gradually assuming salience from the late seventeenth century. No longer an economic unit of production extending to kinship ties as remote as grandparents, aunts and uncles, cousins and more, all ruled by exclusive patriarchal control and maintaining unclear boundaries via-á-vis the outside world, the new institution was a small independent familial group, created anew with each marriage and more clearly separated from the surrounding community. As a new economy of wage labor and workplaces removed from the home emerged, the family also became a unit of consumption. The new form of family was (expected to be) higher in affect and psychological commitment. Between husband and wife, romantic love became a normative expectation.[6]

Love's centrality signaled a problematization of alternative bases for the marital union – those associated with statuses, which circumscribed the marrying couple with predetermined societal belongings and engulfed

6 For a concise general account see Steven Horwitz, "Capitalism and the Family," *Freeman* 26 (July/August 2007). See Lawrence Stone, *The Family, Sex and Marriage in England 1500–1800* (New York: Harper & Row, 1977) for a classic articulation of the history (with much-criticized progressive tones, though interestingly Stone described the nineteenth century as a setback to the rise of what he called "affective individualism"); John Tosh, *A Man's Place: Masculinity and the Middle-Class Home in Victorian England* (New Haven, CT: Yale University Press 1999), Chapter 1. Tosh emphasizes the historical uniqueness of the nineteenth century, when the separation of work from home became widespread and dramatic, and so altered the meaning of the domestic.

Controversies of course abound, from both economic and feminist perspectives, as this and the next chapter make clear. For a general critical review of accounts identifying the family's importance in its ideological role see Louise A. Tilly, "Review: The Family and Change," *Theory and Society* 5, no. 3 (1978), 421–34. Tilly argues that the family's importance lay not in its ideological construction (primarily as a realm of personality development), but in its ability to supply the resources required in an evolving economic world: it sponsored migration, found jobs, provided services for workers, and raised the

their relation with social expectations of fit pertaining to pedigree, wealth, and politics. Niklas Luhmann explains the rise of love as the importation of a semantics into the family which brought about a historical transformation from a traditional stratified social order into a functionally differentiated one.[7] While describing a process that began in the seventeenth century, he attributes to the nineteenth century the invention of love as the *positive* principle on which the choice of partner should rest; an earlier stage, in the eighteenth century, emphasized inability to love as reason to *refuse* to marry.[8]

Class (with its modern basis in wealth[9]) was thus challenged by love. Literary courtship plots increasingly suggested that persons motivated by class aspirations were marrying for the wrong reason, their decision suspect, a notion that still resonates today.[10] Gender hierarchies too were challenged; love evoked an image of equality between man and woman. As Luhmann puts it, moral sentimentalism involved a rejection of the structural subordination of women.[11] Wendy Jones explains the effect of love in terms of contract, where both signal progressive equality: Consensual married love, she claims, implied a "contractual subjectivity" for women that was seen by many as incompatible with women's subjection, and that undermined rigid conceptions of sexual difference.[12]

future workforce. De Vries argues that families chose consumer goods which required labor investment, and so in effect participated in production. Jan De Vries, *The Industrious Revolution: Consumer Behavior and the Household Economy, 1650 to the Present* (Cambridge: Cambridge University Press, 2008).

See Susan Moller Okin, "Women and the Making of the Sentimental Family," *Philosophy & Public Affairs* 11, no. 1 (1982): 65–88 for a critical feminist review. See Ruth Perry, *Novel Relations: The Transformation of Kinship in English Literature and Culture:, 1748–1818* (Cambridge: Cambridge University Press, 2004) for a review of the history and claim that women were weakened by the transformation, which isolated them from their extended families while putting them, propertyless, under husbands' control. I return soon to controversies about the ideological interpretation of this history.

7 Niklas Luhmann, *Love as Passion: The Codification of Intimacy*, trans. Jeremy Gaines and Doris L Jones (Cambridge: Harvard University Press, 1986).

8 Luhmann, *Love as Passion*, Chapter 13.

9 I use "class" as a form of status (ascription), and elide the distinction between rank and wealth as its basis, for this chapter's interest is the question of hierarchy broadly understood. For the distinction and interrelation between "status" and "class" in historical terms see Michael McKeon, *The Origins of the English Novel 1600–1740* (Baltimore, MD: Johns Hopkins University Press, 1987), 162–7.

10 The idealization of love supported additional liberal commitments, like the significance of ordinary life and personality development. See for instance Charles Taylor, *Sources of the Self* (Cambridge: Cambridge University Press, 1989), 285–302.

11 As well as the transference of political hierarchy into the family. Luhmann, *Love as Passion*, 131. But, as discussed below, on many feminist accounts love served as an ideological solution for continued subordination that individualism per se threatened.

12 Wendy S. Jones, *Consensual Fictions: Women, Liberalism, and the English Novel* (Toronto: University of Toronto Press, 2005), 5. As Nomi Stolzenberg observes, the backlash against

Contract and love both signaled a regime of choice and mobility for core social institutions, over a regime of status.[13] And so statuses were problematized. Yet "problematization" is very far from elimination. The imagery in accounts of the historical rise of late modern love and contract often intimates that statuses were meant to be eliminated. Consider for instance Anthony Giddens' argument that the ideal of love, the "pure relationship," was "explosive in its connotations for preexisting forms of [...] power,"[14] which resonates with Luhmann's "rejection" of subordination. Or listen to Dicey describing, much earlier, the nineteenth-century individualist embrace of contract as a mode of abolition of "antiquated institutions."[15] Elimination was never in the cards. Class had never lost its relevance to conjugal families, and patriarchy lurked in the enduring power of Victorian gender roles, and on many accounts deepened in historically unprecedented ways. Economic relations, like familial ones, were never worked pure of status biases, despite the popularity of Maine's aphorism. The promise of marriage was a contract in which women, whose role in the economy was a source of anxiety, and whose legal agency was widely denied under the doctrine of coverture,[16] were necessary parties. But here as elsewhere, gender roles, alongside class divisions, were paramount, making for decades of critique by feminist and market historians.

Forms of power and old institutions were significantly stirring but hardly exploded. The following discussion explores a new assessment of this history through the patterns of containment and withdrawal.

Containment

Containment is a concept developed in cultural theory to describe processes whereby forms of power employ their own terms to license threatening elements in culture that end up subverting them. It was classically articulated by Stephen Greenblatt in *Invisible Bullets*.[17]

legal reforms which signaled gender equality in consequence of "romantic liberalism" continued to be felt late into the twentieth century. Nomi M. Stolzenberg, "Liberalism in a Romantic State," *Law, Culture and the Humanities* 5, no. 2 (2009): 194–215.

13 For a broader account of the rise of consent as the basis of political authority see Holly Brewer, *By Birth or Consent: Children, Law, and the Anglo-American Revolution in Authority* (New York: University of North Carolina Press, 2005).

14 Anthony Giddens, *The Transformation of Intimacy* (Stanford, CA: Stanford University Press, 1994), 2. Giddens refers particularly to gender power.

15 Albert V. Dicey, *Lectures on the Relation Between Law and Public Opinion in England During the Nineteenth Century*, 2nd ed. (London: Macmillan, 1962), 151.

16 Full contractual capacity was given to married women only in the interwar years.

17 Stephen Greenblatt, "Invisible Bullets: Renaissance Authority and Its Subversion," in *Glyph. Johns Hopkins Textual Studies* 8, ed. Walter Benn Michaels (Baltimore, MD: Johns Hopkins University Press, 1981), 40–61.

I proceed from the perspective of liberalism rather than status, and so reverse the historical trajectory often applied in discussing containment, where the old power contains the new.[18] While I do not rely on the same trajectory, the concept of containment is helpful in signaling an inclusive move in the sense of cultural theory and history. I ask how, from the perspective of the new (liberal ideals), the old – and acknowledged – power of statuses was conceptualized and treated. (I use "old" and "new" provisionally, to gesture at perceptions more than historical accuracy, for both gender and class bore a distinctly Victorian content, which was not fully mandated by older forms of hierarchy. Yet, when liberal ideals challenged hierarchies they were experienced as the new thing.) This direction too is not unfamiliar. Raymond Williams theorized such relations in terms of dominance, and used the close concept of "incorporation." Any culture, he said, includes elements of its past – the residual – which are still active, effective elements of the present. Some residual elements are oppositional or alternative to the dominant culture, while others have been incorporated into it by reinterpretation, dilution, projection, or discriminating inclusion and exclusion.[19] While my own analysis owes much to Williams's theory, I retain "containment" (and will later distinguish it from withdrawal, both of which resonate with William's "incorporation"), while using it backward as it were, because I seek to evade, provisionally, an account of dominance. I attempt a description of living liberalism as a form of thought that neither rejected statuses nor simply embraced them. I do not point to a clear trajectory whereby either statuses or liberal ideals had or were bound to have the upper hand, but rather to the terms of coexistence.

Under containment patterns, liberal frameworks faced statuses by making them part of the governing structure, effectively turning the status logic to use within the discourse of free will, choice, and agency. The effect was preservation together with a reduction in magnitude and a redirection

18 A dominant example of this trajectory in Victorianist scholarship is the "relative economic decline debate." The question was (and remains), what caused Britain's perceived loss of Western economic lead after its short-lived mid-Victorian zenith (1850–70)? The dominant explanation speaks to a containment of the newer middle-class values within aristocratic ones. Martin Weiner, of the best known proponents of the cultural argument for economic decline, argues that the new dominant bourgeois culture was "gentrified," bearing the imprint of old aristocracy. The debate about this argument (which appears to have left no marks on discussions of liberalism and status, perhaps because its explanatory focus has not been the question of hierarchy/mobility, but rather a concern with economic performance), relies on the historical trajectory in which old status contains (or not) new forces. See W.D. Rubinstein, *Capitalism, Culture and Decline in Britain, 1750–1990* (London: Routledge, 1993); Martin J. Wiener, *English Culture and the Decline of the Industrial Spirit, 1850–1980* (Cambridge: Cambridge University Press, 2004).

19 Raymond Williams, *Marxism and Literature* (Oxford: Oxford University Press, 1977), Chapter 8.

of effects and relevance. The conceptual process brings to mind a wonderful children's book by Mercer Mayer, *There's a Nightmare in My Closet* (1968). A child, afraid of a monster hiding in his closet every night, overcomes his fear by bringing the creature into his bed. The child now lies with a monster, his own place in the bed shrunken, while the monster has been domesticated.

I begin by reading central features of breach of promise law as a way of containing class and gender biases within classical contract thought. I then read instances of containment of the same hierarchies in courtship plots in *Bleak House* and *Middlemarch.* The two registers of discussion trace statuses' conceptual entanglements with Victorian liberal ideals, and the transformations those entanglements encouraged.

Containing Status in Contract

The action for breach of promise in England reached its nineteenth-century form following a gradual decline in the availability of ecclesiastical remedies that reached its peak with the Hardwicke's Marriage Act of 1753[20] and developments in the common law civil action. Breach of promise of marriage could be redressed by common law courts from the Interregnum onwards. However, when the classical model of contract rose to prominence in the nineteenth century, the promise of marriage, though theoretically and practically processed as contractual, acquired peculiar characteristics which distinguished it from other contracts as well as from the litigation practice of marriage promises in earlier decades (described below). The rise-and-fall story of the peculiarly-nineteenth-century action has been periodized by historians from the late-eighteenth to the late-nineteenth century, its high tide in mid-century and its slow decline from the 1860s or 1870s, in terms of chances of winning, amounts of damages,[21]

20 Lord Hardwicke's Marriage Act, 26 Geo II, c 33. The Act was intended to stop clandestine marriages by requiring banns or a license as well as a church-administered ceremony, and establishing a mandatory recording of marriages. The Act deprived the ecclesiastical courts of their power to compel marriage on the grounds of a promise of any kind, leaving disappointed promisees with only a claim for damages in civil courts. For a critique of the assumption that until 1753 marriage by consent was easily created see Rebecca Probert, *Marriage Law and Practice in the Long Eighteenth Century: A Reassessment* (Cambridge: Cambridge University Press, 2009), Chapter 2. Probert shows that solemnization was required to bring the marriage into effect. Still, Probert suggests that after the Act the civil action for breach of promise was broadened to enable suits for contracts no longer enforced by the church. Ibid., 221–2. The later history of the civil action I discuss is a historical irony given that a dominant consideration in passing the Act was the threat to class structures by clandestine love marriages.

21 For some figures see Susie L. Steinbach, "Promises, Promises: Not Marrying in England, 1780–1920" (PhD diss., Yale University, 1996), 212–13 and Chapter 5.

and public support.[22] While not abolished until 1970,[23] numbers of suits were in sharp decline from 1900 onwards.

The importance of the contractual framing vis-à-vis the forces of status in the promise's Victorian fortunes is a contested question. Some historians, like Patrick Atiyah, view doctrinal developments at the high point of litigation as significant, a telling sign of the triumph of the classical model of contract, as evident by its effect on an area outside its paradigmatic ambit.[24] Susie Steinbach argues that the promise of marriage, its rise and fall, can make little sense outside the contractual ideology of the Age of Contract.[25] On the other hand, historians who view the class and gender story as paramount, like Ginger S. Frost and Saskia Lettmaier, tend to dismiss the contractual framing as thin cover, if not total misfit, little helpful in explicating what was going on.[26] The middle grounds is perhaps best captured in Michael Grossberg's account of similar developments in American law: "The revamped breach suit illustrates not only the pervasive influence of contractual ideology and romantic love on domestic relations, but more directly a new judicial recognition of the gap between the law's theoretical assumption of contracting equality between men and women and the reality of feminine powerlessness." Put otherwise, liberal ideals and statuses were both influential; the story is one of internal contradictions: a push and pull, with conflicting interpretations about the victorious side.[27]

The conceptual polarization about explanatory frameworks should be reread to make up a single story of living liberalism. The contractual framing cannot be dismissed, or reduced to mere legal fiction or ideological blindness. Its historical salience renders such interpretations unconvincing.

22 Heated public debates followed the amendment of the law of evidence allowing women plaintiffs to act as witnesses in their own suits. Evidence Further Amendment Act of 1869, 6 & Vict. C. 85.

23 Law Reform (Miscellaneous Provisions) Act 1970, c. 33, s. 1.

24 P.S. Atiyah, *The Rise and Fall of Freedom of Contract* (Oxford: Clarendon, 1979), 401. See also Randall Craig, *Promising Language: Betrothal in Victorian Law and Fiction* (Albany, NY: State University of New York Press, 2000), 106.

25 Steinbach, *Promises, Promises.*

26 Ginger S. Frost, *Promises Broken: Courtship, Class and Gender in Victorian England* (Charlottesville, VA: University of Virginia Press, 1995); Saskia Lettmaier, *Broken Engagements, The Action for Breach of Promise of Marriage and the Feminine Ideal, 1800–1940* (New York: Oxford University Press, 2010). Note that Steinbach does not deny the status biases of the action for breach of promise. In fact, her analysis turns on gender and class no less than those of Lettmaier or Frost. Instead, Steinbach argues that women were able to bring and win suits in large numbers due to the influence of contract (and love (sentiment)). Frost, meanwhile, has much to say on the love as well. The dominant arguments of historians, however, suffice here.

27 Michael Grossberg, *Governing the Hearth: Law and the Family in Nineteenth-Century* (Chapel Hill, NC: University of North Carolina Press, 1988), 38. Grossberg seems to ultimately view gender as the dominant framework, the "larger goal." Ibid., 39.

The power of gender and class too cannot be discounted. Yet contradiction and compromise do not exhaust this history; the continual maintenance of a contractual framing for a gender-and-class problem exposes the containment of forces of statuses within liberal frameworks in a manner that altered them all.

The following discussion first introduces central aspects of the history of breach of promise. To do so I draw primarily on three studies: Ginger S. Frost's *Promises Broken*, Saskia Lettmaier's *Broken Engagements*, and Susie Steinbach's *Promises, Promises*.[28] These studies serve my methodological effort to examine not only discourse but also broader social phenomena: they offer elaborate accounts of litigation and surrounding practices; they contain details of parties, procedures and evidence, claims and defenses, and figures for the assessment of damages.[29] At the same time, the studies represent, as noted, competing explanations of this history. I then explain the history as a pattern of containment.

Suing for Breach of Promise

Nineteenth-century plaintiffs seeking to substantiate a claim for breach of promise had to establish both contract and breach in accordance with classical contract doctrine. Classical doctrine required promise and acceptance supported by consideration for a binding contract to exist. Mutual promises would constitute both acceptance of one another and consideration, therefore a plaintiff's writ would customarily state that the couple had promised to marry one another; plaintiff then had to prove these mutual promises. The plaintiff also had to claim and prove breach of contract. The writ would customarily submit that the defendant had "neglected and refused" to marry her, and that the plaintiff had always been "ready and willing" to marry him, and evidence brought to show the defendant's refusal.[30] The statement of defense would deny or admit the contract, deny or admit its breach, if denied – add several contractual defenses in case the denial failed, and in any event add claims aimed at mitigating damages, all

28 See also Denise Bates, *Breach of Promise to Marry: A History of How Jilted Brides Settled Scores* (Los Angeles, CA: Pen & Sword History, 2014), that generally aligns with these histories' findings.

29 Frost examined 875 breach of promise suits in English assize courts, most of them between 1850 and 1900. Lettmaier examined 250 cases decided by a variety of English courts, most of them between 1800 and 1940. Steinbach examined 345 cases, 322 of which were between 1780 and 1920 – the period she defines as the rise (1780–1870) and fall (after 1870) of breach of promise suits.

30 Often suits were brought only after the defendant had married another woman. However, breach could also be proved by showing that the defendant had evinced unwillingness to marry toward the plaintiff, her family, or friends.

of which were pursued at trial.[31] Within this general contractual framework, historians point to peculiarities of the promise of marriage, arising primarily from perceptions of gender.

First, while formally available to both men and women, in practice the action was restricted to women: over 90 percent of plaintiffs in the nineteenth century were women. Moreover, unlike other contractual causes of action, the action for breach of promise was personal,[32] and did not survive the decease of the plaintiff, solidifying the effective limitation of the cause to women. Women were not only near-exclusive plaintiffs, but usual winners. Judges usually found for women; the tendency was exacerbated by juries, who were more likely to ignore judges' summations when they found for defendants; judges in turn confirmed these trends: they did not set aside jury decisions, though they could. Men plaintiffs stood a good chance of losing, and even when they won were often awarded minimal damages, and possibly denied compensation for legal costs which could be considerable. Men were thus actively discouraged from filing suits for breach of promise. The bias toward women plaintiffs stands in contradistinction to earlier periods in which both filing suits and winning them were distributed more equally among men and women.

Women's prominence in breach of promise cases was part of a construction of gender differences in courtship, whereby women were wooed, men the wooers. Proof of the promise reflected an expansive evidentiary policy heavily reliant on social courting expectations, with signs such as intimate attention or gifts of jewelry as part of the evidentiary array alongside witnesses, letters, and, after a 1969 amendment of the law of evidence, a testimony by the plaintiff corroborated by material evidence – a category leaving latitude to courts. The array of evidence and the fact that it was needed – for most promises were oral and between the couple alone – reinforced a picture of courting in which proactive men entice passive women. The counter-promise was, within this picture of gender roles, more difficult to prove, and here the promise of marriage evinces a marked departure from classical contract doctrine: Silence on the part of the woman was construed as acceptance of the promise (and counter-promise and consideration), in contradistinction to the standard denial of silence as acceptance of an offer.[33]

31 There is some controversy about the standard move by defendants. While Frost argues that denial was customary, Frost, *Promises Broken*, 21, Steinbach argues that in most cases defendants admitted to both the promise and its breach, Steinbach, *Promises, Promises*, 141. The question is not central in considering the contractual framework of breach of promise.

32 The rule was set in Chamberlain, Administrator of Ann Chamberlain, *Deceased v. Williamson*, 148 (1814) 2 M & S 408.

33 In addition, the promise could be oral despite some equivocality about the applicability of the Statute of Frauds, and no stamp tax was required for written evidence to be admitted.

Another peculiarity lies in the pursuit of defense. Defendants could raise the defense of unchastity, an instance idealizing female sexual virtuousness and men's expectation of sexual exclusivity.[34] Lettmaier argues that the theoretical basis for the defense within contract doctrine was never made clear, although one case came close in conceptualizing it as failure to disclose a material fact.[35]

Other peculiarities included the question of exoneration, which, for male defendants, was practically impossible to prove despite its theoretical availability here as in other contracts. The passive picture of women that made for inaudible acceptance was also reluctant to imagine them willfully withdrawing from their engagements.

The investment in gender roles favored women in these cases; men defendants were locked into prescribed roles which limited their ability to defend their position. While women played into the deceived-maiden role, men assumed that of the responsible initiator in control of the relationship, and were reluctant to appear weak and victimized.[36]

Important in its peculiarity was the award of damages. An earlier focus on pecuniary loss,[37] was eclipsed by a focus on psychological damage, with compensation conceptualized as addressing damages for loss of happiness – and health in consequence, injured feelings, wounded honor, humiliation, and social degradation (while still allowing for pecuniary

34 In the course of the nineteenth century unchastity was gradually limited to physical unchastity, i.e. sexual intercourse, although "mere" loose conduct could impact damages. The defense had a few qualifications: Unchastity had to be proven; it had to have been unknown at the time of the promise, had to be the reason for breaking it; and had to have been with another man, not the defendant himself. Note that holding the defendant responsible for sexual intercourse between himself and the plaintiff was part of the construction of men as the aggressive sex, the only side to push for intercourse, and the one expected to assume responsibility for it. The point of the defense of unchastity, then, was not simply the sexual purity of women, but a more complex construction of the interaction between the couple: men were entitled to purity and exclusivity, but if they had knowingly forgone them, they bore responsibility for the decision.

35 Lettmaier, *Broken Engagements*, 44 (referring to *Beachey v. Brown*, 114 (1860) EB & E 796). Even this formulation did not clearly fall within classical doctrine, which protected from fraud narrowly, and did not generally offer redress for nondisclosure. Atiyah, *Rise and Fall*, 468–9.

36 See Frost, *Promises Broken*, Chapter 3, for a detailed account of gender expectations and their contradictions.

37 Damages were calculated to compensate for the pecuniary value of a lost marriage, or, if that expectation could not be proved, for out-of-pocket expenses in preparation for marriage. Lettmaier, *Broken Engagements*, Chapter 1. Steinbach agrees that the focus until 1780 was on pecuniary loss, but suggests that most cases had been based on part-executed contracts, and so damages were addressing reliance rather than pure expectation. Steinbach, *Promises, Promises*, 184. This despite the fact that a wholly-executory promise of marriage was theoretically held actionable from the seventeenth century.

losses).[38] Damages were part of a picture of virtue in distress. Punitive damages, usually unacknowledged in contracts, were available for plaintiffs in the presence of aggravating circumstances, important among them seduction under promise of marriage.[39] Here too women were pictured as trusting and liable to misuse, while sexual virtue was confirmed as a critical condition of marriageability. On the other hand, damages could be reduced, possibly to negligible levels, under mitigating circumstances, important among them an unfeminine conduct of the plaintiff.[40] Looks too were relevant to damages, with youth and beauty securing higher awards. As Lettmaier puts it, everything that brought the plaintiff closer to the ideal of the angelic child-woman would enhance, everything that separated her from it detract from the damages she would receive.[41]

Peculiarities speak to an idealization of gender roles in courtship. While each alone could possibly be explained away, gender historians convincingly identify their striking cumulative effect. Lettmaier carefully analyzes the construction of true womanhood as virtuous, submissive, and delicate – and by the same token an object, article of the man's ability to pay, arguing that this vision molded the action into its specifically-Victorian form. Frost, meanwhile, brings into the picture the idealization of manhood, which she argues was more important than that of womanhood for the history of breach of promise.[42] The construction of manhood in terms of the independent provider in charge of the relationship, Frost argues, entailed limits as well as benefits, and explains historical developments.

Class was also a driving force behind the legal picture, particularly the level of damages. Amounts awarded were on average relatively high until the closing decades of the nineteenth century, when the action fell out of favor.[43] The action was recognized at its high tide and afterwards as one aimed at assisting and protecting relatively low-class women – most

38 These were general damages, which did not have to be proved. According to Lettmaier, they were the chief source of legal classificatory trouble, seemingly more appropriate for tort than contract. Lettmaier, *Broken Engagements*, 48–9 and n. 130; see also Steinbach, *Promises, Promises*, 118–19. But Steinbach also notes that despite the departure from standard contractual damages, the centrality of heartbreak also meant that otherwise wholly executory contracts were actionable, in line with the classical model of contract. Ibid., 190.

39 For a calculation of the average increase in damages in cases of seduction see Lettmaier, *Broken Engagements*, 50–1. For the newness of these damages in the action's history see Grossberg, *Governing the Hearth*, 45–9.

40 For instance, if she had been the one doing the courting.

41 Lettmaier, *Broken Engagements*, 72.

42 Frost, *Promises Broken*, 46.

43 The median amount found by Steinbach was £200, which could have supported a middle-class family comfortably for one year. Steinbach, *Promises, Promises*, 224. Frost's median is £100, but her calculations cover a period excluded by Steinbach – after 1869. Frost, *Promises Broken*, 159.

plaintiffs were lower-middle or upper-working class – whose economic prosperity was seriously threatened by broken engagements. The question of class also reached deeper, with levels of damages varying in relation to class differentials between plaintiff and defendant. Steinbach's analysis indicates that juries were more sensitive when there was no class difference, and less generous when there was, with damages lower the greater the class disparity between the couple. Put differently, juries were suspicious toward cross-class marriages.[44] Class, like gender, had an important role to play in the legal response to breach of promise.[45]

Breach of Promise Law as Containment

The overall picture is one of a contractual legal framing (and here we can read it *with* contracts histories in terms of atomistic individualism, for in relation to statuses the tension is presumably more patent), in which peculiarities driven by forces of status play a key role. The combination was not a curtailment of contract for gender and class, nor contract's ultimate victory, but rather containment structure.

The point of departure, that critics of Atiyah have been too quick to dismiss, was the classic insistence that in the presence of manifest choice, courts would hold promisors to their obligations. The contractual framing was not mere procedure or empty rhetoric; it was substance, enacting the individualist reluctance to second-guess the desirability of a contract. Liability depended on the existence of a valid contract; whether upholding it was desirable or just was beside the point; whether the couple could form a functioning marriage was an irrelevant question in determining legal liability. Determinations of liability on a formal basis validated the idealist liberal picture of social relations created by individuals needing no social policing. Classical contract's main conceptual underpinning, that of respecting whatever individuals chose to do, thus remained put.

While choice was upheld, there was an element of direct social policing in the level of damages, which would be low in the absence of affection. From the perspective of the status/contract tension, however, this did not dramatically undermine the liberal framing. First, the celebration of affection was itself a conceptual investment in the liberal frame of reference; denying high damages in its absence was not damaging for the liberal framework. Second, a major goal of filing a suit for breach of

44 Steinbach, *Promises, Promises*, 231. Cases of class disparities were a relative minority (34% or less). Frost, *Promises Broken*, 232.

45 Class also had a role in the background for litigation: Frost argues that class was a major factor in break-ups leading up to suits in assize courts. Most frequently, the interplay between the desire for love and an economic inability to sustain it made for broken promises, in a complex interaction between class and the romantic ideal. Frost, *Promises Broken*, Chapter 5.

promise was reestablishing the woman's virtuousness. As Ruth Perry observes, after the Hardwicke's Act, law was the dividing line between the good and the fallen woman.[46] And so, holding a promisor liable for breach carried expressive meanings which were not exhausted by the level of damages. Indeed, the very agreement to marry a woman was a sign of her virtuous character (which explains why breach was so damaging) – a dramatic enactment of the classical paradigm in which value is definitively signified by consent.[47]

The idiosyncratic rules and practices on proof of counter-offer and acceptance, on unchastity and exoneration as defenses, and on damages for psychological distress, despite their departure from classical doctrine, operated within the classical attribution of liability based on choice, and targeted the promisor as a responsible individual. Because his counterparty was a woman, and of relatively low class, he was, if anything, extremely responsible. Positioning women as plaintiffs only, allowed courts to rehearse the logic of contractual agency and responsibility with few qualms. Men as sole defendants were treated as contracting individuals expected to meet their obligations. The practical unavailability of exoneration, for example, meant that responsibility was individualized and located in only one party, with the other having no possible role to play, in a construction bringing the ideal picture of the autonomous contractor to the verge of caricature, reminiscent of Hardy's portrayal of compulsory masculinity as victimhood. At the same time, women's submissiveness, neediness, economic dependence, were channeled through the contractual position of a promisee demanding performance of a contract. The problematization of the ideal contracting individual which would come about if roles had been reversed and women were to assume the position of responsible promisors, was avoided.[48]

Since only men were cast into the role of the autonomous individual, breach of promise cases could exhibit some of the extremities associated with the arm's-length competitive ideal of atomistic individualism in contracts, among them the often-used example of the new Victorian refusal to let men off the hook because of ill health:[49] this is the kind of refusal to allow equitable sharing and consider changed circumstances that had won classical law its disrepute.

46 Perry, *Novel Relations*, Chapter 6.

47 For a discussion of some of these points see Steinbach, *Promises, Promises*, 24, 158–9, 195–7.

48 The gendered division of labor between the contract parties here explains why historians of the action, like Frost and Lettmaier, disagree whether the cultural construction manhood or womanhood was more important for the story: one can emphasize either men's enhanced responsibility in these cases, or women's diminished agency; the two aspects, however, were complementary.

49 The change is attributed to *Hall v. Wright* [1860] 120 E.R. 688 (Exch.).

The delimitation of the action to women in the nineteenth century allowed classical contract law to contain gender differentials, even turn them to effective use, while maintaining individualistic terms of art.

Containment explains a point customarily seen as an inherent contradiction in the promise of marriage. The legal action, historians note, was founded on a paradox: it framed women as submissive and fragile just when they were taking the initiative and appearing in a public arena for themselves.[50] The ideal of female delicacy was threatened by the agency and often also vindictiveness and money-seeking motives associated with filing a suit. Female submissiveness under marital coverture, a formal annulment of agency, is similarly hard to square with the agency involved in suing for breach: the action seemed to depend on an agency erected only to be annulled. The paradox disturbs otherwise neat stories of gender and class. However, it largely disappears when viewed as part of a containment structure; in this form gender roles could function within the liberal contractual framework. What appears as an irreconcilable contradiction from a gender-only perspective becomes a viable pattern when read through the demands of contract which were asserted by containing status ascriptions.

The doctrinal structures of breach of promise and their Victorian application clarify that statuses were not eliminated, but instead reinforced by the contractual framework; concurrently, however, their workings altered: social roles were channeled to serve a liberal picture of the promise of marriage based on freedom of choice, rather than signal an alternative. This channeling not only reinforced, for those who came to courts, read and talked about them, the liberal commitment to respect whatever individuals chose to do, it also unsettled the implications of status: by letting low-class women appear in courts and win hundreds of suits, it unsettled gender as well as class power. This effect, note, was not a matter of significant material redistributions – though some redistribution took place – but rather a stirring of symbolic social roles. Whether these suits served to co-opt real change in social hierarchies or to prompt it in the final analysis[51] – is debatable.[52] And

50 Nineteenth-century women could not be judges, barristers or jurors, and their appearance as plaintiffs was usually in their roles as wives, mothers, or workers. Lettmaier's analysis centralizes this paradox, reading the evolving treatment of women plaintiffs as different ways of coming to terms with it.

51 On the difficulties involved in identifying "bottom lines" see my critique of functional assessments in Chapter 6, under "Ideology Critique."

52 There is probably some frame of reference to support either position. On this problematic in general see Gerald Graff, "Co-optation," in *The New Historicism*, ed. Aram H. Veeser, (New York: Taylor & Francis, 1989), 173. Moments of seeming empowerment can be interpreted as in fact a weakness, and vice versa. A classic example is Hartog's analysis of resistance emerging from a full internalization of the oppressing demands of coverture. Hendrik Hartog, "Abigail Bailey's Coverture: Law in a Married Woman's Consciousness," in *Law in Everyday Life*, eds. Austin Sarat and Thomas R. Kearns (Ann Arbor, MI: University of Michigan Press, 1993), 63–108.

that is the point to see. A debate indeed ensued and continues: Victorians and their historians remained deeply unsure whether the action was empowering or disempowering for women and men, for the low classes and the upper ones. The very disagreement both indicated and created a disturbance to an ordered picture of the social world from both status and idealist liberal perspectives, its resolvability itself needing explanation.

Containing Status in Love

Novels were engaged in a complex negotiation of the viability of love vis-à-vis statuses. Much of the burden of negotiation was laid on promises of marriage which allowed close assessments of motivations for marriage. Somewhat like the tensions in the legal action, novels often seemed to speak in two voices. On the one hand, investments in the ideal of unencumbered love, and obsessive differentiations between status and romantic motivations for marriage, have been widely observed by criticism.[53] On the other hand, novels registered the continuing force of statuses, among them class and gender.

Ian Watt famously identified the courtship plot as the defining feature of the realist novel, marking the shift from the patriarchal to the conjugal family. His argument sparked extensive debates in and beyond English studies.[54] Research of recent years has been challenging love's exclusivity in marriage plots and complicating its implications. Talia Schaffer, Kelly Hager, Sharon Marcus, and Elsie Michie are among the critics who recover alternative models of marriage that pervade novels.[55] As in law, here too my interest is in complications; in particular, I ask how the plot of love stands in relation to alternatives that signal social hierarchy. As Jones says, the novel's appropriation of courtship as its primary subject, and its cultural centrality, render it a privileged site for untangling the ideological complexities of love, marriage and gender[56] – and one might add,

53 Research has identified not just the status/love tensions but additional challenges to the romantic paradigm, among them materialism and vocationalism. Talia Schaffer subsumes these and other alternatives under the model of the "familiar marriage" premised on a rational decision, see Talia Schaffer, *Romance's Rival: Familiar Marriage in Victorian Fiction* (New York: Oxford University Press, 2016). While I focus specifically on status, I do not deny the slippage to other non-romantic motivations for marriage. As Elsie Michie's study of the marriage plot reveals, slippages (in her study between materialism per se and status) require an analytic choice of focus. Elsie B. Michie, *The Vulgar Question of Money: Heiresses, Materialism, and the Novel of Manners from Jane Austen to Henry James* (Baltimore, MD: Johns Hopkins University Press, 2011).

54 Ian Watt, *The Rise of the Novel: Studies in Defoe, Richardson and Fielding* (Berkeley, CA: University of California Press, 1957), Chapter 5.

55 For an extensive review of the literature see Schaffer, *Romance's Rival*, Chapter 1.

56 Jones, *Consensual Fictions*. 64.

class.[57] Apparent opposites, I will argue, here too were often reconciled through a containment pattern.

To examine containment in novels, I return to *Bleak House*, to Esther's parentage plot. I first emphasize the extent of its dependence on the love/status tension in marriage. Esther's narrative is framed by two stories of never-materialized promises of marriage – between her parents, and between her and Jarndyce – which tie social evils with the frustration of love by status in marriage decisions, and social prosperity with the rule of love. I then examine how forces of status are not so much made irrelevant in the love match, as made newly relevant within a liberal logic, through a containment pattern, here also with a digression to *Middlemarch*.

Love, Not Status

Lady Dedlock was engaged to marry Hawdon, an engagement broken under untold circumstances. Hints of Hawdon's despair and Lady Dedlock's guilt are woven throughout the plot, telling a story of passionate love sacrificed for social capital. Apparently, Lady Dedlock broke the engagement under pressure to hide the shame of Esther's birth and marry better, finally marrying the aristocratic Sir Leicester who bears the role of generational status, and adopting an openly metaphoric family name bespeaking her unhappiness. Her regret is acted out most clearly in her effort to secure love for her maid Rosa. The love between Rosa and Watt Rouncewell is staged as an explicit – and socially mobile – alternative to status (the Dedlock patronage), which Lady Dedlock pursues to the amazement of her husband. Sir Leicester sees here "the whole framework of society ... receiving tremendous cracks ..." (455).

Hawdon's and Lady Dedlock's broken engagement is the root of the parentage plot; their love, suppressed under class considerations and gender discipline, becomes the source of spreading forms of unhappiness, from the poor, lonely Hawdon and the rich yet miserable Lady Dedlock, through their illegitimate Esther, and outward in all directions, to the entire bleak plot. The marriage to the Dedlocks, observe, also ties the parentage story with the Chancery story, for Sir Leicester is a party in the suit. In formal terms, the denial of an affective union is the root of social evils explored in the novel. The narration, broken and dispersed, reiterates the problematic in dialogue with the theme of "connexion" I explored in Chapter 3: while the story of the broken engagement must be made

57 We need not think of the ideological process at stake in opposition to a conscious effort to transform the social order at large. From the 1850s, Kathy Psomiades argues contra Nany Armstrong's classic argument in *Desire and Domestic Fiction*, plots were consciously (theoretically) engaging the question of marriage to think about political life. Kathy Alexis Psomiades, "The Marriage Plot in Theory," *Novel* 43, no. 1 (2010): 53–9.

comprehensible as everything must in *Bleak House,* the violation of love as unifying element is dramatized by making the labor of connection a painful and unsure effort.

The closure of the parentage plot arrives with the happy marriage of Esther and the admired self-made physician Woodcourt. Yet to arrive there Dickens narrated another promise of marriage which undermines the novel's stability, that between Esther and Jarndyce. The problem is not breaking the promise, but keeping it; it therefore becomes clear that motivations are at stake, not formalities of performance: here too the problem is the violation of the ideal relationship of love. In proposing to Esther, Jarndyce leverages his power as rich guardian, aware that she does not love him. He makes his offer in a letter – a suspected instrument in *Bleak House*[58] – which seemingly says everything possible to free Esther to make any choice, as she reports:

> It addressed me as if our places were reversed: as if all the good deeds had been mine, and all the feelings they had awakened, his. It dwelt on my being young, and he past the prime of life … It told me that I would gain nothing by such marriage, and lose nothing by rejecting it … I was always to remember that I owed him nothing, and that he was my debtor.
>
> (690–1)

Yet as soon as Esther reads the letter she feels she "had but one thing to do" (692), as Jarndyce must have known she would. As Gary Watt argues, Jarndyce evades responsibility in ignoring the power he has gained by the bond of gratitude.[59] Nothing could emphasize Esther's indebtedness to Jarndyce more than its utter denial. Despite the socioeconomic merits of this marriage, Esther, who loves Woodcourt, sobs at the prospect.

The proposal's problematic resonates with a broader uneasiness about the integrity of Jarndyce's beneficence. Jarndyce's letter tells Esther that she had wrought changes in him since he first saw her in a stage coach, when she was fourteen. This confession recalls that first meeting: Esther was leaving her childhood home, crying in the coach; Jarndyce, a stranger, over fifty, oddly wrapped in furs, wiped her eyes with his sleeve, offered tempting foods hidden in his pockets, and made her afraid. The same problem is hinted when Esther first arrives at Bleak House; as she recalls,

58 Allan Christensen, "'Not a Love Letter': Epistolary Proposals of Marriage and Narrative Theory in *Bleak House* and *Middlemarch,*" in *Letter(s): Functions and Forms of Letter-Writing in Victorian Art and Literature,* eds. Mariaconcetta Costantini *et al.* (Rome: Aracne, 2009), 59–9.

59 Gary Watt, *Equity Stirring: The Story of Justice Beyond Law* (Oxford: Hart Publishing, 2009), 19.

Jarndyce "had one of his arms round Ada's waist and the other round mine, and kissed us both in a fatherly way" – but her telling intuition is to be "demonstrative" (82). When Jarndyce proposes marriage Esther's initial fears become a shrewd intuition. The proposal likewise throws new light on Jarndyce's assigning to Esther the role of housekeeper and giving her old nicknames. These hints of attraction add up to Jarndyce's tendency to aid young people and his preference for child-like characters. With all these pieces put together Jarndyce's benevolence appears sexually charged, and at moments with the troubling light of pedophilia. As Timothy Peltason argues, he mixes the fatherly and the erotic.[60] Jarndyce's offer to Esther undermines his impartial, almost superhuman benevolence and authoritative worldviews.[61] The promise, in other words, undermines the moral outlook offered in *Bleak House*: it imperils the text, not just Esther.

Jarndyce finally releases Esther from her promise, apologizes for it, and gives a home to her and Woodcourt. Why put his character and the novel's moral outlook under threat in the first place? One answer is Dickens' idealization of unencumbered love. Just like the under-narrated broken promise between Lady Dedlock and Hawdon, so this over-narrated waived promise dramatizes a counterimage to the resolution offered in the relationship of love. The promises' formal role is representing dangers greater than themselves: The Hawdon-Lady Dedlock broken promise is the figurative source of *Bleak House's* spiraling miseries; the Jarndyce-Esther promise is the figurative cause of collapse of the textual moral vision meant to undo these miseries; both promises create deeply disturbing counterimages, amplifying the significance of the happy ending in a marriage of love.

Dickens drove the point to the extreme by keeping the force of status operative until the very last moment. From Esther's acceptance of Jarndyce's promise until the last chapters, Dickens kept her under obligation and repeatedly narrated her sexual discomfort with Jarndyce. The narrated motivation is to make the surprise replacement of Jarndyce with Woodcourt felt to the full – by Esther and implicitly by readers. The awkward tool chosen is a sadistic traffic in the novel's protagonist; this is a pathological instance of Esther's status-weakness, bringing to a height its implications which the love match finally ends.

60 Timothy Peltason, "Esther's Will," *ELH* 59, no. 3 (1992): 684.

61 Jarndyce's equivocal naming becomes less surprising from this perspective. The name resembles jaundice, which relates to a disease and also means to affect with envy or jealousy, or to tinge the views or judgment. These meanings seem to undermine Jarndyce's view point as does his marriage proposal. These resonances have also to do with the Chancery case of this name, another threat over Jarndyce's character. See "Jaundice" in *The Oxford English Dictionary Online*, http://dictionary.oed.com/cgi/ findword?query_type=wordandqueryword=jaundice. See also Watt, *Equity Stirring*, 57–8 for a discussion of the pun.

Status Not Gone, But Contained

Yet Esther's triumph does not simply do away with status hierarchies. When Jarndyce gives her as a "willing gift" (966) to Woodcourt, the uncertainty of love is already present: Esther is an agent ("willing") but she is also an object of male gifting in the most traditional sense which invokes both total female subordination and the class differentials between Jarndyce and Woodcourt.[62]

To explore the persistence of status I examine this and additional elements: Esther's dependence on the impersonal narrator who represents status in the novel, and revealing statements when she closes the novel, all speaking to class and gender in the context of the love match. All of these, while operating on different levels of the text, from a comprehensive element of form, through content, to a minute play with words, together reveal the ineradicable force of status in a world concurred by the love marriage. All, I suggest, were managed through a containment pattern.

The codependence of Esther and the narrator as inverse voices that divide between them the novel's labor – whether as two characters, as often suggested, or as two sides of a single narrator[63] – has been a central theme of *Bleak House* scholarship. One line of inversion and mutual dependence is the narration's relation to class: The impersonal voice is the almost exclusive narrator of aristocracy, and more crucially, the unrelenting admonisher of the evils of a classed society, the defining evil being an (im)morality of abstraction. As the narrator complains, "fashion" is "a world wrapped up in too much jeweler's cotton and fine wool, and cannot hear the rushing of the larger worlds, and cannot see them as they circle around the sun" (20). He provides what Amanda Anderson calls the sociological critique of class from a totalizing perspective, and what Judith Wilt calls judgment.[64] Esther meanwhile is both the outcast victim of that society and an optimist insistently deferring judgment, refusing despair, and eventually achieving mobility, providing the vision of the embedded social actor.[65] The split registers the power of hierarchy within a liberal vision insistent on social mobility: The narrator cannot be simply done away with; not only is his world at the roots of Esther's story as illegitimate child, but he and Esther complement one another in formal terms of plot coverage

62 See Gayle Rubin, "The Traffic in Women: Notes on the 'Political Economy' of Sex," in *Toward an Anthropology of Women*, ed. Rayna R. Reiter (New York: Monthly Review Press, 1975), 157–210.

63 Judith Wilt, "Confusion and Consciousness in Dickens's Esther," *Nineteenth-Century Fiction* 32, no. 3 (1977): 285–309.

64 Amanda Anderson, "Dickens, the Brontës, Gaskell: Politics and Its Limits," in *The Cambridge History of the English Novel*, eds. Robert Caserio and Clement Hawes (Cambridge: Cambridge University Press, 2012), 345–6. Wilt, "Confusion and Consciousness".

65 Ibid.

and comprehension. The world of status is in this sense ineradicable, the incompatibility of visions unresolved as Hillis Miller argued.[66] But, it is containable. Dickens' liberal effort to overcome class occurs through Esther's ability by the end of the novel to not only escape but encircle the narrator's narrative – the status-world which initially encircled her.

As many readers have argued, Esther's perspective becomes increasingly knowing in terms of plot "connexions," even as she insists on her uncertainty. Her formal closing of the novel is ultimately a performance of containment in which she switches places with the narrator who opened it. Anderson observes that Esther and the narrator sometimes adopt each other's formal and rhetorical strategies.[67] At the novel's end the crucial ability that Esther achieves is imparting a sense that her way of knowing is a powerful form of omniscience otherwise reserved for the totalizing outlook of the narrator. Or, as Audrey Jaffe puts it, Esther has established that omniscience is itself an imaginary wholeness existing only as a reflex of the first person subject.[68] The uncertainty and doubling of vision that Esther represents, and that readers have learned by the end of the novel to interpret and thus to rely on, are a mobility asserted against the certainty of a status-world. Esther's refusal to properly close the novel, that Wilt highlights, asserts her way of seeing over that of the narrator. The narrator closes the curtain on the aristocratic world of Chesney Wold in the chapter before last, moving with the class exclusivity he narrated into 'dull repose' (985); his presence, like that of status, has been toned down. Esther gets the last chapter; her victorious narration makes the final stamp and contains the world of status within her narrative.

Esther's power is crucially enhanced when Woodcourt is around, that is, when the love match is in view. When Jarndyce gives Esther to Woodcourt he says, "Allan Woodcourt stood beside your father when he lay dead – stood beside your mother" (965), effectively reading the love match back in time to empower Esther's narrative. As Alexander Welsh suggests, Woodcourt in a sense creates Esther by presiding over the deaths of the parents who had sinned,[69] and, I would add, who never followed through their love match. (Woodcourt's role is one reason that I emphasize the class- rather than gender side of the contrast between Esther and the narrator; from a gendered perspective Esther does not quite outgrow the narrator-as-male on her own. But more on gender in a moment.)

66 J. Hillis Miller, "Interpretation in *Bleak House*," in J. Hillis Miller, *Victorian Subjects* (London: Harvester Wheatsheaf, 1990), 198.

67 Anderson, "Dickens, the Brontës, Gaskell."

68 And vice versa. Audrey Jaffe, *Vanishing Points: Dickens, Narrative, and the Subject of Omniscience* (Berkeley, CA: University of California Press, 1991), Chapter 4.

69 Alexander Welsh, *Dickens Redressed: The Art of "Bleak House" and "Hard Times"* (New Haven, CT: Yale University Press, 2000), 32–3.

Yet victory is fragile, not least because the voice of mobility is also that of instability. John Jordan argues that Esther loses herself in the final chapter – a point I complicate below – and therefore reads her back into the narrator's chapter – the one before last.[70] While I suggest that the formal order of chapters deserves more emphasis than Jordan allows, I share with him the sense of fragility of Esther's emergence, which makes *Bleak House's* efforts of containment very vivid.

Before examining Esther's contested ending, which moves the discussion from class to gender, it is worth pausing on her love for Woodcourt. Esther just happens to fall in love with a person more appropriate than Jarndyce to her ambiguous class. Chris Vanden Bossche argues that Esther and Woodcourt resist class discourse altogether.[71] While they do not opt for direct discourse, they nonetheless appeal to middle-class values, not least those of vocation and domesticity, even as Esther's position, as I observe in a moment, is equivocal. On either interpretation, it is noteworthy that their match is less class-obtrusive than the Jarndyce match. This narrative choice, I suggest, represents an effort to narrate class-fit between loving couples. Such efforts speak to the need to reconcile love and status. Their logic exposes the pattern of containment whereby love drives the marriage, while class compatability appears as an unintended convenient consequence.

Along narrations of direct class compatibility, a second strategy for maintaining class-fit can be observed in narrations of class-crossing (a rare narrative choice[72]) neutralized for all practical and symbolic purposes. To place it alongside Dickens' treatment of Esther I return for a moment to *Middlemarch*.

Michie describes two kinds of fit strategies in cases of class-crossing. One is as an uplifting of the husband in terms other than economic so as to compensate for a woman's elevated status.[73] Eliot's treatment of Dorothea and Will fitted the strategy. Like Dickens, Eliot contrasted love with class. Will's social and economic inferiority, of amphibious status as Elizabeth Langland calls it,[74] invokes shock and anger in Dorothea's circle, while her insistence on marrying him sets apart love from class as marriage motivations. Eliot relied on Dorothea's love marriage explicitly to signal freedom.

70 John O. Jordan, *Supposing* Bleak House (Charlottesville, VA: University of Virginia Press, 2011).

71 Chris R. Vanden Bossche, "Class Discourse and Popular Agency in *Bleak House*," *Victorian Studies* 47, no. 1 (2004): 7–31.

72 On its rarity, especially for working-class women, see Elizabeth Langland, *Nobody's Angels: Middle-Class Women and Domestic Ideology in Victorian Culture* (Ithaca, NY: Cornell University Press 1995).

73 Elsie B. Michie, *The Vulgar Question of Money*, 13–14.

74 Ibid., 204.

As Raymond Williams observed, Will is free not just in name; in him Eliot sought to think and feel beyond the restrictions and limitations she was recording.[75] In Chapter 4 I discussed the anticlimax of the union, but here we should observe that it is disappointing precisely in proportion to the expectation of liberally-schooled readers, accustomed to the rule of love, to have narrative desire fulfilled. You await the union, hence the anticlimax of economizing talk which cannot exceed itself. Yet Dorothea's economizing is only the small trouble. The defiance of class that it represented was the daring move, and the narrative contains the pressure by privileging other realms, like art and intellectualism, in which Will excels, so as to diffuse class transgression.

Michie also points to a second strategy: leveling down, where the woman is downgraded to the man's economic position. On the surface, Eliot seemed to engage that strategy too when she let Dorothea lose Casaubon's fortune, but the crucial thing that is *not* sacrificed is the Brooke succession. Eliot daringly lifted love to the level of socioeconomic power. In the novel's finale it turns out that Dorothea's learning of costs was a shallow, if not empty gesture. The narrator tells readers that Dorothea "never repented that she had given up position and fortune," but a paragraph later undoes the main sacrifice: no "lasting alienation" with her family holds on account of the improper marriage with "low blood" (783); following an easy reconciliation, Brooke is happily talked out of cutting Dorothea's son off the entail, and the transfer of estate, the classic signal of old status and the source of income for the future, continues with Dorothea and Will. The solution disrupts expectations of endogeneity that Michie argues applied to heiresses, yet, we should observe that it is portrayed as continuity. Analyzing the similar convergence of love and land in *The Way We Live Now* (Hetta and Paul), Supritha Rajan argues that the solution supplies a fiction that the system of endogamous inheritance has not been interrupted.[76] Or we might view the same point in terms of the conflict that Perry analyzes between consanguineal and conjugal ties, to see that these ties are reconciled.[77] Observe the implication: Rank is made subservient to love and to a woman's love at that, but at the same time the significance of traditional status markers is confirmed. Readers in the last moment must know that estate inheritance (or the wholeness of traditional consanguineal kinship) can be the happy

75 Raymond Williams, *The English Novel from Dickens to Lawrence* (London: Hogarth Press, 1984), 93.

76 Supritha Rajan, *A Tale of Two Capitalisms: Sacred Economics in Nineteenth-Century Britain* (Ann Arbor: The University of Michigan Press, 2015), 210.

77 Perry, *Novel Relations*.

background of love.[78] As Rajan says, at stake is a joining of the holiness of love with the traditional one of land. Far less conservative than narrations of class-fit though Dorothea's plot is (and even empowering from the perspective of gender, if we accept Perry's analysis of the benefits of consanguineal models for women), here too we see a tribute to the power of status.

The important point in these plots is that status retained significance, but with a twist: it could no longer occupy the active place of motive; its explanatory role in marital decisions was diminished while it became an element, a welcomed one, of what readers were placed to accept as an anyway-established relation. Status, while neither goal nor explanation, was a stabilizing force.

A similar pattern is evident with gender hierarchies that plagued the love marriage at its height. What is a "willing gift" – as Esther is? The grammatical logic enwraps the gift in the active will, yet it is very hard to breathe life, and particularly a liberal will, into an object. Having willed to be exchanged Esther celebrates her love in an ending that has enraged many readers:

> The people even praise Me as the doctor's wife. The people even like Me as I go about … I owe it all to him … They like me for his sake, as I do everything I do in life for his sake."
>
> (988–9)

Hierarchy appears to have captured love's victory.[79] As Mill would later charge, "All the moralities tell them that it is the duty of women, and all the current sentimentalities that it is their nature, to live for others; to make complete abnegation of themselves, and to have no life but in their affections."[80] Mill did not like *Bleak House* and charged Dickens with ridiculing

78 Another form of containing class within love returns to law. Recall juries' aversion to cross-class engagements, manifest in their damage awards (note 44 and accompanying text). The aversion was not conceptualized through a straight-forward admission that crossing class is inappropriate in itself; this would be a problematic assertion if love is the only relevant consideration in marriage decisions. And so, class-crossing was rationalized as an *absence* of love – it was considered a sign of gold-digging which replaced love. In effect, class-belonging retained relevance to promises of marriage, but its relevance was not acknowledged as a problem of protecting status as such – status could no longer function as a goal or explanation for marriage; instead class was processed through the liberal frame of reference which highlighted the importance of affection.

79 Claims of her effacement come in psychoanalytic and not just feminist terms. Jordan's psychoanalytic account suggests that Esther slips here into her old "good" self, an underworld in which she is not fully alive, rooted in mother-daughter deficiencies. Jordan, *Supposing* Bleak House.

80 John Stuart Mill, *The Subjection of Women* (Penn State University (electronic classics), 1999) (1869), 21.

the rights of women.[81] Esther appears to enact subjection to its utmost, yet her gesture frustrates readers because by this point it is inconsistent: her self-annihilating discourse had been doubled from the very start, and eventually denied as she became the novel's center. This problematic is central to Esther's narration. From *Bleak House's* publication onwards, readers have been debating whether or not she was a failed character. Feminist criticism generally agrees that Esther represents a set of female virtues, some embraced by (some) feminists, others rejected as oppressive: an ethic of care, a tendency to self-renunciation, and an ideal domesticity[82] – but splits on whether she is ultimately a powerful individual or a subjectified consciousness.[83]

As with other cases of tension between liberal ideals and statuses, the point here too is irresolvability. The stakes often lay in reconciling the poles of subjection and power. For instance, Langland argues that Esther's seeming disappearance depends on her own skillful sleight of hand, in line with the powerful domestic ideology she represents.[84] What requires emphasis is Dickens' effort to preserve a liberal subjectivity attained by love, and contain the gender hierarchy of domestic ideology and of the construction of womanhood more broadly within it. Even on the face of the page and the simple lines, Esther at once disappears and emerges. Observe the double, capitalized "*Me*" that Kathleen Blake views as a win along with love.[85] Esther's subjectivity, seemingly denied in her discourse, is equally emphasized; she succeeds in emerging salient and capitalized from the abnegation she narrates as a consequence of her love marriage, exceeding textual content through textual form – in the most direct sense of visual perception of the letters on the page. Esther's *Me* emphasizes the individual self, insisting that it carry the weight of a gendered model of individuality without collapsing. Esther's *Me* is Dickens' effort to breathe

81 John Stuart Mill, A Letter to Harriet Taylor, March 20, 1854, in *Charles Dickens: The Critical Heritage*, ed. Philip Collins (London: Taylor & Francis, 2005), 311.

82 E.g., Allison Case, "Gender and History in Narrative Theory: The Problem of Rhetorical Distance in David Copperfield and Bleak House," in *A Companion to Narrative Theory*, eds. James Phelan and Peter J. Rabinowitz (Malden, MA: Blackwell, 2005), 312–21.

83 E.g., Suzanne Graver, "Writing in a 'Womanly' Way and the Double Vision of *Bleak House*," *Dickens Quarterly* 4 no. 1 (1987): 1–15. Graver argues that ultimately Dickens subjected Esther's complexity to a separate-spheres patriarchal ideology; Virginia Blain, "Double Vision and the Double Standard in *Bleak House*: A Feminist Perspective," *Literature and History* 11, no. 1(1985): 31–64. Blain argues that the separation of spheres is the source of violence condemned in the novel; Wilt, "Confusion and Consciousness." Wilt argues for Esther's power by reading the impersonal narrator as part of her voice. For a review of debates see Kathleen Blake, "*Bleak House*, Political Economy, Victorian Studies," *Victorian Literature and Culture* 25, no. 01 (1997), 13–15.

84 Langland, *Nobody's Angels*, 96.

85 Blake, "*Bleak House*, Political Economy," 15.

willfulness into female objects. He did not simply register a tension between gender and love; gender hierarchy was turned into a relational modality within a liberal account of love as self-fulfillment. As historians often argue, patriarchal and passionate marriages were never stark opposites.[86] Not only did thinkers like Dickens find ways of reconciling love with patriarchal authority – a reconcilement that, as Luhmann observes, had deep roots in the Christian conception of one's relation to God[87] – but we can see here the structural terms of reconcilement.

Feminists have long criticized the ideological side of accounts of female power rooted in models of care and self-denial; Mill's claim that women's minds had been enslaved to produce sentiment to go along with obedience articulated that critique.[88] But we should see that something beyond apologetics was taking place in such efforts: gender hierarchy was secured, but at the same time could no longer be an *alternative* explanation of marital relations; it had to fit into love. We might read the move as a cultural attempt to eliminate the possibility of the "bad man" as Mill described the unloving husband-master whom the law should imagine in structuring married women's rights.[89] Containment in love reduced pressures, like Mill's, toward equality; after all, without bad men there was less urgency. But containment also, and uncynically, denied legitimacy from sheer mastery as the logic of marriage.

In Perry's account, gender subordination is ultimately a capitalistic project. The ideology of love, she argues, was a rationalization for the reality of marriages institutionally serving economic imperatives: the capitalistic consolidation of property and management of financial liabilities.[90] It is hard to dispute the conjugal family's relation to capitalism even if you are reluctant to commit to a functional unidirectionality (a point I revisit in Chapter 6). But it is nonetheless important to appreciate the ways hierarchy could and could not operate inside this system.

Withdrawal

I now turn to examine a different pattern of liberal ideals' entanglement with statuses. While containment reflected an insistence on keeping the liberal frame of reference extensive, and controlling and reconciling the forces of status to liberal conceptual structures, withdrawal signified taking

86 E.g., James Hammerton, *Cruelty and Companionship: Conflict in Nineteenth-Century Married Life* (New York: Routledge, 1992), 2; Ben Griffin, *The Politics of Gender in Victorian Britain: Masculinity, Political Culture and the Struggle for Women's Rights* (Cambridge: Cambridge University Press, 2012), at 46.

87 Luhmann, *Love as Passion*, 130.

88 Mill, *Subjection*, 18.

89 Ibid., 42.

90 Perry, *Novel Relations*, Chapter 5.

a step back; it reflected a willingness to narrow down the application of the liberal frame of reference in order to keep it coherent, ideal indeed. With withdrawal statuses were made room for, and the hope of liberal mobility preserved elsewhere. Yet this was not the full conceptual move: the crucial addition in withdrawal was to treat that elsewhere as more important, and so channel cultural energies to areas of culture responsive to liberal idealizations.

I begin again with law, reading central features of breach of promise law as a way of withdrawing contract so that it need not include status biases within its positive ambit, and yet retain its centrality for the marital relation. I then turn to the withdrawal of love in *Middlemarch*. Eliot acknowledged that love did not overcome nor coherently contain statuses, but still navigated it to a central conceptual place in the order of things.

Withdrawing Contract

Victorian contract law at times withdrew its formal application from areas in which statuses too clearly held sway. Two curious instances were the classical contractual theory of the promise of marriage, and the foundations of legal liability for its breach.

By the time civil marriage was made universal toward the mid-nineteenth century – apparently a step toward contractualism – the view of marriage as contract depended on the nominally consensual aspect involved in choosing a spouse or agreeing to marry. Other than this element, from early in the century the incidents of marriage were largely prescribed by the state.[91] This fact posed a difficulty for classical theorists of contract: if roles, rights and obligations in marriage were determined by the state, and husband and wife, the parties to the initial contract of the promise of marriage, could little alter the terms, marriage hardly fitted into the vision of contract as a self-imposed, freely-willed law. Coverture meant the legal death of married women as contracting parties, itself a doctrine in stark opposition to the idea of the marital relation as contract, hence the traditional

91 Sandra Berns, "Women in English Legal History: Subject (Almost), Object (Irrevocably), Person (Not Quite)," *University of Tasmania Law Review* 12, no. 1, (1993): 26–72; John V. Orth, "Contract and the Common Law," in *The State and Freedom of Contract*, ed. Harry N. Scheiber, (Stanford, CA: Stanford University Press, 1998), 52 ("the contract of marriage carries the parties, as it were, to the threshold of their new status, but not beyond"). For an expansive account of models of marriage in the Anglo-American tradition, see John Witte Jr., *From Sacrament to Contract: Marriage, Religion, and Law in the Western Tradition* (Louisville, KY: Westminster/John Knox Press, 1997). Witte argues that the contractarian model of the Enlightenment, in which marriage was in essence a voluntary bargain with terms set by the parties themselves, was adumbrated in the eighteenth century, elaborated theoretically in the nineteenth, but implemented legally only in the twentieth century. The model could not transform the law of the nineteenth century, though it induced greater protections for wives and children. Ibid., 10, 194–215.

feminist invocation of contract to attack coverture, prevalent in the nineteenth century. Mary Lyndon Shanley describes the position of Victorian political feminism as an individualistic critique of law resisted by a patriarchal understanding of marriage.[92] As a matter of public debate in the Victorian era, Geoffrey Searle recounts, the contractual view of marriage was up against a concurrence between the Christian emphasis on marriage's sacramental quality which united man and woman into one person, and separate-spheres apologetics which combined a denial of gender equality and a concern about the ruthless world of the market from which one had to find shield and protect the family.[93] As Marcus observes, both opponents and proponents of contractual marriage assumed that it signified a progress narrative of gender equality.[94] And so, in both meanings of status – as social ascription and as reference to state-made law, marriage posed a challenge to the contractual framing.

The consequence of state prescriptions was, as Duncan Kennedy argues, that classical legal writers eventually excluded marriage from their treatises on the law of contract, defining it as status, a process that began with John Austin who used the concept of status vis-à-vis abstract rights and duties to organize the exposition of legal rules.[95] Weber would later distinguish between "status contracts" which involved a change in "the total legal situation (universal position) and the social status of the persons involved" – a mode typical of primitive societies, and "purposive contracts," "aiming solely … at some specific (especially economic) performance or result" – typical of market societies.[96] But classical legal theorists did not contain status in contract in this instance, but rather cut off marriage from contract. William Anson's treatise made the logic explicit when he excluded from his treatment transactions that were "not such as we ordinarily term Contracts"; among these were "[a]greements which affect a change of status immediately upon the expression of the consent of the parties, such as marriage, which, when consent is expressed before a competent authority, alters at once the legal relations of the parties in many ways."[97] The formal reasoning, we can see, did not explain the

92 Mary Lyndon Shanley, *Feminism, Marriage, and the Law in Victorian England, 1850–1895* (Princeton, NJ: Princeton University Press, 1989). See also Jones, *Consensual Fictions*, Chapter 1; Sharon Marcus, *Between Women: Friendship, Desire, and Marriage in Victorian England* (Princeton, NJ: Princeton University Press, 2007), Chapter 5.

93 G.R. Searle, *Morality and the Market in Victorian Britain* (Oxford: Clarendon, 1998), Chapter 7.

94 Marcus, *Between Women*, 216.

95 Duncan Kennedy, *The Rise and Fall of Classical Legal Thought* (Washington, DC: Beard, 2006), Chapter 4.

96 Max Weber, *Economy and Society: An Outline of Interpretive Sociology*, eds. Guenther Roth and Claus Wittich (Berkeley, CA: University of California Press, 1978), vol. 2, 668–80.

97 William Reynell Anson, *Principles of the English Law of Contract* (Oxford: Clarendon Press, 1879), 3; and see discussion in Kennedy, *Rise and Fall*, 204–5.

inapplicability of contract in terms of social hierarchy directly, but rather through a formal legal distinction between state- and individually-made law. Yet the reasoning aligned both meanings of status, because the terms of marriage which the state prescribed had everything to do with gender hierarchies. Kennedy argues that the state provisions that classical theorists excluded were more concerned with communal solidarity than with the legal backing of despotic power – and effectively supported a laissez faire vision which marginalized community. In the case of women's rights in England this would be a strained account, even if the atomistic alternative was little more attractive. Observe that this instance of withdrawal is interestingly resonant of a process of withdrawal in doctrinal developments in courts that Susan Staves finds in the eighteenth century. The application of contract ideology to domestic relations, she says, reveals how it "was felt to lead to consequences so genuinely subversive of patriarchy that after some decades ... courts attacked the relevance of this logic in domestic cases."[98] In excluding marriage from contract, classical thinkers thus created a sharp theoretical distinction between the promise of marriage and marriage itself. While the promise of marriage was a contract, marriage was not.[99] The distinction, I suggest, is an important instance of withdrawal.

Historians of contracts usually attend to the theoretical distinction between marriage and promise of marriage because it reveals the broader process of differentiating status from contract, and the emergent support for the liberal construction of contract in terms of autonomous individual willing. Feminist histories, meanwhile, have paid much of their attention to the "status" part of this history – that of marriage – and have examined women's subjection and forms of resistant agency. It is worth paying more attention, however, to the effect the distinction had specifically on the promise of marriage, standing as it were just on the brink of status.

The distinction between the promise of marriage and marriage brought the promise closer to the ideal contract, because in withdrawing contract law's application from marriage itself, legal thinkers withdrew the ambition to control too much through free will. Once marriage was out, the promise of marriage presumed to embody choice of the identity of a spouse, and no more;[100] the object of choice in this instance (spouse) was isolated from the future relation envisioned by choosing (marriage). This move freed the promise of marriage from much of the conceptual conundrum that plagued the classical model of contract elsewhere.

As discussed Chapter 1, the classical model ran into trouble because it

98 Susan Staves, *Married Women's Separate Property in England, 1660–1833* (Cambridge, MA: Harvard University Press, 1990), 167.

99 Kennedy, *Rise and Fall*, 195–205. Treatises of contract law from the preclassical era included marital obligations in their treatment of contract.

100 This move did not solve the problem of status considerations affecting the choice of spouse; I turn to them shortly.

was overly ambitious in its presumed application to social relations. Critiques of the temporal structure of the model clarify the difficulty: The legal celebration of individual will was captured in contract law's emphasis on the moment of formation. That emphasis came with a discount of circumstances preceding formation, focusing on the exercise of the will as a starting point, thus picturing it as a root cause of contractual relations; and a discount of circumstances that followed formation, thus picturing the exercise of the will as sufficient reference for the contractual relation. Put simply, the classical model's temporal freeze made the exercise of the will a necessary and sufficient condition of contractual relations. Now, this freeze entailed not just considerable injustices but conceptual stretches: expressed wishes at specific moments in time became rationalizations of ongoing relationships in which statuses, as well as other social and interpersonal determinants, emerging from both past and future constraints, had a role to play.[101] These moves, according to many historical accounts, undermined the model's coherence and invited critique. In Part I recounted a relational liberalism in novels and suggested that it may have inflected law in ways which remain unexamined by historians. The promise of marriage seems better suited to the model of atomistic individualism from this perspective, for it was a contract that did *not* presume to formally control the relationship it signaled. Ironically, the association of contract with free will could be more convincing here than it could in more paradigmatic areas of contract law.

While the exercise of the will was formally limited to the identity of spouse, with the rest of marriage beyond its control, the significance of the moment of choice – the promise of marriage – remained enormous. The promise had to carry much of the weight of the idealist attempt to imagine the modern family institution based on new mobilities. This required the second conceptual move involved in withdrawal: trivializing withdrawal's implications. Here the broader classical legacy of core and periphery in private law had a role to play. The conceptual structure of private law in classical legal thought made the will of the parties the core and the will of community a periphery, indicating clearly the hierarchy between them – hence, historians argue, contracts' positioning as the heart of private law. Put simply, the social regulation of the marital relation, with the subjection of women within that context, was conceptualized as secondary in importance to the freedom associated with the point of entry into marriage. That conceptual structure could at once limit the application of the atomistic

101 As I noted in the Introduction, over a hundred years later, Ian Macneil, equating promise with individual willing, articulated the critique by claiming that contract is ridden with "non-promissory" elements; without accounting for them, it cannot be comprehended Ian R. Macneil, *The New Social Contract: An Inquiry into Modern Contractual Relations* (New Haven, CT: Yale University Press, 1980).

ideal in contracts to keep it coherent, and rely on it to explain and justify the institution of marriage *as a whole*.

Even in this shrunken form, freedom at the point of entry into marriage was not free from status. What about the motives for choosing one's spouse? Here a second instance of withdrawal can be observed.

Formal enforcement of promises of marriage depended, recall, on proving a promise, not its motives.[102] Randall Craig explains the legal reluctance to consider the relation between love and breach of promise as a privatizing tendency, but observe that evasion of motives was an effective withdrawal from an area hardly likely to fit liberal idealizations of either love or contract;[103] class-fit as well as gender inequalities retained power in channeling ideally autonomous choices of future couples.[104] Put differently, upholding choice in the abstract, an enactment of the core ideal of atomistic contractual freedom, was also a mark of the *limits* of contractual analysis. Upholding choice in this manner rid contract law of the need to ask about motives to marry, a locus of status biases.

If contract withdrew from the question of motives, however, this move again required a justification which would make the withdrawal unimportant. This was available in the construction of autonomy in atomistic liberal thought: The liberal outlook, explains Alan Brudner, assumes an individual abstracted from relation to another, as a fixed and stable existence. Given this assumption, contractual rights and duties are grounded by abstracting from all concrete intentions (seen as mere subjective preferences) to the bare capacity of choosing as the only capacity worthy of respect. From this perspective, motives have no rational significance. They are not the expression of freedom but particularistic inclinations from which thought must abstract in order to arrive at a foundation for obligations.[105] The important thing, quite simply, was abstract choice where contract reigned supreme; motives, susceptible to status, were of no "rational significance."

102 Reluctance to scrutinize motives was also evident in the denial of a defense based on suspect motives: the argument that a woman was undemonstrative was unacceptable: if the woman appeared not to love the man, this was no excuse for breaching a promise. Lettmaier, *Broken Engagements*, 47. It did influence damages, as noted earlier.

103 Craig, *Promising Language*.

104 To clarify, the argument here is not causal, but structural: what matters is that objectivism in this sense keeps the question of status outside formal contract discourse without resolving it.

105 Alan Brudner, *The Unity of the Common Law*, 2nd ed. (Oxford: Oxford University Press, 2013), Chapter 4; see also Peter Benson, "The Unity of Contract Law," in *The Theory of Contract Law: New Essays*, ed. Peter Benson (Cambridge: Cambridge University Press, 2001), 139–49. Benson explains how, in the doctrine of offer and acceptance, the capacity to choose is abstracted from all internal and external circumstances in which it is exercised.

Was withdrawal a real entanglement of contract and status which altered both, as containment was? Can it be seen as statuses' new interpretation? I return to this question after discussing love's withdrawal.

Withdrawing Love

Middlemarch, like *Bleak House*, ended by highlighting the problem of gender in Victorian marriage. As in *Bleak House*, gender inequalities plague the love relation of Dorothea and Will once achieved: Dorothea disappears into intersubjectivity in a finale reminiscent of Esther's:

> Many who knew her, thought it a pity that so substantive and rare a creature should have been absorbed into the life of another, and be only known in a certain circle as a wife and mother. But no one stated exactly what else that was in her power she ought rather to have done. (783)

Though Dorothea now has a "love stronger than any impulses which could have marred it" (782), Eliot, occupied with the 1860s concern with women's vocational options,[106] refused to ignore her inferior position as social member. Unlike the containment offered by *Bleak House's* capitalized "*Me*," the love Dorothea finds is an express trade-off for a full *Me*, not a form of its attainment. As things stand, Eliot suggested in a far more radical position on gender, this is better than nothing for no one can "state exactly" what a woman might otherwise do, or be. Recall that Dorothea was driven to marriage in the first place through exclusions from political economy. *Middlemarch* offers the love relation not as a utopian end able to contain and redirect social pressure, but as a comfort in its midst.

And yet, despite this express withdrawal, the love Dorothea attains was Eliot's effort at closure. In Chapter 4 I noted the equivocalities of closure, which remained uncertain as a ground of existential meaningfulness, and argued that Dorothea's "incalculably diffusive" (785) effects on the good of the world were a rhetorical trick which did not fully work, not least because of Dorothea's gender subordination. But here I want to highlight the lengths to which Eliot went to centralize love as the *sine qua non* for whatever good *could* be achieved. Her centralization of love sketched an order of significances which placed love high in a world of suffocations.

The question of love in Dorothea's life is brought to the fore in her plot almost despite Dorothea herself, whose idea of achievement lies in being

106 See Schaffer, *Romance's Rival*, Chapter 6; Charles Hatten, *The End of Domesticity: Alienation from the Family in Dickens, Eliot, and James* (Newark, DE: University of Delaware Press, 2010), Introduction.

somehow "greatly effective" (26) in the public realm, and despite Eliot's express framing which opened, as it ended, with the theme of gender inequality. Schaffer argues that Eliot was shaping the "suppressive hypothesis" (her analogue to Foucault's repressive one) which obsessively showed marriage's suppression of the liberal free woman's vocational urge, while failing to imagine alternatives in which happy, successful, working women could exist. On Schaffer's account, the gradual pathologizing of all kinds of marriages other than romantic ones, which may have made sense for women, and the very narrative insistence that heroines marry (and by hypothesis suffer) were themselves part of the suppression.[107] My interest, however, is in the historical assumption that Eliot betrayed as she gave shape to *Middlemarch*, namely, that pressures on women to marry and to relinquish public roles were the background context against which stories of Dorotheas developed. *Middlemarch* bespeaks the assumption that gender hierarchy was an inevitable (and appalling) condition and frame for plots, while love was a signal of mobility, precisely the assumption that feminist histories would overturn in identifying love as part of the problem. The question I want to examine is how love was made to matter in a plot that framed it in liberal terms, yet was too well aware of the force of status hierarchies.

Eliot associated love with social progress on the level of content, while, and more crucially, as a matter of form she allocated narrative attention to love over gender hierarchy. Observe that making love matter in this way is not the typical privatizing urge which flattened political consciousness. Dorothea's gendered subordination in a love marriage is where the novel points to an *admittedly* unaccommodating order of things. This is the interesting side of withdrawal: Rather than try to overcome status with love, Eliot withdrew love's reach, openly pointing to its limits, but salvaged the novel's liberalism by attributing importance to the conceptual apparatus of love.

In content, love becomes the heart of social progress through an equation between Dorothea's positive effects on her social surroundings and the love marriage. Three main phases are easily discernable. To begin with, Dorothea's abilities to help the world are narrowed to naught while married to Casaubon, the absence of affection translated directly into a "moral imprisonment" (258). When Casaubon dies, Dorothea's agency evolves. Her failed marriage allows her to sympathize with Lydgate's similar failure. The parallel to a man, a professional career, and a public good (public health) is significant; Eliot made complex the private/public and gendered divide by having Lydgate experience a parallel, if not quite as dramatic, constriction in consequence of his loveless marriage. The basic condition of love is key for both Dorothea and Lydgate. Economizing, that I discussed in Chapter 4, is itself a practice that love-matches enable in the

107 Ibid.

novel. The lessons of a loveless marriage allow Dorothea to become the agent behind Lydgate's mild rehabilitation. Yet without positive love she is halted, and eventually at a loss. It is crucial that Eliot's acute awareness of gender oppression emerged subordinate to her centralization of love: While oppression is pervasive in Dorothea's life, it is worse when Dorothea is widow than when she is in a relationship of love. On her own, recall, she ended up without access to language. This position is not easily supported by the history of coverture, nor by the options of widows as Schaffer notes,[108] nor by the plot (given Casaubon's material punishment), and reflects a dramatic ideological effort.

And so, when Dorothea marries Will love must free her to do good in the sweeping generalizations of the novel's finale. Rather than observe the details of love's effects on social progress, the retrospective narrator offers us incalculable diffusiveness which typifies not just Dorothea's effects but the abstract manner of (un)narrating them. The closing words claim progress again almost despite themselves (my interventions in brackets): "that things are not so ill *[but still ill]* with you and me as they might *[not surely]* have been, is half owing *[just half, implying that nobody knows]* to the number who lived faithfully a hidden life and rest in unvisited tombs" (785). The wavering claims, made shortly after the narrator's complaints about Dorothea's gender oppression, are revealing of the narrative effort to make love signify while conceding an unobliging world.

Observe that Eliot's equation between the fortunes of love and the fortunes of society, reliant on the reverse mirror imaging of Dorothea's two marriages, turns on the genuineness of mutual love already at the point of decision – formally the promise to marry. This reinforces the promise's conceptual centrality despite its logical redundancy: after all, love could fail or succeed at later points in the relationship, an option Eliot neglected to develop, finding all the relevant signs of success or failure already at the time of the decision to marry. It was the marriage beginning with mutual love that typified the happy ending of domestic plots, while failed love, whether because unilateral or absent, was extensively explored, a point that Hager highlights.[109] Schaffer observes that the idea that love would develop after the wedding became unpopular in the Victorian era.[110] It is equally revealing to observe the reluctance to look into life after the moment of mutual love in protagonists' stories, which was a form of withdrawal into the limited temporal dimension in which liberal idealism could hold sway. As Schaffer suggests in distinguishing the romantic model from the "famil-

108 Schaffer, *Romance's Rival*, Chapter 6.

109 Kelly Hager, *Dickens and the Rise of Divorce: The Failed-Marriage Plot and the Novel Tradition* (Farnham: Ashgate Publishing, 2010).

110 Schaffer, *Romance's Rival*, 3.

iar marriage," the former lives in the present,[111] somewhat like the classical contractual model.

The last point leads to Eliot's manner of making love signify more than hierarchy on the level of form, through *Middlemarch's* allocation of attention. This is where most of the effect is achieved, for in content Eliot had a hard time making Dorothea's accomplishments meaningful. While Dorothea's search for true romantic love takes up the full span of the novel, her subjection under coverture in the love marriage, leaving her as only "wife and mother," is never narrated. The closing commentary remains the only complaint, much like Esther's implicit one in *Bleak House's* finale. This absence stands in contradistinction to the close study of womanly subjection during Dorothea's loveless marriage to Casaubon. The structure allows love to depreciate the meaning of status differentials prompted by marriage, despite their far-reaching implications for all women, loved or not.

Acknowledging love's limits and at the same time making it a core of social relations is no mean feat. In *Middlemarch's* finale the effort is thrown into sharp relief precisely because it is so equivocal, exposing the moves involved in the pattern of withdrawal: give something up, but belittle its meaning in the overall picture of the social order, and invest your energies elsewhere.[112]

Withdrawal appeared to keep liberal ideals and statuses separate and conceptually untouched, unlike the muddier pattern of containment. Put differently, while containment was clearly an entanglement and transformation of liberal ideals and statuses, withdrawal might seem closer to the notion of opposition between them often informing histories of liberalism. But here too, further attention to the separation withdrawal encouraged exposes a nuanced picture.

Withdrawal left certain areas, like married women's opportunities in the public arena, little transformed by liberal idealizations. At the same time, the second move entailed in withdrawal, that of centralizing areas of social life in which liberal ideals more easily applied, was significant in shifting cultural energies to those areas. Critical work has often been skeptical about these conceptual moves no less than about patterns of containment. However, in withdrawal, as in containment, there was more at stake than a rhetorical justification, or mystification, of preserved power structures, and more than a mediation of contradictions.[113] Withdrawal involved a transferal of efforts, and meaning. The private law of contract, and particularly the legal examination of "intention" (but not motive), developed

111 Ibid., 5.

112 For an argument about a similar move in Oliphant's fiction, but also a more radical turn in some of her late novels, see Jones, *Consensual Fictions*, Chapter 5.

113 For an account of the critical notion of mediating contradictions see for example Robert Gordon, "Critical Legal Histories," *Stanford Law Review* 36 nos. 1 and 2 (1984), 114–16.

significantly and intricately in manners still reverberant today; the emphasis on romantic love assumed unprecedented scope and became the very mark of realism, traceable in literature and beyond it ever since. As Nancy Armstrong argued, while the celebration of choice of partner over marital inequality (by writers who used a contractual rhetoric, a sexual contract modeled on the social contract[114]) implicitly justified women's subordination, it also licensed new forms of female authority.[115]

Taking all of this seriously, while observing the areas that withdrawal left out of the reach of liberal ideals, captures seemingly contradictory phenomena. This pattern explains the resilience of multiple gender-and-class hierarchies to change; their resilience was conceptually secured by liberal ideals' withdrawal in a manner clarifying that the elimination of statuses was not a commitment of living liberalism. At the same time, the concentration of cultural efforts in specific areas emerged in conceptual changes in self- and other-portrayals, changes that promised (or threatened) to inflect social spheres beyond the paradigmatic targets of idealist liberal thought. Consciousness fails to observe boundaries, and so the dynamics at work here implicated the stability of statuses. It can explain historical change without implying that the trajectory must be progressive. If Victorian liberalism is understood as an ambitious historical conceptualization of the social order at large, its manner of creating spaces for liberal ideals *and* statuses, while shifting their normative relationalities, should be seriously considered as a viable entanglement, a living liberalism.

* * *

The patterns of containment and withdrawal appear chaotic. One can observe different approaches to class: while at the level of literary discourse I noted primarily containment when it came to class-related motives, at the level of legal doctrine I noted withdrawal. Similarly, gender hierarchies were contained in some cases (as in *Bleak House* or litigation practice), withdrawn from in others (as in *Middlemarch* or legal theory). The patterns of containment and withdrawal were not coherent plans nor principled arguments; yet, despite the disorganized response they both occurred on different levels of culture – and so are not entirely untheorizable nor simply contradictory, and most crucially, they had a common effect. They distanced liberal thought in law as well as literature from an idealist

114 Interestingly, Armstrong used the term more or less concurrently with Pateman's work. Nancy Armstrong, *Desire and Domestic Fiction: A Political History of the Novel* (New York: Oxford University Press, 1987); Carole Pateman, *The Sexual Contract* (Stanford, CA: Stanford University Press, 1988). Armstrong's emphasis is not men's access to women's bodies but the division of labor according to sex that marriage implied.

115 For Armstrong, however, the logic of the process was ultimately coherent, the basis of the middle-class political rise. There is reason to doubt coherence and directionality here, a point I revisit in Chapter 6.

rejection of statuses and turned them into a restatement of statuses' roles. With statuses secured yet losing their roles as explanations and goals of social relations, and becoming a convenient background, social thought was in active search and articulation of new meanings, new routes of speech, new ways of understanding and justification, making for the ideological turbulence that Victorian living liberalism was.

And so, analyses claiming that liberal ideals were a transformative force in the Victorian era are no more wrong than those insisting that statuses were pervasive. But they are not right enough. Both idealist rejections of statuses and unwavering commitments to them were undermined – but not discarded. This chapter began a search for tools that come to terms with these dual dynamics, which seem still relevant today.

One locus of the incarnation of the same dynamics is the politics of recognition (or identity, or difference), and liberal multiculturalism. Discussions in this area emerge from the tension pervading multicultural societies between group-based and individual-based constructions of social relations. The politics of recognition rests on social group-belongings, and an emergent demand that society acknowledge specificity and embrace a differential treatment of persons based on their group identities. At the other end of the spectrum lies the liberal ideal of equal democratic citizenship based on difference-blindness. As Charles Taylor explains, the principle of universal equality is at once part of, and hard to assimilate to, the politics of recognition. This seems to be an intriguing location of the rehearsal of both withdrawal and containment; accounts of liberal citizenship alternate between the two patterns.

Withdrawal captures moves in which, as Taylor argues, fundamental rights are distinguished from a broad range of immunities and presumptions of equal treatment; in the latter difference can prevail and notions of universal difference-blind equality discarded, yet the former continue to be conceptualized as, indeed, fundamental. The significance of the abstract individual bearer of political rights is understood as a thin, yet crucial, framework, an outer bastion guaranteeing a critical minimum.

Under containment, group identities are conceptualized as the very heart of political rights. For supporters of historical liberalism, those whom Taylor calls the "proponents of the politics of dignity" (which replaced the politics of honor, i.e., status), such a conceptualization might appear like a reversal of their principle; in consequence attempts are made to justify these politics on the basis of dignity – a containment pattern; justifications succeed, Taylor reminds us, only up to a point.[116] His remark, which points to the limitations of an analysis based on a contradictory conceptual

116 Charles Taylor, *Multiculturalism and the "Politics of Recognition": An Essay* (Princeton: Princeton University Press, 1994).

relation between liberal- and group-based accounts of social life, seems to invite a rereading of living liberalism today as a complex mutuality of liberal ideals and new notions of group identities.

Ironically, in this round liberal ideals likely serve as a conceptual source of stability, while newly claimed statuses invoke perceptions of social disintegration. The dynamics at work in containment and withdrawal may have come full circle.

Chapter 6

Liberal Anguish

Wuthering Heights and the Structures of Liberal Thought

I circle back to the 1840s, this time to read a single novel, Emily Brontë's *Wuthering Heights* (1847),[1] and not as a historical site of liberal thinking in which to observe particular patterns, but instead as a conceptual commentary on those patterns, specifically on containment. Brontë relied on the fictionalization of varied promises; she pulled together family, friendship, credit, labor, land and trade, and offered an early and sophisticated argument about the pattern of containment as a dominant liberal mode for handling tensions.

At stake in *Wuthering Heights* is not only the problem of status hierarchies, but a messier set of ideas often considered problematic for liberal idealizations, among them irrationality, untamed passion, and the supernatural. But my motivation is not simply to extend the argument about containment in this manner. Rather, and more importantly, I want to observe an aesthetic enactment of the anguish that liberal structures of complexity were to evoke for generations to follow. The catastrophic qualities of *Wuthering Height* were an aesthetic amplification of the modern anguish of incomprehensibility and eruption at the heart of the liberal order, experienced already at the novel's troubled reception.[2]

Tension

Social Versus Psychic

Brief reminder: *Wuthering Heights* tells the generational history of a small group living in two isolated estates, Wuthering Heights and Thrushcross Grange, in the Yorkshire moors. The narrative is doubly framed, told by Lockwood, a tenant dismayed and attracted by the Heights' haunted

1 All references are to Emily Brontë, *Wuthering Heights: The 1847 Text, Backgrounds and Contexts, Criticism*, ed. Richard J. Dunn (New York: W. W. Norton and Co., 2003).

2 For a discussion of that reception see e.g., Ian Ward, "Emily Bronte and the Terrorist Imagination," *English Studies* 89, no. 5 (2008): 524–51.

quality and its violence; Lockwood records the narrative of the servant Nelly Dean. The embedded story takes off with the arrival of Heathcliff, a deserted child, into the Earnshaw family at the Heights. It recounts Heathcliff's and Cathy Earnshaw's intense love and his degradation by her brother and by the more bourgeois Lintons in the Grange. When Cathy decides to marry Edgar Linton, Heathcliff leaves and returns rich to take possession of the two estates and pursue a plan of demolition and domestic abuse which continues after Cathy dies, half-way through the novel, into the next generation.

Generations of *Wuthering Heights* readers have iterated a sense of duality in the novel, one of the very few elements that divergent readings of *Wuthering Heights* are likely to concede. A partial list going from the late 1940s to our own time includes treatments of the duality in terms of personal vs. social, spiritual vs. practical, necessary vs. agreeable;[3] daemonic depths of the soul vs. limited and limiting lucidities of consciousness;[4] metaphysical (a reservoir of society's unrealized value) vs. social, personal intensity vs. social domain;[5] woman (emotion, desire) vs. man (worldliness, education, travel, novel-reading);[6] passion vs. social intercourse privileging morality, religion, gender and class;[7] Romantic individualism vs. socialization;[8] and passion vs. contending social forces.[9] The sense of duality has also given rise to discussions of genre: *Wuthering Heights* might be treading between Romanticism and realism. Most generally, the sense of duality has generated rich and often contradictory readings, from which *Wuthering Heights* emerges as an elusive text resisting interpretation.[10]

3 Derek Traversi, "Wuthering Heights after a Hundred Years," in *Emily Brontë: "Wuthering Heights,"* ed. Miriam Allott (London: Macmillan, 1970), 157–76.

4 Dorothy Van Ghent, "Dark 'Otherness' in *Wuthering Heights,*" in Allott, *Emily Brontë: "Wuthering Heights,"* 177–83.

5 Terry Eagleton, "Myths of Power in 'Wuthering Heights,'" in *Emily Brontë: "Wuthering Heights,"* ed. Patsy Stoneman (Basingstoke: Macmillan, 1993), 118–30.

6 Nancy Armstrong, *Desire and Domestic Fiction: A Political History of the Novel* (New York: Oxford University Press, 1987).

7 Bette London, "Wuthering Heights and the Text Between the Lines," *Papers on Language and Literature* 24, no. 1 (1988): 34–52.

8 Linda M. Shires, "The Aesthetics of the Victorian Novel: Form, Subjectivity, Ideology," in *The Cambridge Companion to the Victorian Novel*, ed. Deirdre David (Cambridge: Cambridge University Press, 2001), 61–76.

9 Beth Newman, "*Wuthering Heights* in Its Context(s)," in *Approaches to Teaching Emily Brontë's "Wuthering Heights,"* eds. Sue Lonoff and Terri. A. Hasseler (New York: Modern Language Association of America, 2006), 36–43.

10 Discussions of (and disagreements about) the literary descent of *Wuthering Heights* abound. See for example, Mary Ward, "Introduction to *Wuthering Heights,*" in Allot, *Emily Brontë: "Wuthering Heights"*; Jacques Blondel, "Literary Influences on *Wuthering Heights,*" in Allot, *Emily Brontë: "Wuthering Heights,"* 229–41; Nancy Armstrong, "Emily Brontë in and out of Her Time," *Genre* 15 (1982): 243–64; Lyn Pykett, "Gender and Genre in 'Wuthering Heights': Gothic Plot and Domestic Fiction," in Stoneman, *Emily Brontë:*

In the reading that follows I conceptualize the duality in terms of the social and the psychic as two alternative logics for interpreting human experience, both operative in the novel. My reading maintains a dialogue with existing analyses while slightly shifting the emphasis in two senses. First, I emphasize the relation of duality to complexities constitutive of Victorian liberal thought. In the foreword to Part II, I recalled complexities that historians of Victorian liberalism have been examining; many of the dualities discussed in *Wuthering Heights* scholarship map on to these complexities because they essentially deal with the same troubled liberal consciousness.

I also shift the emphasis of existing readings by observing a subtle difference between the social/psychic and other dualities noted by readers. The social/psychic tension does not draw only on familiar complexities in liberalism; it tends to deepen the sense of incoherence by pushing beyond them. Estrangements of familiar dualities deny readers the comfort of readability of social relations and individual actors. Some dualities, such as that between passion and social order, were simply too accessible in the nineteenth century to impart discomfort and so create an *experience*, not just an intellectual understanding, of complexity. In offering experience Brontë moved beyond the familiar zone.

The implications of the social/psychic duality will become clear through my reading but I want to emphasize one implication of estrangement in relation to Chapter 5: From the perspective of this chapter, *both* sides of the hierarchy/progress tension belong to the side of the social, because, as I explain below, the social reads experience through the idea of living in society and speaks the language of social struggle and social order within which that tension made sense, while the psychic refers to combinations that defy its very ontology. I appreciate the confusion that this claim might generate. I therefore want to clarify upfront that the significance of the psychic/social tension for the discussion that follows lies less in the reframed content of familiar dualities, and more in the very act of reframing. Pushing beyond (some) recognizable tensions, the social/psychic relationality enables a particularly acute enactment of complexity – an aesthetics of incoherence capturing a liberal anguish.

"*Wuthering Heights*," 86–99; and U. C. Knoepflmacher, *Emily Brontë: "Wuthering Heights"* (Cambridge: Cambridge University Press, 1989). Readings of *Wuthering Heights* typically open with a review of the history of critical disagreement. For a relatively recent example, see Joseph Carroll, "The Cuckoo's History: Human Nature in *Wuthering Heights*," *Philosophy and Literature* 32, no. 2 (2008): 241–57.

Enabling Tension

Lockwood, the socialized visitor to the psychic Heights, is trapped in social metaphors:

> One state resembles setting a hungry man down to a single dish, on which he may concentrate his entire appetite, and do it justice; the other, introducing him to a table laid out by French cooks. He can perhaps extract as much enjoyment from the whole, but each part is a mere atom in his regard and remembrance.
>
> (49)

For Lockwood, the residents of the Heights form deeper attachments for lack of multitudinousness available in his world. Lack of multitudinousness emerges, however, in a qualitative difference that Lockwood's quantitative metaphors do not capture. It is not that things matter more; they matter differently. Isabella senses something of the qualitative difference: "I cannot recognise any sentiment which those around [at the Heights] share with me" (106).

The social logic in *Wuthering Heights* belongs to "the busy world" (196), a realm of the moderate, the rule-bound, the external, the understandable. The source of all of this is an existence understood and mediated through the comparative abstractions offered by the very idea of sociality, that is through a plurality of associations – including *dis*sociations – with other persons and groups of persons, and individuals' priorities (normative, ontological) vis-à-vis such persons and groups. Functional differentiation – or the capitalist division of labor – is an important aspect of the social logic.

The psychic realm, at the heart of the Heights, is, by contrast a realm of the inconsistent and inexplicable. It is not simply antisocial; its qualities emerge – and here lies the crucial difference – from an existence *un*mediated by a plurality of interpersonal and group associations, and by the functional differentiation of society. The specificity of contact between persons at the Heights emerges from and in psychic combinations which are almost beings, and are incomprehensible through the liberal lens of the social/individual relationality. (Think of the representations of Cathy and Heathcliff, a relationship that lacks psychological boundaries between selves, and even, finally, physical ones.[11]) These combinations gain their meaning without the option of nonspecificity – of remote or generic association, and of *dis*sociation – available in the social; without the option of a coherent individual identity

11 Harvey called this a "psychic decomposition", W.J. Harvey, *Character and the Novel* (London: Chatto & Windus. 1965), 127–9, while Bersani suggests that "certain configurations of characters begin to compete for our attention with the individual characters themselves," Leo Bersani, *A Future for Astyanax: Character and Desire in Literature* (London: Marion Boyars, 1978), 199.

constituted in some relation to various persons and groups and to social functions. Questions of relative abstraction are not part of the processes of meaning-making within the psychic logic. It is not that life in *Wuthering Heights* cannot be understood in social terms; it is that the social is not the controlling frame of reference; the fact that it can be is a constant threat.

The social/psychic tension runs through *Wuthering Heights.* It not only bifurcates the novel down the middle, as has often been argued; it actually bifurcates the novel's entire representational schema.[12] It occurs between frame and embedded stories: the sociality of Lockwood (the frame narrator) is more developed than that of Nelly (the embedded narrator), who is closer to the Heights. It also occurs between houses or families, for example the more social Grange vs. the psychic Heights, the more socialized Lintons vs. the psychic Earnshaws; within individuals, for example in Heathcliff, who embodies psychic and social elements; and between them and their house, for example between Nelly, who embodies some social elements, and the psychic Heights. The tension is importantly enacted in the novel's name: Wuthering Heights signals the social: it is a name of an estate, with the social-status connotations involved (can you help reading even "Heights" in a double sense?), and a name gaining its meaning from a provincial (read: socially decentered) use of language: "'Wuthering' being a significant provincial adjective." Concurrently, the name draws on the psychic – its atmosphere, at once naturalistic and uncanny, and its deep incoherence: "'Wuthering' … descriptive of the atmospheric tumult to which its station is exposed in stormy weather" (4).

Wuthering Heights represents the psychic and the social as incompatible logics. Yet their incompatibility does not rely on there being, anywhere, a "pure" case of either, but instead on textual representations of excess: the core of the Heights is excessively psychic, the periphery frame story excessively social, and so forth. Brontë let her characters (narrators included) process and interpret action predominantly through one construction or the other. At the same time that these logics are structurally inseparable on every level of representation in the novel, each of them, through this setting of excesses, becomes a disturbance to the other.

The social/psychic relationality functions as the novel's enabling tension. Brontë registered her historical moment – the rise of liberal consciousness – through the pervasiveness of the tension: an experience of inescapable complexity. Having grounded this experience, Brontë delineated the structure of containment in two related moves: she marked the

12 Shires argues for a bifurcation between the novel's two halves, yet the middle and end of the novel, on her account, are not committed to either side of the duality (which she views as Romantic individualism/social pressure). Shires, "Aesthetics of the Victorian Novel," 66–7. The analysis can be taken further, as I suggest below.

social's triumph over the psychic – the point at which the story becomes more recognizable for liberally-schooled readers; but she also defined that triumph as a matter of a titling of balance only, one in which the psychic remained a constitutive force, capturing a painful locus of disquiet, inherent and enduring, contained within the social. The formal structure of containment thus transpires in two seemingly opposite effects, as I argued in Chapter 5: it delimits the power of the psychic, and it keeps the psychic alive – conceptually secure within Victorian liberalism. It should come as no surprise that both the social/psychic tension and the process of containment are represented in the novel through promises.

Reading Experience Through the Social/Psychic Tension

Promissory Junctions

Wuthering Heights' embedded plot hinges on three promissory junctions. In the first junction, Heathcliff arrives as a broken promise, in lieu of presents promised by Mr. Earnshaw to his children and Nelly. In the second and third, Heathcliff moves to power over the Earnshaws and the Lintons: he comes to own Wuthering Heights and to dominate Hindley's "representative," Hareton, through an exercise of his rights as mortgagee after Hindley dies unable to repay his accumulated game-debts to Heathcliff; then he comes to own Thrushcross Grange and to dominate Edgar's "representatives," Isabella and Catherine, through his own marriage to Isabella and a marriage between Catherine and his son Linton, in both cases following promises of marriage from the women. Around these promises in the embedded story, there is the frame story of Lockwood, connected to the Heights through yet another promise: a lease contract.

While the centrality of promises for reflections on liberal modernity was pervasive, and *Wuthering Heights* from this perspective relied on a typical narrative tool, promises here were removed from all the frameworks I have so far explored: status-sociality, relationality, or atomism, and from the varied meanings that went along with them. Brontë consistently turned promises into signs of doom. Lockwood ends his lease contract dismayed. In the embedded story, the first promissory failure by Mr. Earnshaw and the next promissory "successes" by Heathcliff are all junctions contributing to his destructive passion. The common theme informing all of these representations is the social/psychic tension that makes for the fatal role of promises. The social's rise to dominance is signaled in the gradual move in the final chapters of the novel from promises, where the tension is open and turbulent, to money, a social medium which works to contain and delimit the psychic's presence, not least because money cannot register history as promises can, an assumption I explored in Chapter 2, and one that Brontë shared and developed further: Promises for Brontë were responsive to the richness of humanity – good and evil – and to its diverse and conflicted ways of meaning-making, as money could not be.

Frame and Embedded Narratives: Lockwood's Lease Contract

Lockwood's frame story surrounds the psychic landscape of the Heights with sociality, a connection achieved through a lease contract. Arnold Kettle explained his (and Nelly's) view: "[Nelly's and Lockwood's] function ... is partly ... to comment on it [the story] from a common-sense point of view and thereby to reveal in part the inadequacy of such common sense."[13] Not just inadequate, Lockwood's overly socialized framing of a psychic world is untenable. The tension carries calamity for this bewildered tenant: attacked, insulted, and turned ill, Lockwood soon realizes that he and Heathcliff are anything but "a suitable pair to divide the desolation" (3). They do not share a joint understanding of desolation, and therefore have nothing to divide.[14] In a comic opening, friendly Lockwood describes Heathcliff: "A capital fellow! He little imagined how my heart warmed towards him when I beheld his black eyes withdraw so suspiciously under their brows" (3). The opening is matched by an equally blind and amusing soliloquy of Lockwood toward the close of the novel: "What a realization of something more romantic than a fairy tale it would have been for Mrs. Linton Heathcliff [Catherine], had she and I struck up an attachment ... and migrated together into the stirring atmosphere of the town!" (232). Lockwood relies on socialized concepts bearing no relation to the psychic state of the Heights; he cannot decipher what he sees. His effort throughout is to impose his own terms on the story. Social sense-making, however, will require overbearing the Heights, and terminating the contract. In the interim (the embedded story), the tension brings disaster.

A Triple Promise: Fiddle, Whip, and Fruit

When Earnshaw comes home with Heathcliff, his children's and Nelly's expectations of promised presents are disappointed. The combined reaction of the disappointed promisees contains a mixture of psychic and social

13 Arnold Kettle, *Introduction to the English Novel*, 2 vols. (London: Hutchinson House, 1951), I, 141. The choice of "social" narrators goes deeper still. The psychic is the unnarratable; it escapes language. By definition, narrators cannot come from the psychic alone.

14 And, as Knoepflmacher noted, a true misanthropist can hardly join another as a "suitable pair." Knoepflmacher, *Emily Brontë: "Wuthering Heights,"* 13. Observe, however, that Lockwood, like everyone and everything else in *Wuthering Heights*, contains something of the psychic, but in him it can only appear in his dreams, given his overly socialized character – and even in a dream Lockwood rejects the psychic which, he feels, belongs to the Heights, not to himself.

terms. That reaction, convergent on Heathcliff, propels the plot of his degradation and revenge.

Hindley asks his father for a fiddle, a figure of careless gaiety but also one of delicacy and deeper notes. When the fiddle is "crushed to morsels," literally by Heathcliff who is carried by the betraying father, Hindley's untroubled childhood is crushed with it. Crushed to morsels: irretrievable, not merely functionally but visually, Hindley's hopes are irrestorable. Hindley reacts with tears; this reaction is more insightful than Nelly credits when she wonders at his "blubber[ing] aloud" (30). Hindley can never overcome his crushed-to-morsels fiddle, and he retaliates against Heathcliff. Heathcliff's ensuing revenge is an internalization of the same refusal to readjust. Extreme emotional states in *Wuthering Heights* are about perfections and crushings. Yet Hindley cannot account for the results alone: he is too plain, too understandable to account for the psychic state of *Wuthering Heights.* The inverse image of his sister is required here.

Cathy asks for a horse whip. She is barely six and already more complex than her brother. Cathy can "ride any horse in the stable" (29), she senses her power and asks for the instrument that confirms it. Unlike Hindley's crushed fiddle, Cathy's whip is simply lost. The lost whip is replaced by Heathcliff, a new object of power. Sandra Gilbert therefore argues in her fairy-tale analysis of the children's wishes, that Cathy's wish was figuratively fulfilled and that she therefore achieves an extraordinary fullness of being.[15] Cathy's "fullness of being," I will argue below, is a complex (and less than ideal) reaction to the less-than-perfectly-fulfilled promise. Cathy spits and grins at Heathcliff, not simply expressing loss but reacting to and through Heathcliff himself; she at once announces disappointment at the change of terms and reveals her understanding that there is no change of substance. Cathy's reaction to her broken promise is reproduced in the following years, most crucially in her decision to marry Edgar, made of dual sentiments: Cathy feels it would degrade her to marry Heathcliff (the sentiment of repulsion introduced at the loss of her promised whip), but she also wishes to create a safe haven for him at the Grange (the sentiment of attraction introduced when Heathcliff arrives in lieu of the whip). Cathy's dually motivated desertion ignites Heathcliff's lifelong revenge, which is an internalization not only of Hindley's rigid breakdown, but also of the depths of troubled attachment that Cathy is capable of.

Cathy's story has another twist: she sees *herself* in Heathcliff; her reactions to Heathcliff are figuratively an internal dialogue. Cathy's double

15 Sandra Gilbert, "Looking Oppositely: Emily Brontë's Bible of Hell," in Stoneman, *Emily Brontë: "Wuthering Heights,"* 137–8.

sense of anger and attraction thus alters the meaning of her promise: if the promise began as a sign of an emotional relation to her father, then its breaking signifies a turn inward. While Hindley remains isolated without his promise, an isolation signifying his unwholeness at the breakdown of the father-son relationship, Cathy's turn inward unravels an emotional independence.

A third angle is still missing. Between emotional breakdowns and emotional ties, emotional dependence and emotional independence, there exists the more earthly idea of enabling conditions that underlie Heathcliff's fall and rise, pain and revenge. Here comes Nelly: she contributes the social, practical angle.

Nelly's promise of apples and pears signifies the unstable position she occupies from childhood between servant and family member. Nelly is not forgotten when other children are promised; yet she does not get to choose her promised gift, and, more important, she is not kissed. The paragraph narrating Earnshaw's departure registers Nelly's promise as a symbolic replacement of a kiss; the paragraph ends: "He promised to bring me a pocketful of apples and pears, and then he kissed his children good-bye, and set off" (29). Placing her promise alongside the kisses, at the closing sentence of the scene after which everything changes, reveals Nelly's unspoken desire to be more than a servant, to become part of the emotional ties at the Heights.

When Nelly's promise is broken she is made to stay within socially defined ties: a servant. Thrust back into the social, she never mentions her broken promise. She narrates the children's reactions, and nothing about herself. But her own story is implicit: in criticizing Hindley's outburst, inappropriate for his (and her) age, Nelly narrates her own appropriate silence. Criticizing excessive emotional outbursts in other persons marks Nelly's social role. Nelly also takes action: she leaves Heathcliff on the stairway, "hoping it might be gone on the morrow" (30). Unable as servant to express expectations, and critical of uncontrolled passion, she denies her action's relation to the promise, framing it instead as mere senselessness. Nelly is banished from the house as punishment and returns on her own initiative; she insists on finding a place at the Heights. From here on, Nelly acts out her social-status (class) anxiety, seeking to surmount her servant position.

At key points in the narrative, Nelly's discretion, reflecting a constant denial of her inferiority, conditions the turn of events. Nelly is responsible, for instance, for Heathcliff's painful misconstruction of Cathy's emotions and his flight, for Cathy's inability to prevent Heathcliff's violent marriage to Isabella, for Catherine's marriage to Linton, and the list goes on. Nelly at one point muses: "I [was] … passing harsh judgment on my many derelictions of duty; from which, it struck me then, all the misfortunes of my employers sprang. It was not the case, in reality … but it was, in my imagination" (211). Or was it? Criticism has long explored her agency.[16] Nelly symbolizes causality: she is a practical facilitator in Heathcliff's story, a role suitable for a social component.

Nelly's status anxiety could be easily processed within social terms, but not in the psychic realm of the Heights. The characters never think about Nelly in these terms. They absorb her into their world, heedless of her danger, and the incompatibility of logics wreaks havoc.[17] The combination made up of the emotional alternatives represented in Hindley and Cathy and the social angle added by Nelly sets the terms for the rest of the story.

Heathcliff, arriving as a broken promise, not only acts on the psychic and social terms supplied by the three disappointed promisees, but also embodies within him the same tension, a quality allowing him to act on both logics equally well. Heathcliff vacillates between the social and the psychic; ostensibly the most socially untamed character, acting on passion and living for it alone, Heathcliff is also the most socially aware person in the little group.[18] The Grange and Heights residents grew up in a well-defined, secluded world. Heathcliff, by contrast, has two blanks in his past: his early childhood in Liverpool, and his three years away somewhere in society. His arrival itself is disruptive of the Heights' perfectly secluded

16 Discussions of Nelly's involvement in the plot go a long time back. See, for example, Knoepflmacher, *Emily Brontë: "Wuthering Heights"* for an analysis of Nelly as an outsider coveting an insider position, an appropriator of homes which are not hers; Ward, "Introduction to *Wuthering Heights,*" notes Nelly's role and complains about the clumsiness with which it was created; Carl R. Woodring, "The Narrators of *Wuthering Heights,*" *Nineteenth-Century Fiction* 11, no. 4 (1957): 298–305, discusses Nelly's imprint on the action, at times motivated and at others not; James Hafley, "The Villain in *Wuthering Heights,*" *Nineteenth-Century Fiction* 13, no. 3 (1958): 199–215, declares that Nelly is the villain of the novel, her villainy rooted in her wish to be considered a social equal. See also John Fraser, "The Name of Action: Nelly Dean and *Wuthering Heights,*" *Nineteenth-Century Fiction* 20, no. 3 (1965): 223–36, for an argument set against Hafley's analysis, claiming that Nelly's interventions are generally sound and reasonable, and her confrontation of the world of the Heights admirable.

17 For a discussion of Nelly's position as servant, as well as differences between her and other servants in the novel, particularly Joseph (whom I discuss below), see Carolyn Steedman, *Master and Servant: Love and Labour in the English Industrial Age* (Cambridge: Cambridge University Press, 2007), 193–216.

18 For claims linking Heathcliff directly with the social order, see for example John T. Matthews, "Framing in *Wuthering Heights,*" *Texas Studies in Literature and Language* 27, no. 1 (1985): 25–61. Matthews argues that Heathcliff reflects the violence of the social order itself, that he observes social codes. See also Daniela Garofalo, "Impossible Love and Commodity Culture in Emily Brontë's *Wuthering Heights,*" *ELH* 75, no. 4 (2008): 819–40. Heathcliff, I argue, cannot be reduced to the social alone; he embodies a more complex tension that neither represents nor serves the social order. Discussing the lack of a certain route into Heathcliff's mystery, Bloom argues that aesthetically "this is more of a gain than not, since it saves Heathcliff from psychoanalytic or sociological reductions." Harold Bloom, *Heathcliff* (New York: Chelsea House, 1993), 2. Heathcliff, for Bloom, escapes time and received traditions of representation.

existence and provides readers with the first sense of threat of incompatible logics; Heathcliff's physical blackness and gibberish language are the figurative representation of the unknown lives that might exist in Liverpool. He is a racial Other. The Liverpool port was a major slave-trade center, was extensively populated by transient foreigners, and was also a refuge for the Irish who fled famines. Whatever his origins, Heathcliff is aware of multiple forms of human stratification, unknown meanings suddenly bursting on a limited and familiar world. He understands the social meaning of savagery and degradation much better than his acquaintances. He also understands Nelly better.

Heathcliff's name creates a double intimacy with a lost son at the same time that it excludes him from the Earnshaw family. He changes from "it" to a double Heathcliff, the doubleness at once distancing and maintaining his "it" quality. The naming represents the same emotional-social tension in Heathcliff's biographical depiction: he is made to appreciate both depths of feeling and longing, and depths of social exclusion.

Both Heathcliff's treatment *by* Hindley and Edgar and his revenge *on* them is conducted in social terms of power, acquisition, and interest, and Nelly serves him in the process. Yet Heathcliff mediates it all through his passion for Cathy. He turns the story linear through a psychic construction, delineating the story's social parts in emotional terms; yet the strength and peril of his totality stem not from his passion alone, but from his ability to enlist and submit the social to its idolization.

Daniela Garofalo suggests that Heathcliff is an early example of making engagement with capitalism a form of personal self-expression, and maintains that Heathcliff's passion-motivated accumulation of assets offers an origin story that explains capitalism and lends it an aura of virility and excitement.[19] In other words, she argues for compatibility between the psychic and the social, the former serving the latter. The argument resonates with Nancy Armstrong's claim that *Wuthering Heights* (and the Brontës' fiction more broadly) was historically crucial in producing universal figures of modern desire cast in psychological terms. While Armstrong observes the different ontological plane on which identity is construed in *Wuthering Heights,* she reads it as the other side of the social incompatibility pervading passion in the novel.[20] Such arguments require a twist: self-expression is not just a problematic term for the slippery concept of selfhood in the novel; as much as it can be viewed as self-expression, Heathcliff's passion is not directly translated into the basis of a social system. His acquisitions, being mixed up with the psychic, are a source of catastrophe; a social system emerges here only with struggle. In other

19 Garofalo, "Impossible Love," 828.

20 Armstrong, *Desire and Domestic Fiction,* 186–99.

words, I suggest that Emily Brontë's ontology is not simply a figure for social incompatibilities, but a form that moves outside their logic. If Heathcliff's passionate acquisitions are constitutive of a liberal outlook or supportive of a capitalist system, they are so not as direct origins but as an ineradicable possibility that requires a constant, and painful, effort of containment.

* * *

To recapitulate, we have a triple promise (fiddle, whip, and fruit), representing potential attachments bearing emotional and (for Nelly) social implications, as well as a link to a distant, unknown social world. It is broken through a symbolic thrusting of the social on the scene (outcast Heathcliff), and emerges in three disappointed promisees tied together by Heathcliff, featuring as the replacement of the promised objects. We have a promisee (Hindley) who could not do without an emotional relationship and is thus broken, a promisee (Cathy) who did away with the relationship and denies that the new one is at all external to her (and is thus too whole), and a promisee (Nelly) whose need of the relationship is mediated through her social position and who continues to reenact her class anxiety when emotionality is denied to her. Heathcliff revenges on the breakdown of the first promisee (Hindley), absorbs into the internal wholeness of the second (Cathy), and does both through the third (Nelly). Heathcliff can use these elements in his revenge because he appreciates both the social and the psychic terms at work here.

Using Contracts: Possessing the Heights, Possessing the Grange

Heathcliff gains power by manipulating weaknesses. He becomes Hindley's mortgagee and creditor (and so obtains the Heights) in dice and card games with a broken alcoholic. Similarly, Catherine promises to marry Linton under coercion, having been imprisoned at the Heights while her father is dying (and so Heathcliff obtains the Grange). With these promises, the novel carefully treads the line between legality and illegality. The rights over the Heights are perfected with a lawyer who confirms their validity (144–6); Catherine declares that she had promised to marry Linton of her own accord (209).[21] Yet both cases are not clearly legal: in the first story (possessing the Heights) there is a constant current of complaint

21 I do not address the property laws applicable assuming the validity of the mortgages and marriages; rather, I am concerned with the promissory moments at stake. For an analysis of the property rights that Heathcliff did and did not gain over the various properties see C. P. Sanger, *The Structure of "Wuthering Heights"* (London: Hogarth Press, 1926). Sanger argued, for instance, that as a matter of property laws Heathcliff would not have had any right to an estate for life over the Grange through his marriage to Isabella or as Linton's father. The centrality of promises for the novel's world means that questions of land rights are set aside; the turn of events depends on the role of promises.

about the injustice done to Hareton (Hindely's heir): "Hareton ... [is] quite unable to right himself, because of his friendlessness, and his ignorance that he has been wronged" (146). In a similar vein, the lawyer's corruptness casts doubt on the legality of procedures. In the second story (the Catherine-Linton marriage) there is similar effort to keep things in the gray zone through a careful narration of the exchange between Heathcliff, Catherine, and Nelly: while Catherine declares her free will to marry Linton, Nelly frames the scene as unlawful coercion, and Heathcliff draws on both elements, telling Nelly: "she [Catherine] must either accept him, or remain a prisoner ... If you doubt, encourage her to retract her word" (210) – both force and the word.

By contrast to these two unsure cases, Heathcliff's marriage to Isabella – the last element in Heathcliff's revenge – is represented as clear of legal doubt. Isabella was infatuated; she ignored the warnings of her friends, and she ignored Heathcliff who never made pretences:

> She [Isabella] cannot accuse me [Heathcliff] of showing one bit of deceitful softness. The first thing she saw me do ... was to hang up her little dog ... was it not the depth of absurdity – of genuine idiocy – for that pitiful ... brach to dream that I could love her?
>
> (118)

And Heathcliff is careful to maintain legality: "I keep strictly within the limits of the law. I have avoided ... giving her the slightest right to claim a separation" (118). We are legally in the clear.

Heathcliff's victims react inversely to their legal position. Hindley, and then Hareton, never challenge the promissory processes by which Heathcliff obtained ownership of the Heights. Catherine, though miserable, never challenges the consequences of her marriage to Linton.[22] Isabella, by contrast, cannot rest. She is looking to undo her own folly, escaping from Heathcliff in the (vain) hope of removing her son from his power. This discrepancy relies on the social/psychic opposition. Hindley and Catherine are acting on the psychic plane, moved solely by emotional concerns, unmediated by social conventions and institutions. Hindley was acting out his enmity with Heathcliff and was, in this sense, experiencing fair play; Hareton after him was acting out his emotional dependence on Heathcliff: "Earnshaw [Hareton] took the master's [Heathcliff's] reputation home to himself, and was attached by ties stronger than reason could break" (245). Catherine was trapped by a loving wish to unite with her

22 There is one exception: immediately before Heathcliff's death, Catherine talks Hareton into planting flowers in the garden, in a symbolic act of repossession. She soon comes to repent that line of revolt given Hareton's refusal to accept its deeper implications. I discuss the scene below.

dying father and by an emotional commitment to Linton. She too experiences a sense of fair play within these terms. That the social-legal terms may tell a different story using the same facts, is for them uninteresting. Isabella, by contrast, was not acting on an emotional attachment, but on a fantasy of romance. This fantasy is a socially constructed one: it reflects a conventional expectation about romantic intercourse (apparently picked up from literature, as Heathcliff suggests: "picturing in me a hero of romance" (118)). Isabella, to begin with, was acting within the social and not within the psychic.

In a double inversion, then, it is in the stories that lack liberal "free will" and "rationality" (recall, "stronger than reason could break" – a lack of reason is supposedly at stake) that we find a consistency of logic, while in the story containing a formally "free will" we find the opposite: "I can hardly regard her [Isabella] in the light of a rational creature," says Heathcliff (118). The promissory stories complicate the view of these three events as similar, cynical manipulations of the law by Heathcliff and expose a more complex picture of the play of the emotional, psychic, and irrational, with the social, moderate, and rational in promise.[23] And these motives mix further: the alternatives represented by Hindley and Catherine, on the one hand, and Isabella, on the other, are not mutually exclusive; rather, Isabella's story is trapped between the other two promissory contexts. It is through his possession of the Heights that Heathcliff learns about Linton's arrival and seizes him despite Isabella's efforts. It is then through Catherine's marriage to Linton that Heathcliff secures his rights to the Grange – Isabella's home, beyond doubt. Psychic rationality and social irrationality are mixed together, locating promises in a complex and often unacknowledged conceptual region.

The Ascendance of the Social: From Transaction to Money

When Cathy is dying, Heathcliff asks Nelly to let him see her. Nelly is reluctant, but makes a promise:

> in the long run he forced me to an agreement. I engaged to carry a letter from him to my mistress; and should she consent, I promised to let him have intelligence on Linton's next absence from home, when he might come … I fear it was wrong, though expedient.
>
> (120)

23 The same inversion occurs in Lockwood's contract: he is the one seeking social ties and love, while his passionate landlord Heathcliff insists on the contract's thin rationality.

Nelly eventually gives the letter to Cathy, but at that moment Heathcliff walks in anyway. Nelly's promise in this case was clearly irrelevant to the turn of events, yet she narrates it in detail and meditates on her moral dilemma. Why?

This is a turning point in the novel, followed by the climactic scene between Cathy and Heathcliff, and leading to the second-generation story. At this point Nelly is torn between the psychic and the social on all levels: the Heights and the Grange, Heathcliff and Edgar, her unclear position as family and servant, her emotional and social (or contractual) involvement. The significance of this turning point is marked by a change in narrators: after Nelly's account of her promise to Heathcliff, Lockwood tells us that *he* from now on continues the history, only a little condensed, in Nelly's "own words. She is, on the whole, a very fair narrator" (121). But Lockwood had been reporting to the reader Nelly's stories all along anyway. This rhetorical intervention is Lockwood's subtle move to domination: it is a mark in the slow ascendance of the social achieved through a distancing from the psychic scene, shifting attention to the literary technique and Lockwood's role, away from the embedded tale. The extended attention to Nelly's promissory quandary builds on this promise's location at the peak of the social/psychic tension, just before the scales begin to tilt.

The final ascendance of the social is represented through another servant, Joseph. Like Nelly, Joseph lives the family/servant tension: he lived in the house until banished to the kitchen by Hindley; he too had held a position of more than servant, assuming responsibility for the Earnshaws' religious observance. And Joseph becomes, from this position, the character introducing the final containment of the Heights in the social.

Joseph's world is shaken in the closing chapters of the novel when the "perfect misanthropist's heaven" (3) loses its character: Catherine and Hareton become lovers, and Heathcliff, dying, loses his will to inflict pain. As the process builds up, the text dramatizes escalating encounters, through Joseph, with the idea of bare materiality, culminating in abstract money as the source of relations. If promissory ties in *Wuthering Heights* contain psychic and social elements in a complex entanglement in which measurability and abstract value had been lacking, then at these final stages measurable material objects assume prominence, with money displacing the more layered and historically-laden concept of promise. The move to money involves the abstractions of the social logic, foreign to the psychic.

Three stages make up the symbolic erosion of the psychic. First, when Joseph discovers the affection between Catherine and Hareton he is "perfectly aghast" (241). Too confounded to voice an observation, "his emotion was only revealed by the immense sighs he drew, as he solemnly spread his large Bible on the table, and overlaid it with dirty bank-notes from his pocket-book, the produce of the day's transactions" (241). Using explicit imagery, Joseph's Bible as a source of superiority is replaced by his relation to the world of nameless bank-note-producing transactions. Joseph perceives that his catechizing days have been superseded by abstract materialism, an idea so far foreign to the Heights. Until this point, transactions sealed by social institutions, like Heathcliff's contracts and property rights, had been specific both with regard to subject matter and with regard to parties, and had been between characters in the two houses. Now, by contrast, dealings are not with another character mediated by the social world, but dealings *with* the social world, and they can have no meaning but the dirty one of money. Yet abstraction here is not complete: Joseph's transactions work to sooth his anxiety at the Heights; he is seeking another source of power in his own world. The transactions represented by the notes are spread over the Bible and maintain contact with the never-acknowledged servant/family trouble plaguing the tale, mixing psychic with social terms.

In Joseph's next disaster Hareton pulls up black-currant trees, which are "the apple of Joseph's eye" (242), in order to plant flowers for Catherine (note the change to a milder plant, but also one that does not bear fruit – signaling an end). Joseph is "unmanned" (244) by this act, bitterly complaining to Heathcliff. While Hareton is speechless in the face of Heathcliff's anger, Catherine voices a material complaint: "You shouldn't grudge a few yards of earth for me to ornament, when you have taken all my land!.. And my money … And Hareton's land, and his money" (244). Catherine's logic reduces Joseph's distress to a material struggle, and translates the tensions at the Heights into property-tuned ones. This struggle had been there, as a potential, all along, but had been found wanting, and now it suddenly gains grounds. After a fury, Heathcliff uncharacteristically withdraws. Catherine's logic is not crushed and Heathcliff does not have the last word. Yet here too the psychic retains a role. Despite her apparent victory, Catherine avoids further voicing of the material idea, because Hareton resents its implications for his emotional attachment to Heathcliff. Materialism raises its head and is suppressed, but it has made its mark: Catherine now chooses to give up a line of thought which is found relevant. The choice of removing materialism from affective relations is already part of a more familiar Victorian sociality, with its attention to the division of labor and the separation of spheres. This kind of thinking had been absent in the earlier transformations of land acquisition in *Wuthering Heights.* The terms of interaction begin to fall into more recognizable patterns as the psychic quality wears down.

The final stage of the social's ascension occurs at the closing of the novel. Lockwood, the representative of the social, exits the Heights for the last time. Lockwood leaves through the kitchen – the servants' space representing the complex passage between the Heights' psychic quality and the social world. The last person Lockwood sees is Joseph, and he shapes Joseph's opinion: "[Joseph], fortunately, recognised me for a respectable character by the sweet ring of a sovereign at his feet" (258). As the psychic loses its dominance, bare materialism in the form of a gold coin is thrust on the scene. The coin is of the social: Joseph is made not only to pick up the coin thrown so contemptuously at his feet, but also thus to recognize Lockwood's respectability.

If Joseph's turn to bank-notes had been in the hope of finding a new source of power and consolation within the Heights, then the next stage, in which property struggles replace his more complex intuitions, hints at the futility of his hopes, and the coin already marks their reversal. The three-stage escalation, transactions-property-money, marks the stages from the social/psychic mixture in which promises function in *Wuthering Heights*, to a dominant social logic, where abstract money is the new determinant of relationships, blind to unrepeatable, ungeneralizable contacts behind them.

This last scene, marking the social's rise to final dominance, is a convergence of the novel's frame and embedded narratives: Nelly's narrative has been brought "back to the present," and Lockwood takes over. The two narratives had been kept in a social/psychic tension; at this closing point the distance has been narrowed through their convergence, and the socialized Lockwood has the last word – not the last word in the frame story, but within the embedded story. Edward Mendelson notes that Lockwood also initiated the change in the Heights with his visionary dream of Catherine at the beginning of the novel, causing Heathcliff to forgo his demolition plan.[24] The social surrounds the psychic Heights and contains it. John Matthews concludes: "the survival of the narrators at the cost of their protagonists defines the triumph of framing this fiction."[25] It is significant, however, that the triumph is a matter of a changed balance. There remains a psychic element that cannot be banished.

The coin is thrown at Joseph, but he is beyond socialization. His reaction to the coin is thus mediated to the reader through Lockwood's social interpretation, while Joseph remains unseen and keeps an unnarrated and uncontrolled space, symbolized in the kitchen. Joseph will remain in the Heights' kitchen while the rest of the house is shut up. The psychic plane is literally narrowed down, but cannot be eradicated. Indeed, the centrality of promises, no less than money, for the liberal order, implied the presence of psychic irritants to a greater extent than Joseph's dimmed light. In the closing words of the novel Lockwood wonders "how any one could ever imagine unquiet slumbers for the sleepers in that quiet earth" (258). This last thought begs the question and leaves it open, like Joseph's kitchen. At once minimized and centralized, the room left in the Heights, the question

24 Edward Mendelson, *The Things That Matter: What Seven Classic Novels Have to Say About the Stages of Life* (New York: Pantheon, 2006), 72–3.

25 Matthews, "Framing in *Wuthering Heights*," 65.

left by Lockwood, the sense of unsure closure left with the reader, the experience of anguish – all of which secured the novel's problematic reception, and still do – keep the psychic an active element for a liberal delineation of experience at the same time that they curtail its conceptual reach.

Liberal Experience

Wuthering Heights did and does feel remarkable within the Victorian canon. If the critical mood has changed since the awry Victorian reception, the governing sense that its reception requires discussion remains cogent. Ian Ward recounts the many assaults on common morality and subversions of accepted cultural norms that *Wuthering Heights* stood for – the home, the hearth, the feminine, the clerical, domestic harmony (national too) – any and all of which explain the historical antipathy.[26] This chapter's argument does not dispute such claims so much as insists that we appreciate that the sense of discomfort stemmed, and stems still, not from the marginality of threats of this kind – or the psychic logic more generally, but on the contrary, from its ineradicable power within liberalism. As Ward shows, readers have acknowledged the undeniable truth of the dark side explored in the novel. Its liminal quality lay there; the discomfort arose from Brontë's ability to take apart and lay bare the experience of complexity pervading Victorian liberalism. At stake was a generally valid Victorian experience, in amplified form; the novel textually imparted, early on, an experience that made for decades of critique. Brontë's use of the familiar metaphors of promise and money to explore that experience invoked its broad applicability, and resisted marginalization. I therefore concur with Linda Shires when she recognizes in *Wuthering Heights* a central paradigm of Victorianism, rather than an aberration.[27]

The estrangements of *Wuthering Heights* offer a sense of disturbances contained at the core of a liberal order, at once viable and limited. I concur with Shires that tensions in *Wuthering Heights* are kept in play rather than healed or resolved.[28] Not only is there no historical – or plot-designed – resolution here, but there is in fact a specific form of lived tension, that of containment; this is an equally significant part of the history of liberalism captured by Brontë. Containment accounts not only for unresolved tensions, but also for the structural relation that set the interaction among their constitutive elements. Containment kept tensions alive, but also transformed such elements as irrationality, passion, nonsocial mediation of

26 Ward, "Emily Bronte and the Terrorist Imagination."

27 Shires is interested in the irresolvability of ideological tensions and examines their relation to the novel's form, arguing that the fissures in *Wuthering Heights* were to inform the realist genre's aesthetics, their presence deserving of no less attention than realism's ideological solutions. Shires, "Aesthetics of the Victorian Novel."

28 Ibid., 66–7.

relationships, brute power – and much else – from within liberal thinking, and delimited their modes of reach in late modernity. The psychic remained a pounding locus, lurking, demanding attention, yet set within limits that justified, for those so inclined, attempts to downplay its role within large parts of human experience.

Ideology Critique

Scholarship theorizing complexity has been creating new conversations in ideology critique. In conclusion I want to develop one angle which seems particularly important for the discussion of the place of statuses, where complexity as a viable option, familiar from scholarship on other tensions in liberalism, remains undertheorized.

The difficulty that containment as well as withdrawal pose is that they are not satisfactorily explicable in functional terms. Social theory of both liberal and radical hues has for a long time exhibited a commitment to an assumption of functionality: ideology, on this assumption, must be *serviceable* for some social interest, power, or normative program. This assumption comes up against historical complexity in ideological constellations. The overall picture that containment and withdrawal reveal is this: We have conceptual frameworks which pull in different directions in terms of interests, powers, and normative programs, yet they viably coexist in patterned manners across culture in modernity. This complexity is dysfunctional from the perspective of any one of the identified interests or programs, and demands some sort of theoretical response.

I briefly discuss two kinds of responses that we can glimpse from scholarship sensitive to the power of statuses in liberal modernity. One response is to downplay dysfunction – there are many and often competing ways to do that, as I explain, but they all share an implicit commitment to the assumption of functionality for they insist on functionality in the final account. Another response is to accept dysfunction as pervasive, but then to still betray a theoretical expectation of functionality. The expectation is betrayed in tendencies to associate dysfunction with particular areas of culture (say, subversive art), rather than examine dysfunction's broad application. It is also betrayed in portrayals of the overall picture as contradictory. Emphases on contradiction and on localism implicitly keep the assumption of functionality alive as a dominant possibility in the operation of ideology.

After explaining how the assumption of functionality retains dominance in scholarship, I examine a possible alternative.

A Pervasive Assumption of Functionality

Ideological dysfunction has been brushed off by accounts that identify complexity – for example, histories observing that contract and class both had a role to play in Victorian betrothals despite their contradictory meanings – but argue that overall conceptual structure tilts to one side more than the other. The debates among historians reviewed in Chapter 5 about the law of promise of marriage proceed along this route: Status and contract in law are treated in terms of coexisting yet incongruent visions serviceable to differing interests and normative visions, with analyses split on which had the upper hand – but jointly committed to the goal of identifying a marginal "winner," a commitment which implicitly confirms the assumption of functionality.[29] A similar point can be made about readings of *Wuthering Heights* that identify the ultimate "winner" in the dualities they analyze, be they frame/embedded narrator, passion/socialization or else.

Another way to downplay dysfunction has been to treat the very idea of complexity as chimerical in the following sense: Apparently contradictory elements turn out to function together logically toward establishing a coherent social order, be it modern patriarchy, modern capitalism and bourgeois rule, or both. These positions sometimes view one side of the tension, typically liberal ideals, as ideological smokescreen, so that ultimately there is no real tension. However, just as often historians propose a complicated account in which liberal ideals are not empty but rather historically revolutionary ideas that nonetheless coherently operate with status hierarchies in the service of the needs of a particular order. For instance, in Armstrong's *Desire and Domestic Fiction*, the affective basis of domesticity and the contractual discourse on marriage created a modern female authority at the same time that they naturalized sexual difference and made it the political basis of middle-class dominion.[30] In Carole Pateman's *The Sexual Contract*, the contractual idea at the basis of marriage is both revolutionary and tied with the domination of women by men, which makes up the missing half of the mythology of modern equality: the subordinated agree to their subordination – a truly modern form of gender inequality.[31]

29 A Victorian example is mentioned by Jones, who discusses contradictory stances in Trollope with regard to gender equality, and recounts his own justification of these contradictions as a form of careful – rather than too rushed – progress, the assumption (of Trollope) being that the overall direction is decidedly progressive. Wendy S. Jones, *Consensual Fictions: Women, Liberalism, and the English Novel* (University of Toronto Press, 2005), 152–4. The effect of identifying the marginal "beneficiaries" is a downplaying of the problem of inherent complexity. I return to this point below.

30 Armstrong, *Desire and Domestic Fiction*. See also Mary Lyndon Shanley, *Feminism, Marriage and the Law in Victorian England* (Princeton, NJ: Princeton University Press, 1989) for a complex argument essentially suggesting that capitalism benefited from certain forms of status hierarchies, particularly gender, alongside a certain liberation of economic forces.

31 Carole Pateman, *The Sexual Contract* (Stanford, CA: Stanford University Press, 1988); see also Charles W. Mills and Carole Pateman, *Contract and Domination* (Cambridge: Polity Press, 2007), Chapter 7. (In *The Sexual Contract* Pateman would not use "gender," but sex.) See also Christopher Tomlins, *Freedom Bound: Law, Labor, and Civic Identity in*

Brook Thomas's work on contract and American literary realism, with which I share many methodological as well as substantive alignments, provides an account in which "the failed promise of contract" to create mobility and equality, assessed as such already in his title,[32] has at least two roots. According to Thomas, the failure of contract was a consequence of a historical process in which emerging corporate powers rapidly undid "the promise of contract," but he also suggests that the failure was internally underwritten from the start by contract's covert preservation of race, class and gender hierarchies. These two explanations (which incidentally preserve an (historically unrealized) utopian ideal of contract), offer a sophisticated analysis of historical complexity, yet exemplify the two manners of downplaying dysfunction: Thomas both identifies ultimate winners and losers, and points to ways in which contract in fact serves statuses. On both fronts the assumption of functionality is implicitly retained.

The willingness to downplay dysfunction is challenged by containment and withdrawal. These patterns did not purge either liberal ideals or statuses of real historical content and effect; they brought about mutual transformations. In their inescapability, these patterns promised – or threatened – to complicate and redirect the conceivable interests of any social class or power, and recast any normative program. The anguish that Brontë successfully imparted to her readers was an experience of irresolvable complication which was always just on the verge of shifting its directionality.

A different response to ideological dysfunction has been to actually turn it into the fulcrum of history, rather than downplay it. I opened Part II with Williams' call for analyses that recognize contradictions. Responses along these lines include a host of accounts that speak to a persistent gap between ideology's reality as a complex conceptual structure and its theoretical functionality, and provide possible explanations for it. For instance, a familiar account in law focuses on the contradictions of experience playing out in

Colonizing English America, 1580–1865 (New York: Cambridge University Press, 2010), Chapter 8, for an account of the theoretical dependence of contractualism on patriarchalism in English political theory, and the centrality of the household in which various authoritative relations sustained the production and reproduction of liberal free persons. Tomlins shows how patriarchy assumed a power in late modern thought that it did not have earlier, arising together with contractualism.

For other examples see for instance Okin's argument that the ideology of love – that she called the sentimental family – acted as a modern way of reinforcing patriarchal relations threatened by early modern individualism, Susan Moller Okin, "Women and the Making of the Sentimental Family," *Philosophy and Public Affairs* 11, no. 1 (1982): 65–88. See also Perry's argument that the rise of the nuclear family was "the great disinheritance" of women. Ruth Perry, *Novel Relations: The Transformation of Kinship in English Literature and Culture, 1748–1818* (Cambridge: Cambridge University Press, 2004).

32 Brook Thomas, *American Literary Realism and the Failed Promise of Contract* (Berkeley, CA: University of California Press, 1997).

doctrine, as developed by Critical Legal Studies. The argument is often channeled through the concept of the indeterminacy of legal doctrine.[33] Another account, that has become a staple of cultural critique, is the indiscipline of language which can be expected to subvert any intended social meaning. Yet another centers on the argument that particular discursive fields exhibit forms of partial autonomy from social powers, and so retain a nonfunctional relation to political interests while developing internal complexity. The modern differentiation of genres provides rich grounds for these arguments; it explains how law, literature, or other sites of social thought develop long-term internal characteristics and so maintain a distance from other sites of culture, and from loci of social struggle. Terry Eagleton, for instance, ties complexity with the cultural location of art in modernity. He argues that the modern aesthetic artifact is inseparable from the dominant ideological forms of the modern class-society, but at the same time provides a powerful challenge and alternative to these dominant forms, and is in this sense an eminently contradictory phenomenon.[34]

As these cursory references clarify, responses that accept dysfunction often localize their claims to certain levels of existence, like language, or certain fields of social action, like law or aesthetics, rather than make room for the possibility that the same phenomena repeat themselves in discourse and practice, and across fields. Containment and withdrawal clarify why that room is required; they are not entirely reducible to particular forms of ideological production. As the history of the promise of marriage shows, they can be traced not only in literary discourse, but also in broader phenomena like litigation practice, and abstracting ones like legal theory, nor are they reducible to the relative autonomy of particular sites, hence their repetition in law and literature, and, as I suggested at the close of Chapter 5, likely elsewhere.

Responses that take dysfunction to be a foundational phenomenon of modernity also share a tendency to emphasize contradiction rather than conceptualize a viable entanglement between different commitments, like gender and contract, or love and class. The language of contradiction often

33 I remain unsure, however, about Critcial Legal Studies' level of comfort with the dysfunction of ideology. Leading critics have tended to treat legal conceptual structures as an enabling (and sometimes enabled) consciousness of political change despite contradictions, a functional notion. For a critical discussion see Christopher Tomlins, "How Autonomous Is Law?" *Annual Review of Law & Social Science* 3, no. 1 (2007): 45–68. At the same time, indeterminacy does emphasize an irresolvable complexity: political change is enabled by mediating contradictions, not solving them, and so there remains an inherent risk of collapse.

34 Terry Eagleton, *The Ideology of the Aesthetic* (Oxford: Blackwell, 1990), 3. As I observed in the Introduction, in interdisciplinary analyses of law and literature the same positioning of literature as subversion of dominant ideologies sometimes emerges. For a brief discussion and references on law see Robert Gordon, "Critical Legal Histories," *Stanford Law Review* 36, nos. 1 and 2 (1984): 88–93.

also dominates analyses that downplay dysfunction. An emphasis on contradiction implicitly retains functionality as a conceptual norm: why think of this history as contradictory if not because it subverts functionality? The viability of the entanglements between apparent contradictions has been revealed by recent scholarship. Containment and withdrawal clarify some of its force and implications.

Beyond Functionality

To conceptualize the ideological dysfunction involved in Victorian liberalism it seems necessary to approach ideology as a culturally-embedded conceptual structure, without seeking a deeper *ongoing* rationale. The broad direction would be to take seriously the proposition that imagination, courses of decision, and terms of normative evaluation, are all channeled through patterns of thought, sometimes acknowledged, sometimes unacknowledged; visible or invisible, conceptual patterns emerge in specific historical moments, and, through their embeddedness in cultural sites, become facts in themselves – lacking any deeper identifiable rationale, but entrenched. The argument that ideas become entrenched while the original logic is lost is hardly new theoretically, and has also been developed in a variety of historical contexts.[35]

Human agency is not necessarily denied by this suggestion;[36] it is just set aside analytically for a particular gain. The gain lies in the redirection of critical attention toward the internal patterns of ideology, quite conceivably dynamic, irreconcilable with known interests, powers or normative programs, and entirely viable – all at once. This approach seems to have had the least use in the study of statuses in Victorian liberalism. Certainly in studies of contract and love, class and gender, the sense of contradiction and locality, and often the search for marginal winners, has been an overwhelming presence. Containment and withdrawal reveal the ongoing dynamics of freedom and subjection, a tormenting condition of the oxymoronic free subjects of modernity. As I have argued, no teleology can be implied.

35 An elaborate example is Veblen's account of "barbarian" distinctions between modes of occupation which were "rational" at their historical inception, became accepted, and remain established in modern thought. Veblen considered this a generally valid process of "cultural code" dissemination. Thorstein Veblen, *The Theory of the Leisure Class* (Oxford: Oxford University Press, 2007). Another well-known argument is Weber's, who saw the continued force of religious asceticism in capitalism as a ghostly presence that remains long after its roots have been forgotten. Max Weber, *The Protestant Ethic and the Spirit of Capitalism*, ed. Stephen Kalberg, 3rd ed. (New York: Oxford University Press, 2007). To be sure, these arguments do not in themselves challenge functionality, but they do highlight historical moments in which the beneficiaries of an ideology are unclear.

36 On the nondeterminism of structures see Luc Boltanski and Ève Chiapello, *The New Spirit of Capitalism*, trans. Gregory Elliott (New York: Verso 2007).

Epilogue

History Is Always in the Future

After all seems to have been said and done in contracts histories; after they have been written and rewritten for well over a hundred years; after they have undergone doctrinal, internalist, liberal, radical, feminist, cultural and perhaps some other revisions; after they have expanded from theory to consciousness, from high-court precedent to small-claims litigation, from books to practice, and have extended their idea of context in multiple directions, there remain untouched residues of agreements which make up a common sense of the past beyond all controversy, and which merit more attention.

"Liberalizing Contracts" in my title speaks to two inseparable questions of the Victorian era: What it meant for the concept of contract to be a liberal idea, and what it meant to live in an order liberalized by contracts, that is, what Victorian liberalism was, viewed through the prism of contract. On both questions, and on both ends of the status-to-contract formula, realist fiction illuminatingly speaks to and with legal histories. The dominance of relationality as the basis of contracts and of the capitalist economy, and the patterned entanglements of contracts with statuses, open up new angles on Victorian liberalism. Such angles allow us to see liberal complexity with both its lights and shadows.

Where lights are and where shadows lie depends on your point of view. Relational sociality could be sentimentalized or suspected. It could be read against the alienations of atomism or as a denial of larger political communities. It could be read for its enclaves of hope or for its suffocations. Entanglements of contracts with status hierarchies could be assessed by their persistent subordination of women or lower classes, or by the new areas of mobility and authority they introduced, or perhaps today, be embraced, counterintuitively for some, as acknowledgements of treasured identities. The history of Victorian liberalism always lies in the future of its assessments.

Recent years have seen reassessments of liberalism's normative appeal, generally leaning toward the affirmative or at least the hesitant, after years of censure. Is Victorian liberalism, understood on the terms explored here, to be reembraced or newly rejected? Having endeavored so far to keep in view both lights and shadows, I remain unsure that history should finally turn normative in such a strong sense. By way of holding final answers at bay we might return one last time to Emily Brontë. What should we make of the liberal anguish she so skillfully imparted? It could be a warning, a critique of liberalism. But Brontë did not lament the loss of some better world, nor hint at some finer vision; one would be hard pressed to find those in her tale. A more productive way to read *Wuthering Heights'* liberal anguish would be to treat it for what it was, and is: an effect of art. Brontë was reminding readers, and perhaps we still need reminding, that ideological stances depend on – as much as they enable – aesthetic satisfaction.

Bibliography

Ablow, Rachel. *The Marriage of Minds: Reading Sympathy in the Victorian Marriage Plot.* Stanford, CA: Stanford University Press, 2007.

Adams, James Eli. *A History of Victorian Literature.* Malden, MA: Wiley-Blackwell, 2009.

Agnew, Jean-Chrisophe. *Worlds Apart: The Market and the Theater in Anglo-American Thought, 1550–1750.* Cambridge: Cambridge University Press, 1986.

Alexander, D.M. "Trollope's Cosmopolitanism." *Trollopian* 2, no.1 (1947): 3–10.

Anderson, Amanda. *Tainted Souls and Painted Faces: The Rhetoric of Fallenness in Victorian Culture.* Ithaca, NY: Cornell University Press 1993.

Anderson, Amanda. *The Powers of Distance: Cosmopolitanism and the Cultivation of Detachment.* Princeton: Princeton University Press, 2001.

Anderson, Amanda. "Dickens, the Brontës, Gaskell: Politics and Its Limits." In *The Cambridge History of the English Novel,* edited by Robert Caserio and Clement Hawes, 345–6. Cambridge: Cambridge University Press, 2012.

Anderson, Benedict. *Imagined Communities: Reflections on the Origin and Spread of Nationalism.* London: Verso, 1991.

Anson, William Reynell. *Principles of the English Law of Contract.* Oxford: Clarendon Press, 1879.

Arendt, Hannah. *The Human Condition.* Chicago, IL: The University of Chicago Press, 1958.

Armstrong, Nancy. "Emily Brontë in and out of Her Time." *Genre* 15 (1982): 243–64.

Armstrong, Nancy. *Desire and Domestic Fiction: A Political History of the Novel.* New York: Oxford University Press, 1987.

Armstrong, Nancy. *How Novels Think: The Limits of British Individualism From 1719–1900.* New York: Columbia University Press, 2005.

Atiyah, P.S. *The Rise and Fall of Freedom of Contract.* Oxford: Clarendon, 1979.

Atiyah, P.S. *An Introduction to the Law of Contract,* 5th ed. Oxford: Clarendon, 1995.

Attwood, Nina. *The Prostitute's Body: Rewriting Prostitution in Victorian Britain.* Toronto: Toronto University Press, 2011.

Baker, J.H. "Book Review of The Rise and Fall of Freedom of Contract by P.S. Atiyah." Modern Law Review 43 no. 4 (1980): 467–9.

Bates, Denise. *Breach of Promise to Marry: A History of How Jilted Brides Settled Scores.* Los Angeles, CA: Pen & Sword History, 2014.

Bauman, Zygmunt. *Liquid Modernity.* Oxford: Blackwell, 2000.

Beer, Gillian. *Darwin's Plots: Evolutionary Narrative in Darwin, George Eliot and Nineteenth-Century Fiction,* 2nd ed. Cambridge: Cambridge University Press, 2004.

Benjamin, Walter. "Critique of Violence." In Walter Benjamin, *Walter Benjamin: Selected Writings, Volume 1: 1913–1926*, edited by Marcus Paul Bullock and Michael W. Jennings, 236–52. Cambridge, MA: Belknap Press, 1999.

Benson, Peter. "The Unity of Contract Law." In *The Theory of Contract Law: New Essays*, edited by Peter Benson, 139–49. Cambridge: Cambridge University Press, 2001.

Ben-Yishai, Ayelet. "Trollope and the Law." In *The Cambridge Companion to Anthony Trollope*, edited by Carolyn Dever and Lisa Niles, 155–67. Cambridge: Cambridge University Press, 2011.

Ben-Yishai, Ayelet. *Common Precedents: The Presentness of the Past in Victorian Law and Fiction*. Oxford: Oxford University Press, 2013.

Berman, Marshall. *All that Is Solid Melts into Air: The Experience of Modernity*. New York: Simon & Schuster, 1982.

Berns, Sandra. "Women in English Legal History: Subject (Almost), Object (Irrevocably), Person (Not Quite)." *University of Tasmania Law Review* 12 no. 1, (1993): 26–72.

Bhabha, Homi K, ed. *Nation and Narration*. New York: Routledge, 1990.

Bigelow, Gordon. *Fiction, Famine and the Rise of Economics in Victorian Britain and Ireland*. Cambridge: Cambridge University Press, 2003.

Bigelow, Gordon. "The Cost of Everything in *Middlemarch*." In *Economic Women: Essays on Desire and Dispossession in Nineteenth-Century British Culture*, edited by Lana L. Dalley and Jill Rappoport, 97–109. Columbus, OH: Ohio State University Press, 2013.

Blain, Virginia. "Double Vision and the Double Standard in *Bleak House*: A Feminist Perspective." *Literature and History* 11, no. 1 (1985): 31–64.

Blake, Kathleen, ed. *Approaches to Teaching Eliot's* Middlemarch. New York: The Modern Language Association of America, 1990.

Blake, Kathleen, ed. "*Bleak House*, Political Economy, Victorian Studies." *Victorian Literature and Culture* 25, no. 1 (1997): 1–21.

Blondel, Jacques. "Literary Influences on Wuthering Heights." In *Emily Brontë:* Wuthering Heights, edited by Miriam Allott, 229–41. London: Macmillan, 1970.

Bloom, Harold. *Heathcliff*. New York: Chelsea House, 1993.

Blumberg, Ilana M. *Victorian Sacrifice: Ethics and Economics in Mid-Century Novels*. Columbus, OH: Ohio State University Press, 2013.

Boltanski, Luc, and Ève Chiapello. *The New Spirit of Capitalism*. Translated by Gregory Elliott. New York: Verso, 2007.

Bossche, Chris Vanden R. "Class Discourse and Popular Agency in *Bleak House*." *Victorian Studies* 47, no. 1 (2004): 7–31.

Bourdieu, Pierre. *Distinction: A Social Critique of the Judgement of Taste*. Translated by Richard Nice. London: Routledge & Kegan Paul, 1984.

Brantlinger, Patrick. *Fictions of State: Culture and Credit in Britain 1694–1994*. Ithaca, NY: Cornell University Press, 1996.

Brewer, Holly. *By Birth or Consent: Children, Law, and the Anglo-American Revolution in Authority*. New York: University of North Carolina Press, 2005.

Brontë, Emily. *Wuthering Heights: The 1847 Text, Backgrounds and Contexts, Criticism*. Edited by Richard J. Dunn. New York: W. W. Norton and Co., 2003.

Brudner, Alan. *The Unity of the Common Law*, 2nd ed. Oxford: Oxford University Press, 2013.

Carrier, James G. *Gifts and Commodities: Exchange and Western Capitalism Since 1700.* New York: Routledge, 1995.

Carroll, Joseph. "The Cuckoo's History: Human Nature in *Wuthering Heights.*" *Philosophy and Literature* 32, no. 2 (2008): 241–57.

Case, Allison. "Gender and History in Narrative Theory: The Problem of Rhetorical Distance in *David Copperfield* and *Bleak House.*" In *A Companion to Narrative Theory*, edited by James Phelan and Peter J. Rabinowitz, 312–21. Malden, MA: Wiley-Blackwell, 2005.

Christensen, Allan. "'Not a Love Letter': Epistolary Proposals of Marriage and Narrative Theory in *Bleak House* and *Middlemarch.*" *In Letter(s): Functions and Forms of Letter-Writing in Victorian Art and Literature*, edited by Mariaconcetta Costantini et al, 59–69. Roma: Aracne, 2009.

Coleman, Dermont. *George Eliot and Money: Economics, Ethics and Literature.* Cambridge: Cambridge University Press, 2014.

Collins, Hugh. *The Law of Contract*, 2nd ed. Austin, TX: Weidenfeld and Nicolson, 1993.

Connell, R.W. *Masculinities*, 2nd ed. Berkeley, CA: University of California Press, 2005.

Cormack, Bradin. *A Power to Do Justice: Jurisdiction, English Literature, and the Rise of Common Law, 1509–1625.* Chicago, IL: University of Chicago Press, 2007.

Cornish, W. R., and G. de N. Clark. *Law and Society in England 1750–1950.* London: Sweet & Maxwell, 1989.

Cottom, Daniel. *Social Figures: George Eliot, Social History, and Literary Representation.* Minneapolis, MN: University of Minnesota Press, 1987.

Craig, G. Armour. "On the Style of *Vanity Fair.*" In *Twentieth Century Interpretations of* Vanity Fair: *A Collection of Critical Essays*, edited by Michael G. Sundell. Englewood Cliffs, NJ: Prentice-Hall, 1969.

Craig, Randall. *Promising Language: Betrothal in Victorian Law and Fiction.* Albany, NY: State University of New York Press, 2000.

D'Albertis, Deirdre. *Dissembling Fictions: Elizabeth Gaskell and the Victorian Social Text.* New York: Palgrave Macmillan, 1997.

Dames, Nicholas. Introduction to, *Vanity Fair: A Novel Without a Hero*, by William Makepeace Thackeray, xiii–xxviii. New York: Barnes & Noble Classics, 2003.

Darwin, Charles. *On the Origin of Species by Means of Natural Selection, or the Preservation of Favored Races in the Struggle for Life*, 1st ed. London: John Murray, 1859.

Davidoff, Leonore, and Catherine Hall. *Family Fortunes: Men and Women of the English Middle Class, 1780–1850.* Chicago, IL: University of Chicago Press, 1987.

Dawson, John P. "Economic Duress: An Essay in Perspective." *Michigan Law Review* 45, no. 3 (1947): 253–90.

Deakin, Simon. "Legal Origin, Juridical Form and Industrialization in Historical Perspective: The Case of the Employment Contract and the Joint-Stock Company." *Socio-Economic Review* 7, no. 1 (2009): 35–65.

Deane, Bradley. *Masculinity and the New Imperialism: Rewriting Manhood in British Popular Literature, 1870–1914.* Cambridge: Cambridge University Press, 2014.

Delany, Paul. *Literature, Money and the Market: From Trollope to Amis.* Hampshire: Palgrave Macmillan, 2002.

Devereux, Joanna. *Patriarchy and Its Discontents: Sexual Politics in Selected Novels and Stories of Thomas Hardy.* London: Routledge, 2003.

De Vries, Jan. *The Industrious Revolution: Consumer Behavior and the Household Economy, 1650 to the Present.* Cambridge: Cambridge University Press, 2008.

Dicey, Albert V. *Lectures on the Relation Between Law and Public Opinion in England During the Nineteenth Century,* 2nd ed. London: Macmillan, 1962.

Dickens, Charles. *Bleak House.* Edited by Nicola Bradbury. New York: Penguin Books, 2003.

Dodd, Nigel. *The Social Life of Money.* Princeton, NJ: Princeton University Press, 2014.

Dolin, Kieran. *Fiction and the Law: Legal Discourse in Victorian and Modernist Literature.* Cambridge: Cambridge University Press, 2009.

Dunlop, C.R.B. "Debtors and Creditors in Dickens' Fiction." *Dickens Studies Annual* 19 (1990): 25–47.

Duncan, Ian. *Scott's Shadow: The Novel in Romantic Edinburgh.* Princeton, NJ: Princeton University Press, 2007.

Dutta, Shanta. "Hardy and his Mayor: A Gendering of Critical Response." *The Thomas Hardy Journal* 19, no. 2 (2003): 33–40.

Dyson, A.E. "*Vanity Fair*: An Irony Against Heroes." In *Twentieth Century Interpretations of* Vanity Fair: *A Collection of Critical Essays,* edited by Michael G. Sundell, 73–90. Englewood Cliffs, NJ: Prentice-Hall, 1969.

Eagleton, Terry. *The Ideology of the Aesthetic.* Oxford: Blackwell, 1990.

Eagleton, Terry. "Myths of Power in 'Wuthering Heights.'" In *Emily Brontë*: "*Wuthering Heights,*" edited by Patsy Stoneman, 118–30. Basingstoke: Macmillan, 1993.

Ehrlich, Eugen. *Fundamental Principles of the Sociology of Law.* Cambridge, MA: Harvard University Press, 1936.

Eisenberg, Melvin A. "Why There Is No Law of Relational Contracts." *Northwestern University Law Review* 94, no. 3 (2000): 805–82.

Eliot, George. *Middlemarch: A Study of Provincial Life.* Edited by David Carroll. Oxford: Oxford University Press, 1996.

Epstein, Richard A. "Contracts Small and Contract Large: Contract Law Through the Lens of Laissez-Faire." In *The Fall and Rise of Freedom of Contract,* edited by F.H. Buckley, 25–60. Durham, NC: Duke University Press, 1999.

Ermarth, Elizabeth Deeds. "Negotiating *Middlemarch.*" In Middlemarch *in the Twenty First Century,* edited by Karen Chase, 107–32. Oxford: Oxford University Press, 2010.

Farnsworth, Allan E. "The Past of Promise: An Historical Introduction to Contract." *Columbia Law Review* 69, no.4 (1969): 576–607.

Feinman, Jay, and Peter Gabel. "Contract Law as Ideology." In *The Politics of Law: A Progressive Critique,* edited by David Kairys, 497–510. 3rd ed. New York: Basic, 1998.

Ferguson, R.B. "The Horwitz Thesis and Common Law Discourse In England." *Oxford Journal of Legal Studies* 3, no.1 (1983): 34–58.

Ferguson, R.B. "Commercial Expectations and the Guarantee of the Law: Sales Transactions in Mid-Nineteenth Century England." In *Essays in the History of English Law,* edited by. G.R. Rubin and David Sugarman, 192–208. Abingdon: Professional, 1984.

Finn, Margot C. *The Character of Credit: Personal Debt in English Culture, 1740–1914.* Cambridge: Cambridge University Press, 2003.

Flint, Kate. "'… As a Rule, I Does Not Mean I': Personal Identity and the Victorian Woman Poet." In *Rewriting the Self: Histories from the Renaissance to the Present*, edited by Roy Porter, 156–66. London: Routledge, 1997.

Forster, E.M. *Aspects of the Novel.* New York: Harcourt, 1927.

Foucault, Michel. *The History of Sexuality: An Introduction (vol. 1).* Translated by Robert Hurley. Harmondsworth: Penguin Books, 1978.

Frank, Cathrine O. *Law, Literature, and the Transmission of Culture in England, 1837–1925.* Farnham: Ashgate, 2010.

Franklin, Jeffrey J. "Anthony Trollope Meets Pierre Bourdieu: The Conversion of Capital as Plot in the Mid-Victorian British Novel." *Victorian Literature and Culture* 31, no. 2, (2003): 501–21.

Fraser, John. "The Name of Action: Nelly Dean and *Wuthering Heights.*" *Nineteenth-Century Fiction* 20, no. 3 (1965): 223–36.

Friedman, Lawrence M. *Contract Law in America: A Social and Economic Case Study.* Madison, WI: University of Wisconsin Press, 1965.

Friedman, Milton. *Capitalism and Freedom.* 4th ed. Chicago, IL: University of Chicago Press, 2002.

Frost, Ginger S. *Promises Broken: Courtship, Class, and Gender in Victorian England.* Charlottesville, VA: University of Virginia Press, 1995.

Fryckstedt, Monica Correa. *Elizabeth Gaskell's* Mary Barton *and* Ruth*: A Challenge to Christian England.* Uppsala: Uppsala University, 1982.

Gagnier, Regenia. *Individualism, Decadence and Globalization: On the Relationship of Part to Whole,* 1859–1920. Basingstoke: Palgrave Macmillan, 2010.

Gallagher, Catherine. *The Industrial Reformation of English Fiction: Social Discourse and Narrative Form 1832–1867.* Chicago, IL: University of Chicago Press, 1985.

Gallagher, Catherine. "George Eliot: Immanent Victorian." *Representations* 90, no. 1 (2005): 61–74.

Gallagher, Catherine. *The Body Economic: Life, Death, and Sensation in Political Economy and the Victorian Novel.* Princeton, NJ: Princeton University Press, 2006.

Gallagher, Catherine. "The Rise of Fictionality." In *The Novel, Volume 1: History, Geography, and Culture,* edited by Franco Moretti, 336–63. Princeton, NJ: Princeton University Press, 2006.

Ganz, Melissa J. "Binding the Will: George Eliot and the Practice of Promising." *ELH* 75, no.3 (2008): 565–602.

Garofalo, Daniela. "Impossible Love and Commodity Culture in Emily Brontë's *Wuthering Heights.*" *ELH* 75, no. 4 (2008): 819–40.

Gaskell, Elizabeth. *Ruth.* Edited by Alan Shelton. Oxford: Oxford University Press, 1985.

Giddens, Anthony. *The Transformation of Intimacy.* Stanford, CA: Stanford University Press, 1994.

Gilbert, Sandra. "Looking Oppositely: Emily Brontë's Bible of Hell." In *Emily Brontë: "Wuthering Heights,"* edited by Patsy Stoneman, 137–8. Basingstoke: Macmillan, 1993.

Gilmore, Grant. *The Death of Contract.* Columbus, OH: Ohio State University Press, 1974.

Goodlad, Lauren M.E. *Victorian Literature and the Victorian State: Character and Governance in a Liberal Society.* Baltimore, MD: Johns Hopkins University Press, 2003.

Goodlad, Lauren M.E. "*The Eustace Diamonds* and 'The Great Parliamentary Bore.'" In *The Politics of Gender in Anthony Trollope's Novels: New Readings for the Twenty-First Century*, edited by Margaret Markwick, Deborah Denenholz Morse, and Regenia Gagnier, 99–116. Farnham: Ashgate, 2009.

Goodlad, Lauren M.E. "Liberalism and Literature." In *The Oxford Handbook of Victorian Literary Culture*. Edited by Juliet John, 103–23. Oxford: Oxford University Press, 2016.

Goodrich, Peter. *Oedipus Lex: Psycholanalysis, History, Law*. Berkeley, CA: University of California Press, 1995.

Goodrich, Peter. "Friends in High Places: Amity and Agreement in Alsatia." *International Journal of Law in Context* 1 (2005): 41–59.

Goodrich, Peter. "The Posthumous Life of the Postal Rule: Requiem and Revival of *Adams v. Lindell*." In *Feminist Perspectives on Contract Law*, edited by Linda Mulcahy and Sally Wheeler, 75–90. London: Glasshouse, Press 2005.

Gordley, James. *The Philosophical Origins of Modern Contract Doctrine*. Oxford: Clarendon, 1991.

Gordley, James. "Contract, Property, and the Will: The Civil Law and Common Law Tradition" In *The State and Freedom of Contract*, edited by Harry N. Scheiber, 66–88. Stanford, CA: Stanford University Press, 1998.

Gordon, Robert W. "Critical Legal Histories." *Stanford Law Review* 36, nos. 1 & 2 (1984): 57–126.

Gordon, Robert W. "*Britton v. Turner*: A Signpost on the Crooked Road to 'Freedom' in the Employment Contract." In *Contract Stories*, edited by Douglas G. Baird, Chapter 7. New York: Foundation, 2007.

Gottlieb, Stacey. "'And God Will Teach Her': Consciousness and Character in *Ruth* and *Aurora Leigh*." *Victorians Institute Journal* 24 (1996): 57–85.

Graeber, David. *Debt: The First 5,000 Years*. New York: Melville House Publishing, 2012.

Graff, Gerald. "Co-optation." In *The New Historicism*, edited by Aram H. Veeser, 168–81. New York: Taylor & Francis, 1989.

Granovetter, Mark. "Economic Action and Social Structure: The Problem of Embeddedness." *American Journal of Sociology* 91, no. 3, (1985): 481–510.

Graver, Suzanne. "'Writing in a 'Womanly' Way and the Double Vision of *Bleak House*." *Dickens Quarterly* 4, no. 1 (1987): 1–15.

Graver, Suzanne. "'Incarnate History': The Feminisms of *Middlemarch*." In *Approaches to Teaching Eliot's* Middlemarch, edited by Kathleen Blake, 64–74. New York: The Modern Language Association of America, 1990.

Greenblatt, Stephen. "Invisible Bullets: Renaissance Authority and Its Subversion." In *Glyph. Johns Hopkins Textual Studies* 8, edited by Walter Benn Michaels, 40–61. Baltimore, MD: Johns Hopkins University Press, 1981.

Greiner, Rae. "Thinking of Me Thinking of You: Sympathy Versus Empathy in the Realist Novel." *Victorian Studies* 53, no. 3 (2011): 417–26.

Greiner, Rae. *Sympathetic Realism in Nineteenth-Century British Fiction*. Baltimore, MD: Johns Hopkins University Press, 2012.

Griffin, Ben. *The Politics of Gender in Victorian Britain: Masculinity, Political Culture and the Struggle for Women's Rights*. Cambridge: Cambridge University Press, 2012.

Grossberg, Michael. *Governing the Hearth: Law and the Family in Nineteenth-Century*. Chapel Hill, NC: University of North Carolina Press, 1988.

Hack, Daniel. "Close Reading at a Distance: The African Americanization of *Bleak House*," *Critical Inquiry* 34, no. 4 (2008): 729–53.
Hacking, Ian. "Nineteenth Century Cracks in the Concept of Determinism." *Journal of the History of Ideas* 44, no. 3 (1983): 455–75.
Hadley, Elaine. *Living Liberalism: Practical Citizenship in Mid-Victorian Britain.* Chicago, IL: University of Chicago Press, 2010.
Hafley, James. "The Villain in *Wuthering Heights*." *Nineteenth-Century Fiction* 13, no. 3 (1958): 199–215.
Hager, Kelly. *Dickens and the Rise of Divorce: The Failed-Marriage Plot and the Novel Tradition.* Farnham: Ashgate Publishing, 2010.
Hamburger, Philip A. "The Development of the Nineteenth-Century Consensus Theory of Contract." *Law and History Review* 7, no. 2 (1989): 241–329.
Hammerton, James. *Cruelty and Companionship: Conflict in Nineteenth-Century Married Life.* New York: Routledge 1992.
Hardy, Thomas. *The Mayor of Casterbridge.* Edited by Dale Kramer. Oxford: Oxford University Press, 1998.
Hartog, Hendrik. "Abigail Bailey's Coverture: Law in a Married Woman's Consciousness." In *Law in Everyday Life*, edited by Austin Sarat and Thomas R. Kearns, 63–108. Ann Arbor, MI: University of Michigan Press, 1993.
Harvey, W.J. *Character and the Novel.* London: Chatto & Windus, 1965.
Hasday, Jill. "Intimacy and Economic Exchange." *Harvard Law Review* 119, no. 2 (2005): 491–530.
Haskell, Thomas L. "Capitalism and the Origins of the Humanitarian Sensibility, Part 2." In *The Antislavery Debate: Capitalism and Abolitionism as a Problem in Historical Interpretation,* edited by Thomas Bender, 136–60. Berkeley and Los Angeles, CA: University of California Press, 1992.
Hatano, Yoko. "Evangelicalism in *Ruth*." *Modern Language Review* 95, no. 3 (2000): 634–41.
Hatten, Charles. *The End of Domesticity: Alienation from the Family in Dickens, Eliot, and James.* Newark, DE: University of Delaware Press, 2010.
Hayek, F.A. "The Use of Knowledge in Society." *The American Economic Review* 35, no. 4 (1945): 519–30.
Heilmann, Ann. "Marriage." In *Thomas Hardy in Context,* edited by Phillip Mallett, 351–62. Cambridge: Cambridge University Press, 2013.
Heineman, Helen K. *Three Victorians in the New World.* New York: American University Studies Series No. 4: English Language and Literature, 1992.
Helsinger, Elizabeth K., et al., *The Woman Question* vol. 3. Manchester: Manchester University Press, 1983.
Henry, Nancy. "'Ladies Do It?': Victorian Women Investors in Fact and Fiction." In *Victorian Literature and Finance,* edited by Francis O'Gorman, 111–32. Oxford: Oxford University Press, 2007.
Henry, Nancy. "George Eliot and Finance." In *A Companion to George Eliot,* edited by Amanda Anderson and Harry E. Shaw, 323–37. Oxford: Wiley-Blackwell, 2013.
Hensley, Nathan K. "Mister Trollope, Lady Credit and *The Way We Live Now*." In *The Politics of Gender in Anthony Trollope's Novels: New Readings for the Twenty-First Century,* edited by Margaret Markwick et al., 147–60. Farnham: Ashgate, 2009.
Higonnet, Margaret R. "Hardy and His Critics: Gender in the Interstices." In *A Companion to Thomas Hardy,* edited by Keith Wilson, 117–29. Malden, MA:

Blackwell Publishing, 2009.

Hilton, Boyd. "Moral Disciplines." In *Liberty and Authority in Victorian Britain*, edited by Peter Mandler, 224–46. Oxford: Oxford University Press, 2006.

Hirschman, Albert O. *The Passions and the Interests: Political Arguments for Capitalism Before Its Triumph*. Princeton, NJ: Princeton University Press, 1977.

Hirschman, Albert O. "Rival Interpretations of Market Society: Civilizing, Destructive, or Feeble?." *Journal of Economic Literature* 20, no. 4 (1982): 1463–84.

Hobsbawm, Eric J. *The Age of Capital 1848–1875*. Harmondsworth: Penguin Books, 1979.

Hobsbawm, Eric J. *The Age of Revolution 1789–1848*. New York: Vintage Books 1996.

Horwitz, Morton J. *The Transformation of American Law 1780–1860*. Cambridge, MA: Harvard University Press, 1977.

Horwitz, Steven. "Capitalism and the Family." *Freeman* 26 (July/August 2007).

Houghton, Walter E. *The Victorian Frame of Mind, 1830–1870*. New Haven, CT: Yale University Press, 1957.

Ibbetson, D.J. *A Historical Introduction to the Law of Obligations*. Oxford: Oxford University Press, 1999.

Iser, Wolfgang. *The Implied Reader: Patterns of Communication in Prose Fiction from Bunyan to Beckett*. Baltimore, MD: Johns Hopkins University Press, 1974.

Jaffe, Audrey. *Vanishing Points: Dickens, Narrative, and the Subject of Omniscience*. Berkeley, CA: University of California Press, 1991.

Jaffe, Audrey. "Under Cover of Sympathy: Ressentiment in Gaskell's *Ruth*." *Victorian Literature and Culture* 21 (1993): 51–65.

Jaffe, Audrey. "*Cranford* and *Ruth*." In *The Cambridge Companion to Elizabeth Gaskell*, edited by Jill L. Matus, 46–58. Cambridge: Cambridge University Press, 2007.

Jaffe, Audrey. "Trollope in the Stock Market: Irrational Exuberance and *The Prime Minister*." *Victorian Studies* 45, no. 1 (2002): 43–64.

Jaffe, Audrey. *The Affective Life of the Average Man: The Victorian Novel and the Stock-Market Graph*. Columbus, OH: Ohio State University Press, 2010.

Jones, Tod E. "Michael Henchard: Hardy's Male Homosexual," *Victorian Newsletter* 86 (1994): 9–13.

Jones, Wendy S. *Consensual Fictions: Women, Liberalism, and the English Novel*, 2nd ed. Toronto: University of Toronto Press, 2004.

Jordan, John O. *Supposing* Bleak House. Charlottesville, VA: University of Virginia Press, 2011.

Jumeau, Alain. "*The Way We Live Now*; or, Trollope in Vanity Fair." *Cahiers Victoriens et Eduardiens* 58 (2003): 57–70.

Kahn, Victoria. *Wayward Contracts: The Crisis of Political Obligation in England, 1640–1674*. Princeton, NJ: Princeton University Press, 2004.

Kaufmann, David. *The Business of Common Life: Novels and Classical Economics Between Revolution and Reform*. Baltimore, MD: Johns Hopkins University Press, 1995.

Kennedy, Duncan. "Form and Substance in Private Law Adjudication." *Harvard Law Review* 89, no. 8 (1976): 1685–1778.

Kennedy, Duncan. "Distributive and Paternalist Motives in Contract and Tort Law, with Special Reference to Compulsory Terms and Unequal Bargaining Power." *Maryland Law Review* 41, no. 4 (1982): 563–658.

Kennedy, Duncan. "From the Will Theory to the Principle of Private Autonomy: Lon Fuller's 'Consideration and Form.'" *Columbia Law Review* 100, no. 94 (2000): 94–175.

Kennedy, Duncan. *The Rise and Fall of Classical Legal Thought.* Washington, DC: Beard, 2006.

Kent, Susan Kingsley. *Sex and Suffrage in Britain 1860–1914.* Princeton, NJ: Princeton University Press, 1987.

Kermode, Frank. Introduction to *Anthony Trollope, The Way We Live Now,* edited by Frank Kermode. Harmonsworth: Penguin Books, 1994.

Kettle, Arnold. *Introduction to the English Novel,* 2 vols. London: Hutchinson House, 1951.

Klaver, Claudia C. *A/Moral Economics: Classical Political Economy and Cultural Authority in Nineteenth-Century England.* Columbus, OH: Ohio State University Press, 2003.

Knoepflmacher, U. C. *Emily Brontë: "Wuthering Heights".* Cambridge: Cambridge University Press, 1989.

Konings, Martijn. *The Emotional Logic of Capitalism: What Progressives Have Missed.* Stanford, CA: Stanford University Press, 2015.

Kornbluh, Anna. *Realizing Capital: Financial and Psychic Economies in Victorian Form.* New York: Fordham University Press, 2014.

Kraus, Jody. "The Correspondence of Contract and Promise." *Columbia Law Review* 109, no. 7 (2009): 1603–49.

Kreisel, Deanna K. *Economic Woman: Demand, Gender, and Narrative Closure in Eliot and Hardy.* Toronto: University of Toronto Press, 2012.

Kreitner, Roy. *Calculating Promises: The Emergence of Modern American Contract Doctrine.* Stanford, CA: Stanford University Press, 2007.

Kucich, John. *Repression in Victorian Fiction: Charlotte Brontë, George Eliot, and Charles Dickens.* Berkeley, CA: University of California Press, 1987.

Lacey, Nicola. "Gamblers and Gentlefolks: Money, Law and Status in Trollope's England." *Law, Society and Economy* (2016): 1–24. Accessed February 2016. doi:10.2139/ssrn.2745378.

Langland, Elizabeth. "Hardy and Masculinity." In *Thomas Hardy in Context,* edited by Phillip Mallett, 374–83. Cambridge: Cambridge University Press, 2013.

Langland, Elizabeth. *Nobody's Angels: Middle-Class Women and Domestic Ideology in Victorian Culture.* Ithaca, NY: Cornell University Press 1995.

Langford, Paul. *Englishness Identified.* Oxford: Oxford University Press, 2000.

Latour, Bruno. *The Making of Law: An Ethnography of the Conseil d'État.* Translated by Marina Brilman and Alain Pottage. Cambridge: Polity Press, 2010.

Leff, Arthur A. "Contract as Thing." *American University Law Review* 19, no. 2 (1970): 131–57.

Lennard, Davis J. *Factual Fictions: The Origins of the English Novel.* New York: Columbia University Press, 1983.

Leo, Bersani. *A Future for Astyanax: Character and Desire in Literature.* London: Marion Boyars, 1978.

Lettmaier, Saskia. *Broken Engagements, The Action for Breach of Promise of Marriage and the Feminine Ideal, 1800–1940.* New York: Oxford University Press, 2010.

Levine, Caroline. "Narrative Networks: *Bleak House* and the Affordances of Form." *Novel* 42, no. 3 (2009): 517–23.

Levine, George. *The Realistic Imagination: English Fiction from Frankenstein to Lady Chatterly.* Chicago, IL: University of Chicago Press, 1981.

London, Bette. "Wuthering Heights and the Text Between the Lines." *Papers on*

Language and Literature 24, no. 1 (1988): 34–52.
Lovett, Denise M. "Economic Exchange and the Discourse of Contract in the Victorian Novel 1846–1875." PhD diss., University of Connecticut, 2011.
Luhmann, Niklas. *Love as Passion: The Codification of Intimacy.* Translated by Jeremy Gaines and Doris L. Jones. Cambridge, MA: Harvard University Press, 1986.
Lukes, Steven. *Individualism.* Oxford: Blackwell, 1973.
Lynch, Deidre Shauna. *The Economy of Character: Novels, Market Culture, and the Business of Inner Meaning.* Chicago, IL: University of Chicago Press, 1998.
MacDonald, Tara. *The New Man, Masculinity and Marriage in the Victorian Novel.* New York: Pickering & Chatto, 2015.
Macfarlane, Alan. *The Origins of English Individualism.* Cambridge: Cambridge University Press, 1978.
Mackenzie, Catriona, and Natalie Stoljar. "Introduction: Autonomy Refigured." In *Relational Autonomy: Feminist Perspectives on Autonomy, Agency, and the Social Self,* edited by Catriona Mackenzie and Natalie Stoljar, 3–33. Oxford: Oxford University Press, 2000.
Macneil, Ian R. "Contracts: Adjustment of Long-Term Economic Relations Under Classical, Neoclassical, and Relational Contract Law." *Northwestern University Law Review* 72, no. 6 (1978): 854–905.
Macneil, Ian R. *The New Social Contract: An Inquiry Into Modern Contractual Relations.* New Haven, CT: Yale University Press, 1980.
Macneil, Ian R. "Relational Contract Theory: Challenges and Queries." *Northwestern University Law Review* 94 (2000): 877–908.
Macneil, Ian R. "Restatement (Second) of Contracts and Presentiation." *Virginia Law Review* 60, no. 4 (1974): 589–610.
Maine, Henry Sumner. *Ancient Law: Its Connection with the Early History of Society and Its Relation to Modern Ideas.* New York: Henry Holt, 1906.
Maitland, Frederic W., and Francis C. Montague. *A Sketch of English Legal History.* Edited by James F. Colby. New York: G.P. Putnam's Sons, 1915.
Malachuk, Daniel S. "George Eliot's Liberalism." In *A Companion to George Eliot,* edited by Amanda Anderson and Harry E. Shaw, 370–84. Oxford: Wiley-Blackwell 2013.
Mantena, Karuna. *Alibis of Empire: Henry Maine and the Ends of Liberal Imperialism.* Princeton: Princeton University Press, 2010.
Marcus, Sharon. *Between Women: Friendship, Desire, and Marriage in Victorian England.* Princeton: Princeton University Press, 2007.
Martha, Nussbaum C., and Alison L. LaCroix, eds. *Subversion and Sympathy: Gender, Law, and the British Novel.* New York: Oxford University Press, 2013.
Marx, Karl, and Friederich Engels. *The Communist Manifesto* (1848).
Matthews, John T. "Framing in *Wuthering Heights.*" *Texas Studies in Literature and Language* 27, no. 1 (1985): 25–61.
Mauss, Marcel. "A Category of the Human Mind: The Notion of Person; the Notion of Self." In *The Category of the Person: Anthropology, Philosophy, History,* edited by Michael Carruthers et al., 1–25. Cambridge: Cambridge University Press, 1985.
Mauss, Marcel. *The Gift.* Translated by W. D. Halls. New York: W.W. Norton & Company, 2000.
McColla, Charles J. *Breach of Promise Its History and Social Considerations.* London: Pickering & Co., 1879.

McGann, Tara. "Literary Realism in the Wake of Business Cycle Theory: *The Way We Live Now* (1875)." In *Victorian Literature and Finance*, edited by Francis O'Gorman, 133–56. Oxford: Oxford University Press, 2007.

McKeon, Michael. *The Origins of the English Novel 1600–1740.* Baltimore, MD: Johns Hopkins University Press, 1987.

McMaster, Juliet. *Thackeray: The Major Novels.* Toronto: University of Toronto Press, 1971.

Mehta, Uday Singh. *Liberalism and Empire: A Study in Nineteenth-Century British Liberal Thought*, 2nd ed. Chicago, IL: University of Chicago Press, 1999.

Mendelson, Edward. *The Things That Matter: What Seven Classic Novels Have to Say About the Stages of Life.* New York: Pantheon, 2006.

Mensch, Betty. "Freedom of Contract as Ideology." *Stanford Law Review* 33, no. 75 (1981): 753–72.

Michie, Elsie B. *The Vulgar Question of Money: Heiresses, Materialism, and the Novel of Manners from Jane Austen to Henry James.* Baltimore, MD: Johns Hopkins University Press, 2011.

Mill, John Stuart. *On Liberty.* London: Penguin Books, 1974.

Mill, John Stuart. *The Subjection of Women.* Penn State University (electronic classics), 1999.

Mill, John Stuart. A Letter to Harriet Taylor, March 20, 1854, in *Charles Dickens: The Critical Heritage.* Edited by Philip Collins. London: Taylor & Francis, 2005.

Miller, Andrew. *Novels Behind Glass: Commodity Culture and Victorian Narrative.* Cambridge: Cambridge University Press, 1995.

Miller, D.A. *The Novel and the Police.* Berkeley, CA: University of California Press, 1989.

Miller, J. Hillis. *Charles Dickens: The World of His Novels.* Cambridge, MA: Harvard University Press, 1958.

Miller, J. Hillis. *Thomas Hardy: Distance and Desire.* Cambridge, MA: Harvard University Press, 1970.

Miller, J. Hillis. "Interpretation in *Bleak House.*" In J. Hillis Miller, *Victorian Subjects*, 179– 99. London: Harvester Wheatsheaf, 1990.

Miller, J. Hillis. "A Conclusion in Which Almost Nothing is Concluded: *Middlemarch's* Finale." In *Middlemarch in the Twenty First Century*, edited by Karen Chase, 133–56. Oxford: Oxford University Press, 2010.

Mills, Charles W., and Carole Pateman. *Contract and Domination.* Cambridge: Polity Press 2007.

Moretti, Franco. *The Way of the World: The Bildungsroman in European Culture.* New York: Verso, 2000.

Morgan, Susan. "Gaskell's Heroines and the Power of Time." *Pacific Coast Philology* 18 (1983): 43–51.

Morse, Deborah Denenholz. "The Way He Thought Then: Modernity and the Retreat of the Public Liberal in Anthony Trollope's *The Way We Live Now*, 1873." In *BRANCH: Britain, Representation and Nineteenth-Century History*, edited by Dino Franco Felluga (Extension of Romanticism and Victorianism on the Net) (2014).

Mulcahy, Linda. "The Limitations of Love and Altruism – Feminist Perspectives on Contract Law." In *Feminist Perspectives on Contract Law*, edited by Linda Mulcahy and Sally Wheel, 1–19. London: Glasshouse Press, 2005.

Muldrew, Craig. *The Economy of Obligation: The Culture of Credit and Social Relations in Early Modern England.* Basingstoke: Palgrave Macmillan, 1998.

Murphy, Sara. "The Law, the Norm and the Novel." In *Studies in Law, Politics and Society: Special Issue – Law and Literature Reconsidered,* edited by Austin Sarat, 53–78. London: Emerald, 2008.

Musselwhite, David. *Social Transformations in Hardy's Tragic Novels: Megamachines and Phantasms.* Houndmills: Palgrave Macmillan, 2003.

Nead, Lynda. *Myths of Sexuality: Representations of Women in Victorian Britain.* New York: Blackwell Publishers, 1988.

Nead, Lynda. "Mapping the Self: Gender, Space and Modernity in Mid-Victorian London." In *Rewriting the Self: Histories from the Renaissance to the Present,* edited by Roy Porter, 167–85. London: Routledge, 1997.

Nedelsky, Jennifer. *Law's Relations: A Relational Theory of Self, Autonomy, and Law.* Oxford: Oxford University Press, 2011.

Newman, Beth. "*Wuthering Heights* in Its Context(s)." In *Approaches to Teaching Emily Brontë's "Wuthering Heights,"* edited by Sue Lonoff and Terri. A. Hasseler, 36–43. New York: Modern Language Association of America, 2006.

Newsom, Robert. *A Likely Story: Probability and Play in Fiction.* New Brunswick, NJ: Rutgers University Press, 1988.

Nietzsche, Friedrich. *On the Genealogy of Morality.* Edited by Keith Ansell-Pearson. Translated by Carol Diethe. Cambridge: Cambridge University Press, 2006.

Nockleby, John T. "Tortious Interference with Contractual Relations in the Nineteenth Century: The Transformation of Property, Contract, and Tort." *Harvard Law Review* 93, no.7 (1980): 1510–39.

Nolan, Donal. "The Classical Legacy and Modern English Contract Law." *Modern Law Review* 59 (1996): 603–19.

Ohno, Tatsuhiro. "The Structure of *Ruth*: Is the Heroine's Martyrdom Inconsistent with the Plot?" *Gaskell Society Journal* 18 (2004): 16–36.

Okin, Susan Moller. "Women and the Making of the Sentimental Family." *Philosophy & Public Affairs* 11, no. 1 (1982): 65–88.

Olsen, Frances E. "The Family and the Market: A Study of Ideology and Legal Reform." *Harvard Law Review* 96, no. 7 (1983): 1497–578.

Orth, John V. "Contract and the Common Law." In *The State and Freedom of Contract,* edited by Harry N. Scheiber, 44–65. Stanford, CA: Stanford University Press, 1998.

Page, Norman. *Thomas Hardy: The Novels.* New York: Palgrave, 2001.

Pateman, Carol. *The Sexual Contract.* Stanford, CA: Stanford University Press 1988.

Peltason, Timothy. "Esther's Will." *ELH* 59, no. 3 (1992): 671–91.

Perry, Ruth. *Novel Relations: The Transformation of Kinship in English Literature and Culture, 1748–1818.* Cambridge: Cambridge University Press, 2004.

Pettit, Mark Jr. "Freedom, Freedom of Contract, and the 'Rise and Fall'." *Boston University Law Review* 79 (1999): 263–354.

Polanyi, Karl. *The Great Transformation.* Boston, MA: Beacon Press, 1967.

Pollock, Frederick. *Principles of Contract at Law and in Equity.* London: Stevens and Sons, 1876.

Poovey, Mary. *Making a Social Body.* Chicago, IL: University of Chicago Press, 1995.

Poovey, Mary. *A History of the Modern Fact: Problems of Knowledge in the Sciences of Wealth and Society.* Chicago, IL: University of Chicago Press, 1998.

Poovey, Mary. *Genres of the Credit Economy: Mediating Value in Eighteenth- and Nineteenth-Century Britain.* Chicago, IL: University of Chicago Press, 2008.

Porter, Roy, ed. *Rewriting the Self: Histories from the Renaissance to the Present.* London: Routledge, 1997.

Posner, Eric A. "The Decline of Formality in Contract Law." In *The Fall and Rise of Freedom of Contract,* edited by F.H. Buckley, 61–77. Durham, NC: Duke University Press, 1999.

Pound, Roscoe. "Liberty of Contract." *Yale Law Journal* 18, no. 7 (1909): 454–87.

Pound, Roscoe. "The End of Law as Developed in Juristic Thought (Part 1)." *Harvard Law Review* 27, no. 7 (1914): 605–28.

Pound, Roscoe. "The End of Law as Developed in Juristic Thought (Part 2)." *Harvard Law Review* 30 (1917): 201–25.

Pound, Roscoe. "The Role of the Will in Law." *Harvard Law Review* 68 (1954): 1–19.

Powell, Neil. "Thomas Hardy's *The Mayor of Casterbridge.*" In *British Writers Classics, Vol. 2,* edited by Jay Parini, 177–94. New York: Charles Scribner's Sons, 2004.

Probert, Rebecca. *Marriage Law and Practice in the Long Eighteenth Century: A Reassessment.* Cambridge: Cambridge University Press, 2009.

Psomiades, Kathy Alexis. "The Marriage Plot in Theory." *Novel* 43 no. 1 (2010): 53–39.

Pykett, Lyn. "Gender and Genre in 'Wuthering Heights': Gothic Plot and Domestic Fiction." In *Emily Brontë: "Wuthering Heights,"* edited by Patsy Stoneman, 86–99. Basingstoke: Macmillan, 1993.

Rajan, Supritha. *A Tale of Two Capitalisms: Sacred Economics in Nineteenth-Century Britain.* Ann Arbor, MI: University of Michigan Press, 2015.

Rappaport, Erika. "'A Husband and His Wife's Dresses': Consumer Credit and the Debtor Family in England, 1864–1914." In *The Sex of Things: Gender and Consumption in Historical Perspective,* edited by Victoria de Grazia and Ellen Furlough, 163–87. Berkeley, CA: University of California Press, 1996.

Reed, John R. *Victorian Will.* Columbus, OH: Ohio University Press, 1989.

Reynell, William A. *Principles of the English Law of Contract.* Oxford: Clarendon Press, 1879.

Rich, Adrienne. "Compulsory Heterosexuality and Lesbian Existence." *Signs: Journal of Women in Culture and Society* 5, no. 4 (1980): 631–60.

Robbins, Bruce. "Telescopic Philanthropy: Professionalism and Responsibility in *Bleak House.*" In *Nation and Narration,* edited by Homi K. Bhabha, 213–30. London: Routledge, 1990.

Robbins, Bruce. *Upward Mobility and the Common Good: Toward a Literary History of the Welfare State.* Princeton. NJ: Princeton University Press, 2007.

Rosenberg, Anat. "The History of Genres: Reaching for Reality in Law and Literature." *Law & Social Inquiry* 39, no. 4 (2014): 1057–79.

Rosenberg, Anat. "Commodity Fetishism and Fear of the Social Between Trollope and Law." In *The Edinburgh Companion to Anthony Trollope,* edited by Frederik Van Dam, David Skilton, and Ortwin de Graef (forthcoming).

Rubin, Gayle. "The Traffic in Women: Notes on the 'Political Economy' of Sex." In *Toward an Anthropology of Women,* edited by Rayna R. Reiter, 157–210. New York: Monthly Review Press, 1975.

Rubinstein, W.D. *Capitalism, Culture and Decline in Britain, 1750–1990.* London: Routledge, 1993.

Sanger, C.P. *The Structure of "Wuthering Heights"*. London: Hogarth Press, 1926.

Sartori, Andrew. *Liberalism in Empire: An Alternative History*. Berkeley, CA: University of California Press, 2014.

Schaffer, Talia. *Romance's Rival: Familiar Marriage in Victorian Fiction*. New York: Oxford University Press, 2016.

Scheiber, Harry N. "Economic Liberty and the Modern State." In *The State and Freedom of Contract*, edited by Harry N. Scheiber, 122–60. Stanford, CA: Stanford University Press, 1998.

Searle, G.R. *Morality and the Market in Victorian Britain*. Oxford: Clarendon Press, 1998.

Sedgwick, Eve Kosofsky. *Between Men: English Literature and Male Homosexual Desire*. New York: Columbia University Press, 1985.

Seidman, Robert B. "Contract Law, the Free Market, and State Intervention: A Jurisprudential Perspective." *Journal of Economica Issues* 7, no. 4 (1973): 553–75.

Select Committee on Debtors (Imprisonment), Report, HC 1909–239, q. 2249 q. 3163.

Sennett, Richard. *The Fall of Public Man: On the Social Psychology of Capitalism*. New York: Vintage Books, 1978.

Seyla Benhabib, *Situating the Self: Gender, Community and Postmodernism in Contemporary Ethics*. Cambridge: Polity Press, 1992.

Shanley, Mary Lyndon. *Feminism, Marriage and the Law in Victorian England, 1850–1895*. Princeton, NJ: Princeton University Press, 1989.

Shires, Linda M. "The Aesthetics of the Victorian Novel: Form, Subjectivity, Ideology." In *The Cambridge Companion to the Victorian Novel*, edited by Deirdre David, 61–76. Cambridge: Cambridge University Press, 2001.

Shires, Linda M. "'And I Was Unaware': The Unknowing Omniscience of Hardy's Narrators." In *Thomas Hardy: Texts and Contexts*, edited by Phillip Mallett, 31–48. Basingstoke: Palgrave Macmillan, 2002.

Shoemaker, Robert B. *Gender in English Society: 1650–1850: The Emergence of Separate Spheres*. New York: Longman, 1998.

Showlater, Elaine. "The Unmanning the Mayor of Casterbridge." In *Critical Approaches to the Fiction of Thomas Hardy*, edited by Dale Kramer. 99–115. London: Palgrave Macmillan, 1979.

Simmel, Georg. *The Philosophy of Money*. Translated by Tom Bottomore and David Frisby. Edited by David Frisby. 3rd ed. New York: Routledge, 2004.

Simpson, A.W.B. "The Horwitz Thesis and the History of Contracts." *Chicago Law Review* 46, no. 3 (1979): 533–601.

Simpson, A.W.B. "Contract: The Twitching Corpse." In *Legal Theory and Legal History: Essays on the Common Law*, 321–33. London: Hambledon Press, 1987.

Simpson, A.W.B. "Innovation in Nineteenth Century Contract Law." In *Legal Theory and Legal History: Essays on the Common Law*, 171–202. London: Hambledon Press, 1987.

Singer, Joseph William. "Legal Realism Now." *California Law Review* 76, no. 2 (1988): 465–544.

Smiles, Samuel. *Self-Help: National and Individual*. Cambridge: Cambridge University Press, 1859. Accessed July 2016. doi: http://dl4a.org/uploads/pdf/Samuel%20Smiles%20-%20Self-Help%20-%20National%20and%20Individual.pdf.

Stanley, Amy Dru. *From Bondage to Contract: Wage Labor, Marriage, and the Market in the Age of Slave Emancipation*. New York: Cambridge University Press, 1998.

Staten, Henry. "Is *Middlemarch* Ahistorical?." *PMLA* 115, no. 5 (2000): 991–1005.
Staten, Henry. *Spirit Becomes Matter: The Brontës, George Eliot, Nietzsche.* Edinburgh: Edinburgh University Press, 2014.
Staves, Susan. *Married Women's Separate Property in England, 1660–1833.* Cambridge, MA: Harvard University Press, 1990.
Steedman, Carolyn. *Master and Servant: Love and Labour in the English Industrial Age.* Cambridge: Cambridge University Press, 2007.
Steinbach, Susie L. "Promises, Promises: Not Marrying in England, 1780–1920." PhD diss., Yale University, 1996.
Steinberg, Marc W. *England's Great Transformation: Law, Labor and the Industrial Revolution.* Chicago, IL: University of Chicago Press 2016
Steinfeld, Robert J. *Coercion, Contract, and Free Labor in the Nineteenth Century.* Cambridge: Cambridge University Press 2001.
Stolpa, Jennifer M. "What's in a Name? Echoes of Biblical Women in Elizabeth Gaskell's *Ruth.*" *Gaskell Society Journal* 18 (2004): 50–64.
Stolzenberg, Nomi M. "Liberalism in a Romantic State." *Law, Culture and the Humanities* 5, no. 2 (2009): 194–215.
Stone, Lawrence. *The Family, Sex and Marriage in England 1500–1800.* New York: Harper & Row, 1977.
Stone, Lawrence. *Road to Divorce: England 1530–1987.* New York: Oxford University Press, 1995.
Suk, Julie C. "The Moral and Legal Consequences of Wife Selling in *The Mayor of Casterbridge.*" In *Subversion and Sympathy: Gender, Law and the British Novel,* edited by Martha C. Nussbaum and Alison LaCroix, 27–47. New York: Oxford University Press, 2013.
Swain, Warren. "Contract as Promise: The Role of Promising in the Law of Contract. An Historical Account." *Edinburgh Law Review* 17, no. 1 (2013): 1–21.
Swain, Warren. *The Law of Contract 1670–1870.* Cambridge: Cambridge University Press, 2015.
Swinden, Patrick, ed. *George Eliot, Middlemarch: A Casebook.* London: Macmillan, 1972.
Taylor, Charles R. *Philosophy and the Human Sciences: Philosophical Papers 2.* Cambridge: Cambridge University Press, 1985.
Taylor, Charles R. *Sources of the Self: The Making of Modern Identity.* Cambridge: Cambridge University Press, 1989.
Taylor, Charles R. *Multiculturalism and the "Politics of Recognition": An Essay.* Princeton, NJ: Princeton University Press, 1994.
Thackeray, William Makepeace. *Vanity Fair: A Novel Without a Hero.* New York: Barnes & Noble Classics, 2003.
Thomas, Brook. *American Literary Realism and the Failed Promise of Contract.* Berkeley, CA: University of California Press, 1997.
Thomas, David Wayne. *Cultivating Victorians: Liberal Culture and the Aesthetic.* Philadelphia, PA: University of Pennsylvania Press, 2004.
Thompson, E.P. *The Peculiarities of the English.* London: the Socialist Register, 1965.
Thompson, E.P. *Customs in Common.* London: Penguin 1991.
Tillotson, Kathleen. "Vanity Fair." In *Twentieth Century Interpretations of* Vanity Fair: *A Collection of Critical Essays,* edited by Michael G. Sundell, 40–54. Englewood Cliffs, NJ: Prentice-Hall, 1969.

Tilly, Louise A. "Review: The Family and Change." *Theory and Society* 5 no. 3 (1978), 421–34.

Tomlins, Christopher. "How Autonomous Is Law?" *Annual Review of Law & Social Science* 3, no. 1 (2007): 45–68.

Tomlins, Christopher *Freedom Bound: Law, Labor, and Civic Identity in Colonizing English America, 1580–1865.* New York: Cambridge University Press, 2010.

Tosh, John. *A Man's Place: Masculinity and the Middle-Class Home in Victorian England.* New Haven, CT: Yale University Press 1999.

Traversi, Derek. "Wuthering Heights after a Hundred Years." In *Emily Brontë: "Wuthering Heights,"* edited by Miriam Allott, 157–76. London: Macmillan, 1970.

Trilling, Lionel. *Liberal Imagination: Essays on Literature and Society.* New York: Viking Press, 1950.

Trollope, Anthony. *An Autobiography.* New York: Dodd, Mead & Company, 1883.

Trollope, Anthony. *The Way We Live Now.* Edited by Frank Kermode. England: Penguin Books, 1994.

Tucker, Irene. *A Probable State: The Novel, the Contract, and the Jews.* Chicago, IL: University of Chicago Press, 2000.

Turner, Victor. *From Ritual to Theatre: The Human Seriousness of Play.* New York: Performing Arts Journal Publications, 1982.

Unger, Roberto Mangabeira. *The Critical Legal Studies Movement.* Cambridge, MA: Harvard University Press, 1986.

Van, Annette. "Ambivalent Speculations: America as England's Future in *The Way We Live Now.*" *Victorian Structures of Feeling* 39, No. 1(2005): 75–96.

Van Ghent, Dorothy. "Dark 'Otherness' in *Wuthering Heights.*" In *Emily Brontë: "Wuthering Heights,"* edited by Miriam Allott, 177–83. London: Macmillan, 1970.

Veblen, Thorstein. *The Theory of the Leisure Class.* Oxford: Oxford University Press, 2007.

Vernon, John. *Money and Fiction: Literary Realism in the Nineteenth and Early Twentieth Centuries.* Ithaca, NY: Cornell University Press, 1984.

Wahrman, Dror. *The Making of the Modern Self: Identity and Culture in Eighteenth Century England.* New Haven, CT: Yale University Press, 2004.

Walkowitz, Judith R. *Prostitution and Victorian Society: Women, Class and the State.* Cambridge: Cambridge University Press, 1980.

Ward, Ian. "Emily Brontë and the Terrorist Imagination." *English Studies* 89, no. 5 (2008): 524–51.

Ward, Ian. *Sex, Crime and Literature in Victorian England.* Oxford: Hart Publishing, 2014.

Ward, Mary. "Introduction to *Wuthering Heights.*" In *Emily Brontë: "Wuthering Heights,"* edited by Miriam Allott. London: Macmillan, 1970.

Watt, Gary. *Equity Stirring: The Story of Justice Beyond Law.* Oxford: Hart Publishing, 2009.

Watt, Ian. *The Rise of the Novel: Studies in Defoe, Richardson and Fielding.* Berkeley, CA: University of California Press, 1957.

Weber, Max. *Roscher and Knies: The Logical Problems of Historical Economics.* Translated by Guy Oakes. New York: The Free Press, 1975.

Weber, Max. *Economy and Society: An Outline of Interpretive Sociology.* Edited by Claus Wittich and Guenther Roth. Berkeley, CA: University of California Press, 1978.

Weber, Max. *The Protestant Ethic and the Spirit of Capitalism.* Edited by Stephen Kalberg, 3rd ed. New York: Oxford University Press, 2007.

Welsh, Alexander. *The City of Dickens.* Oxford: Oxford University Press, 1971.

Welsh, Alexander. *Dickens Redressed: The Art of* Bleak House *and* Hard Times. New Haven, CT: Yale University Press, 2000.

White, Hayden V. *Metahistory: The Historical Imagination in Nineteenth-Century Europe.* Baltimore, MD: Johns Hopkins University Press, 1975.

Wiener, Martin J. *English Culture and the Decline of the Industrial Spirit, 1850–1980.* Cambridge: Cambridge University Press, 2004.

Williams, Melanie L. "Coercion and the Labour Contract – Revisiting Glasbrook Brothers and the Political Fiction of Lewis Jones." *International Journal of Law in Context* 8, no. 1 (2012): 1–25.

Williams, Raymond. *The English Novel from Dickens to Lawrence.* London: Hogarth Press, 1984.

Williams, Raymond. *The Long Revolution.* London: Chatto and Windus, 1961.

Williams, Raymond. *Marxism and Literature.* Oxford: Oxford University Press, 1977.

Williston, Samuel. "Freedom of Contract." *Cornell Law Quarterly* 6 (1921): 365–80.

Wilt, Judith. "Confusion and Consciousness in Dickens's Esther." *Nineteenth-Century Fiction* 32, no. 3 (1977): 285–309.

Witte, John Jr. *From Sacrament to Contract: Marriage, Religion, and Law in the Western Tradition.* Louisville, KY: Westminster/John Knox Press, 1997.

Woloch, Alex. *The One vs. the Many: Minor Characters and the Space of the Protagonist in the Novel.* Princeton, NJ: Princeton University Press, 2003.

Wonnell, Christopher T. "The Abstract Character of Contract Law." *Connecticut Law Review* 22 (1990): 437–98.

Woodring, Carl R. "The Narrators of *Wuthering Heights.*" *Nineteenth-Century Fiction* 11, no. 4 (1957): 298–305.

Yuran, Noam. *What Money Wants: An Economy of Desire.* Stanford, CA: Stanford University Press, 2014.

Zelizer, Viviana A. *Economic Lives: How Culture Shapes the Economy.* Princeton, NJ: Princeton University Press 2011.

Zelizer, Viviana A. "How I Became a Relational Economic Sociologist and What Does That Mean?" *Politics & Society* 40, no. 2 (2012): 145–74.

Index

For Product Safety Concerns and Information please contact our
EU representative GPSR@taylorandfrancis.com Taylor & Francis
Verlag GmbH, Kaufingerstraße 24, 80331 München, Germany